Islamic Capital Markets and Products

Founded in 1807, John Wiley & Sons is the oldest independent publishing company in the United States. With offices in North America, Europe, Australia and Asia, Wiley is globally committed to developing and marketing print and electronic products and services for our customers' professional and personal knowledge and understanding.

The Wiley Finance series contains books written specifically for finance and investment professionals as well as sophisticated individual investors and their financial advisors. Book topics range from portfolio management to e-commerce, risk management, financial engineering, valuation and financial instrument analysis, as well as much more.

For a list of available titles, visit our Web site at www.WileyFinance.com.

Islamic Capital Markets and Products

Managing Capital and Liquidity Requirements Under Basel III

SIMON ARCHER
RIFAAT AHMED ABDEL KARIM

WILEY

This edition first published 2018

© 2018 Simon Archer and Rifaat Ahmed Abdel Karim

Registered office

John Wiley & Sons Ltd, The Atrium, Southern Gate, Chichester, West Sussex, PO19 8SQ, United Kingdom

For details of our global editorial offices, for customer services and for information about how to apply for permission to reuse the copyright material in this book please see our website at www.wiley.com.

Wiley publishes in a variety of print and electronic formats and by print-on-demand. Some material included with standard print versions of this book may not be included in e-books or in print-on-demand. If this book refers to media such as a CD or DVD that is not included in the version you purchased, you may download this material at http://booksupport.wiley.com. For more information about Wiley products, visit www.wiley.com.

Designations used by companies to distinguish their products are often claimed as trademarks. All brand names and product names used in this book are trade names, service marks, trademarks or registered trademarks of their respective owners. The publisher is not associated with any product or vendor mentioned in this book.

Limit of Liability/Disclaimer of Warranty: While the publisher and author have used their best efforts in preparing this book, they make no representations or warranties with respect to the accuracy or completeness of the contents of this book and specifically disclaim any implied warranties of merchantability or fitness for a particular purpose. It is sold on the understanding that the publisher is not engaged in rendering professional services and neither the publisher nor the author shall be liable for damages arising herefrom. If professional advice or other expert assistance is required, the services of a competent professional should be sought.

Library of Congress Cataloging-in-Publication Data

Names: Archer, Simon, editor. | Abdel Karim, Rifaat Ahmed, editor.
Title: Islamic capital markets and products : managing capital and liquidity requirements under Basel III / [edited] by Simon Archer, Rifaat Ahmed Abdel Karim.
Description: Chichester, United Kingdom : John Wiley & Sons, 2017. | Series: Wiley finance | Includes bibliographical references and index. |
Identifiers: LCCN 2017026729 (print) | LCCN 2017038796 (ebook) | ISBN 9781119218838 (pdf) | ISBN 9781119218814 (epub) | ISBN 9781119218807 (cloth)
Subjects: LCSH: Finance—Islamic countries. | Finance—Religious aspects—Islam. | Capital market—Islamic countries. | Financial institutions—Islamic countries. | Financial institutions—Religious aspects—Islam.
Classification: LCC HG3368.A6 (ebook) | LCC HG3368.A6 I854 2017 (print) | DDC 332/.0415091767—dc23

LC record available at https://lccn.loc.gov/2017026729

Cover Design: Wiley
Cover Image: © Anna Poguliaeva/Shutterstock

Set in 10/12pt Sabon by SPi Global, Chennai, India

Printed in Great Britain by TJ International Ltd, Padstow, Cornwall, UK

10 9 8 7 6 5 4 3 2 1

To our wives, Eveline and Iglal, and the children of the second author, Alameen, Tassneem, Asma and Al-Sideeq.

Contents

Foreword

Professor Simon Archer and Professor Datuk Rifaat Ahmed Abdel Karim are very well known in the field of Islamic finance, to which they have made great contributions over the years. In this new book, they lead a team of expert contributors who write on the subject of Islamic Capital Markets and Products, with a particular emphasis on that important aspect of it which concerns managing capital and liquidity requirements under Basel III. They are uniquely qualified to do this, Prof. Rifaat having been CEO of the International Islamic Liquidity Management Corporation (the IILM), which is headquartered in Malaysia, between 2012 and 2016, and Prof. Archer having consulted for the major bodies in Islamic finance over a range topics.

These are technical requirements under Basel III that benefit from clear expositions by a number of practising professionals, but the book valuably traverses a wider terrain. In particular, there are numerous case studies particularly on sukuk issues which bring together practical information on particular issues. Although the focus is on sukuk, there are contributions on Islamic equities, collective investment schemes, and collateralisation, the latter being an important prerequisite of liquidity. The focus is also on Malaysia, the authors pointing to the consistent support from the authorities as explaining why, for example, Malaysia continues to dominate the global sukuk market, though other important players are not neglected, there being a chapter on Bahrain and much material from elsewhere in the Islamic world.

Amidst the detail there are wider remarks, for example as to the roots of sukuk in the Middle Ages as papers denoting obligations arising from commercial transactions, and a contribution by a leading scholar which emphasises the role of the Shari'ah in Islamic finance as a live body of jurisprudence that can be understood in the light of contemporary circumstances.

The authors' primary concern in this work, however, is with liquidity, and the management of risk, recognising the challenges which Islamic finance faces in this respect, challenges which in one form or another are faced by all financial institutions. The value of the work lies in the solutions that are to be found in its pages. Prof. Rifaat and Prof. Archer are to be congratulated for bringing together a group of authors who share their commitment to the continuing growth of Islamic Capital Markets, in which they themselves are such leading participants. Everyone who works in this growing field will be glad to have this book on their shelves.

Sir William Blair
Judge in Charge of the Commercial Court
Royal Courts of Justice in London
September 2017

Acknowledgements

The authors would like to acknowledge the helpful support of Farrah Mohamed Aris and Noor Erni Surya Hj Noordin of the International Islamic Liquidity Management Corporation.

About the Editors

Professor Simon Archer is a Visiting Professor at the ICMA Centre, Henley Business School, University of Reading, UK. He qualified as a Chartered Accountant with Arthur Andersen in London and then moved to Price Waterhouse in Paris, where he became Partner in charge of Management Consultancy Services. Since the beginning of his academic career, Professor Archer has undertaken numerous consultancy assignments, including acting as consultant to the Accounting and Auditing Organization for Islamic Financial Institutions (AAOIFI), the Islamic Financial Services Board (IFSB) and the International Islamic Liquidity Corporation (IILM). He is the author or co-author of a considerable number of academic papers on Islamic finance and a co-editor of and contributor to several books on the subject, including three published by Wiley. In 2010, he received an award from the Central Bank of Bahrain and Kuwait Finance House for his 'outstanding contribution to the Islamic financial services industry'.

Professor Rifaat Ahmed Abdel Karim has an international reputation as a leader and authority in the Islamic financial services industry (IFSI) at both the professional and academic levels.

Professor Rifaat was the CEO of the International Islamic Liquidity Management Corporation during the period October 2012–December 2016. He has served as the inaugural Secretary-General at both the AAOIFI and the IFSB. Professor Rifaat is an Adjunct Research Professor at INCEIF, Malaysia, and Visiting Professor at the ICMA Centre, Henley Business School, University of Reading, UK. He is the author or co-author of a considerable number of academic papers on Islamic finance and a co-editor of and contributor to several books on the subject, including three published by Wiley.

Professor Rifaat's contribution to the IFSI has been recognised by the many prestigious international awards that he has received during his career over three decades, which has been dedicated to high achievement in professional activities, as well as in research and academic work. These awards notably include the (inaugural) 2004 Euromoney Outstanding Contribution in the Development of Islamic Finance, the 2010 Islamic Development Bank Prize in Islamic Banking and Finance and the Malaysian Royal Award in Islamic Finance 2016.

In 2010, the King of Malaysia awarded Professor Rifaat the Royal Malaysian Honorary Award of Darjah Kebesaran Panglima Jasa Negara (PJN), which carries the title 'Datuk'.

CHAPTER 1

Overview of the Islamic Capital Market

By Simon Archer, Brandon Davies and
Rifaat Ahmed Abdel Karim

This chapter provides an extensive overview of the Islamic capital market (ICM), or more broadly the Shari'ah-compliant finance industry, and its various segments, including equities, *sukuk* (Islamic investment certificates), investment funds and Islamic banks. This overview is presented in the context of the international capital markets of which the ICM forms a growing part. Later chapters in this volume deal in more detail with various aspects of the ICM, including Islamic equities, *sukuk*, Islamic investment funds and legal, Shari'ah and regulatory issues.

HISTORY OF THE ICM

The beginning of the modern Islamic financial industry can be dated to the mid-1970s. Fundamentally different in some important respects from the conventional financial model, Islamic finance has its religious identity and is based on the principles of Shari'ah (Islamic law) and the rules of *Fiqh al Muamalat* (Shari'ah commercial jurisprudence).

Total assets of Shari'ah-compliant financial institutions have grown by an average of 15–20 percent per annum over the past five years, suggesting strong demand for Islamic investing. It is expected that Islamic finance will continue to grow at this rate for the next few years. The figure for total assets in Islamic finance was around USD2.0 trillion at the end of 2015.

The growth in Shari'ah-compliant finance has also been mirrored in the growth of Shari'ah-compliant investment funds. It is estimated that currently there are more than USD75 billion under management in Shari'ah-compliant investment funds, while *sukuk* outstanding now amount to around USD300m (Table 1.1).

TABLE 1.1   Breakdown of Islamic finance segments by region (USD billion, 2015 YTD)

Region	Banking Assets	Sukuk Outstanding	Islamic Funds' Assets	Takaful Contributions
Asia	209.3	174.7	23.2	5.2
Gulf Cooperation Council countries	598.8	103.7	31.2	10.4
The Middle East and North Africa (MENA) region (exc. GCC)	607.5	9.4	0.3	7.1
Sub-Saharan Africa	24.0	0.7	1.4	0.5
Others	56.9	2.1	15.2	-
Total	1,496.5	290.6	71.3	23.2

Note: Data for banking and *takaful* as of 1H2015, while for *sukuk* and funds as of 11M15.
Source: IFSB Secretariat Workings

The majority of Shari'ah-based assets are, however, still banking assets which comprise around 75 percent of the total Shari'ah assets, but this represents a significant opportunity for *sukuk* (Shari'ah-compliant investment certificates which take the place of bonds) issuance. If we contrast major companies in the GCC area with major international companies the funding differences are stark. Major GCC companies average less than 50 percent bond versus bank funding, whereas major international companies average over 90 percent bond funding. This indicates that there is a significant opportunity for growth in the corporate *sukuk* market in GCC countries in particular.

GEOGRAPHIC SPREAD

Overall, Shari'ah-compliant finance assets are heavily concentrated in the Middle East and Asia, although the number of new markets is expanding, especially in Malaysia and other parts of South East Asia. The GCC region, with around 38 percent of total Shari'ah-compliant assets, accounts for the largest proportion of Islamic financial assets, as the sector sets to gain mainstream relevance in most of its jurisdictions. The Middle East and North Africa (MENA) region (excluding GCC) ranks a close second, with around a 35 percent share. Asia ranks third, representing around a 22 percent share in the global total, largely due to the size of the Malaysian Shari'ah-compliant finance marketplace (Table 1.2).

The Shari'ah-compliant finance industry is deepening its significance in key traditional markets, mainly concentrated in the GCC and select countries in Asia. Aside from Iran and Sudan, which operate fully Shari'ah-compliant banking systems, Shari'ah-compliant banking has also now achieved systemic importance in seven other countries: Brunei, Kuwait, Malaysia, Qatar, Saudi Arabia, the United Arab Emirates (UAE) and Yemen. These markets operate a Shari'ah-compliant finance sector alongside the conventional finance sector within a dual financial system. They have each achieved at least 15 percent market share of total banking assets for their Shari'ah-compliant banking systems and/or hold more than 5 percent of the total global Shari'ah-compliant banking assets.

TABLE 1.2   Shari'ah banking assets

Country	% total
Saudi Arabia	51%
Brunei	41%
Kuwait	38%
Yemen	27%
Qatar	25%
Malaysia	22%
UAE	17%
Bangladesh	17%

In addition Bahrain, Bangladesh, Jordan, Pakistan and Turkey are witnessing rapid growth in Shari'ah-compliant banking, in many instances supported by regulatory and legal developments.

On a global front there continue to be new innovations in Shari'ah-compliant financings, notably those coming from the London market, where in addition to the development of public/private partnership financings there have also been important developments in Shari'ah-based aircraft financings.

In *sukuk* issuance, Malaysia is dominant both in government and corporate issuance (Figure 1.1).

As a result of Malaysian dominance the Malaysian ringgit remains the dominant currency for *sukuk* issuance, with USD issues, which have a broad appeal to global investors, comprising some 21 percent of issuance (Figure 1.2).

KEY PRINCIPLES FOR SHARI'AH-COMPLIANT FINANCIAL INSTRUMENTS

There are a number of key concepts which are central to Shari'ah and which must be taken into account when structuring any Islamic finance transaction. The interpretation of these basic concepts may, however, differ according to the school of Islamic jurisprudence followed by particular Shari'ah-compliant investors and/or by Shari'ah scholars. Some of the key concepts in Shari'ah-compliant finance are:-

Riba
Riba is most commonly understood as the prohibition of charging interest. However 'interest' is only one component of *riba*; it also covers any unjustified payment such as a penalty payment for late payment. Shari'ah law requires that any return on funds be earned by way of profit derived from a commercial risk taken by the provider of finance (even if this is only very briefly). Any return on money cannot simply be for the use of money, that is to say, charging a 'pure rent for money' is prohibited.

Gharar
Contracts where there is uncertainty about the fundamental terms of a contract such as price, time, delivery, and each party's obligations and rights are not permitted under Shari'ah law. The inference of *gharar* is that the uncertainty encourages

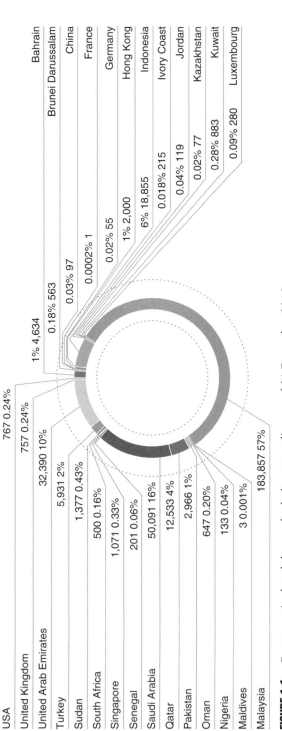

USA 767 0.24%
United Kingdom 757 0.24%
United Arab Emirates 32,390 10%
Turkey 5,931 2%
Sudan 1,377 0.43%
South Africa 500 0.16%
Singapore 1,071 0.33%
Senegal 201 0.06%
Saudi Arabia 50,091 16%
Qatar 12,533 4%
Pakistan 2,966 1%
Oman 647 0.20%
Nigeria 133 0.04%
Maldives 3 0.001%
Malaysia 183,857 57%

Bahrain 1% 4,634
Brunei Darussalam 0.18% 563
China 0.03% 97
France 0.0002% 1
Germany 0.02% 55
Hong Kong 1% 2,000
Indonesia 6% 18,855
Ivory Coast 0.018% 215
Jordan 0.04% 119
Kazakhstan 0.02% 77
Kuwait 0.28% 883
Luxembourg 0.09% 280

FIGURE 1.1 Country-wise breakdown of sukuk outstanding, as of 31 December 2015

Source: IIFM Sukuk Database

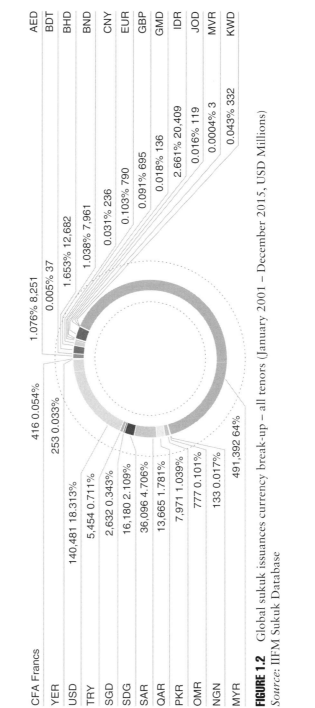

CFA Francs	416 0.054%		AED
YER	0.005% 37		BDT
USD	140,481 18.313%	1.076% 8,251	BHD
TRY	5,454 0.711%	1.653% 12,682	BND
SGD	2,632 0.343%	1.038% 7,961	CNY
SDG	16,180 2.109%	0.031% 236	EUR
SAR	36,096 4.706%	0.103% 790	GBP
QAR	13,665 1.781%	0.091% 695	GMD
PKR	7,971 1.039%	0.018% 136	IDR
OMR	777 0.101%	2.661% 20,409	JOD
NGN	133 0.017%	0.016% 119	MVR
MYR	491,392 64%	0.0004% 3	KWD
		0.043% 332	

253 0.033%

FIGURE 1.2 Global sukuk issuances currency break-up – all tenors (January 2001 – December 2015, USD Millions)
Source: IIFM Sukuk Database

speculation where a return is subject to chance rather than earned by the assumption of commercial risk. The influence of *gharar* on contracts creates a need for transparency where all parties to a contract understand the risks borne by, and returns accruing to, each other party to the contract. This need for transparency is often extended to disallowing contracts that are dependent upon one another or where the overall effect of the contracts is not clear.

Maisir
In Shari'ah, gambling or speculation (known as *maisir*) is prohibited, which leads to some contracts, such as derivative contracts including futures and options contracts being considered unacceptable as they can be used for speculative purposes.

Bay' Al-Dayn
This term relates to the sale of debts. Under Shari'ah, the transfer of debt obligations other than at face value is prohibited, and therefore the buying and selling of debt certificates is generally prohibited.

Bay' Al Inah
Many scholars disapprove of *bay' al inah*, which refers to the sale and subsequent buy-back of an asset at an increased price, which they consider is a disguised loan. The transaction cannot be confined to two persons, seller and buyer. Rather, it must involve a third party.

In the context of Shari'ah-compliant financial products, the effect of these principles can be summarised as:

- a preference for profit and loss sharing and risk sharing
- prohibition of interest
- asset-backing principle
- prohibition of uncertainty.

In addition to the principles, Shari'ah-compliant financial institutions must avoid the business with *haram* (an act forbidden in Islam) sectors such as:-

- alcohol
- pornography
- pork.

By applying these principles, the Shari'ah-compliant or Islamic financial industry (IFI) has been established to take into consideration, in addition to its religious aspects, moral, ethical and social dimensions.

It is also considered by some economists to be more stable than the conventional system, especially during crisis periods.[1] This is primarily because of the avoidance of debt-financed asset bubbles which are a major cause of financial instability.

---

[1]Arouri, M. E. H., H. Ben Ameur, F. Jawadi, N. Jawadi and W. Louhichi (2013) 'Are Islamic finance innovations enough for investors to escape from a financial downturn? Further evidence from portfolio simulations', *Applied Economics*, 35(24), 3412–3420.

SHARI'AH-COMPLIANT INSTRUMENTS

The creation of Shari'ah-compliant financial products hinges on the use of a number of Shari'ah-compliant legal instruments, based on the nominate contracts of *Fiqh al Muamalat*, which may be used individually or in combination to create the desired financial products. The nominate contracts most frequently used are briefly explained in Appendix A.

SHARI'AH-COMPLIANT INVESTORS

Owing to the prohibition of interest, the need for equity markets as a financial investment is greater in Shari'ah-compliant finance than in conventional finance. In addition, a number of recent innovations in terms of product design and risk management have taken place with the growth of the Shari'ah-compliant capital markets. One of the aspects of these innovations was the launching of Shari'ah-compliant indices and as a consequence the creation of funds.

Funds cannot pay fixed or guaranteed return on capital, as this would be considered *riba*. Instead of borrowing and lending, Shari'ah-compliant finance relies on sharing or transferring the ownership of assets and therefore risk and profit/loss.

As debt is disapproved of, investment in highly leveraged companies is not acceptable (see Chapter 7 for a more detailed treatment).

Companies involved in activities considered *haram* cannot be part of a Shari'ah fund strategy. Prohibited business activities can relate to food (production and sales of alcoholic beverages including pubs and restaurants, pork products, tobacco), gambling (casinos, online gambling, betting, lottery schemes), adult oriented (video, magazines, online material, strip clubs), dubious, immoral and illicit trades (prostitution, drugs).

Shari'ah forbids gambling or speculation in any form (*maisir*). Consequently, derivatives, options and futures are prohibited, as are a number of common trading practices such as short selling and margin trading. Opinion differs about forwards, but in general they are not considered permissible. Moreover, this prohibition extends to day trading, as the difference between the multi-day settlement period for the underlying instrument and the intra-day trading of the securities means that day traders are effectively trading on credit for which they pay.

Because of these restrictions, it has generally been considered that Shari'ah-compliant investors have less opportunity to spread their investment risk, resulting generally in their investments having a higher volatility of returns when compared to those of conventional investors. However, considering systematic risk, in general Shari'ah indices are considered to have lower portfolio betas relative to conventional equity indices. The lower portfolio beta of Shari'ah-compliant indices is a logical result of Shari'ah screening. As Shari'ah screening eliminates stocks with high financial leverage, the resulting portfolio beta is likely to be lower because a stock's beta is reflective of the underlying business risk and financial risk, which is greater the higher the leverage of the company.

SHARI'AH-COMPLIANT EQUITY INDICES

What is an 'index'?

Put simply, it is a hypothetical portfolio that represents the market as a whole, or the sub-group of the market the investor wishes to track.

The weighting of each stock or bond in the hypothetical portfolio will reflect its proportion in the whole or sub-group. The proportion may, however, be assessed in different ways and investors should take note of the proportioning methodology. This is important, as the different assessment and proportioning methodologies require a great deal of understanding in order to see both the strengths and the weaknesses of indices. The days of indices being simple averages are long gone.

Global indices now have a huge effect on investors and markets. Passive investment has been a huge growth industry in recent times; indeed there are actually more indices in the markets today than there are stocks. The biggest indexer S&P Dow Jones publishes over 1 million indices every day.

Moreover, indices are the dominant structural component for mutual fund assets in the US, covering some USD9.4 trillion of assets – a position that has been reinforced by the development of exchange-traded funds (ETFs), which are index tracking and now cover some USD3 trillion of assets globally.

Indeed, there is some evidence that Shari'ah-compliant equity funds, which screen out highly indebted companies, perform better than simple corporate equity indices. Conventional investors either in corporate bonds or equities may find this research especially useful when looking at risk-adjusted performance.

A note on market index providers is given in Appendix B.

Chronologically, indices of Shari'ah-compliant equity investments were launched for the first time in the late 1990s, beginning in April 1998 with the index DMI 150 (Dar al Mal al-Islami) launched jointly by two private banks (Faisal Finance and Bank Vontobel) in order to track the performance of the 150 largest global publicly traded companies. Another index which was created in November of the same year was SAMI (Socially Aware Muslim Index), which measured the performance of 500 Shari'ah-compliant companies.

After this beginning, several financial markets launched their own Shari'ah-compliant indices as a new alternative for investors seeking investment opportunities without compromising their religious beliefs. Hence, Dow Jones created the Dow Jones Islamic Market (DJIM) Index in February 1999 and FTSE Group launched Global Islamic Index Series (GIIS) at the London Stock Exchange in October 1999. The index provider S&P created the Global Benchmark Shari'ah indices in December 2006 and MSCI Barra launched its global family of Islamic indices in March 2007. In February 2011, STOXX Limited introduced the first set of Shari'ah-compliant indices for Europe and the Eurozone; these indices measure the performance of Shari'ah-compliant companies selected from the universe of STOXX Europe 600 index.

In addition to the above indices which have an international geographical coverage, some financial markets such as Malaysia, India, Pakistan, Saudi Arabia, Taiwan, Bahrain, Turkey and Egypt have introduced their own Islamic indices with a local focus.

Some further information on the main Shari'ah-compliant indices is given below.

Dow Jones Islamic Indices

Dow Jones Islamic Market (DJIM) Indices include:-

- DJIM ™ Titans 100 Index: Covers the US, Europe and the Asia/Pacific region.
- DJIM ™ Asia/Pacific Titans 25 Index.
- DJIM ™ Europe Titans 25 Index.
- DJIM ™ US Titans 50 Index.
- DJIM ™ CHIME 100 Index.
- DJIM ™ China/Hong Kong Titans 30 Index: Covers companies whose primary operations are in mainland China and Hong Kong and trade on HKEx.
- DJIM ™ International Titans 100 Index: Represents ex-US companies.
- DJIM ™ Malaysia Titans 25 Index.

FTSE Shari'ah-Compliant Indices

In addition to the FTSE Shari'ah Global Equity Index Series, which is based on the large and mid-cap stocks in the FTSE Global Equity Index Series universe, the FTSE calculates a number of other Shari'ah-compliant indices based on other universes, including those listed below:-

- FTSE NASDAQ Dubai Index Series.
- FTSE Bursa Malaysia Hirjah Shari'ah and EMAS Shari'ah indices.
- FTSE SET Shari'ah Index.
- FTSE TWSE Taiwan Shari'ah Index.
- FTSE/JSE Shari'ah indices.
- FTSE SGX Shari'ah Index Series.
- FTSE Shari'ah Developed Minimum Variance Index.

S&P Shari'ah-Compliant Indices

The S&P Shari'ah Market Indices include:-

- The S&P 500® Shari'ah, which includes all Shari'ah-compliant constituents of the S&P 500, the leading benchmark for the US equity market.
- The S&P Global BMI Shari'ah, which offers investors a comprehensive global Shari'ah-compliant benchmark.

MSCI Barra Islamic Indices

MSCI Barra Market Indices includes the MSCI World Islamic Index (USD).

STOXX Islamic Indices

STOXX Market Indices include:-

- STOXX® Europe Islamic.
- EURO STOXX Islamic 50.

Other Islamic Indices Providers

In addition to these equity indices there are a number of others, including:-

- Credit Suisse HS50 Sharia Index.
- Dubai Shari'ah Hedge Fund Index.
- Jakarta Islamic Index, Indonesia.
- Thomson Reuters' Islamic indices:
  - Regional Indices, e.g. MENA, BRIC, ASEAN, OIC.
  - Country Indices, e.g. UAE, Malaysia, Bahrain, Indonesia.
  - Sector Indices, e.g. Global Energy, Global Technology, Global Healthcare.

SHARI'AH-COMPLIANT COLLECTIVE INVESTMENT SCHEMES

Shari'ah-compliant Collective Investment Schemes (CIS) include equity funds, commodities funds and Islamic real estate investment trusts (REITs). Some restricted profit-sharing investment accounts, which are offered by some Islamic banks, may also be considered as a type of CIS, but are classified as banking products rather than capital market products.

These types of Islamic CIS are described in more detail in Chapter 4.

TAKAFUL (ISLAMIC INSURANCE) INSTITUTIONS

Takaful institutions are actors in the ICM, as they buy and hold Islamic equities and *sukuk* in the funds that they manage and, in family *takaful*, offer savings and investment products similar to CIS, except that they come bundled with a whole life insurance policy. The operation of the *mudarabah* contract allows the bank to take a large share of the income from the investments – up to 70 percent.

SUKUK

The *sukuk* market is a key part of the ICM, as it provides seekers of funds and investors with a Shari'ah-compliant alternative to the conventional bond market. *Sukuk* (plural of *sakk*) is an Arabic word which means 'certificates'. *Sukuk* are structured to yield returns that do not involve interest. They may be issued by either sovereigns (governments) or corporates (including Islamic banks). *Sukuk* are discussed in more detail in later chapters. The present section provides an extensive overview of the *sukuk* market.

There are three main types of *sukuk*: asset-backed, asset-based and equity-based. These are described in detail in Chapter 3. A special case is the *sukuk* issued by the International Islamic Liquidity Management Corporation (IILM), which are short-term instruments to be held by Islamic financial institutions as High Quality Liquid Assets (HQLA) in order to meet Basel III requirements (see Chapter 11).

Sukuk in 2014

The issuance of *sukuk* in 2014 was dominated by government issuance, making it a very unusual but also very welcome year for the *sukuk* market, especially as several of the government issuers in 2014 were new to the market (see Figures 1.3 and 1.4). The Maldives, Senegal, South Africa and the Emirate of Sharjah made their debut in the market, and there were also sovereign debuts by conventional financial centres such as Luxembourg, Hong Kong and the United Kingdom (Table 1.3). In 2014, the UK became the first non-Muslim sovereign government to issue *sukuk* when it sold a GBP200 million ($307 million) issuance in June. In September, Luxembourg sold EUR200 million ($240 million) of five-year Islamic *sukuk*, Hong Kong raised USD1 billion and South Africa tapped the market for USD500 million.

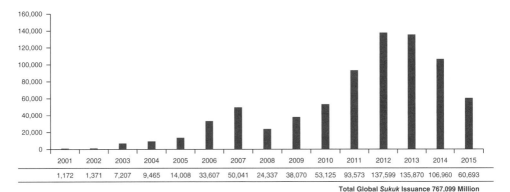

FIGURE 1.3 Total global *sukuk* issuances (January 2001 – December 2015, USD Millions)
Source: IIFM Sukuk Database

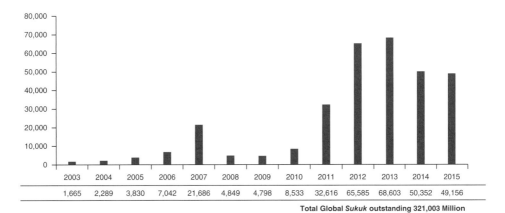

FIGURE 1.4 Total global *sukuk* outstanding as of 31 December 2015
Source: IIFM Sukuk Database

While the number of sovereign *sukuk* sales rose in 2014, the amount raised dropped 30 percent from a year earlier to USD20.4 billion, the lowest level of issuance since 2010. Corporate issuers raised USD78.6 billion through 501 sales. Total outstanding issuance, however, rose in 2014 to just below USD300 billion equivalent, and issuance in the year was just below the USD120 billion equivalent of 2013 and substantially below the peak outstanding issuance of over USD130 billion equivalent in 2012.

Sukuk in 2015

In 2015, the *sukuk* market entered a period of consolidation with total global *sukuk* issuance falling to just over the equivalent of USD60 billion from over 100 billion in 2014 and over 135 billion in 2013 and a peak of just over 137 billion in 2012 (Table 1.4).

While a major talking point in 2015 was the very significant drop in short-term issuance by Bank Nagara Malaysia, which resulted in a fall in total global *sukuk* issuance of around USD40 billion, both Malaysian sovereign and corporate issuance increased in 2015 over their 2014 issuance to respectively USD14.3 billion from USD8.1 billion and to USD11.57 billion from USD9.96 billion.

A mix of the maturity of a number of major international *sukuk* and a slowing of new issuance due to economic uncertainty also saw international *sukuk* issuance fall by USD6.0 billion from its 2014 peak of USD26.4 billion.

Apart from Malaysia domestic *sukuk* issuance in aggregate rose slightly in 2015. Saudi Arabia issued the equivalent of USD4.5 billion in 2015 as against USD2.5 billion the previous year, Bahrain more than doubling domestic issuance to the equivalent of USD3 billion and Turkey quadrupled its domestic issuance to the equivalent of USD920 million.

TABLE 1.3   Selected hallmark global *sukuk* issuances in 2014 (USD 500 Million or >)

Issuer	Issuance Currency	Millions USD or USD Equivalent	Average Tenor Years
The International Finance Facility for Immunisation	USD	500	3
Government of Pakistan	USD	1,000	5
FlyDubai	USD	500	5
Bahrain Mumtalakat	USD	600	7
DIFC Investments	USD	700	10
Government of South Africa	USD	500	6
Goldman Sachs	USD	500	5
Government of Sharjah	USD	750	10
Government of Hong Kong	USD	1,000	5
Government of Indonesia	USD	1,500	10
Islamic Development Bank	USD	1,000	5
Kuveyt Turk Katilim Bankasi	USD	500	5
Emaar Malls	USD	750	10
Khazanah Nasional Berhad	USD	500	7

Source: IIFM Sukuk Database

TABLE 1.4   Selected hallmark global *sukuk* issuances in 2015 (USD 500 Million or >)

Issuer	Issuance Currency	Millions USD or USD Equivalent	Average Tenor Years
Axiata	USD	500	5
Government of Oman	OMR	647	5
Majid Al Futtaim	USD	500	10
APICORP	USD	500	5
Qatar Islamic Bank	USD	750	5
Arab National Bank	SAR	533	10
Jimah Energy Ventures	MYR	2,006	5
Islamic Development Bank	SAR	514	5
Garuda Indonesia	USD	500	5
Government of Hong Kong	USD	1,000	5
Government of Indonesia	IDR	2,000	10
Dubai Islamic Bank	USD	750	5
Noor Bank	USD	500	5
Emirates Airlines	USD	913	10
Government of Ras Al Khaimah	USD	1,000	10
Sharjah Islamic Bank	USD	500	5
Islamic Development Bank	USD	1,000	5
Petroliam Nasional	USD	1,250	5
Government of Bahrain	BHD	660	5
National Commercial Bank	SAR	740	Perpetual
Riyad Bank	SAR	1,070	Perpetual
Qatar Islamic Bank	QR	550	Perpetual
Dubai Islamic Bank	USD	1,000	Perpetual
Al Hilal Bank	USD	500	Perpetual

Source: IIFM Sukuk Database

International *Sukuk* Issuance

The total of international *sukuk* issuance has risen more than tenfold since 2001 (Figure 1.5).

There are a number of different structures that support *sukuk* issuance and the most commonly used are described below.

In issuance terms, the *sukuk al ijarah* has remained the most popular structure since 2001 with just over 40 percent of the market. For international issuers the structural similarities between the *ijarah* structure and a conventional sale and lease back structure does make this structure an easier 'sell' to international investors and therefore issuers.

Sukuk al musharaka in the period 2001 to 2008 was the second most popular at 23 percent, but this fell to 6 percent in 2009 to 2012 and only 1 percent in 2013

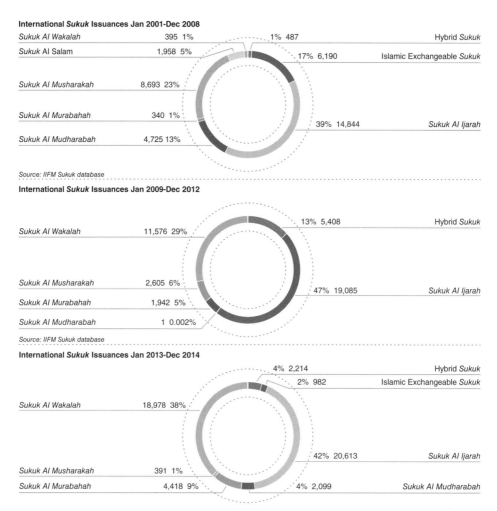

International *Sukuk* Issuances Jan 2001-Dec 2008

Sukuk Al Wakalah	395 1%	
Sukuk Al Salam	1,958 5%	
Sukuk Al Musharakah	8,693 23%	
Sukuk Al Murabahah	340 1%	
Sukuk Al Mudharabah	4,725 13%	

1% 487 — Hybrid *Sukuk*
17% 6,190 — Islamic Exchangeable *Sukuk*
39% 14,844 — *Sukuk Al Ijarah*

Source: IIFM Sukuk database

International *Sukuk* Issuances Jan 2009-Dec 2012

Sukuk Al Wakalah	11,576 29%
Sukuk Al Musharakah	2,605 6%
Sukuk Al Murabahah	1,942 5%
Sukuk Al Mudharabah	1 0.002%

13% 5,408 — Hybrid *Sukuk*
47% 19,085 — *Sukuk Al Ijarah*

Source: IIFM Sukuk database

International *Sukuk* Issuances Jan 2013-Dec 2014

Sukuk Al Wakalah	18,978 38%
Sukuk Al Musharakah	391 1%
Sukuk Al Murabahah	4,418 9%

4% 2,214 — Hybrid *Sukuk*
2% 982 — Islamic Exchangeable *Sukuk*
42% 20,613 — *Sukuk Al Ijarah*
4% 2,099 — *Sukuk Al Mudharabah*

FIGURE 1.5 Structural break-up of international *sukuk* issuances – all tenors (January 2001 – December 2014, USD Millions)
Source: IIFM Sukuk Database

to 2014. The popularity of *musharaka* structures in property finance does make this structure prone to the global property cycle and in part may account for this trend.

The *sukuk al wakala* replaced the *sukuk al musharaka* in popularity in the 2009 to 2012 period, taking a 29 percent market share up from only 1 percent in 2001 to 2008. This popularity continued to gain momentum in 2013 to 2014 with the market share rising to 38 percent – very close to the *ijarah*'s 42 percent.

This does contrast with domestic *sukuk* issuance where *sukuk al murabaha* is consistently the most popular structure.

One of the major changes over the whole period has been the fall in the diversity of structures used in international issuance. Four structures each had over 10 percent of the market in 2001 to 2008, but this fell to three in 2009 to 2012 and to only two in 2013 to 2014. Standardisation is in general to be welcomed in capital markets as it concentrates liquidity and in the process aids price discovery.

Ijarah

The most common structures used for the creation of *sukuk* is the *sukuk al ijarah*. Set out in Figure 1.6 is a simplified structure diagram and brief description of the *ijarah* structure and principal cash flows to assist in understanding the transaction structure.

Assets which are capable of being leased, including land or tangible assets such as plant and machinery, are appropriate for *ijarah* structures. Transactions involving real estate will require analysis as to whether registration or other formalities are required to effect a transfer of real estate or any interest therein.

1. A special purpose vehicle ('issuer SPV') issues Sukūk, which represent a right against the SPV to payment of the Periodic Distribution Amount (i.e. profit) and the Dissolution Amount (i.e. principal) on redemption.
2. Certificate holders purchase Sukūk and pay the proceeds to the SPV (the 'Principal Amount'). The SPV then typically declares an English law trust over the proceeds and the assets acquired using the proceeds (i.e. the land and contractual rights) and thereby acts as trustee on behalf of the Certificate holders (the 'Trustee'). Each Certificate is thereby intended to represent an undivided beneficial ownership interest in the relevant assets underpinning the trust.
3. The Company enters into a Sale and Purchase Agreement with the Trustee, pursuant to which it sells land or other tangible assets to the Trustee in consideration for an amount equal to the Principal Amount.
4. The Trustee leases the land or other assets back to the Company pursuant a lease agreement between the parties (Ijārah) in consideration for the periodic payment of Rental by the Company (which, minus certain expenses, will serve to produce the 'Periodic Distribution Amount' payable by the Trustee to the Certificate holders).
5. The SPV pays Periodic Distribution Amounts to the Certificate holders using the Rental.

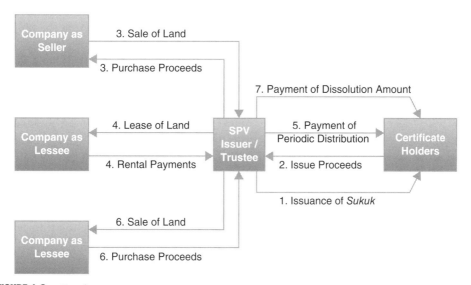

FIGURE 1.6 *Ijarah* structure

6. Upon (i) the occurrence of an event of default or maturity, or (ii) the exercise of any applicable put or call options (including a tax call), the Trustee will sell, and the Company will repurchase, the land or other assets pursuant to the exercise of a Sale Undertaking or Purchase Undertaking (as applicable). The consideration for such sale/repurchase will be payment of the 'Exercise Price', being a sum equal to the Principal Amount plus any accrued and unpaid Periodic Distribution Amounts owing to Certificate holders.
7. The SPV pays the 'Dissolution Amount' to the Certificate holders in an amount equal to the Exercise Price.

Criticisms of *Sukuk* Issuance Practices

During the course of 2007, Sheikh Taqi Usmani, the chairman of the Shari'ah board of the AAOIFI (Accounting and Auditing Organization for Islamic Financial Institutions), criticised a number of *sukuk* structures used in the market, in particular certain equity *sukuk* structures (*mudaraba, wakala* and *musharaka*) on the basis that, in his view, they were not Shari'ah-compliant.

For example, in *sukuk mudaraba*, in order to achieve the economic result of the investors receiving a predetermined amount on redemption and periodic profit distributions in the interim, a combination of a purchase undertaking and liquidity facility was used. The liquidity facility received criticism as it was felt to run contrary to the principle that the investor (*rab-al-maal*) should solely bear the loss on the investment.

In effect, the combination of the purchase indemnity and the liquidity facility were seen to serve to grant a guarantee in favour of the *rab-al-maal* and therefore negate the risk to which the *rab-al-maal* should be exposed. There was also criticism of the 'incentive fee' for the *mudarib* being linked to a benchmark, rather than to profits based on the skill exercised by the *mudarib* with respect to investments made.

Another area of criticism was that without the investment plan specifying that the proceeds are required for the purposes of investment in physical assets, the money invested by the *rab-al-maal* amounts to a loan.

Criticism was also extended to the use of purchase undertakings from the obligor in other Shari'ah structures for the same reasons regarding negating risk, because the purchase price is pre-agreed on the issue date of the *sukuk* instead of it being determined at the time of sale in the future by reference to the market value of the asset.

For a period of time there was uncertainty as to the Shari'ah ruling in respect of *sukuk* that had previously been issued in the market. AAOIFI soon clarified in discussions with market participants that *sukuk* which had been approved previously, together with the fatwas relating to such *sukuk*, remained intact.

Furthermore, in February 2008 the AAOIFI Shari'ah board, having met on various occasions both among themselves and with a number of market participants, issued the following guidance on *sukuk* issuance:[2]

- *Sukuk* must represent ownership in real or physical assets which may also include services or usufruct. The originator/obligor must be able to prove the transfer of

---

[2]In its first Shari'ah Roundtable, the International Islamic Liquidity Management Corporation (IILM) agreed with the participating Shari'ah scholars that there should be a difference in the guidance on *sukuk* issuance between sovereign assets, which back all the IILM short-term *sukuk*, and corporate assets.

title in its records and may not retain title to its assets sold or transferred under the *sukuk* structure;
- *Sukuk* may not represent receivables or debts unless as part of a sale of all assets by a financial or commercial institution;
- The obligor (be it *mudarib*, partner in a *musharaka* or agent/*wakeel*) may not provide a liquidity facility;
- A *mudarib*, partner in a *musharaka* or agent (*wakeel*) may not undertake to purchase the *mudaraba* or *musharaka* assets at the face value of the *sukuk* but such purchase must instead be at the market value or a value to be agreed upon at the time of purchase; and
- A lessee in an *ijarah sukuk* may redeem the *sukuk* by purchase of assets at a pre-agreed price provided the lessee is not a *mudarib*, partner in a *musharaka* or agent.

The issue of this AAOIFI guidance has resulted in current *sukuk* being structured to conform to the guidance, except for sovereign issuances where legal title to the assets is retained by the sovereign and the issuer SPV receives beneficial title in an 'asset-based' structure. In particular, the market has moved away from the once-prevalent 100 percent *ijarah* structure towards hybrid structures, which for instance combine *ijarah* assets with a smaller proportion of *murabaha* assets within a *wakala*- or *mudaraba*-based structure to give more flexibility with respect to the types of assets that can be used. These have the additional advantage of allowing a commodity *murabaha* transaction to form part of the asset base, up to a maximum percentage (less than 50 percent) of the total asset value. As a result, issuers are able to issue *sukuk* on a more 'asset efficient' basis than previously.

Sukuk Indices

The Criteria for *sukuk* to be included in a Shari'ah-compliant Index comprise the following:

- The issuance is certified by a reputable Shari'ah supervisory board.
- The issue must comply with the standards for tradable *sukuk* laid down by AAOIFI.
- The underlying assets to be securitised in *sukuk* must be screened for Shari'ah principles.

S&P Dow Jones has a trio of bond and *sukuk* indices aimed at MENA and Islamic investors. They include the S&P MENA Bond & Sukuk Index and two sub-indices, the S&P MENA Bond Index and S&P MENA Sukuk Index.

The S&P MENA Bond & Sukuk Index comprises a universe of USD-denominated debentures that seeks to measure the performance of bonds and *sukuk* in the MENA region. This region incorporates Algeria, Bahrain, Egypt, Iran, Iraq, Jordan, Kuwait, Lebanon, Libya, Morocco, Oman, Palestine, Qatar, Saudi Arabia, Syria, Tunisia, UAE and Yemen.

The S&P MENA Bond Index comprises a universe of USD-denominated debentures that seeks to measure the performance of bonds issued by companies domiciled in the MENA region. This index is, however, not Shari'ah-compliant.

The S&P MENA Sukuk Index is designed to provide exposure to *sukuk* issued by companies domiciled in the MENA region and is Shari'ah-compliant.

To be eligible for inclusion in these indices, each security must have maturity greater than or equal to one year from the rebalancing date and a minimum par amount of

USD200 million at each rebalancing. Fixed or floating rate coupon instruments are eligible. The minimum credit rating for inclusion is BBB– / Baa3 / BBB–.

Sukuk Trust Certificate Programmes

A *sukuk* trust certificate programme allows the issuer to issue multiple tranches of trust certificates at the same time based on the same programme documentation. The issuer may also may issue certificates with different features such as:

- Fixed or floating profit rate
- Callability and puttability
- Currency flexibility
- Tenor.

Due to their flexibility and repeatability of issuance, the economics of these programmes favour those who are seeking multiple issuances each year and require speed to market; this is achieved because all documentation is agreed before any issuance under the programme takes place.

Trust certificate programmes also allow for a flexible response to investor demand, even allowing for private placement if required, and can be structured to allow issuance to both GCC domestic and international investors, including compliance with US regulations Rule 144A & Regulation S.

The bulk of international issuance is at ten-year tenors, whereas GCC investors favour three- to five-year tenors.

Rule 144A and Regulation S

Public and private entities can access the US capital markets without registering the offering with the US Securities and Exchange Commission (SEC) by issuing securities under Rule 144A and/or Regulation S of the US Securities Act of 1933, as amended. Rule 144A and Regulation S offerings are frequently conducted simultaneously and give an issuer the flexibility to offer its securities inside the US in reliance on Rule 144A at the same time as it offers its securities outside the US in reliance on Regulation S.

Private entities, including foreign issuers, view Rule 144A and Regulation S offerings favourably, because such offerings provide an opportunity to raise capital without subjecting themselves to the burdensome periodic filing requirements of the SEC or the internal controls requirements imposed by the Sarbanes-Oxley Act of 2002 (SOX). Because of the absence of SEC registration and review, Rule 144A and Regulation S offerings are also typically accomplished at a lower cost than a registered US underwritten offering.

International Islamic Liquidity Management Corporation (IILM)

Set up though the actions of Bank Negara's then governor Tan Sri Dr Zeti Akhtar Aziz, the organisation's initial membership of 13 includes Saudi Arabia, Qatar, Luxembourg and the Islamic Development Bank.

The IILM's first objective was to issue Shari'ah-compliant financial instruments to facilitate more efficient and effective liquidity management for the Shari'ah-compliant banking industry and to start with is focusing on issuing short-term paper in US dollars. This will make a very important contribution to resolving the problems caused by the separate national 'pools' of liquidity in Shari'ah-compliant markets.

On 9 July 2015, IILM announced that it had successfully reissued USD860 million three-month tenor *sukuk* priced at 0.58325 percent profit rate. This was the seventeenth series of short-term IILM *sukuk* that are rated A1 by Standard and Poor's Rating Services. As at July 2015, the IILM *sukuk* that have been issued and reissued amounted to USD10.84 billion.

IILM *sukuk* based on A1 ratings are recognised by Bank Negara Malaysia as Level 1 HQLA, subject however to a 20 percent risk weight under the Basel II Pillar 1 Standardised Approach for credit risk. A number of other banking regulators have accepted, or are in the process of accepting, IILM *sukuk* as HQLA under the Basel III rules and wider acceptance will no doubt come in due course.

The recognition of these instruments in a European context is of primary importance as the European Union (EU) is moving towards replacing banking directives with banking regulation. Directives, while published across the EU, were incorporated nationally, leaving significant room for nation states to adapt the directive to local requirements. Regulations lack this form of adaptability, and it is all too easy to envisage the specific needs of EU-based Shari'ah-compliant banks, all of which are UK domiciled, being overlooked in this new regulatory environment.

It is of course possible that, after the UK's exit from the EU, the Bank of England (BoE) will have greater regulatory flexibility.

BANKS: CAPITAL AND REGULATORY ISSUES

As noted at the start of this chapter, Islamic banks are still the dominant providers of capital in Shari'ah-compliant finance. More pertinently for the purpose of this chapter, they are also important investors and arrangers of Shari'ah-compliant capital markets products such as *sukuk* and lease products.

Banks were, however, hit by, and were a source of contagion from, the series of financial markets and banking crises that affected a number of economies following the Lehman crisis of 2007. Because of this, the re-regulation of banks, undertaken as a result of the Basel III global regulatory initiative, is having a major effect upon them as both providers and arrangers of financial products.

Why did the pre-financial crisis capital regime fail to provide the necessary protection to the financial system when the crisis hit?

There were two major flaws with the pre-crisis capital regime for banks:

1. The definition of capital.
2. The capital weights of banking and especially trading book assets, i.e. both the numerator and denominator of the Capital Adequacy Ratio (CAR) were wrongly specified.

The Definition of Capital

The flaws of the pre-crisis regime started with the definition of capital. Prior to the crisis, it was possible to operate with no more than 2 percent of risk-weighted assets in the form of common equity. This was largely because the then existing regime allowed hybrid debt instruments to count as Tier 1 capital, even though they had no principal loss absorbency capacity on a going concern basis.

That is to say, they only absorbed losses after a bank's common equity (ordinary share capital and reserves) was either exhausted by losses or the bank was in insolvency.

But in many cases the insolvency procedure could not in fact be used because the essence of the concept of 'too big (or too systemically important) to fail' was that large banks could not enter insolvency as the consequences were too damaging for customers, financial systems and economies more broadly.

The big lesson from this history is that going concern capital instruments must comprise mainly common equity, and all other instruments contributing to Tier 1 capital must unambiguously be able to absorb losses when the bank is a going concern.

At present, Shari'ah-compliant banks are at a competitive disadvantage because their capital structures are of necessity dominated by equity because they cannot use lower cost debt capital. Consequently, a conventional bank will offer investors a significantly higher return than an Islamic financial institution with a similar balance sheet. This advantage has been substantially reduced by two recent developments. Firstly, Basel III will force conventional banks to hold much more equity. Secondly, Islamic banks are starting to issue equity *sukuk* which meet the Basel III criteria for Tier 1 capital (see Chapter 14).

Moreover, the pre-crisis regime also allowed hybrid debt capital instruments to support the required deductions from the capital calculation, such as:

- goodwill,
- expected losses (introduced later under Basel II with the internal models regime for credit risk) and
- investments in other banks' capital instruments.

However, this had a perverse effect, since according to international financial reporting standards (IFRS) any losses arising from these items are deducted from common equity in the going concern state. Hence, the result of applying these deductions at the level of total capital had the effect of overstating the core equity capital ratio.

A further flaw was that deferred tax assets (DTAs) were not deducted from capital, and minority interest assets were recognised in full. But the value of DTAs depends on future profitability (which is not assured), and minority interests are not fully transferable to absorb losses for a group.

There were also problems in relation to the treatment of provisions. Under the currently applied IFRS, provisions are based on actual asset impairments, i.e. incurred rather than expected losses. However, this will change with the imposition of IFRS9, which will require all companies to recognise provisions on an expected loss basis. The implementation of this reporting standard is likely to raise bank provision numbers by between 50 percent and 100 percent, which is a major revision. The standard is mandatory for financial reporting as from 1 January 2018.

Until that happens, the Basel III bank capital framework *de facto* acts as a partial substitute means of achieving more forward-looking provisioning, through the internal models regime for credit risk, which requires the deduction from capital of expected losses in excess of incurred loss based provisions numbers.

The Capital Weights of Banking and Trading Book Assets

Basel I risk weights applied only to credit risk and provided little insight into how firms measured and managed risk, tending to create incentives for banks to increase the average level of riskiness of their assets.

Basel II was not in place properly when the crisis broke, though the 1986 Market Risk Amendment was.

The Market Risk Amendment and Basel II dramatically increased the complexity of the capital framework, and while it was intended to increase the scope of risk capture in the regulatory capital measure it ended up creating new opportunities for 'optimising' (in practice reducing) regulatory capital.

The Basel Committee recognised that across internationally active banks, Basel II, by permitting such banks to use internally determined credit risk weightings (IRB), would likely lead to an overall reduction in the required capital compared with that required under Basel. Indeed, for a set of 17 major international banks (designated as Global Systemically Important Banks, or G-SIBs) average risk weights fell almost continuously from 70 percent in 1993 to below 40 percent in 2012. But this fall in average risk weights did not represent a systematic reduction in risk within the banking system.

Thus the level of Basel II Pillar 1 risk-weighted capital was wrong, with too little capital being required. This was not corrected by the imposition of the Pillar 2 capital requirements. In 2008, the major UK banks had a Pillar 2 capital requirement £22bn (equivalent to 10 percent of the then Pillar 1 capital requirement).

In summary, the system was flawed in terms of the definition of capital, the quality and the quantity of capital banks were required to hold.

Under the Basel II regime, the Pillar 1 minimum requirement was £38bn of the highest quality capital for the five largest UK banks. Compared with this, taking both capital minima and capital buffers together when Basel III is fully implemented the equivalent figure, as measured in September 2013 (according to the BoE), would be £271bn, or some seven times the Basel II Pillar 1 requirement.

Stress Testing

A major principle of the new framework is that there is no single 'right' approach to assessing capital adequacy. The very important role that is now given to stress tests illustrates the point. This is a key device to examine and mitigate tail risks, and like all good forecasting exercises, the stress test is designed to probe important issues rather than just provide a single answer.

Resolution

A second key principle of capital adequacy is that of establishing a clear boundary between the going concern and gone concern (or resolution) rules for loss absorbency. This is one reason why the work on resolution and gone concern loss absorbency is so important but still incomplete. The Total Loss Absorbent Capital (TLAC) regime applies only to G-SIBs and comprises instruments that should be legally, feasibly and operationally available to absorb losses when needed; this includes Common Equity Tier 1, Additional Tier 1 instruments, Tier 2 instruments, Senior Subordinated Debt and subject to certain restrictions Senior Debt.

Basel III and Islamic Banks

The details relating to the implementation of Basel III are complex and mainly relate to the methodologies banks may employ in calculating their capital weights. In general, however, the changes from Basel II consist of increasing the risk weights for those banks using the simple (Standardised) approach and to introducing additional risk factors for the model-based (Advanced) approaches.

There are also specific problems for banks which may hold financial assets as long-term investments (banking book treatment) which pushes them towards the same capital treatment as if they were held for trading purposes (trading book treatment), with an emphasis on market risk. This may be of greater relevance to Islamic banks, which are likely to invest in (say) Shari'ah-compliant equity or *sukuk* funds.

The Basel Committee outlines its prudential framework for banks' equity investments in funds as follows:[3]

The prudential framework comprises a hierarchy of approaches for banks' equity investments in funds:

1. The Look Through Approach (LTA) is the most granular approach. Subject to meeting the conditions set out for its use, banks employing the LTA must apply the risk weights of the fund's underlying exposures as if the exposures were held directly by the bank.
2. The Mandate Based Approach (MBA) provides an additional layer of risk sensitivity that can be used when banks do not meet the conditions for applying the LTA. Banks employing the MBA assign risk weights on the basis of the information contained in a fund's mandate or in the relevant national legislation.
3. When neither of the above approaches is feasible, the Fall Back Approach (FBA) must be utilised. This applies a 1,250 percent risk weight to a bank's equity investment in the fund. This is equivalent to requiring a capital charge of 100 percent.

To ensure that banks have appropriate incentives to enhance the risk management of their exposures, the degree of conservatism increases with each successive approach.

The Committee also agreed to incorporate a leverage adjustment to the risk-weighted assets derived from the above approaches to appropriately reflect a fund's leverage.

Clearly the LTA approach for Islamic (i.e. Shari'ah-compliant) banks that hold high quality equities is likely to favour them over conventional banks, as the Shari'ah-compliant equity funds they hold will usually display lower individual stock volatility and a lower beta than their conventional counterparts.[4] Where emerging market equity funds are concerned, however, it will be important for national regulators to craft regulation that allows implementation of the MBA approach. The need to implement the punitive FBA approach should be avoided, as it would be prohibitively costly in terms of its impact on banks' capital. The leverage adjustment should, however, favour Islamic banks with their low leverage, as they have a higher proportion of common equity in their capital than conventional banks.

---

[3]Basel Committee on Banking Supervision, Capital requirements for banks' equity investments in funds, December 2013.

[4]Beta (β) is a measure of a stock's risk of volatility compared to the overall market (systematic risk). The market's beta coefficient is 1.00. Any stock with a beta higher than 1.00 is considered more volatile than the market, and therefore riskier to hold, whereas a stock with a beta lower than 1.00 is expected to rise or fall more slowly than the market, and thus be less risky.

Intended and Unintended Consequences

Like all revisions to regulation these revisions are an attempt to create a set of intended consequences; in this case they can be summed up by the phrase 'creating a more resilient banking sector'.

Unfortunately, all regulatory changes also produce unintended consequences and in the case of the banks this is already manifesting itself in the amount of capital devoted to trading and market making for Currencies, Commodities and Fixed Income Securities (CCF) in particular. This will produce major issues for the liquidity of these markets, notably bond markets, which as long-term instruments are particularly affected by the changes in capital requirements for the holding of such securities.

There will be inevitable spillover effects from lower market liquidity in conventional bond markets into the *sukuk* market, not least because the effects of Basel III regulation affect both conventional and Shari'ah-compliant banks.

Liquidity Issues

Liquidity of the banking system differs from the liquidity of a market. The latter relates to the ability to sell an asset and is frequently measured by the bid–offer spread of the assets market price.

Banks, especially US banks (because of their greater reliance on the so-called originate and distribute model), do rely upon markets to sell assets into. This is the banks' so-called market liquidity. Banks, however, also rely upon their ability to fund through their deposit base their holding of illiquid loan assets. This is known as funding liquidity.

Liquidity of the Banking System and the Net Stable Funding Ratio

At present, banks have access to funding liquidity, which is based on their funding structures. If a bank has plenty of stable retail deposits and medium- to long-term contractual funding, through say bonds, certificates of deposit or profit- and loss-sharing accounts, the bank can use these stable sources to fund its asset base, even in difficult economic circumstances. New Basel III rules will impose minimum requirements for stable funding upon banks through what is known as the Net Stable Funding Ratio (NSFR), ensuring much greater levels of match funding between the term of lending and of their funding.

Liquidity Coverage Ratio (LCR) and High Quality Liquid Assets (HQLA)

The concept behind the Basel III LCR measure of liquidity is that banks should compute their cash flow in and out over a period of 30 days under stress conditions and hold HQLA sufficient to be able to provide a cash inflow to offset any cash deficit over the period.

The Basel rules are relatively simple. The LCR has two components:

1. The value of the stock of HQLA; and
2. The total net cash outflow, which is expressed as:

Stock of HQLA/Total net cash outflows over the next 30 calendar days $\geq$ 100 percent

HQLA are discussed in more detail in Chapter 11.

Market Liquidity

Liquidity can also be increased by selling securities in markets, enabling a bank to turn its assets into cash either by selling them or pledging them in order to borrow funds. Market liquidity has grown substantially in recent years, largely due to the growth of so-called 'repo' (repurchase) transactions where banks can pledge assets to back their receipt of loan funds.

Conventional banks have been able to take advantage of this market's growth to fund new business in areas where they have been less able to attract retail deposits or issue debt securities. In contrast, Shari'ah-compliant asset products lack this degree of standardisation, sometimes even within national boundaries, and where national markets have developed they have not been able to support international growth.

To address this problem it is necessary to create international product structures which will lead to the creation of common product features and legal contracts on which asset transfers can be based. In doing so, however, it should be remembered that the short-term nature of repo markets did make them a potentially unstable source of funding. During the financial crisis, lenders became unsure:

- of the capability of the underlying assets to be a secure source of repayment for the loans, and
- of their ability to trace their collateral and reclaim it due to the operation of certain borrowers (notably Lehman's London-based operations) in re-hypothecating (transferring) the collateral.

It should be possible for the Islamic sector to avoid this problem, as transparency and reference to assets with readily observable cash flows are both features of Shari'ah-compliant assets.

In addition to the LCR, the NSFR is intended to address liquidity over a 12-month horizon. This may benefit the Islamic financial sector insofar as it is less reliant on term deposits as a source of funds, but there are nonetheless challenges which have to be addressed.

The emphasis of some Islamic banks on Unrestricted Profit and Loss Sharing (PLS) accounts as a secure source of funding, as a Shari'ah-compliant alternative to interest-bearing deposits, must be qualified. The nature of the so-called 'profit equalisation reserves' and 'investment risk reserves' typically held against these accounts in order to 'smooth' or 'stabilise' the returns paid to Unrestricted Investment Account Holders (UIAH) is likely to be problematic for bank regulators, who in many countries have fought a long battle to eliminate so-called 'reserve accounting' as used in the banking industry to 'smooth' profits (and above all to hide losses), and for accountants because the IFRS, as implemented, makes it virtually impossible to maintain this type of reserve accounting.

An inability to 'smooth' payouts to UIAH is likely to make PLS deposits less attractive. There are already signs of this in Malaysia where the Bank Negara (central bank) has banned such reserves and Islamic banks are taking more deposits in the form of commodity *murabaha*-based term deposits. It is unlikely that steps can be taken to reform their structure so as to enhance the stability of payouts without this being considered unacceptable by regulators and accountants.

Their reliance on retail funding also tends to lock Islamic banks into their domestic economy. The lack of standardised products internationally, and the often very specific national regulation of Islamic banks means that the often-quoted USD1.5 trillion of Shari'ah 'liquidity' globally is something of a myth. In practice the liquidity is locked into individual national 'pools' and there is only a limited capability to move surplus liquidity to countries which may have investment potential but a shortage of funds.

HQLA and Islamic Banks

Basel III stresses the need for banks to maintain a stock of assets (HQLA) that can easily be turned into cash at reliable values either through markets or, should such markets cease to function, through central bank cash from a 'discount window'. The governments of a number of states where Islamic banks are based issue *sukuk* which can provide assets that qualify for discount window access, and a number of central banks have started to accept IILM *sukuk* as providing access to Shari'ah-compliant liquidity facilities. Nevertheless, a number of countries important to international banks, including the US and the overwhelming majority of EU member states, do not do so.

While these countries will accept as bank stock liquidity some assets issued by AAA-graded countries and a limited number of international institutions (this is complicated in the case of the EU countries by obligations under EU treaties), there are, even so, very few *sukuk* issuances that meet the needs of international banks. The exceptions are the largely USD-denominated *sukuk* issued by the Islamic Development ment Bank (IDB), and the UK Treasury issuance in June 2014 of a five-year *sukuk* for GBP200m, and the issuance by Luxembourg. The position regarding IILM *sukuk* is as yet unresolved.

The problems of matching supply to demand for these high quality issues are, however, amply demonstrated by the order book for the UK Treasury *sukuk*, which amounted to some GBP2.3 billion. This mismatch inevitably results in the issue being bought by long-term investors which in turn results in an illiquid market for the securities as they can be easily sold but cannot be readily bought as virtually no supply is available. As a result banks fear to trade their liquid assets in case they are bought by long-term holders making them difficult to re-acquire.

To address this gap in the market it is necessary to have liquid AAA government *sukuk* issued across a range of maturities in significant quantity. This will provide stock liquidity to international Islamic banks (and domestic banks in countries where there are no government *sukuk*) and the issuing governments with attractive funding. The profit rate on the UK Treasury *sukuk* was set at 2.036 percent, in line with the yield on gilts of similar maturity.

Crucially, a significant issuance of such *sukuk* across a range of maturities would also help create a zero credit risk profit rate curve; that is, a profit rate curve showing different rates for different tenors of funds. Zero (credit) risk yield curves allow conventional banks to price their own credit and that of their customers of differing credit risk quality, by reference to such a curve.

Today, the lack of an equivalent benchmark against which to adjust for the credit standing of those entities to which Islamic banks advance funds and thus to price those funds accurately creates problems of pricing financing assets for Islamic banks and for capital market (*sukuk*) issuance across a range of credits and terms. When this is combined with generally illiquid Shari'ah-compliant product markets, the result is that sovereign and corporate *sukuk* issues trade at what often appear to be illogical prices in relation to their relative credit standing.

Rather than wait for the liquid AAA sovereign *sukuk* market to happen, there are initiatives that have been taken by those countries with a strong interest in developing Shari'ah-compliant banking and finance, including the development of a leading role for the IILM.

The effects of introducing the Basel III regime for bank capital are illustrated in Box 1.1.

BOX 1.1   EFFECTS OF BASEL III CHANGES TO BANK CAPITAL

Table 1.5 shows a simple illustration of the effect of the Basel III changes to the definition of capital on Islamic and on conventional banks' cost of capital, respectively.

Under Basel III, the majority of junior subordinated bonds (so-called Tier 1 and Upper Tier 2 bonds) will cease to qualify as bank capital and their use must be phased out in stages beginning 2013. Combined with the requirement for more common equity and the use of Additional Tier 1 (AT1) capital to meet the Tier 1 requirement, a possible result may be somewhat as shown below. AT1 capital is loss absorbent while the bank is a going concern (going concern capital).

Given the immediate reduction in the cost of capital to Islamic banks, regulators in countries with Shari'ah-compliant banking sectors may consider allowing banks to adopt Basel III at the earliest possible date, while those with common equity above the Basel III requirement could raise AT1 capital and repay equity.

TABLE 1.5   The effect of Basel III Changes on Islamic and conventional banks

Today		
Conventional Bank	Common Equity	25 Units Required Return 20%
	Debt Capital	75 Units Cost 10% Average Cost of Capital = 12.5%
Islamic Bank	Common Equity	100 Units Required Return 20% Average Cost of Capital = 20%
Tomorrow in a Basel III world		
Conventional Bank	Common Equity	75 Units Required Return 20%
	AT1 Capital	25 Units Cost 10% Average Cost of Capital = 17.5%
Islamic Bank	Common Equity	75 Units Required Return 20%
	AT1 Capital (*sukuk*)	25 Units Cost 10% Average Cost of Capital = 17.5%

MARKET LIQUIDITY: THE OUTLOOK FOR MARKETABLE ASSETS

In this concluding section, we consider the issues of possible market disruption raised by the eventual 'tapering off' by the US Federal Reserve (the Fed) of its policy of reducing interest rates to a minimum through quantitative easing (QE). In such market disruption, the IFI and its capital markets would not be spared. Indeed, as these are primarily situated in emerging market economies, and because of Shari'ah restrictions on asset reallocation, the effects could be particularly severe.

What is 'Liquidity' in Markets?

When it comes to marketable assets, there are a number of different definitions of liquidity. For the purposes of this section we have defined liquidity risk in the context of market liquidity as: 'The risk stemming from the lack of marketability of an investment that cannot be bought or sold quickly enough to minimise loss. Liquidity risk is typically reflected in unusually wide bid-ask spreads or large price movements, especially to the downside.'

This should be contrasted with liquidity as covered in many documents relating to securities or indices and their trading, where typical statements include 'Liquidity – Stocks are screened to ensure that the index is tradable' – a much weaker test.

Market liquidity is important to Islamic banks in view of their limited access to funding liquidity because of the lack of Shari'ah-compliant money markets in most countries.

This difference in definitions highlights the importance of extreme price movements with regard to liquidity. Such movements are perceived as the main risk posed by, say, the likelihood that the Fed will raise its benchmark interest rate once its long period of supporting the economy (and, in particular, asset prices), through the suppression of interest rates, comes to an end.

We have taken this definition in this context because the Fed's future action in this regard, and the markets' reaction to it, is perhaps the biggest single risk to the global economy over the next decade.

Why Now?

In the summer of 2013, a surge in volatility hit global financial markets – an event that became known as the 'taper tantrum' (Figure 1.7).[5] This 'acting out' by the markets followed statements by the Fed on its QE programme, which led the market to expect the Fed to wind down its bond-buying programme and to tighten US monetary policy. The brunt of the 'tantrum' was felt most in emerging markets.

It was, of course, already well appreciated that changes in US monetary policy, or even signals of such changes, could affect the world outside of the US. What was more of a surprise was the strength of the markets' reaction (Figure 1.8).

---

[5]Sahay, Ratna, Vivek Arora, Thanos Arvanitis, Hamid Faruqee, Papa N'Diaye, Tommaso Mancini-Griffoli and an IMF Team (2014) 'IMF Discussion Note: Emerging Market Volatility: Lessons from the Taper Tantrum', IMF, September.

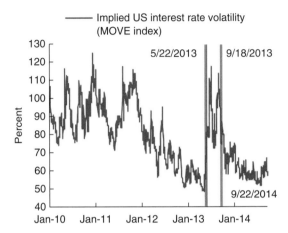

FIGURE 1.7 Implied volatility in US interest rates
Source: IMF

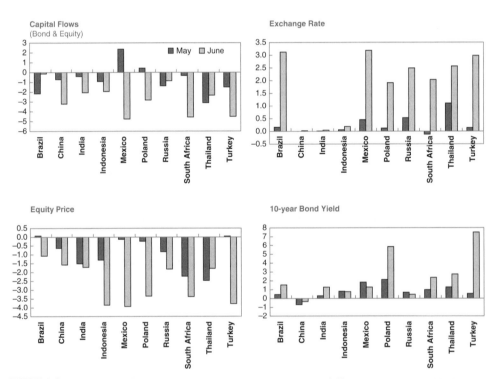

FIGURE 1.8 Variation of asset price responses across countries following May–June 2013 monetary policy shocks (z-scores)
Source: IMF

This reaction was why, in the aftermath of the taper tantrum, it was considered important to prepare properly for the moment when the Fed would not just talk about raising interest rates, but actually do so. Market participants would have to be able to absorb the effects of the Fed's action on asset reallocation. This was where there was one particularly pressing question: Does liquidity matter? Some argued that the lack of liquidity was a primary reason for the way markets behaved in the aftermath of the taper tantrum.

This is of great importance to Shari'ah-compliant investors. Shari'ah-compliant financial assets suffered significantly in the market illiquidity that affected securities markets after 2007, since despite the advances in creating a broader spread of prime credit issuers of *sukuk* in particular, the market issuance of *sukuk* is still dominated by emerging market issuers.

Equity issuance is still dominated by US, European and Japanese issuances and hence, while emerging market equity issuance has grown in relative terms, the portfolios of global investors, including Shari'ah-compliant investors, are still dominated by these major economies' equities.

Has Market Liquidity Declined in Recent Years?

The simple answer to this is 'yes'. The often-quoted example is that US corporate bond markets have grown over the last decade from USD2.8tn in outstanding issuance to USD5.0tn, while market makers' stock positions have fallen from USD300m to USD60m. (A market maker is a mix of the now historic roles of jobber, who makes a market by providing their own capital to purchase assets for sale before selling them on, and broker who finds the longer-term holders who wish to buy such assets. In the end, virtually all of the assets will end up with longer-term investors, as jobbers are simply short-term intermediaries.)

Why are banks no longer holding as much bond 'stock'? Almost every major bank has repositioned its Fixed Income, Currency and Commodity (FICC) businesses in the wake both of numerous FICC scandals and the reforms to capital regulation of banks that are actual and impending (the Fundamental Review of the Trading Book). Regulatory reforms have and will continue to make such businesses less commercially attractive to banks.

This comes at the same time as bond markets have grown dramatically over the last decade, thanks to an overall increase in debt in a world of ultra-low interest rates and ultra-high government deficits. The level of outstanding bond debt rose by some $57 trillion between Q4 2007 and Q2 2014 (Figure 1.9).[6]

Could There be a Market Panic?

In the light of the taper tantrum, market participants are understandably obsessed with divining the date when the Fed will begin to raise interest rates. Moreover, with ten-year fixed income government bond yields being negative out to five years across

---

[6]Dobbs, Richard, Susan Lund, Jonathan Woetzel, Mina Mutafchieva (2015) 'Debt and (Not Much) Deleveraging', McKinsey Global Institute, February (http://www.mckinsey.com/global-themes/employment-and-growth/debt-and-not-much-deleveraging).

Global debt has increased by $57 trillion since 2007, outpacing world GDP growth

Global stock of debt outstanding by type[1]
$ trillion, constant 2013 exchange rates

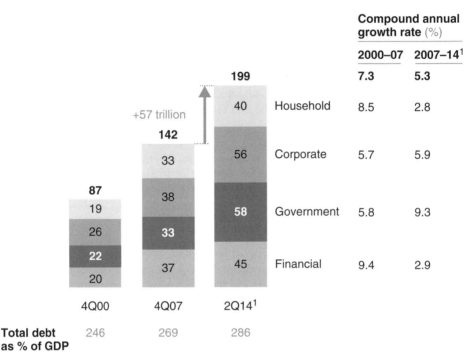

	Compound annual growth rate (%)	
	2000–07	2007–14[1]
199	7.3	5.3
40 Household	8.5	2.8
56 Corporate	5.7	5.9
58 Government	5.8	9.3
45 Financial	9.4	2.9

+57 trillion

142

87

	4Q00	4Q07	2Q14[1]
Total debt as % of GDP	246	269	286

1 2Q14 data for advanced economies and China; 4Q13 data for other developing economies.
NOTE: Numbers may not sum due to rounding.

FIGURE 1.9   Global stock of debt outstanding to end Q2 2014
Source: McKinsey Global Institute

much of Europe, it is likely that many investors are simply front-running European Central Bank (ECB) purchases of government bonds. These investors are certainly not long-term investors. Given this, they are poorly positioned to absorb losses and will react quickly to any perceived change in asset prices.

An interest rate rise need not, in itself, have a destabilising effect on markets. However, it is equally true that market makers' capital need not necessarily absorb the effects of such a rise. There is a genuine concern that the change of stance by the Fed will be a shock to markets. Given the sheer size of the bond markets, all of the shock absorbers available to the Fed need to be functioning when it implements its policy rate change.

By far the most important of these shock absorbers is the Fed's own communication with the markets; that is what sets expectations and, by extension, prices. However, adequately capitalised market makers who can hold the large trades that will inevitably appear in the fixed income market – and then find a buyer – are another vital damping mechanism. This is particularly the case if the market wants to prevent asset price falls that are greater than those that would result purely from adjustments to new current and expected future interest rates.

What sort of price falls might we see? Even a minor increase in the Fed funds rate will be a big deal for financial markets, as can be seen from Table 1.6.[7]

In these circumstances, some investors will 'take the money and run' and, if they are impeded from doing so by an illiquid market place that either delays their exit or is seen to penalise them with a significant fall in market prices not in line with market interest rate expectations, panic could ensue.

Shari'ah-compliant investors are rightly characterised as being, by and large, 'long-term holders for value' of assets. Moreover, there is good reason to believe that the flash point for the markets is unlikely to be the bond market or even securitised asset-backed bonds as in 2007, much less *sukuk*. But panic selling in any securities market eventually affects every market and especially market makers. So where might the flash point be?

TABLE 1.6 Percentage change in bond prices when interest rates change

4% Coupon Bond

Years to Maturity	Interest Rates Change By 1%		Interest Rates Change By 2%	
	Rates Rise	Rates Fall	Rates Rise	Rates Fall
1	−1.0%	1.00%	−1.9%	2.00%
5	−4.4	4.6	−8.5	9.5
10	−7.8	8.6	−14.9	18
20	−12.6	15	−23.1	32.8
30	−15.5	19.7	−27.7	45

6% Coupon Bond

Years to Maturity	Interest Rates Change By 1%		Interest Rates Change By 2%	
	Rates Rise	Rates Fall	Rates Rise	Rates Fall
1	−0.9%	0.90%	−1.8%	1.90%
5	−4.1	4.3	−8.1	8.9
10	−7.1	7.7	−13.5	16.3
20	−10.6	12.5	−19.7	27.3
30	−12.4	15.4	−22.6	34.7

Data Source: The American Association of Individual Investors

---

[7]AAII Journal (2008) 'How Interest Rate Changes Affect the Price of Bonds', January (https://www.aaii.com/journal/article/how-interest-rate-changes-affect-the-price-of-bonds.mobile).

The flash point for such panic could be the mutual funds and ETF markets. In both of these, investor liquidity is assumed and investors expect to be repaid at par – just as though they were running a deposit account. The problem is that there is no 'deposit guarantee' for MMF (Money Market Fund) and ETFs. Investors are fully exposed to market risk.

The growth of mutual funds and ETFs has been remarkable over the last decade, as can be seen from Figure 1.10.

What Liquidity, in the Form of Market Makers' Capital, Can Do and What It Cannot

Market makers' holdings of assets are there to be turned over; as is often pointed out, banks are 'in the moving business not in the storage business'. Placing assets with investors is not an assured process; in particular it is not assured as to price. However, the more market makers there are and the more capital they can bring to bear, the more likely it is that investors who want to sell can exit from assets at a reasonable price and that new investors can be found. This can take time. Investors do not necessarily appear instantly and any hint that a market maker is having trouble selling stock is likely to depress bids. While the market-making processes should be reasonably transparent, transparency can result in costs and even in market disruption. Investors in a market that looks as though it will fall, so shutting off

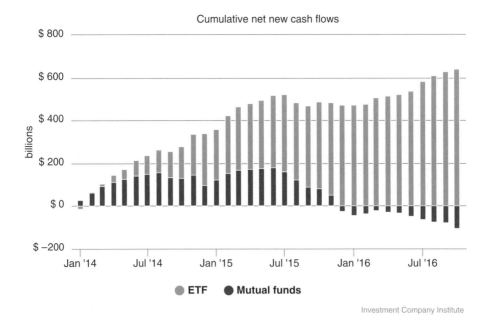

FIGURE 1.10   Cumulative flow into mutual funds and ETFs

demand, can become concerned that 'if the door closes they won't all fit through the cat flap'.

When looking at this, it is important not to confuse the role of market maker and proprietary trader. Investment banks fulfil both roles, but a proprietary trader holds assets not to lubricate the operations of a market, but to execute a view on the value to be derived from holding, selling or selling short.

The Current State of Play

The US Financial Industry Regulatory Authority (FINRA) called a meeting of market participants for 18 June 2015 to discuss 'the extent and severity of the liquidity downturn'. It was proposing to receive views on 15 July 2015 on how, in the light of the lack of liquidity, market rules might be changed to make market disruption less likely.

This would strongly suggest that some regulators had real concerns about the potential for market disruption stemming from the Fed's impending actions.

Should Regulators be Worried?

It is tempting to dismiss market makers' concerns as self-serving. As has often been pointed out, bank market makers were often conspicuous by their absence during the financial crisis. However, both FINRA and the Fed are concerned not about who will actually end up owning particular assets, but about the path of price adjustment – a path that needs to be as smooth and as swift as possible.

Market makers, through their broking and jobbing activities, can contribute to smoothing this path. This is why we might expect market makers to be given more time to place large sell orders without making them public and, possibly, to be allowed some capital relief on stock that is turned over. We can also be sure to see regulators remind MMF and ETF investors that cashing out is not assured.

What If This Does Not Work?

There is a very real possibility that, despite the Fed publicising its likely interest rate actions well in advance and assuring markets as to the likely path of such rate rises, there could be panic sales in bond markets should the Fed need to raise rates more rapidly than the market expects. This is important because the market expects rates to rise slowly but there is ample historic precedent for more rapid increases as shown in Figure 1.11.

What should the Fed do if this happens?

If a panic is confined to US assets, it may be that the Fed could support markets by buying, say, US corporate bonds. This would be a capital markets equivalent of the Fed's emergency funding of US banks. There is, however, one very significant problem,

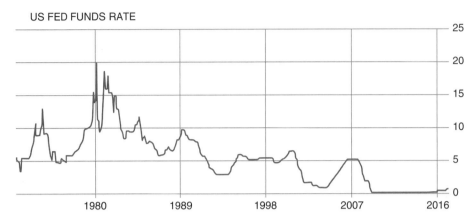

FIGURE 1.11   United States Fed funds rate 1971–2017
Data Source: US Federal Reserve

even if the political hurdles to such actions could be overcome. Bond structures are very diverse – there are over 49,000 separate corporate issues in the US – and there is no easy way to assess the risks and values of all the assets in the market. This means that, in turn, it would be very hard to know what impact any intervention would have on the Fed's balance sheet.

It is also quite likely that the problems will not primarily affect US assets but rather US dollar issues of emerging market issuers, as happened in the taper tantrum.

New Policies

Such problems would have significant implications for *sukuk* markets. The only way to contain another tantrum would be coordinated action by emerging market central banks supported by swap arrangements between the Fed and the relevant national central banks. This level of coordination seems very unlikely to happen in the countries where it would be most needed.

We should not ignore the liquidity problems of the markets and those of the corporate bond and *sukuk* markets in particular. Very low interest rates have, arguably, created a bubble and one that could easily burst in an explosive fashion.

Ten years ago, and with much greater capital, market makers would, arguably, have struggled to provide liquidity of the size needed today, a size largely created by central banks' QE activities. However, now that regulation has made it much more expensive to capitalise market making, there is only a very small buffer to absorb unusual levels of asset sales. That makes the threat of market disruption very real. The response to that threat should, surely, be to support market making by banks – not penalise it.

CONCLUSION

This chapter has provided a wide-ranging introduction to ICMs, which are beginning to occupy an important place in global markets. ICM products offer asset diversification to investors and portfolio managers, as well as either regulatory capital instruments or (so far to a limited degree) liquid assets for Islamic financial institutions. The remaining chapters of this volume, written by practising professionals, examine in more detail the various aspects of ICMs.

CHAPTER 2

Islamic Capital Markets and Islamic Equities

By Nor Rejina Abdul Rahim

'The future has many names. For the weak, it's unattainable. For the fearful, it's unknown. For the bold, it's ideal.'

– Victor Hugo

Since the Asian financial crisis of 1997, great inroads have been made into Islamic finance by the non-conformist country Malaysia. While many of its neighbours imposed austerity measures and borrowed from the World Bank, Malaysia imposed capital controls in 1998 which were effective in insulating the Malaysian economy from further deterioration caused by the domino effects seen in the Asian markets during the Asian financial crisis. The ringgit peg of MYR3.80 to the USD imposed in September 1998 was imposed till July 2005.[1] One of the policy implementations made after the crisis was the initiatives shown by the Central Bank of Malaysia's Financial Masterplan and the Securities Commission's Capital Market Masterplan, where Islamic finance was a major proponent for the development of the Malaysian capital market.[2] The foresight shown by Malaysia has reaped multiple benefits for the country, which is now seen as a global leader of Islamic finance.

Reference to Islamic finance immediately points to Islamic banking as the main thrust of Islamic capital markets (ICMs) and in most markets, banking is where the focus starts and remains. The Central Bank of Malaysia and the Malaysian capital market regulator, the Securities Commission, recognised the fact that banking alone was insufficient. As one of the early adopters of Islamic finance with the world's first Hajj fund established in the 1960s, Malaysia put in place other incentives that have contributed to it being the most comprehensive ICM in the world.

---

[1] See www.bnm.gov.my

[2] The Minister of Finance launched the Capital Market Masterplan, of which 13 recommendations were formulated, establishing Malaysia as an international centre for ICM activities (2001).

This chapter aims to provide the reader with the practical reality of the Islamic equities segment of ICMs as currently practised, rather than approaching it from the theoretical and religious perspective commonly found in Islamic finance books. Thus, there will more emphasis on current application of real world examples than an academic discourse on ICMs, which has been written numerous times.

ICMs by definition aim to bridge the financial sector and the real economic sector in a Shari'ah-compliant manner. The term 'financial sector' here refers to both capital markets as well as the banking sector. This chapter, however, will only examine Islamic finance from the capital markets perspective, with particular reference to Islamic equities.

Globally, there are a few major Islamic economic regions (Table 2.1).

There are 57 Muslim countries globally with a population of approximately two billion people. Islam is also the fastest growing religion in the world,[3] and yet the lack of penetration of Islamic finance seems incongruent to this fact. With regards to Islamic banking assets, 95 percent are currently concentrated in nine markets, namely: Saudi Arabia, Bahrain, Qatar, Kuwait, UAE, Turkey, Pakistan, Malaysia and Indonesia.[4] Those majority Muslims typically reside in predominantly emerging and developing economies, while Muslims in developed economies are usually a minority with an immigrant family background. The average Muslim is typically younger than their developed market counterpart and not typically affluent. It is such demographics that may explain why the growth of ICMs has been slow in the non-GCC markets. Yet Malaysia, whose GDP is substantially lower than that of the GCC, has a more matured ICM infrastructure than its GCC counterparts. So how far have we come? Let's take a step back to see what has been accomplished so far in the ICM (Figure 2.1).

In 2014, there were interesting developments within the ICMs, but whether or not true innovation has occurred to mainstream Islamic finance remains to be seen. With the global economies still crawling out from the aftershocks of the global financial crisis that started in 2007, the growth in Islamic finance appears to be selective with its capital markets still in embryonic stages in most markets and only passably mature in a handful of markets (Figure 2.2).

TABLE 2.1   Islamic economic regions

Region	Share of Global Islamic Banking
GCC	33%
ASEAN	14%
South Asia	12%
Turkey and Rest of the World	5%

Data Source: EY's World Islamic Banking's Competitiveness Report 2014/2015

---

[3]Pew Research.
[4]EY's World Islamic Banking Competitiveness Report 2014/2015.

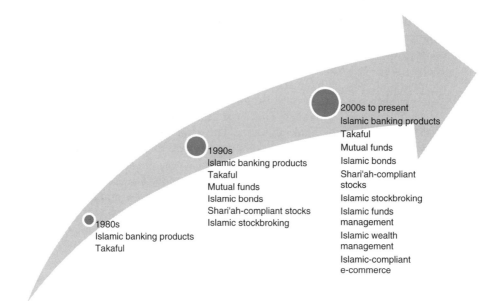

FIGURE 2.1 Evolution of Islamic capital market products

In order for us to examine Islamic finance's ability to compete with conventional finance and help secure a more ethical financial future for everyone, we need to examine how far we have evolved. Irrespective of conventional or Islamic, there are four basic elements of a capital market:

1. Equities (the main focus of this chapter)
2. Debt/*sukuk*
3. Derivatives
4. Foreign Exchange

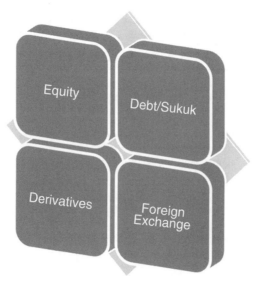

FIGURE 2.2 Basic elements of a capital market, conventional or Islamic

Both Shari'ah-compliant equities and *sukuk* have matured to an extent where the investment universe is sufficient to support growth in the *takaful* and funds management industry. The derivatives element of a complete ICM, however, is still contentious as derivatives' ability to be used for arbitrage and speculative purposes make them a bugbear to Shari'ah scholars. The controversy surrounding derivatives has not stopped the development of Islamic derivatives such as Islamic profit rate swaps, which are based on *wa'ad* and *sukuk*. However, not all scholars have accepted such instruments and thus many investors err on the cautious side and do not allow investments in Islamic derivatives within their investment guidelines.

The Employees Provident Fund of Malaysia (EPF) introduced a Shari'ah-compliant account for its 14.8 million plus members in January 2017. With approximately over USD170 billion (MYR731 billion) in assets under management (AUM) as of end of December 2016, the EPF has approximately 45 percent of its assets under management in Shari'ah-compliant assets currently.[5] Given its sheer size as one of the Top 20 pension funds globally, its Shari'ah-compliant pension assets make it the biggest Shari'ah-compliant pension fund in the world. As the demand for Shari'ah-compliant pensions grows, EPF's foray into providing a Shari'ah-compliant account should result in an increase in the use of Islamic derivatives as a part of the risk management of their foreign currency exposure. With such a large AUM, EPF would help deepen the breadth and depth of available Islamic investments going forward.

In a world where technology has helped bridge communities and changed the face of democracy, global connectedness has increased dramatically. The humble mobile phone now allows communities who have trouble accessing finance to have micro financing made available to them. Technology has changed the face of trading and many elements of the global financial markets, but in Islamic finance we have not utilised technology as far as we should. The Malaysian Securities Commission in February 2015 released crowdfunding guidelines and has since announced the approval and launch of six licensed equity crowdfunding platforms.[6] It is technology that will be providing a level playing field for ICMs, as competition of the future comes not only from the big institutions but also from game changers who are willing to adopt disruptive technology for the end consumer's good. The financial industry has always been slow to adopt innovation, but with the advent of wearable and further advances in technology, personal finance will likely be provided for by either telecommunication or technology companies and not the traditional financial institutions. Watch this space. Skynet is happening.

SHARI'AH COMPLIANCE CRITERIA FOR EQUITIES

The expectation for a single Shari'ah standard globally is as naive as it is impracticable. Islam is practised globally under four major schools of thought or *madhabs* for the *Sunni* Muslims and there are also *Shia* Muslims. Islamic finance is no different from ESG investments in that it too is multifaceted and, similar to Christianity and Judaism, is practised with variations globally. The past two years have seen Malaysia making changes within its capital markets to move towards a more harmonised standard that would meet the GCC's Shari'ah requirements. The Malaysian Securities Commission's Shariah Advisory Council (SAC) introduced a two-tier quantitative approach to their

---

[5]Employees Provident Fund Annual Report, 2016.
[6]https://www.sc.com.my/post_archive/sc-announces-six-peer-to-peer-financing-operators/

ground rules in 2013 (Table 2.2). Where previously only business activity benchmarks were used, there is now an additional financial ratio benchmark in place. The additional screening method has resulted in a fall in the number of Shari'ah-compliant stocks on Bursa Malaysia from 88 percent in May 2013 to 75 percent in May 2017.[7]

TABLE 2.2   Shari'ah screening comparison: Malaysia versus Dow Jones

	Benchmark Activity	Dow Jones Islamic Market Indices	Malaysia Revised Methodology	Malaysia Previous Methodology
Sector screen	Cannot exceed 5% of revenue	Alcohol, pork-related products, conventional financial services, tobacco, entertainment, weapons and defence	Alcohol and alcohol-related activities, pork and pork-related activities, non-*halal* food and beverages, conventional banking, conventional insurance, interest income from conventional accounts and instruments, tobacco and tobacco-related activities, Shari'ah non-compliant entertainment, gambling	Sectors with benchmark activities spread over a range of 5%, 10%, 20% and 25%
	Cannot exceed 20% of revenue	N/A	Hotel and resort operations, stockbroking business, share trading, rental received from Shari'ah non-compliant activities	
		Total debt divided by trailing 24-month average market capitalisation	Debt over total assets. Debt will only include interest bearing debt	N/A
Financial screen	Cannot exceed 33%	The sum of a company's cash and interest bearing securities divided by trailing 24-month average market capitalisation	Cash over total assets. Where cash will only include cash placed in conventional accounts and instruments	
		Accounts receivable divided by trailing 24 month average market capitalisation		

Data Source: Cerulli Asian Monthly Product Trends December 2014, Issue #34, Rising Shari'ah Recognition.

---

[7]List of Shari'ah Compliant Securities published by the Shari'ah Advisory Council of the Securities Commission Malaysia, May 2013 and May 2017.

The move by the Malaysian authorities bodes well for further harmonisation across markets, thus opening further opportunities for Islamic fund managers to move beyond their home markets.

Islamic finance is based on five core principles, as shown in Table 2.3, of which the first three are well known. Principles four and five, however, are the principles which make Islamic finance extremely attractive in a post credit crunch world where too many financial products were developed and sold without any real assets underlying these financial transactions. At the end of 2007, US financial assets were 4.79 times larger than the US GDP.[8] Since the global financial crisis, this amount has decreased to 4.05 times and[9] financial assets remain significantly larger than the real economy. The unconstrained growth in financial assets does not bode well for the global economy, as clearly the global economy has not fully recovered. The loose monetary policies imposed since then have caused a shift towards higher risks investments where even the largest pension fund of the world, Japan's GPIF, has decided to raise their exposure to equities as part of the government's initiative to jumpstart the Japanese economy.

In advancing ICMs, it would be better if the adoption of Shari'ah principles were not promoted as being exclusively faith-based Islamic laws. The attraction of Shari'ah principles from an ethical point of view lies in the fact that they are largely shared with other major religions, notably Christianity, and thus can be considered to transcend all religions and beliefs. The gap between financial assets and real assets, if too large, results in asset bubbles and financial crises. This can be minimised for the greater good of society rather than profit maximisation for the benefit of the privileged few. This will be achieved if the major sovereign wealth funds (SWF) take the lead to show how adoption of Shari'ah-compliant investments can not only provide investment returns but also enhance the quality of life for the general public; I am quite certain the adoption of Shari'ah principles would be seen as a positive undertaking from the general conventional investing community. One just needs to look at the United Nation's Principles of Responsible Investing, as well as the membership requirements of the Financial Action Task Force (FATF) to see how similar ethical and ESG principles are with Shari'ah's core principles. Part of the delay for the deepening of ICMs within the Muslim countries lies in the very fact that the biggest SWFs found globally do not have a strategic asset allocation to Shari'ah-compliant investments. Norway's Future Fund interestingly, as a SWF from a non-Muslim country, has a more transparent and ethical investment policy than her SWF peers from other Muslim countries. Food for thought indeed.

TABLE 2.3   Core principles of Islamic finance

Principle No. 1	The ban on *riba* or interest
Principle No. 2	The ban on *gharar* or uncertainty and *maisir* or speculation
Principle No. 3	The ban on *haram* or unlawful elements such as pork and alcohol
Principle No. 4	The obligation to share profits and losses
Principle No. 5	The obligation to back any financial transactions with assets

[8]Includes stock market capitalisation, bank assets and debt securities (source: Bureau of Economic Analysis, Federal Reserve Bank from Bank of America Merrill Lynch estimates).
[9]As at end of December 2016.

SECURITIES, FUNDS AND MARKETS: ISLAMIC EQUITIES

Simply put, Islamic equities are predominantly listed stocks that are Shari'ah-compliant. The degree of Shari'ah compliance is where the contentious issues usually lie. For example, the degree of transparency and investor engagement in the US listed equities differs greatly from those from the global emerging markets in such countries as China. The lack of transparency and information sharing by these public listed entities results in a lack of depth of information necessary in the screening of these stocks. Earlier in this chapter, the changes adopted by the Malaysian Securities Commission's Shariah Advisory Council in 2013 were mentioned. Benchmark providers, as well as Shari'ah and Ethical screening providers such as Ideal Ratings, have helped investment managers greatly in getting the right information necessary to support their investment decision making process.

In examining the growth of Islamic equities in Malaysia and other GCC markets, it can be deduced that the growth in demand is commensurate with the increase in demand from the major institutional funds. The government-linked institutional funds in Malaysia only invest in ethical and Shari'ah-compliant securities. The major institutional funds in the Middle East have similar ethical considerations.

One major issue currently faced by Shari'ah-compliant fund managers is the timeliness of the flow of information that would determine a public listed company's Shari'ah compliance. Many fund managers rely on index providers or a list from the respective country's Shari'ah authority to provide the investment universe. In Malaysia, for example, the Securities Commission's Shariah Advisory Council comes out with its Shari'ah list every six months with no prior notification of a stock remaining to be on the list or not. Thus, if the internal Shari'ah compliance or Shari'ah advisers disagree with the list, a decision needs to be made as to which takes precedence, and if the requirement to comply is immediate, this may result in instant recognition of loss in the portfolio to the detriment of the investor. Although most managers practise cleansing, the true '*halal*-ness' of a fund may be incongruent with one's personal interpretation of what is Shari'ah-compliant. Screening providers, as mentioned earlier, has helped in minimising the uncertainty, but the additional screening software is an additional cost and can be a significant cost, thus escalating fund managers' costs further. The costs of complying with Shari'ah principles via additional screening and appointment of external Shari'ah scholars have added to the argument that Shari'ah-compliant funds will not be able to compete on a level playing field with conventional funds on a costs structure basis. Until economies of scale are achieved, costs will remain a challenge to the next phase of growth.

Islamic equity indices

An equity index is essentially an index that serves as a measure of performance of a broad-based market. However, an equity index can be utilised in various ways. For example:

1. Measurement of a market, e.g. the S&P 500 or the Nikkei 225.
2. Comparison for a fund to evaluate a fund or a fund manager's performance.
3. Underlying asset for a structured product and derivatives such as index options, stock index futures.

Most of the broad market indices – such as S&P 500, Hang Seng, EAFE – are typically made up of underlying stocks based on the stock's market capitalisation – the market value of a company's outstanding shares and calculated by multiplying a company's shares outstanding by the current market price of one share. The investment community uses this figure to determine a company's size, as opposed to sales or total asset figures.[10] Market cap-weighted indices tend to favour large capitalised companies and thus the size bias may not truly reflect an investor's fundamental or value investing requirements.

In the last ten years, however, we have seen a shift towards different approaches such as fundamental indexing, whereby instead of market capitalisation, the index constituents will be based on the fundamental values of a stock such as sales figures, cash flows, dividends. The Research Affiliate's Fundamental Indices, for example, have given rise to many copy-cats and the new range of smart beta indices are essentially based on a fundamental index. From the Islamic perspective, the diversification of indices available is still rather limited, but it is moving in the same direction as the growth of available indices given indices' dependence on demand from end investors. Thus, the rise in Islamic finance and specifically Islamic collective investment schemes globally has also increased the demand for indices and their by-products, such as Exchange Traded Funds (ETFs). Passive investing has grown in leaps and bounds on the conventional side and a similar trend should be seen on the Islamic side sooner or later as the demand for Shari'ah-compliant products grows. It is early days yet but the Malaysian market is a good example of a good ICM, where an investor has a fairly diversified choice of investment products. There are currently less than 20 Shari'ah-compliant ETFs globally. Total AUM of Islamic ETFs is approximately USD296 million with 7 asset managers – a drop in the ocean compared to the size of the conventional ETF market at over 4 trillion and over 4000 ETFs globally.[11] Malaysia has the largest number of Islamic ETFs at four, followed by Saudi Arabia with three.[12] ETFs may be a good way to encourage more investment participation in Islamic equities from the individual investor rather than through collective investment schemes, as generally the costs of investing in an ETF are far cheaper than that of a collective investment fund. The only issue is to get enough issuers to come out with Shari'ah-equivalent ETFs. There will be more issuers if there is enough demand.

Islamic equity indices and performance comparisons with conventional indices

In addition to costs, the other major issue in relation to Islamic equities would be the comparison of performance with its conventional counterparts. Of course, from a simplistic point of view, many will argue that during periods where financial stocks are performing badly, as they did in 2008 due to the global financial crisis, Shari'ah-compliant equities should fare better than their conventional counterparts. But let's break down the issue here further by looking into the performance of the top indices – both Shari'ah and conventional (Table 2.4).

---

[10]Market capitalisation definition, Investopedia: http://www.investopedia.com/terms/m/market-capitalization.asp#ixzz3tiAtATyj
[11]etfgi.com as at end July 2017.
[12]Bloomberg as at end July 2017.

TABLE 2.4 Top five global Islamic equity indices (and equivalent conventional benchmarks) and 1, 3, 5 and 7 year performances as at end June 2017.

	RETURNS (%)				RETURNS (ann. %)			
	1y	3y	5y	7y	1y	3y	5y	7y
Islamic								
Dow Jones Islamic Market World Index	11.8	12.4	52.5	84.2	11.8	4.0	8.8	9.1
FTSE Shariah All-World Index	9.9	3.1	38.1	63.4	9.9	1.0	6.7	7.3
Dow Jones Islamic Market World Developed Index	10.8	13.3	56.7	94.7	10.8	4.3	9.4	10.0
MSCI ACWI Islamic USD STRD	8.2	0.1	33.4	55.7	8.2	0.0	5.9	6.5
S&P Global BMI Shariah Index	12.0	12.8	55.3	89.8	12.0	4.1	9.2	9.6
Conventional								
Dow Jones Global Index	13.1	8.8	50.8	75.5	13.1	2.8	8.6	8.4
FTSE All World Index	13.1	8.8	49.8	73.8	13.1	2.9	8.4	8.2
Dow Jones Developed Markets Index	12.3	10.1	56.7	86.0	12.3	3.3	9.4	9.3
MSCI ACWI Index	13.0	8.5	49.0	73.4	13.0	2.7	8.3	8.2
S&P Global BMI in U.S. Dollar Index	13.0	8.9	51.6	77.0	13.0	2.9	8.7	8.5
Out/(under) performance								
Dow Jones Islamic Market World Index	-1.3	3.6	1.6	8.7	-1.3	1.1	0.2	0.8
FTSE Shariah All-World Index	-3.3	-5.7	-11.8	-10.4	-3.3	-1.8	-1.8	-0.9
Dow Jones Islamic Market World Developed Index	-1.6	3.2	0.0	8.7	-1.6	1.0	0.0	0.7
MSCI ACWI Islamic USD STRD	-4.9	-8.3	-15.6	-17.7	-4.9	-2.7	-2.4	-1.6
S&P Global BMI Shariah Index	-1.1	3.9	3.6	12.8	-1.1	1.2	0.5	1.1
Simple Average	-2.4	-0.7	-4.4	0.4	-2.4	-0.2	-0.7	0.0
Simple Median	-1.6	3.2	0.0	8.7	-1.6	1.0	0.0	0.7

Data Source: Bloomberg

Most indices, be they conventional or Shari'ah-compliant, are usually based on market capitalisation and average value traded. Based on our readings, except for Dow Jones Islamic Market World Developed Index, all other Islamic indices mentioned in Table 2.4 are widely used. A bit of general Islamic finance trivia: The Dow Jones Islamic Market Index was actually the first global Islamic index ever launched, back in 1999.

Table 2.4 shows that S&P Global BMI Shariah Index and Dow Jones Islamic Market World Index were the best performers among the top global Islamic indices. These indices had also consistently outperformed their conventional benchmarks in the 3, 5 and 7 years period. This could be explained by the low exposure in financials. Since the last 2008 financial crisis, the technology sector has generally outperformed the broader market while the financial sector underperformed. Meanwhile, MSCI ACWI Islamic Index and FTSE Shariah All-Index had consistently underperformed their conventional benchmarks. This may be attributable to the absence of certain large-cap tech-related stocks such as FAANG stocks such Facebook, Amazon, Apple, Netflix and Alphabet's Google which had done very well in recent years. In addition, high energy sector weight may have also dragged performance in recent years due to declining global crude oil prices.

To summarise, irrespective of whether it is conventional or Shari'ah, the performance of an equity index will always be determined by its constituents. As can be seen from Table 2.4, exposure to selected sectors and stocks does provide significant return differentials, both within the Shari'ah index space as well as in the conventional space. Hence, it is crucial that when selecting a fund or a fund manager, questions on the performance and its relative benchmark should be part of the process in identifying the suitability of the investment or the fund manager. There are many intensive studies made by both academics and practitioners that have concluded that in general Islamic indices perform better than their conventional counterparts due to lower volatility as well as betas. However, I stand by my own reading of Table 2.4 that the stock and sector constituents of these indices play a significant role in explaining the performance differential. At the end of the day, information and statistics are open to individual interpretation and thus it is always a case of *caveat emptor* for the end investor.

REGULATORY ASPECTS: ICM AND BASEL III REQUIREMENTS

Lax capital ratios that were inadequate to absorb the shocks from the global financial crisis were arguably one of the major factors contributing to the global financial crisis. As capital requirements were not tightly defined, many banks used debt to meet the capital requirements, which did not have the same ability to soften the negative impact from the crisis as equity would have had. One consequence was that failing banks had to be 'bailed out' at public expense to avoid greater economic damage.

Malaysian ICM regulations and the Basel III Accord

The Islamic Financial Services Act 2013 (IFSA 2013) was a game changer for the ICMs of Malaysia as well as globally. A more holistic regulatory framework should result from the implementation of the IFSA as the Act aims to provide financial stability through better regulation of the Islamic financial system. The Act effectively codifies and updates the previous legislations governing the Malaysian capital markets, such as the Islamic Banking Act, the Takaful Act, the Payment Systems Act, the Exchange Control Acts – these final two Acts having been in effect from the 1950s, while the Islamic Acts date from the 1980s.[13]

Malaysia has just announced the launch of the Investment Account Platform (IAP) on 17 February 2016. The launch of the IAP provides diversification for Islamic business banking where risk-sharing investment products are easily accessed by the public with particular benefit to the SME segment where they now have an alternative Shari'ah-compliant source of funds available to them. The IAP is made up of a consortium of banks in Malaysia namely: Maybank Islamic, Affin Islamic Bank, Bank Islam, Bank Muamalat, Bank Rakyat and Bank Simpanan Nasional. This is an interesting development for ICMs, as equity investment so far has been limited to Shari'ah-compliant listed shares and private equity with the latter being the exclusive purview of more sophisticated investors. Although the operational details have yet to be released, the launch is a positive step towards applying Islamic finance to segments of society that really need it.

CONCLUSION

More and more news is coming out daily of major financial institutions being slapped with billions-worth of fines, as well as a growing number of politicians currying favour with their electorate with promises of reining in corporate misdeeds and blatant greediness. In light of this growing unease from the failure of conventional financial markets in addressing corporate greed, Islamic equities fit in nicely with the concept of ESG and SRI investing, which is an ideal vehicle to further promote Islamic equities into the mainstream. In order for Islamic equities to make greater inroads into the global capital markets, perhaps we need to address the very basics of how modern finance addresses itself. Profit with a greater social purpose is what ESG and SRI investing is premised upon. Shari'ah compliance is not a mere box-ticking compliance exercise. If practitioners and non-practitioners can truly embrace profit for the greater social good, perhaps we do not need to worry about labelling and classification of equities and the financial markets into what is truly Shari'ah and not.

In general, if we are to truly support Islamic finance and its capital markets to move into the mainstream, a change in how we see corporate profits needs to be addressed. A longer time horizon and a more holistic view of a corporate's health would result in less volatility in the markets and could change the way in which businesses, small and large, are run. Admittedly, there is healthy growth for Islamic finance continuing in its major markets such as the GCC and ASEAN, but the current oil pricing may have

---

[13]Bank Negara Malaysia.

dampened this optimism. More needs to be done to spur growth and development of the ICMs for it to truly provide a holistic infrastructure for Islamic finance and provide balance to the global economy for the greater good. Regulators and central banks need to do more to incorporate elements of risk sharing within individual capital markets to minimise the gap between financial assets and real assets, which in turn will help ICMs prosper. Practitioners need to develop products that promote modern finance as being more than just about GDP growth, but a holistic economic growth that is sustainable for the country and the individual consumer. Debt-driven growth is not the way to go, as can be seen by the example of Greece, which with hindsight we can safely say was not ready to be admitted to the European Union. Many Islamic countries are rich in natural resources, yet sustainability of these resources is very poorly addressed or taken for granted, and most are not the best examples of what the Quran requires of a good and just Islamic society. Islamic finance and its capital markets need to address the individual citizen's well-being by addressing the widening poverty gap and ensuring that rising national economic progress translates to the general population's collective well-being.

At the height of Islamic civilisation, pursuit of knowledge and innovation was highly encouraged. Intellectual discourse to help the advancement of ICMs should be highly encouraged by Islamic scholars, so that financial innovation is not left to be the responsibility of the conventional developed markets' purview exclusively. In order for ICMs to attract the necessary talent pool, the pursuit of knowledge which is the backbone of Islam should be encouraged as *ilm* is a form of *ibadah* as well. Thus market participants need to realise that they need to work with universities and scholars to encourage the positive development and innovation for the future growth of the ICMs and the industry in general. If governments, central banks, SWFs and the private sector can come together to address these social and ethical elements, with the benefit of technology, the future for the growth and expansion of ICMs and Islamic finance is indeed very bright. I look forward to more inclusive and ethical global capital markets where ICM products are a given and not a niche alternative for Muslims and Muslim-driven institutional funds only.

CHAPTER 3

Sukuk – Unlocking the Potential for Economic Development

By Dr Sayd Farook and Redha Al Ansari

Sukuk are widely acknowledged as the posterchild of the Islamic finance industry. Their universal appeal for all types of corporates, the strong captive demand base from Islamic financial institutions and the high-profile issuances of non-Muslim sovereigns have catapulted their visibility and prominence into the big leagues of finance, despite their very modest and niche size in absolute issuance terms.

Indeed, *sukuk* could become a significant tool deployed by governments across the world to diversify their funding pool in order to support economic and infrastructure development, particularly in Islamic countries where economic activity is sensitive to religious values.

However, to capitalise on the transformational effects of *sukuk*, it is critical to appreciate their foundational principles and what makes them both distinct from, and in some ways similar instruments to, conventional bonds. This chapter provides a summary of the key characteristics of *sukuk* without necessarily going into the significant amount of Shari'ah and legal knowledge already available on the way a particularly issuance should be structured (see also Chapters 5 and 6 in this volume).

GENERAL CHARACTERISTICS OF *SUKUK*

The *sukuk* industry is at the growth stage of its life-cycle and still depends heavily on government issuance to prop up markets. Corporates have recently tapped the *sukuk* market to benefit from the high demand from Shari'ah-compliant investors and opportunistic buyers looking for diversification with good credit ratings and attractive yields. Also, in the wake of Basel III, some Islamic banks have issued *sukuk* as Tier 1 or Tier 2 capital instruments.

TABLE 3.1   The differences between *sukuk* and conventional bonds

Islamic	Conventional
Each *sakk* (singular of *sukuk*) or unit represents an ownership right in an underlying asset, pool of assets or venture, or a right to cash flows from such an asset, etc.	Bonds represent pure debt obligations due from the issuer.
Maturity of the *sukuk* corresponds to the term of the underlying asset(s) or venture.	The core relationship is a loan of money, which implies a contract whose subject is purely earning money on money.
The *sukuk* prospectus or accompanying documents set out the Shari'ah rules related to the issue.	The issue prospectus does not refer to any Shari'ah rules.
The underlying asset(s) or venture have to be Shari'ah-compliant (i.e. not dealing with pork-related items, gambling, tobacco, institutions that deal with *riba* (interest) etc.).	There is no underlying asset and the funds can be invested in any sector or industry.
The *sukuk* manager is required to abide by Shari'ah rules	Can be issued to finance almost any purpose which is legal in its jurisdiction.

Sukuk first appeared in Malaysia in 1990 through a corporate issuance by Shell MDS Bhd. Despite the slow growth throughout the 1990s, *sukuk* started being issued increasingly in the early 2000s following sovereign issuances from Bahrain and Malaysia in the USD market, and since then have had a strong and steady growth rate. *Sukuk*, or as some would call them, Islamic bonds, in fact differ from bonds in a number of ways. Table 3.1 summarises the differences.

Sukuk are mainly structured to resemble fixed-income instruments, and thus have to be linked to a suitable income-producing asset or assets, whether the issuance is asset-backed or asset-based.

ASSET-BACKED VS. ASSET-BASED

The difference between asset-backed and asset-based is critical to the understanding of *sukuk*. Asset-backed *sukuk* are the result of a securitisation of mostly tangible assets, with recourse in case of default being to the securitised asset(s), while asset-based *sukuk* are the result of a securitisation of rights to cash flows from such assets, and recourse is normally to the originating or issuing entity (obligor). In an asset-backed issuance, ownership of the underlying assets (which may include the usufruct of tangible assets) is transferred by a 'true sale' to a Special Purpose Vehicle (SPV) which holds them on behalf of the *sukuk* investors and issues the *sukuk*. This is why, in case of default, recourse is to the transferred assets, not to the originator or the issuer. In an asset-based issuance, there is no such transfer of ownership, so that the originator or issuer remains the obligor (unless a third party takes on this role as guarantor).

In practice, *sukuk* pricing is not basically different from that of bonds, in the sense that *sukuk* traditionally utilise similar benchmarks to calculate the rate of return due to investors, such as a specified spread over US Treasuries, London Interbank Offered Rate (LIBOR) or Mid-Swaps. This is because generally those institutions that purchase *sukuk* are doing so to replace conventional fixed-income exposure or to gain diversification within the fixed-income markets.

Sukuk emerged at a time where Shari'ah-sensitive financial institutions needed Shari'ah-compliant investments to absorb their surplus liquidity, although this is still an issue for financial institutions, given the undersupply of *sukuk* in the market. The entry of conventional fixed-income investors has limited the supply available for investors with a mandate to invest only in Shari'ah-compliant instruments.

This undersupply of *sukuk* has forced many investors to hold on to their *sukuk*, which has as a result hindered the liquidity of the secondary markets in the paper. The most liquid market today is Malaysia, which accounts for over 50 percent of the global *sukuk* market, thanks to strong primary market issuance and secondary market infrastructure.

Government efforts that included the establishment of national Shari'ah boards housed within Bank Negara and the Securities Commission in previous decades have helped the Malaysian market to mature and to attract a number of cross-border issuers attracted by its liquidity and investor base. Globally, the *sukuk* market is growing and gaining confidence and is being used even by non-Muslim majority countries as a source of funding.

VOLUME OF SUKUK ISSUED

Sukuk issuances started growing in 2005 after the increase in oil prices in the Gulf Cooperation Council (GCC) and Malaysia and accelerated from USD11.3 billion in 2005 to USD37.6 billion in 2007, before getting hit by the financial crisis in 2008. However, it did not take long for the market to recover; in fact in 2010, *sukuk* issuance had already passed the USD50 billion mark previously attained. In 2012, with quantitative easing in full force, the *sukuk* market became a financing method for Islamic and conventional issuers from all over the world, reaching the highest amount of *sukuk* issuance of USD137.1 billion. In 2013, *sukuk* issuance slightly decreased to USD116.93 billion followed by USD113.7 billion in 2014.

Since 2012, the *sukuk* market has passed a milestone every year as it keeps growing and moving from traditional to non-traditional markets. Having attained the peak level of USD137.14 in 2012, the yearly amounts issued slightly dropped, but 2013 had the highest number of *sukuk* issuances of 834 as compared with 763 in 2012. Conspicuously, 2014 has been known as the best year for the international *sukuk* market, as *sukuk* issuances started moving out from their traditional market, as shown in Figure 3.1. A number of non-Muslim countries issued their debut *sukuk*, including Hong Kong, Luxembourg, South Africa, Senegal and the United Kingdom. In addition, a number of corporate issuers from Japan to the Maldives tapped into the markets for

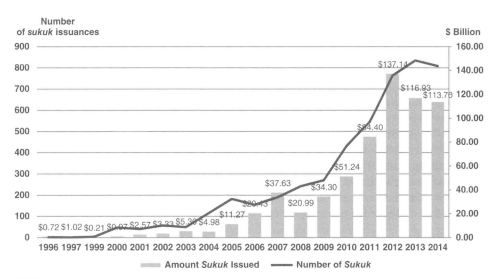

FIGURE 3.1 Global aggregate *sukuk* historical trend (1996–2014)

the highly demanded security. The issuance of *sukuk* by non-Muslim countries indicates great confidence in *sukuk* as an instrument of choice. The year 2014 also witnessed the highest number of jurisdictions issuing *sukuk*, reaching 19 different jurisdictions, compared with 16 in 2013 and 18 in 2012.

ORIGINATORS OF *SUKUK*

Sukuk have served many different issuers from both governments and corporate institutions since their emergence. Initially, governments were the first type of issuers to issue *sukuk* to raise capital for their funding requirements, and this has been well capitalised by many Muslim and non-Muslim governments. As *sukuk* grew, it was then considered as a liquidity management tool by central banks looking for Shari'ah-compliant liquidity tools to serve the Islamic banks and the broader players. Recently *sukuk* have been well used by many financial institutions, especially in the GCC, looking to raise additional capital buffers in order to improve their banking sector's ability to absorb shocks evolving from any unexpected financial and economic crisis. The new regulatory framework of Basel III requires banks to increase the capital buffers, in addition to diversifying the structure of the buffers and its quality. The trend started a few years ago when Abu Dhabi Islamic Bank issued the first capital boosting *sukuk* in 2012.

Sovereign and Quasi-Sovereign

Historically, Bahrain led the way for the first sovereign *sukuk* issuance through the Central Bank of Bahrain (then known as the Bahrain Monetary Authority), establishing its international *sukuk* programme in 2001. In 2002, Malaysia tapped the international market by issuing its first global sovereign *sukuk*. More countries followed Bahrain's and Malaysia's successful *sukuk* issuances. In 2003, Qatar and Saudi Arabia issued their first sovereign *sukuk*, followed by the German state of Saxony-Anhalt and Pakistan in 2005.

After the peak issuance was reached in 2012, slower issuance particularly in Malaysia following general elections in 2013, was offset by more jurisdictions issuing *sukuk*. In 2014, 19 countries were represented in the global market. This is the highest number the industry has ever seen, surpassing the previous high of 18 in 2012. There were notable debut issuers, including a group of sovereigns – UK, Hong Kong, Luxembourg, South Africa and Senegal – and corporates – a real estate company in the Maldives, Goldman Sachs and Bank of Tokyo-Mitsubishi. The strong momentum for sovereign and quasi-sovereign *sukuk* issuance is met by fundamentally solid market demand and appetite for quality papers.

As of end 2014, total sovereign *sukuk* issuance was USD79.7 billion, compared to USD27.3 billion quasi-sovereign and USD36.3 billion corporate issues as shown in Figure 3.2. In the whole of 2013, total sovereign *sukuk* issuances amounted to USD76.26 billion, and quasi-sovereign and corporates totalled USD8.46 billion and USD32.21 billion, respectively. In percentages, total government-related issuance (sovereign + quasi-sovereign as shown in Figures 3.3 and 3.4) accounted for 74.7 percent of the *sukuk* market in 2014 compared to 72.5 percent for the whole of 2013. More sovereigns are looking to tap the market in 2015 and 2016, such as Oman, Egypt, Tunisia, Yemen, Libya, Jordan, Philippines and Morocco. One of the landmark *sukuk*

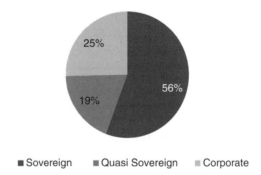

FIGURE 3.2   Sukuk breakdown as of 2014

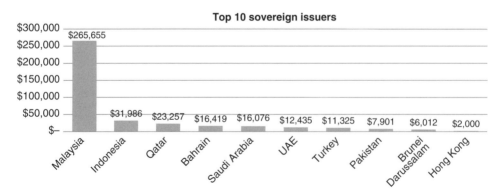

FIGURE 3.3   Top ten sovereign issuers, December 2014

FIGURE 3.4   Quasi-sovereign issuers, December 2014

issuances during 2014 was the UK's GBP200 million sovereign *sukuk* issuances. Its order book reached GBP2.3 billion, making it 11 times oversubscribed. In the same year, Hong Kong, Luxembourg and South Africa issued USD1 billion, EUR200 million and USD500 million, respectively.

Islamic Financial Institutions

Financial institutions, both Islamic and conventional, have been an integral part of issuers in the *sukuk* market since 1996. Cagamas Berhad, Malaysia's national mortgage corporation, was the first financial institution to issue, with a small issuance of USD50 million perpetual *sukuk*. Figure 3.5 shows the top ten financial services issuers by country in 2014.

Islamic financial institutions (IFIs) are confronted with several challenges with regards to their liquidity requirements and capital adequacy. One of the requirements of Basel III is to require all banks to boost their capital position by adding to their higher quality (Tier 1) capital, which would allow the IFIs to better absorb the impact of future financial shocks to prevent a recurrence of the financial crisis. The Basel III rules also require IFIs to hold a higher amount of liquid assets, which would make them less reliant on the short-term money market. Although these requirements will apply to all banks, they have a bigger impact on Islamic banks, which because of Shari'ah constraints have very limited access to liquid financial instruments. For capital adequacy, Islamic banks also have fewer options in terms of Tier 2 and Additional Tier 1 (AT1) capital instruments. The Basel III regulations require banks to maintain a minimum

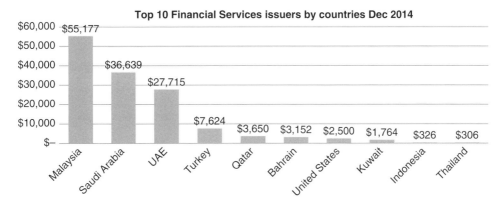

FIGURE 3.5   Top ten financial services issuers by country, December 2014

Tier 1 capital adequacy ratio of 6 percent, including 4.5 percent in the form of Tier 1 common equity capital (previously 2 percent under Basel II) and a total of at least 6 percent in Tier 1 capital (CET1 plus AT1).

Abu Dhabi Islamic Bank (ADIB) was the first to issue *sukuk*, in the form of perpetual Tier 1 bonds in November 2012. These were intended to be Basel III-compliant, with the objective of increasing ADIB's Additional Tier 1 capital, even before the initial implementation of the requirements. Dubai Islamic Bank (DIB) followed in ADIB's footsteps by making the second intendedly Basel III-compliant *sukuk* issuance in March 2013 with the same objective. By end of Q1 2014, three more issuances of similar *sukuk* were issued in Saudi Arabia, from Saudi Hollandi Bank (SHB), Saudi British Bank (SABB) and National Commercial Bank (NCB). Unlike the Emirati banks, the Saudi banks issued the *sukuk* to increase their Tier 2 capital levels. The success stories of the *sukuk* in the GCC have been replicated by Islamic banks in Southeast Asia, especially by AmIslamic Bank, Maybank Islamic, RHB Islamic and Public Islamic (using a *murabaha*-based structure) in Malaysia which aimed to boost the banks' Tier 2 capital.

Corporates

The biggest corporate *sukuk* market is Malaysia; this dominance is a result of decades of efforts exerted by the Malaysian government and regulators Bank Negara Malaysia (BNM) and Securities Commission (SC) to facilitate matters for issuers by standardised laws and regulations. As of 2014, *sukuk* issuances from Malaysia reached USD96 billion, followed by Saudi Arabia and United Arab Emirates (UAE) of USD52 billion and USD48 billion respectively, as shown in Figure 3.6.

Apart from financial institutions (FIs), the construction industry tops the list of the most prolific corporate sector issuers (see Figure 3.7). Out of the 440 *sukuk* issued in construction, 422 were issued in Malaysia, representing a 95.6 percent market share. Notably, about 14 percent of these issuances were in 2014. Saudi Arabia has the second biggest *sukuk* market, even with just seven *sukuk* issuances, although each was significantly larger than most Malaysian corporate *sukuk* issuances. As of December 2014, Saudi Arabian corporates had issued USD2.25 billion. The biggest corporate *sukuk* issuance in Saudi Arabia was made in 2007 by Saad Trading and Contracting Company, a company managed and owned by Maan Al Sanea, one of the leading businessmen in

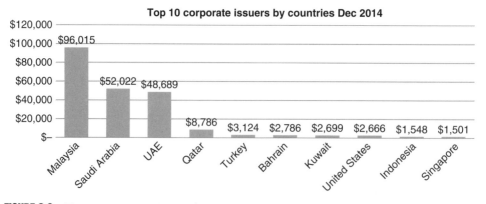

FIGURE 3.6   Top ten corporate issuers by country

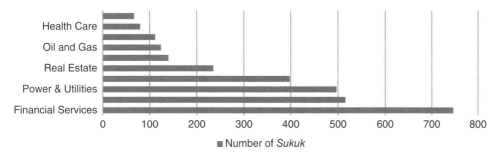

FIGURE 3.7   Top ten global issuers by sector as of 2004

the kingdom. The Maan Al Sanea *sukuk* has also, however, been one of the two major *sukuk* defaults in the Arabian Gulf beside Investment Dar. Interestingly, the *sukuk* defaulted two years after their launch, following the dispute between Maan Al Sanea and the Al Ghosaibi family. The financial crisis has also impacted the financial position of the company, making it unable to meet its financial obligations to the Al Ghosaibi family.

COMMONLY USED CONTRACTUAL BASES AND STRUCTURES FROM ALL *SUKUK* ISSUED

The *murabaha* structure dominates the *sukuk* market, holding a 32.8 percent market share, equivalent to 1,637 issuances as of December 2014, as shown in Figure 3.8. It is a structure that is widely used in Malaysia, the biggest *sukuk* market globally. Malaysia's *sukuk* market leans heavily towards the *murabaha* structure. Outside of Malaysia, for *sukuk* to be accepted as tradable the structure must have underlying assets comprising less than 50 percent of *murabaha* or other debt assets, but as the numbers obviously show, this is not an issue for the domestic local currency Malaysian market. Other debt-based structures such as *bai bithaman ajil*, and to a lesser extent

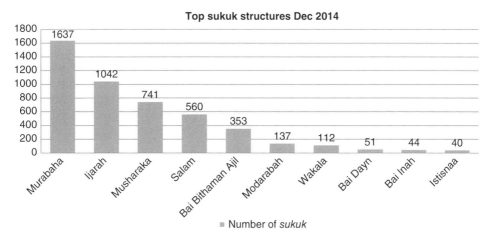

FIGURE 3.8   Top *sukuk* structures as of December 2004

bai inah and *bai dayn*, have also gained popularity within the local Malaysian market; these structures also are generally not accepted outside Malaysia. However, the types of *sukuk* structures used have shifted in the last five years towards the more globally-accepted *mudarabah*, *musharaka*, *wakala* and *ijarah*, as Malaysia moves towards the international markets and a globalisation of its Islamic finance industry. In 2014, *murabaha sukuk* totalled USD53.64 billion or 69.7 percent of Malaysia's total *sukuk* issuance. In October 2014, Prime Minister Najib Razak announced adjustments in the tax structure to favour *ijarah* and *wakala sukuk* until 2018. No such favours were extended to *murabaha sukuk*. This is another telling sign of Malaysia shifting its position to attract more foreign issuers and to narrow differences with the Gulf countries.

In the GCC countries, issuers mainly issue *ijarah sukuk*, a structure that is tradable under AAOIFI standards (Accounting and Auditing Organization for Islamic Financial Institutions) because it represents ownership of a tangible asset and not a debt or financial asset such as *murabaha* or other similar structures. AAIOFI permits issuance of *murabaha sukuk*, but Islamic investors are not able to trade them, significantly limiting their usefulness for a capital market product. Out of the USD29.78 billion of *ijarah sukuk* issued in 2014, 49.8 percent were from Saudi Arabia, UAE, Bahrain and Qatar. Indonesia, Pakistan and Turkey are also active in issuing *ijarah sukuk*, together holding 29.4 percent. Another structure that is widely used in GCC, specifically in Saudi Arabia by the Islamic Development bank (IDB), is the *wakala bil istithmar*, whereby *sukuk* are issued to fund infrastructure developments in the IDB's member countries. In 2014 IDB, an active and regular *sukuk* issuer, issued USD13.02 billion using the hybrid structure where tangible (real) assets like *ijarah* are pooled with a proportion of less than 50 percent of financial assets like *murabaha* receivables in a pool that collectively remains tradable.

'QUASI FIXED-INCOME' *SUKUK* VS. EQUITY-BASED *SUKUK*

Sukuk based on *ijarah* (or pools of *ijarah* and financial assets such as *murabaha* or *istisna'*) are generally considered to be a type of fixed-income instrument, although the income depends on the receipt of *ijarah* rentals and mark-ups on *murabaha*, etc. which are predictable but not guaranteed. In addition, there are other cases where the *sukuk* might be more accurately described as 'quasi fixed-income', such as certain exchangeable *sukuk*, CoCo (contingent convertible) *sukuk*, or Khazanah's social impact *sukuk* which ties returns to specific outcome indicators from its portfolio of funded schools. By 'quasi fixed-income *sukuk*' is meant *sukuk* that involve a structure backed by Shari'ah-compliant assets, e.g. equities of Telekom Malaysia Bhd. The periodic *sukuk* coupon payment is not guaranteed, being based on the profits of the company, a method which is based on sharing profit and risk. However, the 'quasi fixed-income' designation reflects a feature of the structure whereby any shortage of profits for a coupon payment is covered through creation of a sinking fund account for the benefit of investors (similar to a profit equalisation reserve for profit-sharing account holders in an Islamic bank). By this means, profits are set aside to ensure as far as possible the availability of funds to meet the expected coupon payments throughout the life of the *sukuk*.

For the sake of clarity, the difference between exchangeable and convertible *sukuk* is that in exchangeable *sukuk*, investors may get shares in a company other than the issuer, while convertible *sukuk* are convertible only into the issuer's shares. Exchangeable *sukuk*, namely those *sukuk* which are convertible into shares that are not those of the issuer, appeared first in Malaysia in 2006 through the Malaysian government's investment arm, Khazanah Nasional Berhad.

Khazanah Nasional Berhad continued issuing exchangeable *sukuk* following the success and oversubscription of its many previous exchangeable *sukuk* issuances. The latest exchangeable *sukuk* was issued in 2014. This time the *sukuk* were exchangeable into Tenaga Nasional Berhad (TNB) shares. The *sukuk* were interestingly issued at a negative yield (but with an exchange premium), and still drew a demand of about 1.6 times the book size. These exchangeable *sukuk*, announced in autumn 2015, were priced through an accelerated book-building process at a –0.05 percent yield to maturity, with a 15 percent exchange premium that is convertible into TNB shares, thus producing a positive return.

Financial institution issuers are also considering a new structure to hedge against what are described as unfavourable terms for the main shareholders (i.e. dilution of equity) when issuing *sukuk* to outside investors to boost their capital adequacy ratio (CAR). To mitigate this dilution, Islamic banks are considering the use of CoCo *sukuk* – hybrid securities such that the *sukuk* certificates give the investors a contingent right to convert their certificates into common shares. CoCos become convertible when the price of the issuer's common shares rises above a certain amount. The advantage of a CoCo structure is that it helps the banks to meet their capital adequacy funding in addition to providing favourable tax treatment (tax deductibility of returns paid). However, the CoCo structure is immature and the *sukuk* market is still a 'plain vanilla' market; therefore, the issuing of CoCo *sukuk* requires more examination, as there are challenges to overcome before the structure becomes effective. The challenges are in relation to how to avoid uncertainty (*gharar*) and what structure would be ideal to make the structure *gharar*-free. Other challenges are choosing the underlying assets and identifying the source of cash flows. To date, while CoCo bonds have been issued by banks to boost their capital adequacy, the mandate for such bonds has not been introduced under Basel III requirements, as it is believed to require further scrutiny.

ASSET-BACKED AND ASSET-BASED *SUKUK*

Two fundamental types of exchange-based *sukuk* are asset-backed and asset-based, as shown in Figures 3.9 and 3.10. In addition, there are equity-based *sukuk* such as *musharaka*, *mudaraba* and *wakala sukuk*. Project-based *sukuk* are typically equity-based and are to some extent similar to asset-backed, in that the *sukuk* investors have an ownership claim to the underlying project assets (as was shown in the case of the East Cameron Gas *sukuk*). Under the asset-based *sukuk* structure, the investors have beneficial ownership in the asset, in addition to recourse to the originator if there is a shortfall in payments or in case of default. The beneficial ownership is a legal term where specific property rights, such as its use and title belongs to a person even though the legal title of the property belongs to another person. A common example of

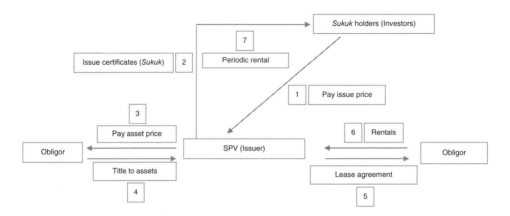

1. *Sukuk* holders subscribe by paying an issue price to the SPV.
2. In response, the SPV issues certificates indicating the percentage of investors' ownership in the SPV.
3. The SPV deploys the funds raised and purchases the asset from the obligor.
4. In return, legal ownership is transferred to the SPV.
5. The SPV as a result, acting as a lessor, leases the asset back to the obligor under an *ijarah muntahia bittamleek* (IMB – lease to buy) agreement.
6. The obligor pays rentals to the SPV, as the SPV becomes owner and lessor of the asset.
7. The SPV then make periodic payments (rental and capital repayment) to the *sukuk* holders.

FIGURE 3.9   Asset-backed structure

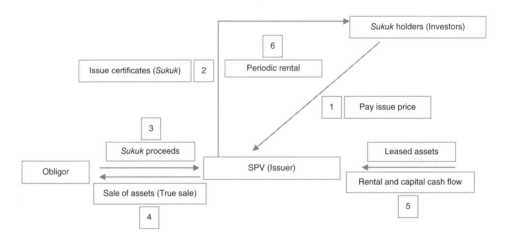

1. *Sukuk* holders subscribe by paying an issue price to the SPV.
2. In response, the SPV issues certificates indicating the percentage of investors' beneficial ownership in the SPV.
3. The SPV deploys the funds raised and purchases the income-producing IMB assets from the obligor.
4. In return, the SPV obtains the title deeds to the leasing portfolio.
5. The leased assets will earn positive returns, which are paid to the SPV.
6. The SPV then makes periodic distributions (rental and capital repayment) to the investors.

FIGURE 3.10   Asset-based structure

beneficial owner is the owner of funds held by a nominee bank or for stocks held in the name of a brokerage firm.

Under asset-based *sukuk*, the *sukuk* holder's beneficial ownership of the asset ends in case of a default with a mandatory repurchase by the originator, whose obligation transforms into an unsecured debt since the investors' recourse is solely against the originator. This is contrasted with asset-backed *sukuk*, where a true sale takes place, the legal ownership of assets is fully transferred to the investors and they have recourse only against the assets in case of default. While for both asset-backed and asset-based *sukuk* the cash flows to investors during the tenor of the *sukuk* come from the underlying assets, in the case of asset-based *sukuk* these assets are not derecognised by the originator (being still on its balance sheet) and in that sense the cash flows come from the originator, while for asset-backed *sukuk* they come solely from the assets). Table 3.2 summarises the main differences.

Shari'ah Issues With Asset-Based *Sukuk*

The controversy surrounding the differences between asset-based and asset-backed *sukuk* started in 2007 when Mufti Taqi Usmani, a prominent Shari'ah scholar, commented that 85 percent of *sukuk* were not Shari'ah-compliant. Referring to equity-based *musharaka* and *mudaraba sukuk*, his criticism was that they offered investors a repurchase undertaking whereby the issuer promises to pay back the face value of the *sukuk* when they mature, or in the event of a default. This promise or guarantee runs against the principles of risk sharing, and mirrors the structure of a conventional bond. His contention was that returns should be solely derived from the performance of the underlying assets, and investors should face the actual consequences of their investments. The same principle should apply to exchange-based *sukuk*. If issuers issue asset-backed *sukuk*, the *sukuk* market would make a fundamental move from a debt-like to a profit-sharing instrument, and that requires a primary

TABLE 3.2 Differences between asset-backed and asset-based *sukuk*

	Asset-Backed *Sukuk*	Asset-Based *Sukuk*
Issuer	SPV	SPV
Obligor	SPV	Originator
Process	Securitisation of underlying assets	Securitisation of rights to cash flows from underlying assets
Characterisation	Based on ownership of underlying assets	Based on rights to cash flows
Sources of payment	The income generated by the underlying assets owned by the investors	The income generated by the underlying assets still legally owned by the originator as obligor
Sukuk holder's ownership	Legal ownership with right to dispose of underlying assets	Beneficial ownership with no right to dispose of underlying assets
Recourse	*Sukuk* holders have no recourse to the originator (recourse only to underlying assets)	*Sukuk* holders have recourse only to the obligor (originator) if there is a shortfall in payments or other default

change of mindset of both investors and issuers to accept *sukuk* as an instrument that merely relies on the performance of the underlying assets. However, such a move would not appeal to most IFIs (and particularly banks) as it would not mesh well within their need for fixed-income type assets that receive favourable risk-weighting under the Basel standards.

Following the announcement in February 2008, AAOIFI issued six new requirements to ensure the Shari'ah compliance (in their view) of newly issued *sukuk*:

1. *Sukuk* to be tradable must be owned by *sukuk* holders with all the rights and obligations of ownership in real assets, whether tangible, usufruct or services. The transfer of ownership should not be shown as the assets of seller or manager.
2. *Sukuk* to be tradable must not represent receivables or debts.
3. It is not permissible for the manager of *sukuk* to offer loans to *sukuk* holders when actual earnings are smaller than expected ones. It is permissible to establish a reserve account for the purpose of covering such shortfalls, provided the same is mentioned in the prospectus.
4. It is not permissible for the investment manager to repurchase the assets from *sukuk* holders for the nominal value when *sukuk* are terminated. It is permissible to purchase on the basis of net value of assets, its market value, fair value or price to be agreed at the time of their actual price.
5. It is permissible for a lessee in *sukuk al-ijarah* to undertake to purchase the leased assets when the *sukuk* are extinguished for their nominal value, provided the lessee is not a partner, investment manager or investment agent.
6. Shari'ah supervisory boards should not limit their role to the issuance of *fatawa* on the structure of *sukuk*, but should also oversee its implementation and compliance at every stage of the operation.

However, it is difficult to say how much this announcement slowed *sukuk* issuances, as the market was also hit by the global financial crisis in 2008.

Specificities of Sovereign *Sukuk*

Ultimately, the main factor driving the selection of a structure is the availability of assets with the issuer to back the *sukuk*, and the second main driver is the investor being targeted as most GCC investors would prefer a structure that is compliant and tradable under AAOIFI standards. For instance, an *ijarah* structure would require a suitable (i.e. leasable) asset or assets to back the *sukuk*. While this is something governments can manage, it should be noted that generally speaking sovereigns do not issue in the same way as corporates do. Sovereign issuers are constrained by the fact that they usually cannot dispose of sovereign property without solid policy backing, and hence they structure *sukuk* based on beneficial ownership as opposed to legal transfer or true sale. On the other hand, many corporations may face difficulties finding a real asset to back their *sukuk* and would face similar limitations on selling assets written into existing debt covenants. Apart from finding the underlying asset, issuers also face a set of legal and tax issues when they use asset-backed structures, including difficulty getting a true sale opinion if they operate in legal jurisdictions where precedent does not guide jurisprudence (see Chapter 5 for more details). For example, under an asset-backed structure, multiple asset transfers may be required for an issue, raising the cost of the paper by creating a heavy tax burden for the issuer unless special legislation is in place.

In most cases, issuers who issue international *sukuk* also take into consideration the demand for their paper. In most cases, the vast majority of investors are from GCC, who prefer *ijarah* structure for its tradability unlike other debt-based structures. In 2014, a number of different non-Muslim countries tapped into the *sukuk* market for the first time by issuing sovereign *sukuk*, and they all used an *ijarah* structure. The new countries which issued internationally, namely Britain, Hong Kong, Luxembourg and South Africa, used this lease-based structure to ensure a wider investor uptake.

The majority of sovereign *sukuk* issuances in 2014 were asset-based. In 2014, 400 sovereign *sukuk* were issued mainly from Malaysia (158 issues), Gambia (140) Indonesia (47) and Bahrain (25). The majority of structures used by the governments were based on the contract of *salam* (forward commodity contract) with 153 issues, followed by *murabaha* (cost plus sale contract) at 123 *sukuk* issuances and *ijarah* (lease) *sukuk* at 87 respectively. The *salam*-based structure was only used in two countries: Gambia which issued nothing but *salam sukuk* in its 140 sovereign issues, and Bahrain in 13 out of 25 sovereign issues. The remaining 12 issues were issued using an *ijarah* structure. Malaysia issued most of its sovereign *sukuk* using a *murabaha* (i.e debt-based) structure. The *ijarah* structure is mainly used in GCC countries and Indonesia, and typically this structure is backed by either beneficial or legal ownership of an underlying asset. Indonesia issued 46 sovereign *sukuk* using an *ijarah* structure, 15 were issued in Brunei Darussalam and 12 in Bahrain.

RATINGS OF *SUKUK*

In most of their forms, rating *sukuk* is not significantly different from rating conventional bonds (see Table 3.3), with the exception of the cost and understanding the flows of obligor rights and responsibilities. For markets dominated by domestic *sukuk*, such as Malaysia, *sukuk* rating may not be as important a consideration as it is for issuers tapping the global markets. *Sukuk* ratings provide an indication of the creditworthiness and the probability of default, either of the issuer or, in the case of asset-backed *sukuk*, of the underlying assets. Most Malaysian *sukuk* are issued in the local currency in the domestic market, where issuers are comfortable with capital market conditions and investors are familiar with the different credit risks. Malaysia has released plans to remove credit rating requirements from 2017 in order to lower transaction costs and attract more issuers. The UAE also released new *sukuk* and bond rules in September 2014, including exempting corporate bonds and *sukuk* from ratings, in a bid to lower costs and encourage more issuance.

Market analysts estimate that issuers can be charged about 0.06 percent of a total *sukuk* issuance size by rating agencies and the annual review can be an additional 0.05 percent. However, for unrated *sukuk* to gain buyers, investors will need to relax their mandates to allow them into the portfolios. Investors would also need to do credit analysis homework either through fund houses or their own investment/credit departments which may require longer approval periods.

Moody's, for example, as an active agency in rating *sukuk*, looks at different aspects of the issuer (or the underlying assets for asset-backed *sukuk*) when rating *sukuk*, but with more emphasis on the structure of the *sukuk*. The process of Moody's *sukuk* rating mirrors the conventional methods when it comes to credit analysis.

---

[1]Beneficial ownership claims give rights to cash flows from the underlying, but not the right of disposal or of recourse in case of default (which is to the originator or issuer as obligor).

TABLE 3.3 Differences between rating *sukuk* and rating conventional bonds

	Sukuk	Bonds
Nature	Certificates of legal or beneficial ownership claims to underlying assets,[1] or business venture.	Pure debt.
Asset backing	A minimum percentage of non-financial assets in order to be tradable.	Not required, but with conventional asset-backed securities (ABS) the underlying are normally financial assets.
Principal and return	Derived from the underlying assets and/or from the contractual commitments of the sponsor (note: our rating approach is based on the contractual commitments).	Obligations of the issuer (depending on the ranking).
Purpose	Raise funds in compliance with Shari'ah/ reduce exposure on balance sheet through securitisation and derecognition of assets (for banks).	Funding purposes.
Risks for investors	Depending on the structure: exposure to the assets, exposure to the credit quality of the obligor, or combination of exposure to the credit quality of the obligor and residual asset risks.	Exposure to the credit quality of the issuer.

Data Source: S&P Rating Services (with editing)

However, Moody's does not take into consideration the compliance of *sukuk* with Shari'ah, as they believe that this is a matter of expert opinion and not objective fact, which could leave room for a possibility of dispute. Issuers who have disputed the validity of the financial obligations created by *sukuk* on the basis of Shari'ah non-compliance have not achieved success, and courts are unlikely to decide differently where Shari'ah is not a basis for the applicable law.

For the purpose of *sukuk* structures, Moody's would grant its ratings primarily on the structure of *sukuk*, i.e. asset-based or asset-backed. Whether the *sukuk* are asset-based or asset-backed plays a significant role in determining the rating. A number of issuers have followed the strategy of issuing asset-backed *sukuk* to get a higher rating on the basis that the asset backing makes them more secure, and may result in a better pricing compared to unsecured *sukuk*. The rating analysis would thus be different when analysing asset-backed as opposed to asset-based *sukuk*. In asset-backed *sukuk*, the rating analysis would be dependent on the assets, while for asset-based *sukuk* it would be dependent on the credit quality of the obligor.

It should be noted that, while it is true that most *sukuk* will have underlying assets in their structure, Moody's will consider them to be asset-backed if and only if the key securitisation elements are taking place to ensure that *sukuk* investors have effective title through a true sale. However, should the *sukuk* issuance have no securitisation in its structure, Moody's rating will likely to be based on the obligor (normally the originator or issuer) and the traditional conventional corporate finance analysis will apply.

S&P rating services, another active rating agency for *sukuk* ratings, has recently revised its rating criteria in January 2015 (see Figure 3.11) to equalise the rating to that of the sponsor's senior unsecured credit rating in the event of the following:

Under the new rating criteria, S&P rating services reports the following:

A credit rating is assigned at the same level as the sponsor's senior unsecured rating, if the next five conditions (A-E) are met:

A. *The contractual payment obligations of the sponsor to the issuer are sufficient for full and timely periodic distributions and final payments of principal (on the scheduled dissolution date or in case of early dissolution);*

B. *The sponsor's contractual payment obligations rank pari passu with the sponsor's other senior unsecured financial obligations (if they do not, but the other four conditions are met, see paragraphs 10 and 25);*

C. *The sponsor's contractual payment obligations are irrevocable;*

D. *The sponsor commits to fully and unconditionally pay all foreseeable costs of the issuer including taxes and costs related to the trustee, service agent, and investment manager through the life of the transaction, in a timely way, so as not to weaken the issuer's ability to meet all payments due in a timely way;*

E. *We assess as remote the risks that conditions, such as those mentioned in paragraphs 16 to 20, jeopardize full and timely payments (as defined by our criteria, see paragraph 12). If we believe these risks are non-remote, we may assign an issue credit rating on the sukuk that is different from the equivalent sponsor issue credit rating according to paragraphs 22 or 24.*

FIGURE 3.11 S&P *sukuk* rating
Data Source: S&P Ratings services

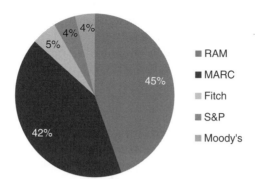

FIGURE 3.12 Top five *sukuk* rating agencies
Data Source: Thomson Reuters Zawya

The Malaysian rating agencies, RAM and MARC, dominate the *sukuk* rating market, as the two combined make up 87 percent of the rated *sukuk* as shown in Figure 3.12. This does not come as a surprise, given that Malaysia is the biggest *sukuk* market, accounting for more than 50 percent of total *sukuk* issuances, and the majority of the *sukuk* issued are domestic. The three giant international rating agencies (Moody's, S&P and Fitch) are more active in the international *sukuk* issuances.

ISSUANCE OF *SUKUK* AND SECONDARY MARKETS

The global volume of outstanding *sukuk* increased by about USD30 billion from 2013 to 2014 (Table 3.4), expanding by 14 percent year-on-year to reach USD263.9 billion as of the end of 2014 (2013: USD233.50 billion). Malaysia remains the biggest secondary market, with *sukuk* outstanding volume reaching as high as USD140 billion, representing 24.4 percent of the total. Saudi Arabia is the second largest secondary *sukuk* market, with its outstanding volume rapidly on the rise in recent years, thanks to long-dated primary market issuances. As of 2014, Saudi *sukuk* outstanding amounted to USD46.4 billion compared to USD34.3 billion in 2013, representing a significant 35 percent growth in volume since the end of 2013. The third largest secondary *sukuk* market globally, the UAE, also expanded notably by 27.5 percent by the end of 2014. Outstanding *sukuk* volumes in the UAE stood at USD26.4 billion from USD20.7 billion in 2013. One of the most impressive growths in outstanding volume comes from Turkey, registering a 79.2 percent increase year-on-year in 2014, up from USD4.7 billion in 2013 to USD8.5 billion as of end 2014. The substantial increase comes mainly from the government's back-to-back *sukuk* issuances. In addition to the existing markets, new markets such as Japan, Senegal, The Maldives and South Africa tapped the *sukuk* market, taking the market into new frontiers.

The UK's *sukuk* was another milestone, indicating confidence in the paper outside the traditional markets. The overall growth of the GCC *sukuk* market also witnessed a considerable 31 percent increase in outstanding value by the end of 2014, amounting to USD89.9 billion in 2014 compared to USD68.4 billion in 2013. This growth in the GCC has mainly come from Saudi Arabia (35 percent), Bahrain and Qatar (29 percent)

TABLE 3.4 Top ten countries by outstanding amounts in 2014

Country	2013 Outstanding	2014 Outstanding	Growth %
Malaysia	$113,897.37	$141,664.89	24%
Saudi Arabia	$34,286.07	$46,368.87	35%
UAE	$20,655.60	$26,375.60	28%
Indonesia	$11,341.38	$15,387.63	36%
Qatar	$10,544.21	$13,565.20	29%
Turkey	$4,728.16	$8,472.55	79%
Bahrain	$2,036.73	$2,636.73	29%
Pakistan	$1,530.50	$3,099.05	102%
Singapore	$739.14	$1,285.41	74%
United States	$165.67	$1,165.67	604%

Data Source: Thomson Reuters Zawya

and UAE (28 percent), while the amounts outstanding in Oman and Kuwait did not change as they did not issue any *sukuk* in 2014. However, the biggest growth rates in *sukuk* outstanding in 2014 (albeit from small bases) were registered in the non-traditional markets such as the US, the UK and Luxembourg.

In terms of performance on *sukuk* instruments in the secondary market, overall the returns on *sukuk* papers fell slightly across the big *sukuk* markets (Malaysia, Saudi Arabia, UAE, Bahrain, Qatar and Turkey) in 2014 (see Table 3.4). Apart from the macroeconomics and political stability of each issuer, the yields of bonds and *sukuk* are somewhat correlated with the US Federal Reserve's tapering policy with respect to quantitative easing.

However, the yields on international *sukuk* were not affected significantly, although they slightly increased right before the scheduled US Federal Reserve's Federal Open Market Committee Meeting (FOMC) on 17–18 June 2015, before again easing down. A rise in interest rates could affect *sukuk* issuance worldwide, as it would become more expensive for the issuers to issue *sukuk*. By contrast, the demand from investors would increase simultaneously, as they would get higher returns on their *sukuk* investments. However, the liquidity may further drop with the increase in interest rates, as *sukuk* would become more expensive through the increase in *sukuk* pricing.

When it comes to secondary market liquidity, the market for high-quality credits is much more liquid as there is a significantly greater demand to purchase the securities. However, the buy-and-hold mentality of the majority of *sukuk* investors leads to less secondary market liquidity, and *sukuk* sometimes struggle to achieve price parity with conventional bonds.

For illustration, we chose two multinational corporations with similar credit ratings and the same maturity, and compared their bid-ask spreads (as a proxy for secondary market liquidity). The IDB *sukuk* and African Development Bank (ADB) bonds were both issued in 2012 and mature in 2017, as shown in Figure 3.13. We can see how tight the bonds market is compared to that for *sukuk*. Initially, the two papers were moving in the same direction, before IDB *sukuk* spreads start widening just after a year

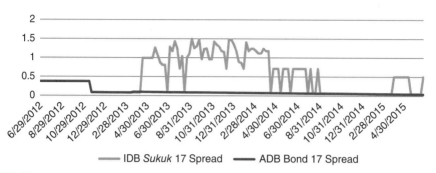

FIGURE 3.13   IDB vs. ADB price spread
Data Source: Thomson Reuters Eikon

from issuance while ADB bond spreads became tighter as they got closer to maturity. The underlying reason for such low tradability in *sukuk* is because the majority of investors come from IFIs, and due to the high demand and low supply of *sukuk*, nearly all IFIs tend to hold these papers to maturity as it would be hard for them to find alternative Shari'ah-compliant investments (this is also known as reinvestment risk). The investment options available to IFIs are limited, and this will continue to hinder the secondary market till more *sukuk* are issued. Another indication of the undersupply of *sukuk* is the oversubscription of many of the international *sukuk* issuances. Notably, in 2014 the United Kingdom's *sukuk* order book reached GBP2.3 billion, making it 12 times oversubscribed.

The oversubscription is also a result of ample liquidity available in Islamic banks mainly in Malaysian and GCC banks. Between 1 May and 30 June 2014, Thomson Reuters conducted a survey of more than 40 Islamic banks and Islamic banking subsidiaries of conventional banks to assess the liquidity positions of these banks, among other things. The survey results show that the average percentage of liquid assets available for investing by GCC Islamic banks is 46 percent, while Malaysian Islamic banks stood at 51 percent, as shown in Figure 3.15. This indicates that once an Islamic bank adds *sukuk* to its portfolio, it is very unlikely the bank would trade them; there is no need to monetise them because of the high liquidity already sitting on its books.

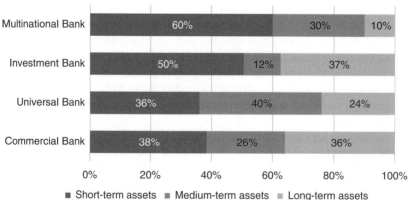

FIGURE 3.14   Average percentage of liquid assets available for investing by type of bank

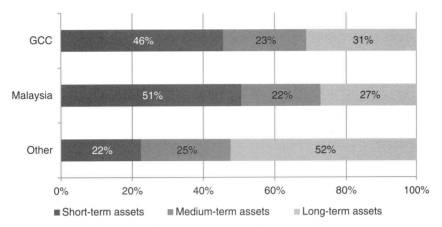

FIGURE 3.15 Average percentage of liquid assets available for investing by region
Data Source: Thomson Reuters Sukuk Report, 2014

Thomson Reuters have also revealed in its yearly *sukuk* report the supply and demand gap which has been derived by taking the demand side from the liquid assets available in IFIs, and the supply from the total outstanding global *sukuk*. The study shows (see Figure 3.16) that the *sukuk* market is undersupplied, and it is expected to be further undersupplied with low *sukuk* issuance in Malaysia, the biggest *sukuk* market in 2015 and 2016.

Demand Side

Fundamentally, there are two types of investors that drive the demand for *sukuk*: Shari'ah-sensitive investors which are mainly IFIs, and other global investors looking for diversification and attractive yields. A conservative approach has been used to measure the projection for the demand from the broadest group of Shari'ah-sensitive investors – the IFIs, as the core base for continued *sukuk* investment. While there is a

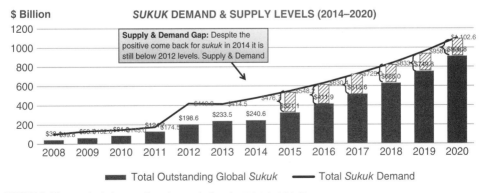

FIGURE 3.16 *Sukuk* demand and supply levels (2014–2020)
Data Source: Thomson Reuters Sukuk Report, 2014

much wider group of investors beyond IFIs, it is the IFI category that forms the most captive investor base that can be relied on regardless of market conditions. Other investors may tend to be cyclical or opportunistic.

The Shari'ah-compliant assets (assets of banks, Takaful, other IFIs, funds and *sukuk*) were conservatively forecasted to grow by 15 percent on an annual basis by Thomson Reuters; this is in line with growth estimates from Ernst & Young, Deutsche Bank and Kuwait Finance House, although their forecasts are higher at around 18–20 percent. According to the data from the ICD-Thomson Reuters Islamic Finance Indicator (IFDI), total Islamic finance assets reached USD1.814 billion as of 2014.

The assumption has been that the average portfolio allocation of *sukuk* required by Shari'ah-sensitive investors is 25 percent. This proportion is supported by data from Islamic commercial banks, which suggests that they hold, on average, 34 percent of liquid assets available for investment or having been invested as per the survey conducted by Thomson Reuters in 2014. The estimation is believed to be conservative, given that Thomson Reuters Sukuk Survey findings in 2014 show that the majority of investors place between 5 percent and 25 percent of their investments in *sukuk*; the 25 percent estimation is just past the mid-mark for *sukuk* holdings.

Supply Side

The decline in 2013 in the *sukuk* market was followed by a strong year again in 2014 due to the high number of issuances, including from Hong Kong, South Africa and the UK. Investors raised their expectations for 2014 and 2015 based on recent market events and pipeline announcements. However, the market took a different direction in 2015 as Malaysia decided to cut short-term *sukuk* issues, which has hindered the growth of *sukuk* issuance.

For total global *sukuk* maturing, the numbers have been derived from Thomson Reuters Zawya as per existing *sukuk* maturity profiles. In addition, Thomson Reuters calculated the average of short-term *sukuk* that were issued and had matured in the same year for the last three years (2011–2014), equal to 30 percent, and subtracted these amounts from the total.

In terms of yield to maturity of five key international *sukuk* compared to five-year US treasury (see Figure 3.17), the performance has been fairly consistent among all the international *sukuk*, which does not come as a surprise, given all global *sukuk* react to the same global trends.

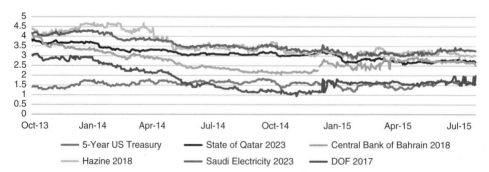

FIGURE 3.17   Five-Year US treasury vs. international *sukuk* bid yield
Data Source: Thomson Reuters Eikon

CONCLUSION

The *sukuk* market will continue to be a prime market for Shari'ah-sensitive investors, given the limited options available to them. The outlook remains sound, especially with the drop in oil prices, as many oil exporting countries, the likes of Bahrain and Saudi Arabia, have already considered *sukuk* as a source of funding to cover their budget deficits. The oil prices could witness a further fall as the supply would rise once the sanctions are fully removed from Iran, another oil exporting country. The increase in global interest rates is another space both issuers and investors are carefully watching. Of course, there are implications for *sukuk*, just like any other financing instruments. However, the only factor distinguishing *sukuk* from other instruments is, without a doubt, the demand. This could be an advantage for the issuers, capitalising on the limited investment options available to Shari'ah-sensitive investors; therefore, issuers could pull a better pricing compared to other instruments. Even with a significant withdrawal of deposits from Islamic banks due to petro dollar liquidity diminishing, Islamic banks will continue to demand liquid assets particularly those with higher investment grade ratings, which have been in acute shortage by a large margin.

Despite being a small market, the *sukuk* market at times shows interesting trends, and data proves that the *sukuk* issuers can be influenced when a heavyweight country like the UK issues *sukuk*. Noticeably, the UK *sukuk* were issued in June 2014; the market took only three months before Hong Kong, South Africa, Luxembourg, Japan's Bank of Tokyo-Mitsubishi UFJ and Goldman Sachs all issued in September of the same year, and it was unlikely to be a coincidence that Hong Kong followed this flurry of issuance in 2014 with another offering in May 2015.

In terms of markets, it is likely, for the foreseeable future, that Malaysia will continue to dominate the global *sukuk* market in terms of volume, despite the fact the central bank (BNM) has decided to cut short-term *sukuk* issuance, a move that was originally targeted to improve the liquidity position of Malaysian institutions, but encountered the problem that most of these *sukuk* were bought by GCC investors. As a result, the global market share for Malaysia has dropped significantly in the first nine months of 2015 to approximately 50 percent, after holding approximately 65 percent for so many years. However, it should be noted that most Malaysian *sukuk* are aimed at the local, not the international market. In terms of sectors, FIs lead all corporate issuances in the market for the first nine months of 2015, followed by Transport, Construction, Real Estate and Conglomerates. The market has also welcomed two new sectors in 2015, which were Information Technology and Consumer Goods, in both of which there were issuances by Malaysian companies.

With *sukuk*, growth is best measured by the entrants of new markets and sectors and not merely by the volume, as the former shows the acceptability of the paper. In 2014, the *sukuk* market is known to have had the best year in its history as the number of jurisdictions tapped by the market reached 19, compared to 16 in 2013 and 18 in 2012. This indicates the acceptance of *sukuk* by a larger group of issuers and investors. It is true that in 2015 the *sukuk* market fell off in issuance volumes, but the fundamentals are built for the instrument to hit the acceleration pedal again in the years ahead.

BIBLIOGRAPHY

AAOIFI. 'Accounting and Auditing Organization for Islamic Financial Institutions (AAOIFI) Shariah Standards'. Bahrain: 2010.

ICD-Thomson Reuters. Islamic Finance Development Report 2015 'Global Transformation'. December, 2015. https://islamic-finance.zawya.com/ifg-publications/IFDI_2015-2411150 73158K/

'Industry at Crossroads', https://islamic-finance.zawya.com/ifg-publications/Sukuk_2016-24111 5073605G/

International Islamic Liquidity Management and Thomson Reuters. 'Global Liquidity Management Regulator's Perspective'. August, 2014. http://www.iilm.com/App_ClientFile/b1c4c838-3d1b-48a9-81cb-f4aa6585e9b9/Assets/150225_Thomson%20Reuters_Liquidity% 20Management_Whitepaper.pdf

S&P Global Ratings 'Methodology For Rating Sukuk'. January, 2015. https://www.standardand poors.com/en_AU/web/guest/article/-/view/type/HTML/id/1609368

Thomson Reuters Sukuk Perceptions & Forecast. 'Global Liquidity Management Regulators' Perspective Whitepaper', December, 2015.

CHAPTER 4

Islamic Collective Investment Schemes

By Simon Archer and Brandon Davies

Shari'ah-compliant Collective Investment Schemes (CIS) include equity funds, commodities funds and Islamic real estate investment trusts. Restricted Profit-Sharing Investment Accounts (PSIAs), which are offered by some Islamic banks, may also be considered as a type of CIS, but are classified as banking products rather than capital market products. In January 2009, the Islamic Financial Services Board (IFSB) issued IFSB-6, *Guiding Principles on Governance for Islamic Collective Investment Schemes*, in the scope of which are included PSIAs that are 'pooled in the form of a CIS and whereby each of the Investment Account Holders (IAH) participates equally in income (whether profit or loss) and is generally governed by the same terms and conditions' (IFSB-6, paragraph 7 (v)).

SHARI'AH-COMPLIANT EQUITY FUNDS

Shari'ah-compliant equity funds are funds that invest in common shares in companies engaged in *halal* (Shari'ah-compliant) business. Companies are also screened in order to check that the extent of any transactions that are not Shari'ah-compliant, such as receipts or payments of interest, does not exceed a screening criterion, and to ensure they are not leveraged beyond a certain level. A company's non-permissible income can be subject to 'purification' (see below and, in more detail, in Chapter 7) so that it can be included in the equity fund.[1]

---

[1]There exists a set of Shari'ah-compliant financial accounting standards issued by the Accounting and Auditing Organization for Islamic Financial Institutions (AAOIFI) which is an Islamic international autonomous not-for-profit corporate body that prepares financial accounting, auditing, governance, ethical and Shari'ah standards for Shari'ah-compliant financial institutions. Its financial accounting standards are, however, applied in only a few countries, including Bahrain (where AAOIFI is based), Jordan and Sudan.

Shari'ah Screening of Equities

To include an equity in a Shari'ah-compliant index, the security must meet certain criteria. A typical Shari'ah advisor's opinion for a Shari'ah equity index would be likely to include a screening out of securities where any issuers' core activities covered:

- Interest-bearing investments.
- Loans and deposits based on interest.
- Forward currency transactions (which rely for their price on currency interest rate differentials).
- Derivatives, including futures, options and contracts for difference.

In addition there will also be a screening out of companies involved in:

- The manufacture or distribution of alcohol or tobacco products, gaming or gambling.
- The manufacture or distribution of weapons and defence-related products.
- Any business activity relating to pork or pork products.
- Conventional banking, insurance or any other interest-based financial services activity.
- The production or distribution of pornographic materials.

There is also likely to be a general 'catch all' disallowing any other activity that is not considered to be permitted under Shari'ah as determined by the entity giving the opinion, at any time.

Once the above screening is completed, an additional test will be conducted screening the resulting stock universe for a set of financial ratios. These typically comprise:

- Debt to total assets ratio to be less than 33 percent.
- Total interest and non-compliant activities income should not exceed 5 percent of revenues.
- Cash and interest-bearing accounts, including liquid instruments, such as certificates of deposit, bills etc., should not exceed a given percentage of total assets. There are two rulings in the market: AAOIFI (Accounting and Auditing Organization for Islamic Financial Institutions) and the Islamic Fiqh Academy. AAOIFI stipulates that cash and debt should not exceed 33 percent, while for the Islamic Fiqh Academy this percentage is 49 percent. The balance, 67 percent for AAOIFI and 51 percent for the Islamic Fiqh Academy, should be tangible assets and services.

For a stock/security to be deemed Shari'ah-compliant it must pass both the business compliance and financial ratios tests (see Chapter 7).

SHARI'AH-COMPLIANT FUNDS – REGULATORY ISSUES

Many banks and other finance companies have created a number of proprietary funds to appeal to the Shari'ah-compliant investor. The funds will typically be created and sold through a dedicated investment company that will issue shares of various classes attached to different sub-funds.

For European investors it will usually be necessary to ensure that the investment company is based in a state that is a member of the European Union (EU) and has structured the funds so as to qualify as an Undertaking for Collective Investment in Transferable Securities (UCITS) fund. There are certain exemptions for states such as Jersey, Guernsey and Switzerland, which for these purposes do qualify as if they were an EU state under what are known as 'passporting' arrangements. Other states such as the Cayman Islands, Hong Kong, Singapore and the US are not currently included in these arrangements.[2] Companies may market UCITS funds directly across all EU states without the need to seek authorisation from the securities regulators of each of the 27 EU states.

Companies establishing Shari'ah-compliant funds will typically ensure that their investment strategy is supervised by an independent committee of Islamic scholars – a Shari'ah Board (SB). These scholars are qualified to issue fatwas on financial transactions and have a deep knowledge of both Islamic law and financial markets. The oversight of such a committee will cover both initial investment, regular review of the investment strategies of the funds and an annual audit of each fund. They will also screen and ensure the investments avoid business that is *haram* and that they conform to certain criteria with respect to their leverage and investments in conventional financial assets. Typically, this will include limits on debt to market capitalisation, cash and interest-bearing securities to market capitalisation and accounts receivable to market capitalisation.

In addition to the Shari'ah committee, the fund managers will also employ investment professionals to structure the fund. These professionals will typically structure the portfolio, taking account of the diversification of the fund on both an industry and country basis, and where tracking an index is the primary objective they will also look to minimise tracking error to the chosen index or composite of several indices, while taking into account both dealing costs and risk based on an absolute and relative returns basis.

SHARI'AH-COMPLIANT AND CONVENTIONAL RETURNS

The general perception of ethical investment is that the ethical investor is likely to earn portfolio returns that are below the market portfolio return. It is argued that ethical investing will underperform over the long term because ethical investment portfolios are subsets of the market portfolio, and lack sufficient diversification.

However, the results from studies on the performance gap between ethically screened and unscreened investments are mixed, with several of these studies reporting no statistically significant difference in their returns.[3]

For Shari'ah-compliant investors, the specific objectives of various academic studies have been to determine whether there is a significant correlation coefficient between

---

[2]As at 3 August 2015 (source: FTfm).

[3]'Does the Shari'ah index move together with the conventional equity indexes?', Kwang Suk Park and Mansur Masih, INCEIF, Malaysia, 20 January 2015.

the Dow Jones Islamic Market (DJIM) Index and other major equity indices such as S&P and DAX.

The majority of these studies followed the same methodologies of comparing the performance of the DJIM Index to other benchmarks, but the choices are quite different from one research study to another in terms of performance measures and benchmarks.

In a study by Hakim and Rashidian (2004), the interdependence theory of financial markets was debased and it was concluded that the Shari'ah-compliant index has unique risk features that are independent from broad equity markets owing to the Shari'ah screening criteria. This contradicts other studies by Hassan (2004) and Girard and Hassan (2008) that provided empirical evidence of Shari'ah-compliant and conventional indices being similar.

As for the Malaysian Shari'ah-compliant stock market, the Kuala Lumpur Shari'ah Index was studied by a number of researchers. Prominent studies by Ahmad and Ibrahim (2002), Albaity and Ahmad (2008) and Yusof and Majid (2007) have addressed various issues of DJIM, FTSE and Malaysian Shari'ah-compliant indices.

Some particular studies focused on other markets such as the Pakistani stock market (Nishat, 2004) or that of Saudi Arabia (Dabbeeru, 2006).

Only a few studies have addressed the issues of the existence of diversification opportunities. Hakim and Rashidian (2004) found that despite investment restrictions, the exclusion of industries from the DJIM did not seem to have hurt its diversification, but may have contributed to reducing its market risk.

Guyot (2011) analysed the same index family and found the absence of co-integration (the absence of co-integration indicates the presence of diversification opportunities in the concerned indices) over the long term between nine pairs of Islamic and conventional indices, while Girard and Hassan (2008) used a multivariate co-integration analysis and found that Islamic and conventional groups of FTSE are integrated.

The Kwang Suk Park and Mansur Masih (2015) study revealed the absence of co-integration between the DJIM and three conventional indexes such as DAX, Hang Seng and KL. This means that diversification opportunities exist for these indexes. But for the S&P and DJIM, the study found that two indexes are moving together and the DJIM was strongly affected by a shock to the S&P index.

The conclusions one may draw from these studies are that while Shari'ah-compliant investors may have somewhat reduced opportunities for diversification in their equity portfolios, the effects of this are small and possibly outweighed by the generally lower risk in a Shari'ah-compliant portfolio that stems from the elimination of highly leveraged firms.

COMMODITIES FUNDS

Commodities funds are funds where the subscription amounts are used to purchase *halal* commodities and which will generate profits by buying and reselling *halal* commodities. Trading profits must be the main source of income for the fund investors. The price of the underlying commodity must be clearly specified and be known to all parties to the transactions.

Because of the restrictions on the use of derivatives and short selling, commodities funds make use of two types of Shari'ah approved contracts: *salam* and *murabaha* (for descriptions, see Appendix A).

In the case of *salam*-based commodity funds, the fund pays in advance for commodities (fungible goods) to be delivered at a given date. The commodities are sold on delivery at a spot price that includes the profit (or loss) of the fund. *Salam* is the reverse of the *murabaha* contract.

The units of the fund can be bought and sold in a secondary market provided the fund owns some commodities at all times. Two examples of Islamic commodity funds are the following:

1. Riyad Capital Bank in Saudi Arabia has two commodity trading funds available to investors. One fund deals in US dollars, and the other deals in Saudi riyals; both are Shari'ah-compliant. The fund manager finances *murabaha* deals through purchasing commodities and goods from established suppliers against immediate payment, and sells them at higher prices on deferred payment terms.

2. Al Rajhi Capital, also in Saudi Arabia, offers three commodity fund products: a US dollar commodity fund, a Saudi riyal commodity fund, and a euro commodity fund. The assets of the fund are invested on a *mudaraba* basis in transactions executed in accordance with Shari'ah principles. The *murabaha* transactions consist of purchasing goods from approved suppliers against immediate payment and selling them to reputed organisations on deferred payment terms with a mark-up, thereby generating a profit.

CIMB also offers an Islamic Global Commodities Equity Fund.

ISLAMIC REAL ESTATE INVESTMENT TRUSTS (iREITs)

Investment trusts (ITs) are a type of collective investment scheme (trusts or corporations) that invests in various asset classes – typically shares and bonds – to provide income to their investors. They may be exchange-traded or non-traded, but in the latter case the secondary market is very limited with only a portion of the shares or units being redeemable each year, offering limited liquidity to investors. Exchange-traded ITs may use debt to leverage their returns, seeking to find a satisfactory balance between higher mean returns and increased volatility.

Real Estate Investment Trusts (REITs) are trusts that invest mainly in income-producing real estate, shares in property companies or real estate financing assets. Investopedia lists five common kinds of REITs: retail, residential, healthcare, office and mortgage REITs. In principle, a REIT may invest in a mixture of these, but there may also be benefits in specialisation through expertise in a particular asset market. REITs may manage as well as own properties.

Islamic REITs (iREITs) are REITs which operate in accordance with Shari'ah requirements, which include having a SB. They are as yet relatively few in number, but given their intrinsic attractiveness to Islamic investors (since many property investments are *halal*) one may expect the number to grow. iREITs are being actively promoted in Malaysia by the Securities Commission, which has issued a set of guidelines for the operation of an iREIT with particular reference to Shari'ah compliance. The Securities Commission has in mind exchange-traded iREITs. In summary, these guidelines are as follows:

- Rental incomes from non-permissible activities must not exceed 20 percent.
- An iREIT cannot own properties where all the tenants operate non-permissible activities (such as: conventional financial services; manufacture or sale of non-*halal* products, armaments or tobacco; 'adult' entertainment; trading in non-Shari'ah-compliant securities).
- An iREIT shall not accept new tenants whose activities are fully non-permissible.
- Tenants engaged in non-permissible activities may occupy no more than 20 percent of the total area.
- For non-space-using activities, decisions must be based on *ijtihad* (juristic reasoning) exercised by the SB.
- All investment, deposit and financing instruments must comply with Shari'ah principles.
- Property insurance must be based on *takaful* schemes. Conventional insurance is permitted if no *takaful* cover is available.

Islamic REITs in Malaysia include a healthcare iREIT, which invests in hospitals, and another which invests in palm oil plantations. CAGAMAS, the Malaysian equivalent of Freddie Mac and Fannie Mae, is in substance an iREIT which invests in Shari'ah-compliant mortgages, although it is not classified as a REIT and its units are in the form of *sukuk* rather than shares.

One approach used by iREITs is sale and leaseback, whereby a property owner sells a property to the iREIT and then leases it back under an *ijarah* contract. This provides the iREIT with a more stable source of income by reducing the risk of having 'void periods' between tenancies.

While iREITs may not use debt finance, an exchange-traded iREIT may issue *sukuk* in the form of *sukuk al-ijarah* (and, in Malaysia, *sukuk al-murabaha*). Whether this would increase its rate of return to shareholders or unit holders obviously depends on whether the rate of return required by the *sukuk* investors is significantly lower than the rate earned by the iREIT on its investments after meeting its operating expenses.

TAKAFUL (ISLAMIC INSURANCE) INSTITUTIONS

As mentioned in Chapter 1, *takaful* institutions offer savings and investment products that are similar to Islamic CIS, except that they come bundled with whole life insurance. As such, they offer consumers an alternative to Islamic CIS.

PROFIT-SHARING INVESTMENT ACCOUNTS

Restricted Profit-Sharing Investment Accounts (RPSIA) operated by Islamic banks acting as asset managers, and based on a *mudaraba* contract, may be pooled in the form of a CIS, as envisaged by the IFSB in its IFSB-6. Nevertheless, they are considered as banking, not capital market, instruments and are regulated as such, not by the capital market regulator. This raises certain governance issues, as such funds have no legal existence separate from that of the Islamic bank managing them as *mudarib* (asset manager). The investment account holders therefore do not benefit from the governance rights available generally to participants in CIS, such as a board of trustees and separate financial statements, although the IFSB recommended in IFSB-4 *Disclosures to Promote Transparency and Market Discipline* (December 2007) that separate financial statements should be provided. Under a *mudaraba* contract, the bank as *mudarib* receives remuneration in the form of a share of the income on the investments, rather than as a percentage of the value of the assets managed.

Unrestricted Profit-Sharing Investment Accounts (UPSIA) are widely used by Islamic banks as a Shari'ah-compliant alternative to conventional interest-bearing deposit accounts. These also are normally operated on the basis of a *mudaraba* contract. Many Islamic banks employ various methods to smooth the returns paid to the account holders and to pay them returns comparable to those on conventional deposits. The operation of the *mudaraba* contract allows the bank to take a large share of the income from the investments – up to 70 percent in some cases. In profitable years, the bank takes its full contractual percentage, while in less profitable years it may take a reduced percentage, so as to pay a competitive return to the UPSIA holders (UIAH). In addition, the contract typically allows the bank to constitute reserves, largely or wholly out of income attributable to the UIAH, which can be used for the purpose of smoothing the returns paid to them, thus reducing any need for the bank to take a lower *mudarib* share of income.

The Bank Negara Malaysia (central bank) has revised its regulations so as to require such accounts to be operated by banks in Malaysia as investment accounts with no such smoothing. Nevertheless, the governance issues mentioned above in the case of RPSIA also arise, perhaps even more acutely, for UPSIA.

CONCLUSION

It should be clear from the above that there exists a range of collective investment schemes that are suitable for Shari'ah-compliant investors. In general, investing in such schemes would seem to offer returns and other conditions no less attractive than those of conventional CISs. We draw attention, however, to the lack of governance rights in the case of RPSIA, which are not regulated as capital market products.

BIBLIOGRAPHY

Ahmad, Z., and H. Ibrahim (2002) 'A Study of Performance of the KLSE Syariah Index', *Malaysian Management Journal*, 6 (1–2), pp. 25–34.

Albaity, M. and R. Ahmad (2008) 'Performance of Syariah and Composite Indices: Evidence from Bursa Malaysia', *Journal of Accounting and Finance*, 4 (1), pp. 23–43.

Yusof, R. M. and M. S. A. Majid (2007) 'Stock Market Volatility Transmission in Malaysia: Islamic Versus Conventional Stock Market', *Journal of Islamic Economics*, 20 (2), pp. 17–35.

CHAPTER 5

Legal and Regulatory Considerations Pertaining to Islamic Capital Markets

By Michael J. T. McMillen*

This chapter provides an overview of select aspects of legal (including regulatory) issues affecting the Islamic Capital Market (ICM). The categories of issues discussed in this chapter are (a) securities laws and regulatory regimes, (b) securitisation laws, which include laws and regulations applicable to *sukuk*, and (c) legal regime matters, including both legal opinion matters that are critical to capital markets transactions and general systemic matters.

Essentially all of these matters are, at core, specific to each jurisdiction in which the relevant capital markets activities occur. Most of the relevant laws, regulations and standards currently in effect have been developed in the context of interest-based instruments and transactions and embody interest-based assumptions and techniques. A challenge to the ICM industry (and the broader Islamic finance industry) is the adaptation between the existing capital markets laws, regulations, standards and practices on the one hand, and the needs of the ICM industry on the other hand. That challenge should be foremost in mind as one considers this chapter.

The chapter begins with a consideration of capital markets (securities) laws and related regulatory regimes. A brief survey of the theories of governmental policy that support capital markets laws and regulations is presented first. This is no abstract undertaking. As a result of the 2007 financial crisis, these theories are the subject of intense contemporary debate: a debate that is influencing the ongoing restructuring of legal and regulatory paradigms in the capital markets context. After this survey, the chapter considers the nature of a security, the types of enforcement mechanisms that exist in the legal and regulatory context, legal and regulatory factors relating to offerings and disclosure in the capital markets, factors influencing access to the capital markets, financial intermediaries, collective investment schemes and secondary markets.

Sukuk and equities are the principal capital markets instruments in the ICM. The *sukuk* segment is the most rapidly growing area of Islamic finance generally, and ICM specifically. *Sukuk* are, at core, securitisations and are and will be subject to securitisation laws and regulations. Thus, the second section of the chapter surveys legal and regulatory requirements applicable to securitisations, including *sukuk*. Brief surveys are provided of relevant definitions, principles, parties, structural considerations and true sales concepts. The true sales concepts are critical to the involvement of private sector entities in the ICM (as well as to existing securitisation concepts, both conventional and Islamic). Thereafter, *sukuk* are considered specifically. This section introduces regulatory regimes that have been developed for asset-based securitisations, despite the fact that these regimes have not been targeted at (or even acknowledged) *sukuk*. Disclosure and investor communication matters are discussed specifically.

The final section of this chapter looks at two aspects of legal regimes generally, given that each of these aspects profoundly influences the development of the ICM. By way of introduction, the extent to which the Shari'ah is incorporated in the secular law of a given country is introduced because the effect of the legal structure at this level will influence every other legal and regulatory matter that is considered in this chapter, as well as the enforceability of any capital markets instrument (and related documents and arrangements). The next sub-section addresses legal opinions (particularly the enforceability or remedies opinion in Shari'ah-compliant transactions and, in particular, in *sukuk* transactions). An enforceability or remedies opinion is (usually multiple enforceability and remedies opinions are) required in virtually every capital markets transaction. Without these opinions, it is not possible to obtain ratings for capital markets instruments. The inability to render these opinions in transactions involving private commercial issuers has been the single largest impediment to development of this segment of the ICM. In addition to general consideration of the enforceability opinion, a select group of topics relating to *sukuk* are surveyed. These topics include true sales, substantive consolidation, lien-free transfers and collateral security structures. The final sub-section takes up structural legal infrastructure matters of different types and their effects on opinion practice in the capital markets context.

As a research aid, the footnotes of this chapter describe sources (often representative sources) for some matters discussed in the chapter. The footnotes are supplemented by the bibliography, which includes both sources included in the footnotes, and other sources that are not included in the footnotes.

SECURITIES LAWS AND REGULATORY REGIMES

The most prominent set of laws of relevance to capital markets activities, including ICM activities, are the securities laws (sometimes referred to as 'capital markets laws') of each relevant jurisdiction. Despite the increasing globalisation of the capital markets, securities laws and the related regulatory regimes are a local matter (national and subnational). And they involve, in different jurisdictions, different combinations of governmental authorities and non-governmental – often self-regulatory – organisations such as stock exchanges and participant associations (SROs). Although this chapter focuses on governmental involvements, the regulatory contribution of SROs is important, particularly in the case of Islamic finance, where matters of Shari'ah interpretation are frequently not embodied in the legal and regulatory regime. The result of this configuration is considerable regulatory disharmony, a matter of increasing concern and attention.[1]

Securities laws deal with three broad categories of activities: (i) disclosure duties; (ii) restrictions on fraud and misrepresentation; and (iii) restrictions on insider trading. Within this general framework, the securities laws regulate a range of different actors and activities. And they provide an array of powers to the regulatory authority, as well as enforcement mechanisms and remedies for violations and non-compliance. These powers include, as primary categories: (i) investigatory powers; (ii) enforcement powers; and (iii) powers to invoke governmental compulsion for non-compliance. These powers are customarily exercisable both administratively and judicially. For example, investigatory powers may include subpoena concepts and enforcement powers may include civil and criminal resorts, including injunctive relief, disgorgement, fines, penalties, contempt remedies, imprisonment and the power to enter into settlements of disputed matters and practices. With increasing globalisation of capital markets, extraterritorial or global enforcement capabilities, transcending national borders, are expanding.[2]

---

[*]Partner and Global Head of Islamic Finance and Investment at the international law firm of Curtis, Mallet-Prevost, Colt & Mosle LLP and Adjunct Professor of Law at the University of Pennsylvania Law School. Copyright 2015 Michael J. T. McMillen; all rights reserved.

[1]See, e.g., Marc I. Steinberg, INTERNATIONAL SECURITIES LAW: A CONTEMPORARY AND COMPARATIVE ANALYSIS (1999) ('Steinberg'), including at 2–3, INTERNATIONAL SECURITIES LAW HANDBOOK, SECOND EDITION, Jean-Luc Solier and Marcus Best, eds. (2005), including at xix–xx., Manning Gilbert Warren III, EUROPEAN SECURITIES REGULATION (2003) (European securities laws, with a particular focus on harmonisation issues), Manning Gilbert Warren III, *Global Harmonization of Securities Laws: The Achievement of the European Communities*, 31 HARVARD INTERNATIONAL LAW JOURNAL 185 (1990), at 186, and Roberta Romano, *Empowering Investors: A Market Approach to Securities Regulation*, 107 YALE LAW JOURNAL 2359 (1998). See also OBJECTIVES AND PRINCIPLES OF SECURITIES REGULATION, INTERNATIONAL ORGANIZATION OF SECURITIES COMMISSIONS (September 1998) (the 'IOSCO Principles'), especially at 18–22; available at http://www.iosco.org/library/pubdocs/pdf/IOSCOPD82.pdf.

[2]Extraterritorial or global financial regulation is not considered in this chapter, despite its currency. For discussions of some of the relevant issues, see, e.g., John C. Coffee, Jr., *Extraterritorial Financial Regulation: Why E. T. Can't Come Home*, 99 CORNELL LAW REVIEW 1259 (2013–2014), David Zarin, *Finding Legal Principle in Global Financial Regulation*, 52 VIRGINIA JOURNAL OF INTERNATIONAL LAW 683 (2012), Chris Brummer, *Territoriality as a Regulatory Technique: Notes from the Financial Crisis*, 79 UNIVERSITY OF CINCINNATI LAW REVIEW 499 (2010), Stephen J. Choi and Andrew T. Guzman, *Portable Reciprocity: Rethinking the International Reach of Securities Regulation*, 71 SOUTHERN CALIFORNIA LAW REVIEW 903 (1998), Jane C. Kang, *The Regulation of Global Futures Markets: Is Harmonization Possible or Even Desirable?*, 17 NORTHWESTERN JOURNAL OF INTERNATIONAL LAW AND BUSINESS 242 (1996), James D. Cox, *Regulatory Duopoly in U.S. Securities Markets*, 99 COLUMBIA LAW REVIEW 1200 (1999), Allen Ferrell, *The Case for Mandatory Disclosure in Securities Regulation Around the World*, JOHN M. OLIN CENTER FOR LAW, ECONOMICS AND BUSINESS, HARVARD UNIVERSITY (October 2004), available at http://papers.ssrn.com/sol3/papers.cfm?-abstract_id=631221, Hendrik Cornelis and Ton Nederveen, *Civil Liability for Prospectus Misstatements under Dutch Law*, 14 INTERNATIONAL FINANCIAL LAW REVIEW 50 (1995), Steven M. Davidoff, *Rhetoric and Reality: A Historical Perspective on the Regulation of Foreign Private*

While this chapter takes the world as it now exists, consideration of existing laws must be made in the context of the theories of governmental policy (including legal policy) that support the laws and their regulatory implementation. This is particularly true at the present time, due to the renewed theoretical debate occasioned by the 2007 financial crisis, the restructuring of the legal-regulatory paradigms that have resulted from this financial crisis, and the unabated globalisation of the capital markets across divergent legal-regulatory systems and environments. Contemporary theoretical debate as to the optimal legal arrangements for governmental approaches to the capital markets is vigorous. A brief summary of that debate is warranted.

There are three general models for government policy and the related legal arrangements.[3] One theory maintains that securities laws are irrelevant or damaging. The other two maintain that securities laws are of relevance and are necessary, although they differ as to what government intervention is optimal.

The first model – characterised as the 'null hypothesis' – argues that the optimal government policy is to leave the securities and capital markets unregulated.[4] It is argued that, in the pure case, and with perfect enforcement, market functioning and existing legal (including contract and tort) mechanisms will serve the goals sought through regulatory intervention. In the disclosure context, it is argued that there is an

---

Issuers, 79 UNIVERSITY OF CINCINNATI LAW REVIEW 619 (2010), Michael Greenberger, *The Extraterritorial Provisions of the Dodd–Frank Act Protects U.S. Taxpayers from Worldwide Bailouts*, 80 UNIVERSITY OF MISSOURI KANSAS CITY LAW REVIEW 965 (2012), Chris Brummer, *How International Law Works (and How It Doesn't)*, 99 GEORGETOWN LAW REVIEW 257 (2011), Wolf-Georg Ringe and Alexander Hellgardt, *The International Dimension of Issuer Liability: Liability and Choice of Law from a Transatlantic Perspective*, 31 OXFORD JOURNAL OF LEGAL STUDIES 23 (2011), available at http://papers.ssrn.com/sol3/papers.cfm?abstract_id=1588112, Wolf-George Ringe, Alexander Hellgardt, Michael D. Mann, Joseph G. Mari and George Lavdas, *Developments in International Securities Law Enforcement and Regulation*, 19 THE INTERNATIONAL LAWYER 729 (1995), Paul G. Mahoney, *Regulation of International Securities Issues*, 14 REGULATION 62 (1991), and Mervyn King, *International Harmonisation of the Regulation of Capital Markets: An Introduction*, 34 EUROPEAN ECONOMIC REVIEW 569 (1990). See also René M. Stulz, *Globalization, Corporate Finance and the Cost of Capital*, 12 JOURNAL OF APPLIED CORPORATE FINANCE 8 (1999) ('Stulz'). Consider also Henry Hansmann and Reiner Kraakman, *The End of History for Corporate Law*, Yale Law School Law and Economics Working Paper No. 235, New York University Law and Economics Working Paper No. 013, Harvard Law School John M. Olin Center for Law, Economics, and Business Discussion Paper No. 280, and Yale International Center for Finance Working Paper No. 00-09 (January 2000), available at http://papers.ssrn.com/sol3/papers.cfm?abstract_id=204528.

[3] This summary tracks the introductory overview in Rafael La Porta, Florencio Lopez-de-Silanes and Andrei Shleifer, *What Works in Securities Laws?*, 61 THE JOURNAL OF FINANCE 1 (2006) ('LaPorta et al.'), although various other formulations are presented in the literature.

[4] This approach follows that of Ronald Coase, *The Problem of Social Cost*, 3 JOURNAL OF LAW AND ECONOMICS 1 (1960), and George Stigler, *Public Regulation of the Securities Market*, 37 JOURNAL OF BUSINESS 117 (1964). Other authors that support this approach include Sanford Grossman, *The Informational Role of Warranties and Private Disclosure About Product Quality*, 24 JOURNAL OF LAW AND ECONOMICS 461 (1981) ('Grossman'), Sanford Grossman and Oliver Hart, *Disclosure Laws and Takeover Bids*, 35 JOURNAL OF FINANCE 323 (1980) ('Grossman and Hart'), and Paul Milgrom and John Roberts, *Relying on the Information of Interested Parties*, 17 RAND JOURNAL OF ECONOMICS 18 (1986) ('Milgrom and Roberts').

incentive to disclose fully because (a) any failure to disclose causes investors to assume the worst, and (b) there are other reputational, legal and contractual consequences of an adverse nature for misreporting.[5] Thus, '[s]ecurities law is either irrelevant (to the extent that it codifies existing market arrangements or can be contracted around), or damaging, in so far as it raises contracting costs and invites political interference in the markets. . . .'[6]

The other two models both maintain that securities regulation is relevant and that the reputational and legal mechanisms are inadequate to prevent adverse consequences to investors (in large part because the reward from misconduct is great, litigation outcomes are too unpredictable, and the costs of litigation are too large).[7]

The first of these other two models favours (i) government involvement to standardise the private contracting framework so as to improve market discipline, and (ii) private litigation. Specifically, the government and the legal mechanisms can (x) mandate the disclosure of specific information in disclosure documents, thereby

---

[5] See, e.g., Grossman, *id.*, Grossman & Hart, *id.*, Milgrom and Roberts, *id.*, Stephen Ross, *Disclosure Regulation in Financial Markets: Implications of Modern Finance Theory and Signaling Theory*, Issues in Financial Regulation, Franklin Edwards, ed. (1979), George Benston, *Required Disclosure and the Stock Market: An Evaluation of the Securities Market Act of 1934*, 63 American Economic Review 132 (1973), Thomas Chemmanur and Paolo Fulghierie, *Investment Bank Reputation, Information Production and Financial Intermediation*, 49 The Journal of Finance 57 (1994), Bradford De Long, Did J.P. Morgan's Men Add Value? An Economist's Perspective on Financial Capitalism, Inside the Business Enterprise: Historical Perspectives on the Use of Information (1991), Daniel Fischel and Sanford Grossman, *Customer Protection in Futures and Securities Markets*, 4 Journal of Futures Markets 273 (1984), and Merton Miller, Financial Innovations and Market Volatility (1991).

[6] LaPorta et al., *supra* note 3, at 2, citing Ronald Coase, *Economists and Public Policy*, in Large Corporations in a Changing Society, J. F. Weston, ed. (1975). See also Jonathan Macey, *Administrative Agency Obsolescence and Interest Group Formation: A Case Study of the SEC at Sixty*, 15 Cardozo Law Review 909 (1994), and Roberta Romano, *The Need for Competition in International Securities Regulations*, 2 Theoretical Inquiries in Law 1 (2001).

[7] See, e.g., James Landis, The Administrative Process (1938) ('Landis'), Irwin Friend and Edward Herman, *The S.E.C. Through a Glass Darkly*, 37 Journal of Business 382 (1964), John Coffee, *Market Failure and the Economic Case of a Mandatory Disclosure System*, 70 Virginia Law Review 717 (1984), Carol Simon, *The Effect of the 1933 Securities Act on Investor Information and the Performance of New Issues*, 79 American Economic Review (1989), Paul Mahoney, *Mandatory Disclosure as a Solution to Agency Problems*, 62 University of Chicago Law Review 1047 (1995), Laura Beny, *A Comparative Empirical Investigation of Agency and Market Theories of Insider Trading*, Harvard Law School John M. Olin Center for Law, Economics and Business Discussion Paper Series, Paper 264 (1999), available at http://lsr.nellco.org/harvard_olin/264, Merritt Fox, *Retaining Mandatory Disclosure: Why Issuer Choice is Not Investor Empowerment*, 85 Virginia Law Review 1335 (1999), Stulz, *supra* note 2, Bernard Black, *The Legal and Institutional Preconditions for a Strong Securities Markets*, 48 University of California Los Angeles Law Review 781 (2001), John Coffee, *The Mandatory/Enabling Balance in Corporate Law: An Essay on the Judicial Role*, 89 Columbia Law Review 1618 (1989), John Coffee, *Understanding Enron: It's About the Gatekeepers, Stupid*, 57 The Business Lawyer 1403 (2002), and William Reese and Michael Weisbach, *Protection of Minority Shareholder Interests, Cross-Listings in the United States, and Subsequent-Equity Offerings*, 66 Journal of Financial Economics 65 (2002).

enhancing investor information, and (y) provide liability consequences for failure to disclose in accordance with the appropriate standards regarding the relevant types of information. And these mechanisms can specify the liability of issuers and intermediaries that violate the relevant standards, thereby reducing uncertainty. Both types of involvement are thought to benefit the markets and market functioning.[8]

The second of these models adds public enforcement to the disclosure regime. Enforcement is implemented by an independent agency (such as a securities or capital markets authority or bank regulator). The enforcement authority acts *ex ante* (clarifying obligations) and *ex post* (providing sanctions). It exercises state power in acquiring and ensuring distribution of information and in the enforcement process, both of which are argued to increase market functioning.[9]

Whatever the theoretical debate, for the purposes of this chapter it is assumed that some type of disclosure regime is embodied in the relevant securities laws and that some type of governmental agency (a 'regulatory authority') oversees the legal (including regulatory) regime. Which is not to say that the theoretical debate is irrelevant; it will influence the nature and composition of the legal regime applicable to the capital markets.

What is a Security?

In considering the securities laws, the first questions relate to what constitutes a 'security' that is subject to the laws. This is true even where the securities laws are characterised as 'capital markets laws'.[10] The definition of securities is usually critical to triggering

---

[8] See, e.g., Bernard Black and Reinier Kraakman, *A Self-Enforcing Model of Corporate Law*, 109 HARVARD LAW REVIEW 1911 (1996), Jonathan Hay, Andrei Shleifer and Robert Vishny, *Toward a Theory of Legal Reform*, 40 EUROPEAN ECONOMIC REVIEW 559 (1996), Edward Glaeser and Andrei Shleifer, *A Reason for Quantity Regulation*, 91 AMERICAN ECONOMIC REVIEW PAPERS AND PROCEEDINGS 431 (2001), Edward Glaeser and Andrei Shleifer, *Legal Origins*, 117 QUARTERLY JOURNAL OF ECONOMICS 1193 (2002), and Nittai K. Bergman and Daniel Nicolaievsky, *Investor Protection and the Coasian View*, MIT SLOAN MANAGEMENT, MIT SLOAN WORKING PAPER 4476-04 (2004), available at http://papers.ssrn.com/sol3/papers.cfm?abstract_id=517022.
[9] See, e.g., Landis, *supra* note 7, Gary Becker, *Crime and Punishment: An Economic Approach*, 76 JOURNAL OF POLITICAL ECONOMY 169 (1968), Mitchell Polinsky and Steven Shavell, *The Economic Theory of Public Enforcement of Law*, 38 JOURNAL OF ECONOMIC LITERATURE 45 (2000), Edward Glaeser, Simon Johnson and Andrei Shleifer, *Coase Versus the Coasians*, 116 QUARTERLY JOURNAL OF ECONOMICS 853 (2001), Chenggang Xu and Katharina Pistor, *Law Enforcement Under Incomplete Law: Theory and Evidence from Financial Market Regulation*, DISCUSSION PAPER NO TE/02/442 (December 2002), available at http://eprints.lse.ac.uk/3748/1/Law_Enforcement_under_Incomplete_Law_Theory_and_Evidence_from_Financial_Market_Regulation.pdf, and Edward Glaeser and Andrei Shleifer, *The Rise of the Regulatory State*, 41 JOURNAL OF ECONOMIC LITERATURE 401 (2003).
[10] Consider, for example, the securities and capital markets laws of Saudi Arabia, the United Arab Emirates, Malaysia, Singapore and Pakistan. The law of Saudi Arabia is Capital Market Law (Saudi Arabia) (the 'Saudi CML'), available (in English) at http://www.cma.org.sa/cma_cms/upload_sec_content/dwfile20/Capital%20Market%20Law.pdf, which defines the base term 'security', based upon Jordanian and Danish constructs, around a defined list of examples

the operation of the various legal and regulatory requirements. In contemporary finance, questions relating to the definition of a security are intricate. However, these questions receive short shrift in this chapter because the assumption is here made that essentially all of the equity and debt instruments that are issued in the ICM constitute securities.[11]

---

of securities (and some exclusions), with a catch-all concept appended. The date of publication of the Saudi CML was June 28, 2003, and the website of the Capital Market Authority specifies issuance by Royal Decree number m/3, date 31 July 2003 (see http://www.cma .org.sa/cma_en/subpage.aspx?secserno=20&mirrorid=278&serno=20). The publication date is taken from Joseph W. Beach, *The Saudi Arabian Capital Market Law: A Practical Study of the Creation of Law in Developing Markets*, 41 STANFORD JOURNAL OF INTERNATIONAL LAW 1 (2005) ('Beach'), discussing the definition of a 'security' at 321–23. Beach assisted Professor James D. Cox in drafting the law and is a useful summary of the 'legislative history' of the Saudi CML, including the sources of the various provisions and concepts embodied in the law. See also Gouda Bushra Ali Gouda, *The Saudi Securities Law: Regulation of the Tadawul Stock Market, Issuers, and Securities Professionals under the Saudi Capital Market Law* 2003, 18 ANNUAL SURVEY OF INTERNATIONAL AND COMPARATIVE LAW 115 (2012) ('Gouda'), discussing the definition of 'security' at 128–34. The United Arab Emirates law is Federal Law No. 4 of 2000 Concerning the Emirates Securities Authority and Market, available at http://www.sca.ae/ english/SCA/Laws/index.asp. The base terms under this law are 'securities' and 'commodities'. Securities are defined (Article 1) as shares, bonds and notes issued by joint stock companies and bonds and notes issued by government entities and 'any other domestic or non-domestic financial instruments accepted' by the Regulatory Authority. The Singapore law is The Securities and Futures Act (Chapter 289), available at http://statutes.agc.gov.sg/aol/search/display/ view.w3p;page=0;query=DocId%3A%2225de2ec3-ac8e-44bf-9c88-927bf7eca056%22%20 Status%3Ainforce%20Depth%3A0;rec=0. Capital markets products include securities (defined in section 2), futures contracts, contracts or arrangements for foreign exchange trading, and other instruments as the Regulatory Authority may designate. The primary enabling legislation in Pakistan is the Securities and Exchange Ordinance, 1969 (Ordinance No. XVII of 1969), available at http://www.secp.gov.pk/corporatelaws/pdf/sep_08_00.pdf, which defines securities in Section 2 and expressly includes *mudaraba* instruments.

[11]The literature on these questions constitutes a fulsome library: there are hundreds of articles, and approximately a thousand published cases in the United States, on the definition of a 'security'. See, e.g., Lewis D. Lowenfels and Alan R. Bromberg, *What is a Security under the Federal Securities Laws?*, 56 ALBANY LAW REVIEW 473 (1993), (1970), Scot FitzGibbon, *What is a Security? – A Redefinition Based on Eligibility to Participate in the Financial Markets*, 64 MINNESOTA LAW REVIEW 893 (1979–1980), John Sobieski, *What is a Security?*, 25 MERCER LAW REVIEW 381 (1974), Park McGinty, *What is a Security?*, 1993 WISCONSIN LAW REVIEW 1033, Marc I. Steinberg and William E. Kaulbach, *The Supreme Court and the Definition of 'Security': The 'Context' Clause, 'Investment Contract' Analysis, and Their Ramifications*, 40 VANDERBILT LAW REVIEW 489 (1987), George F. Jones, *Footnote 11 of Marine Bank v. Weaver: Will Unconventional Certificates of Deposit Be Held Securities?*, 24 HOUSTON LAW REVIEW 491 (1987), William H. Newton III, *What is a Security? A Critical Analysis*, 48 MISSISSIPPI LAW REVIEW 167 (1977), Frederick H. C. Mazando, *The Taxonomy of Global Securities: Is the U.S. Definition of a Security too Broad?*, 33 NORTHWESTERN JOURNAL OF INTERNATIONAL LAW AND BUSINESS 121 (2012–2013), Martin Lipton and George A. Katz, *'Notes' Are (Are Not?) Always Securities – A Review*, 29 THE BUSINESS LAWYER 861 (1974), Martin Lipton and George A. Katz, *'Notes' Are Not Always Securities*, 30 THE BUSINESS LAWYER 763 (1975), Theresa A. Gabaldon, *A Sense of Security: An Empirical Study*, 25 JOURNAL OF CORPORATION LAW 307 (1999–2000)

Definitions of 'securities' generally cast a wide net. In most jurisdictions, definitions of this type include stocks, treasury stocks, transferable shares, investment contracts, voting trust certificates, certificates of interest or participation in profit-sharing agreements, fractional undivided interests in assets or rights (particularly in oil, gas or mineral rights), interests in partnerships, interests in real estate, collateral trust certificates, preorganisation certificates or subscriptions, bonds, notes, certificates of deposit, evidence of indebtedness, various puts, calls, straddles, options and privileges entered into on a national securities exchange, and other instruments that entitle their owner or holder to make a claim upon the assets or earnings of the issuer or the voting power that accompanies such claims.[12] And, in most jurisdictions, certain types of notes and other instruments are excluded from the definition of securities. Examples often include notes secured by a home purchase mortgage and notes secured by accounts receivable.

The issue of what constitutes a security is often one of policy and the substantive economic realities of the relevant instrument and its related transaction.[13] The definitions are commonly open-ended, allowing for adjustments to evolving markets. Thus, while it is here assumed that the capital market instrument in question is a 'security' that is subject to regulation, this assumption should never be made and left unconsidered in a transactional context.

('Gabaldon'), Richard N. Owens, *What is a Security?*, 17 THE ACCOUNTING REVIEW 303 (1942), Jeffrey A. Blomberg and Henry E. Forcier, *But is it a Security? A Look at Offers from Start-Up Companies*, 14 BUSINESS LAW TODAY 48 (2005), Barbara Black, *Is Stock a Security? A Criticism of the Sale of Business Doctrine in Securities Fraud Litigation*, 16 UNIVERSITY OF CALIFORNIA DAVIS LAW REVIEW 325 (1983), Stephen J. Easley, *Recent Developments in the Sale-of-Business Doctrine: Toward a Context-Based Analysis for Federal Securities Jurisdiction*, 39 THE BUSINESS LAWYER 929 (1984), and Robert B. Thompson, *The Shrinking Definition of a Security: Why Purchasing All of a Company's Stock is Not a Federal Security Transaction*, 57 NEW YORK UNIVERSITY LAW REVIEW 225 (1982).

[12] The United States Supreme Court, in interpreting the various securities laws, has emphasised the breadth and open-ended nature of the concept of 'securities', and this pattern is commonplace globally. For example, it is said that the definition of securities is sufficiently broad to encompass virtually any instrument that might be sold as an investment. *Reves v. Ernst & Young*, 494 U.S. 56, at 61 (1990) (the purpose of Congress 'in enacting the securities laws was to regulate investments, in whatever form they are made and by whatever name they are called'), and *United States Housing Foundation, Inc. v. Forman*, 421 U.S. 837, 847–848 (1975). And it includes the 'countless and variable schemes devised by those who seek the use of the money of others on the promise of profits.' *SEC v. W.J. Howry, Co.*, 328 U.S. 293, 299 (1946). See also *Gould v. Ruefenacht*, 471 U.S. 701 (1985), *Landreth Timber Co. v. Landreth*, 471 U.S. 681 (1985), *Marine Bank v. Weaver*, 455 U.S. 551 (1982), *International Brotherhood of Teamsters v. Daniel*, 439 U.S. 551 (1979), *Tcherepnin v. Knight*, 389 U.S. 332 (1967), *SEC v. United Benefit Life Insurance Co.*, 387 U.S. 202 (1967), *SEC v. Variable Annuity Life Insurance Company of America*, 359 U.S. 65 (1959), and *SEC v. C.M. Joiner Leasing Corp.*, 320 U.S. 344 (1943).

[13] See, e.g., the discussion of 'economic reality' tests in the US jurisprudence of definitions of security in Gabaldon, *supra* note 11, at 313–14, noting also Gabaldon's discussion of concepts of exclusion of certain items from the regulatory scheme (such as where the instrument is subject to regulation outside the securities regulatory regime). See also Ronald J. Coffey, *The Economic Realities of a 'Security': Is There a More Meaningful Formula?*, 18 CASE WESTERN RESERVE LAW REVIEW 367 (1966–1967).

Enforcement

The 'teeth' of a capital markets regulatory regime are the enforcement and remedies provisions. Therefore, although enforcement and remedies occur as an end-stage event, it is fruitful to consider them at inception.

The various securities laws differ markedly in the nature of the enforcement structures and remedies that are afforded. Two categories of enforcement exist: governmental enforcement and private enforcement. Governmental enforcement may be by virtue of either, or both, civil actions and criminal actions. Private enforcement is by way of civil actions.

Some jurisdictions allow the regulatory authority to bring a broad range of civil actions. These include cease and desist orders, injunctions, receivership proceedings, monetary fines and penalties, barring of officers and directors, and disgorgement of ill-gotten gains. Failure to comply with judgements in respect of these actions may also result in criminal actions, including fines and imprisonment. SROs may also bring civil actions that correspond to their regulatory role and reach. Thus, securities exchanges may delist securities and, with respect to broker-dealers and other intermediaries, impose bars, censures and monetary fines.

Some jurisdictions rely primarily on criminal actions to enforce their securities laws.[14] Criminal actions tend to be infrequent, however. There is a reluctance to bring criminal actions, primarily because of prosecutorial difficulties resulting from burdens of proof and evidentiary standards.[15]

Private enforcement of securities laws is rare in most countries. It does occur in the United States. The US Supreme Court has recognised private actions under the securities laws as a necessary supplement to governmental and SRO enforcement.[16] Various aspects of the US legal system are supportive of the private enforcement concept. These include acceptance of the contingency fee concept, recognition of class actions and derivative suits, and awards of attorney's fees to a prevailing plaintiff. The legal systems in many countries do not have comparable aspects—and many preclude some or all of these aspects—making private enforcement much less likely.[17] While private enforcement actions are effective, they are also costly in terms of precious resources (individual and systemic).

Modification of existing legal regimes in most Middle East and North African countries to permit (or encourage) private enforcement is not likely to occur, and in many instances is probably inappropriate. Some of these countries, for example, have a cultural, as well as legal, tradition of mediation and arbitration. Legal systems are frequently underdeveloped, with shortages of judges and attorneys. These legal systems have not been designed, and have not evolved, to handle complex financial litigation (although they are increasingly faced with complex financial issues). Often, the enforcement mechanisms are designed to keep this type of complex litigation out of the court

---

[14] See IOSCO Principles, *supra* note 1, at 10–12.

[15] See, e.g., Steinberg, *supra* note 1, at 263–65.

[16] See *J. I. Case v. Borak*, 377 U.S. 426 (1964).

[17] Consider, for example, the position stated by Beach, *supra* note 10, with respect to the structuring of Saudi Arabian enforcement mechanisms in light of this observation.

systems and channel it to more specialised enforcement bodies.[18] Further, the operating practices of many jurisdictions are not such as to realise the benefits of private enforcement in any effective manner: there is insufficient knowledge of enforcement practices and insufficient certainty and predictability of result as a consequence of failures to publish decisions and the reasoning for decisions, the absence of binding precedent (*stare decisis*) systems, and the presence of *ex post facto* legislation, and there are extended timeframes for enforcement, among other factors.[19] At present, allocation of scarce societal resources to the development of incentives to private enforcement such as those present in the US seems inefficient, if not wasteful, in many jurisdictions in which Islamic finance is of the greatest relevance.

The nature of the Shari'ah itself compounds enforcement complexities in many jurisdiction in which the Shari'ah must be enforced (unless the approach is to submit the relevant agreements and practices to purely secular law without deference to the Shari'ah). One major compounding factor is uncertainty as to what in fact constitutes the Shari'ah in any given situation.[20] Different schools of Islamic jurisprudence (*madhahib*; *madhhab* is the singular) interpret Shari'ah principles somewhat differently. It is often unclear which *madhhab*'s principles should or will be applicable in any given case. Should transactional parties be entitled to choose the applicable *madhhab*? Such a question might itself seem contrary to the concept of uniform securities laws within a given jurisdiction. However, in certain jurisdictions the populace is comprised of individuals adherent to various different *madhahib* and, in the present Islamic finance paradigm, the issuer of the relevant security determines the degree of Shari'ah compliance and, by virtue of its Shari'ah board approval, the interpretations that govern the structure and documentation of the instrument in question. What if the choice of the parties is contrary to the prevailing practices in the jurisdiction in which enforcement is sought? This occurs with some frequency in multi-jurisdictional *sukuk* offerings and in *sukuk* offerings within countries (such as the United Arab Emirates or Jordan) where the population is comprised of individuals that subscribe to different *madhahib*. What principles and precepts will then prevail? These are particularly vexing issues relative to practices in the field of Islamic finance.

---

[18] Consider, as but one example, the enforcement entity structure of The Kingdom of Saudi Arabia, described in Michael J. T. McMillen, *Islamic Shari'ah-compliant Project Finance: Collateral Security and Financing Structure Case Studies*, 24 Fordham International Law Journal 1184 (2001) ('McMillen Islamic Project Finance'), at 1193–1203, Beach, *id.*, and Gouda, *supra* note 10.

[19] See the discussion in the section of this chapter entitled 'Systemic Aspects of Legal Regimes – Legal Infrastructure in Shari'ah-Incorporated Jurisdictions'.

[20] Michael J. T. McMillen, Islamic Finance and the Shari'ah: The Dow Jones Fatwa and Permissible Variance as Studies in Letheanism and Legal Change (2013) ('McMillen, Islamic Finance'), provides an introduction to the Shari'ah as applied in Islamic finance (including capital markets activities), the nature and operation of Shari'ah boards (including the nature and functions of *fatawa*), the different *madhahib*, some of the fundamental structures that underlie *sukuk* and other capital markets instruments, and some of the criticisms of contemporary Islamic finance.

Offerings and Disclosure

Primary considerations in essentially all legal regimes regulating capital markets activities relate to offerings, and subsequent resales, of securities. Many – probably most – securities law regimes are disclosure-based.[21] In a common perception, the basic premise is simple; 'all investors, whether large institutions or private individuals, should have access to certain basic facts about an investment prior to buying it and so long as they hold it'.[22] In such a framework, all 'material' information should be disclosed in written offering materials in a timely manner, so that informed decisions may be made on an ongoing basis based upon ongoing (usually periodic) reporting and information requirements.

Most formulations of the matters to be disclosed in connection with effective regulation of securities offerings include:

1. conditions applicable to the securities offering;
2. the content and distribution of offering documents;
3. supplementary documents;
4. advertising in connection with any offering of securities;
5. use of proceeds of the offering;
6. information about ownership and control of, and interests in, the entity offering the securities;
7. information about matters affecting the control of that offering entity, whether by ownership, contract or otherwise;
8. information material to the price or value of an offered security;
9. the financial condition of the entity offering the securities, including assets, liabilities, financial condition, operations, and manager self-dealing;
10. ongoing voting and control matters; and
11. periodic reporting requirements.

In most cases, reasonably accurate financial statements of the issuer prepared in accordance with recognised accounting and auditing standards will be required. Further, there are requirements for the provision of reasonably developed and supportable projections and descriptions of known and reasonably anticipated future developments, events and circumstances which might reasonably be expected to affect the business, affairs and financial condition of the entity issuing the securities. The nature

---

[21] See the discussion in the Introduction sub-section of this section and see IOSCO Principles, *supra* note 1, at 23, and the statement of the 'Purpose of Registration' of the Securities and Exchange Commission of the United States of America (the 'SEC') at https://www.sec.gov/about/laws.shtml. An alternative is a 'merit-based' system in which regulatory authorities may restrict securities offerings, and access to the capital markets, even where fulsome disclosure is made, if the securities offering is unfair, unjust or inequitable (as a result of insider trading, inequitable retention of options or warrants by insiders, or excessive costs). See Steinberg, *supra* note 1, at 268. Disclosure-based systems also address these justice and equitability issues, albeit by leaving determinations to investors and their (scrupulous) advisors, with supplementation by other regulatory devices and fair practice measures, at both the governmental and SRO levels.

[22] The quoted language is taken from the 'Introduction' statement of SEC, at http://www.sec.gov/about/whatwedo.shtml.

and degree of disclosure may be tailored to address different investor bases fairly, efficiently and transparently while reducing or minimising systemic risk.

Shari'ah-compliant businesses may prepare their accounts and financial statements in accordance with standards promulgated by the Accounting and Auditing Organization for Islamic Financial Institutions (AAOIFI) rather than conventional formulations of generally accepted or internationally recognised accounting principles.[23] The AAOIFI-based statements may meet the standards of 'comprehensibility, consistency, relevance, [and] reliability', but they are not likely to meet the 'comparability' standard,[24] at least as compared with financial statements prepared and audited under conventional generally accepted or internationally recognised accounting and auditing standards. This is due to significant differences in risk exposure and adoption that are fundamental to Shari'ah compliance and the relevant AAOIFI standards. Adjustments as between generally accepted accounting principles and internationally recognised accounting principles are relatively easy to make, given that both are prepared on common interest-based assumptions. AAOIFI-based statements are not prepared on an interest-based set of principles, but rather on a shared-risk set of principles with fundamental risk and category assumptions that are quite different, which of course reduces comparability. The comparability issue may be relatively inconsequential where the AAOIFI-based standards supplement other standards (such as international financial reporting standards), such as by specifying treatment of matters that are not addressed in those other standards. If the AAOIFI-based standards are in conflict with these other standards, the comparability issue may be of greater consequence. This is an area that is in need of further study and explication in order to satisfy the principles underlying disclosure requirements.

Capital Markets Access

Access to capital markets occurs in both the initial capital markets and the secondary markets. In the initial capital markets there are three primary offering scenarios that facilitate market access: (i) limited offerings to a finite group of investors having financial acumen; (ii) offerings made to institutional investors that are presumably sophisticated investors; and (iii) offerings to the general public, which will include individuals having limited (or no) financial acumen. Offerings may be public or private. Private offerings may subsequently become public pursuant to sales by private investors.

---

[23] Based upon discussions with market participants, it seems fair to conclude that acceptance of the AAOIFI accounting and auditing standards by operating companies is limited (acceptance by the Islamic banking community is somewhat better, but also inconsistent). Although somewhat dated with respect to acceptance, see Luca Errico and Mitra Farahbaksh, *Islamic Banking: Issues in Prudential Regulations and Supervision*, International Monetary Fund Working Paper WP/98/30 (March 1998) ('Errico and Farahbaksh'), available at http://www.imf.org/external/ pubs/ft/wp/wp9830.pdf. Although issues addressed in Errico and Farahbaksh relate to Islamic banking and have been addressed subsequently by standard setting organisations, this early paper remains helpful in thinking about the differences between Islamic finance generally and conventional finance, particularly with respect to the *mudaraba* construct and the concepts of disclosure and entity governance.

[24] See IOSCO Principles, *supra* note 1, at 26.

The legal regime usually acknowledges these differences and is (ideally) structured so as to realise regulatory objectives with the least cost and the least amount of personal and market interference. Thus, the degree of regulation, including in respect of disclosure requirements, varies with the nature of the offering.

As a general statement, a lesser degree of regulatory requirements applies to limited offerings than public offerings, and the degree of regulation varies with the sophistication (or perceived sophistication) of the prospective investor. The remainder of this sub-section examines some of the major considerations in respect of those variances.

Limited Offerings

In the making of a limited offering there may be no requirement that a disclosure document be filed with the regulatory authority. If all of the offerees are sophisticated investors, there may be no requirement, or quite limited requirements, for the delivery of information in connection with the offering (although the widespread practice is to provide an offering memorandum setting forth essential information). If an offering does not meet the definition of a limited offering, registration of the offering with the regulatory authority is usually required. Even if an offering does satisfy limited offering criteria, prohibitions on fraud often continue to apply.

To constitute a limited offering, the offer of securities must be made to a relatively small number of persons. That number will be determined by the regulatory authority in each jurisdiction, but usually does not exceed 100. Certain jurisdictions, such as the US, also impose monetary ceilings on limited offerings.

In many jurisdictions, particularly emerging market jurisdictions, relevant criteria as to what constitutes a limited offering are often focused on the manner of solicitation, the number of offerees, and restrictions on resale of the offered securities. These factors focus on the sophistication of offerees and the costs of accessing the capital markets, and they provide a basis for efficient balancing at the regulatory level. These factors are indicators of circumstances where investor protection (regarding sufficiency of information for informed decision-making and the potential for fraud), fairness, efficiency, transparency and systemic integrity are thought to be best served by some fundamental level of disclosure. With respect to the manner of solicitation, for example, the use of advertising or other general solicitation methods inclines the regulatory regime towards fuller disclosure, including the required use, and timely delivery to the offerees, of an offering document that adequately describes the issuer and its financial condition (including material financial information), the securities being offered and the terms of the offering. Resale restrictions are an important consideration in connection with any limited offering to ensure that the limited offering device is not a pretext for a public offering pursuant to resale activities.[25]

Institutional Investor Offerings

Institutional investors are generally presumed to be sophisticated investors. 'They have the acumen, experience, personnel and financial wherewithal to make astute

---

[25] Consider, e.g. United States Rule 144, 17 Code of Federal Regulations § 230.144, available at http://www.sec.gov/about/forms/rule144.pdf, and summarised by the SEC at http://www.sec .gov/investor/pubs/rule144.htm.

investment decisions,'[26] and to suffer the economic consequences of poor decisions without disruption of the markets as a whole (the latter being the systemic regulatory consideration). In addition, they have the size, reputation and market presence, particularly when acting in concert, to induce voluntary disclosure of pertinent investment information. In such a case, there are minimal, if any, disclosure requirements, although prohibitions on fraud continue to be applicable.[27] In the context of emerging markets, regulation of institutional investor offerings may be left to SROs or a separate institutional investors' stock exchange might be developed.

Public Offerings

Regulation, including in respect of disclosure, is greatest when public offerings are made because of the involvement and exposure of unsophisticated investors. In addition, prohibitions on, and monitoring for, fraud are imperative.

Filing of disclosure documents, including offering materials, is generally mandated in public offerings. The degree of required disclosure is frequently specified. It generally includes information about the issuer, the offering, the listing, periodic reporting, reports of material events and circumstances, changes in control and similar matters. Further, regulatory requirements often include standards and mechanisms for the ongoing monitoring of those disclosure items.

Investor protection is most strained in this type of offering situation because of the breadth and variety of the offerees and the nature of the adverse consequences for uninformed investment. The investor pool will include individuals who cannot bear losses without devastating personal and societal consequences and social and market disruptions. While those investors cannot be entirely protected from their own folly, the system can be structured to ensure that it is folly, and not insufficient information, that is the cause of any adverse consequences. With the potential for widespread loss and disruption in the public offering context, far greater disclosure and regulation, at far greater cost, are usually deemed appropriate.

Financial Intermediaries

Capital markets regulatory regimes also address the roles and behaviour of financial intermediaries. Intermediaries include those who are in the business of structuring securities and securities transactions, managing portfolios, executing orders, dealing in securities, distributing securities, making markets in securities, trading securities and providing information relevant to the trading of securities.

Secondary markets cannot develop without a sufficient base of intermediaries of different types that have adequate capital to facilitate market liquidity and ensure the presence and effective operation of an acceptable settlement system. Some are essential to the structuring of transactions. Others are essential to the initial placement of offered securities. Still others are necessary for the ongoing operations of secondary markets.

---

[26] Steinberg, *supra* note 1, at 272.
[27] Consider, e.g. United States Rule 144A, 17 Code of Federal Regulations § 230.144A, available at https://www.law.cornell.edu/cfr/text/17/230.144A.

The financial integrity of these intermediaries is a primary focus of the securities regulatory regime, as is the prevention and redress of fraud.

The foci of regulatory regimes applicable to financial intermediaries includes incompetence, negligent management, misappropriation, fraud, front running, manipulation, trading irregularities, insufficiency of capital, and bankruptcy and insolvency.[28] Avoidance of transgressions in these areas is customarily the responsibility of the management of the financial intermediary utilising effective internal controls, risk management tools, and procedures to detect and resolve conflicts of interest. The regulatory objective is to require management to be structured so as to accept responsibility in all areas of its business and to implement the regulatory standards. Other regulations supplement, and ultimately effect and enforce, the defined standards of conduct, but primary responsibility remains with the management of the intermediary.

Frequently, there are both governmental and SRO registration requirements and intermediaries are subject to different levels of oversight and different standards by each regulating body. A base level of regulation of financial intermediaries focuses on (a) entry and ongoing status criteria (authorisation, licensing and registration for the performance of duties as a financial intermediary, such as an investment advisor, broker and dealer), (b) capital and prudential requirements, (c) ongoing supervision and discipline, and (d) the consequences of default and financial failure.[29]

Entry and ongoing status criteria focus on technical competency, reputation, capital sufficiency, and ownership. Each is monitored on an ongoing basis to ensure market integrity. There are periodic reporting requirements. There are usually regulations to ensure that the investor base has access to information regarding the intermediaries. Capital adequacy standards ensure both investor protection and systemic integrity. A focus on both periodic losses and winding-up occurrences is designed to protect against catastrophic losses by investors. Capital adequacy requirements are often continuing and periodically reviewed and reappraised in light of the functioning of the intermediary.

Prudential standards are another essential ingredient of the regulatory regime applicable to intermediaries. These standards usually address both ethical conduct and ongoing risk management. With respect to the latter, standards are designed to ensure the adequacy and effectiveness of risk management systems and processes.

To be effective in regulating financial intermediaries, the regulators are customarily provided with powers to inspect, investigate, monitor, discipline and enforce (including, for example, licence revocation and resort to broader governmental enforcement mechanisms).

Investment advisors present accentuated issues in the regulatory context. Some advisors deal on behalf of both their clients and themselves. Others do not deal, but may still have custody of funds and other client assets. In either case, regulations include those mentioned with respect to all intermediaries, supplemented by detailed requirements with respect to disclosure to clients as to qualifications, reputation, behaviour and conflicts of interest. Additional regulation focuses on issues relating to the use and custody of client assets.

Unique issues arise in the context of Islamic finance, and regulatory mechanisms must be developed to address those specific issues. For example, many Shari'ah-compliant

---

[28] In this chapter, the term 'bankruptcy' is used to include both bankruptcy and insolvency.
[29] See IOSCO Principles, *supra* note 1, at 33–41.

investment arrangements are structured using the *mudaraba* model. A *mudaraba* is a type of joint venture or partnership (it can be either) in which one party (the *mudarib*: a participating advisor or fund or asset manager) contributes services (namely, their investment advice and services), but typically no capital, with the investors (the *rab al-maal*) contributing cash or in-kind capital.[30] Profits are shared. The intermediary in such a case has a direct interest in the outcome of the investment process and is also an investor to some degree (even if it does not contribute capital). Without delving into the niceties and details of the applicable Shari'ah principles, it is important to note at least one Shari'ah precept applicable to losses incurred by a *mudaraba*. The investors will alone bear financial losses; the *mudarib*, having lost its services and, having contributed no financial capital to lose, will not be subject to contribution to financial loss. Capital adequacy standards need to be reconsidered in respect of these types of arrangements (although not in respect of conventional intermediary activities), with due regard to the continuing systemic integrity policies. And ownership criteria may appropriately be more stringent with respect to *mudaraba* arrangements than with respect to conventional arrangements.

Collective Investment Schemes

Open end funds with redemption features of any type and closed end funds that are traded in the secondary markets are an increasingly large segment of the investment economy, including the Islamic economy. Funds are the predominant investment vehicle in Islamic finance, and the current fund structures undoubtedly tend towards collective investment scheme structures. Shari'ah-compliant fund structures frequently take the *mudaraba* form previously discussed, although the entire panoply of entity structures is used.

These funds rely heavily on fund managers and investment managers that have significant discretion regarding the capital and investments of the fund, including rights to delegate performance responsibilities to a wide range of other (often undisclosed) third parties. In some Shari'ah-compliant structures the fund or investment managers may be required, as a matter of Shari'ah compliance, to have essentially complete power over capital and investments. Concomitantly, the rights of investors in collective investment schemes are often quite limited and restricted (and in some structures, may approach non-existence). The constitutional framework for these schemes is often contractual and unburdened by corporate governance and minority protection concepts that are found in laws applicable to corporations, partnerships, companies, trusts and other entities.

As an example, applicable Shari'ah principles and precepts in the *mudaraba* context are particularly limiting. The investors cannot exert control over the management of the investment vehicle (the *mudaraba*). The capital, and returns on capital, provided by the investors cannot be guaranteed or assured, directly or through collateral security arrangements. No pre-established payment or return to the manager (*mudarib*) (such as a percentage of amounts invested) can be assured to the manager; the *mudaraba* is

---

[30] Classically, the *mudarib* was not permitted to contribute capital. In contemporary practice, a *mudarib* may be permitted to contribute capital and, in such a case, the *mudarib* is treated as either a direct *rab al-maal* or a partner in a *musharaka* (partnership) with the other *rab al-maal*.

a profit and loss sharing arrangement. Because the manager of the *mudaraba* bears no risk of monetary loss and is dependent upon the success of the investments, there is an incentive for the relatively unrestricted manager to engage in higher risk investments.[31]

Disclosure principles, standards and imperatives are of particular relevance in the context of collective investment schemes, although the degree of disclosure may still vary depending upon the sophistication of the investors, their ability to absorb losses in respect of their investments, and the risk of market disruption. The nature of the disclosure is not substantively different from that discussed previously in this section. Investors are entitled to understand the nature of the contemplated investment in all the particulars previously noted. They must be informed of the risk-return parameters of the investment, and thereafter make informed decisions as to what risk-return profile best suits them. Given the nature of investment funds, additional disclosure should be required with respect to various categories of matters that have unique formulations or implementations in the context of collective investment schemes, such as:

1. investment objectives, criteria and parameters;
2. fee structures (which are often difficult to understand even by the most sophisticated of investors);
3. valuation of assets, pricing and net asset valuations;
4. redemption rights and restrictions;
5. credit enhancements;
6. yield and payment provisions, including the basis and priority of payments; and
7. asset protection structures, including as they relate to third-party creditors and as they will be enforced in bankruptcy scenarios.

Regulatory frameworks often impose requirements pertaining to eligibility standards for the manager of a collective investment scheme, ongoing supervision of the scheme's operation, and informational requirements and other promoters of transparency and information dispersal, as well as the range of matters discussed elsewhere in this section.

Given the predominance of collective investment schemes in the field of Islamic finance, this is an area that should be given particular consideration and scrutiny.

Secondary Markets

Secondary market activities and institutions are emerging, but limited, in the area of Islamic finance. Secondary market limitations in the field of Islamic finance relate less to the absence of exchanges and trading systems than to the absence of tradable products. Tradable instruments are being developed. Progress is most pronounced in the areas of equities and *sukuk*.

In the conventional markets, secondary markets include stock exchanges, other types of exchanges, bulletin boards, proprietary trading systems and an increasing number of off-market systems.[32] These systems are managed and administered by traditional

---

[31] See Errico and Farahbaksh, *supra* note 23, at 16–17.
[32] See IOSCO Principles, *supra* note 1, at 43–49, with respect to secondary markets issues.

stock exchanges and, increasingly, by other financial intermediaries, including brokers, banks, investment banks, institutional investors and entrepreneurs.

Secondary market activity in the electronic age is truly global, presenting regulators with the need to cooperate internationally at every level of the regulatory process. The plural in secondary 'markets' is of paramount import as these markets become more globalised. Regulatory frameworks vary with the type of intermediary, and their effectiveness depends in part upon the ability to anticipate and include an ever-widening group of intermediaries.

Regulation of secondary market activities frequently is effectuated by both governmental entities and SROs (the exchange or trading systems themselves): 'The level of regulation will depend upon the proposed market characteristics, including the structure of the market, the sophistication of the market users and the rights of access and the types of products traded.'[33] The factors of relevance for any given regulatory regime are, and the variances across jurisdictions relate to: (a) assurances of transparency throughout the system; (b) operator competence; (c) operator oversight; (d) admission of products to trading; (e) admission of participants to the trading system; (f) provision of trading information; (g) routing of orders; (h) trade execution; (i) post trade reporting and publication; (j) supervision of the system and the participants by the operator; (k) trading disruptions; (l) manipulation and unfair trading practices, including insider trading, misleading practices, deceit and fraud (with particular sensitivity to cross-market effects such as manipulation of an equity price so as to affect the pricing of options and warrants); (m) large exposures jeopardising markets, clearing firms, and default procedures and inducing market disruptions; (n) closing, clearing and settlement systems; (o) verification of trades; (p) margining; (q) netting; and (r) short selling and securities lending.

As in other areas, many aspects of the regulatory requirements applicable to the ICM vary little from those applicable to conventional securities. However, some adjustments are appropriately considered with respect to the nature of the Shari'ah parameters. Consider, as but one example, the concept of margins as they might be applicable in the field of Islamic finance. To the extent that the existence of the margin concept entails the existence of a related loan or credit arrangement having *riba* elements, such an arrangement is contrary to the Shari'ah. Innovators have developed techniques that give effect to the economic substance of those loan and credit arrangements without utilising *riba*-based structures, but those techniques frequently involve multiple steps and ownership concepts that are not present in equivalent conventional structures and transactions and that introduce risks not present in the equivalent conventional structures and transactions. Similarly, the Shari'ah prohibits the sale of something that is not owned, which would lead one to conclude that short sale issues would be minimal or non-existent where Islamic financing methods are used. This may not be the case, however. Again, innovation knows no bounds, and structures

---

[33] IOSCO Principles, *id.*, at 43. The matters referred to in this paragraph are discussed in more detail, with recommendations of principles and general practices, in the IOSCO Principles, at 43–49.

have been developed that replicate the economics of the short sale (and preserve the use of back-office characterisation as if the transaction were a short sale) but do not entail the lending of securities; some of these structures make use of back-to-back sales of securities (rather than a loan and subsequent sale), thereby incorporating ownership concepts that are not present in conventional equivalents, which introduces additional regulatory considerations.

In cases such as the foregoing, modifications to the regulatory structure as applicable to the ICM may be necessary. The modifications should be sensitive to the fact that the types of transactional and product structures and market techniques that are used in ICM instruments (and related transactions) will not be the same as those utilised for the equivalent conventional instruments that are the basis of the current regulatory paradigm. Some of these structures and products entail less risk than their conventional equivalents (because of the prohibitions on *riba*-based lending and the trading of assets that do not represent an interest in tangible assets, such as derivatives). Some entail greater risk because of the additional, and often more complicated, structural elements or the risk-sharing nature of Shari'ah principles (such as sequential ownership and sales transactions, often by special purpose entities). Even in the former case, the legal regime may not be sensitive or responsive to the Shari'ah-compliant instruments and participant positions, thereby causing undue burdens on, and discrimination against, the participants in the Shari'ah-compliant markets. In the latter case, protection of the investor and systemic integrity concerns may be undersatisfied.

As another example, consider the essential nature and process of determining Shari'ah compliance and its impact on effective operation of secondary markets. Shari'ah compliance is a matter of individual conscience. However, for all practical purposes, Shari'ah compliance is determined by a Shari'ah board, except in a few jurisdictions that have some type of national Shari'ah authority – such as Malaysia, which has Shari'ah boards within Bank Negara Malaysia (the central bank) and Suruhanjaya Sekuriti (Securities Commission of Malaysia). Shari'ah boards of individual institutions adhere to rulings by the national Shari'ah authority in making their determinations. Due to variations among different *madhahib*, what is compliant for one purchaser may not be compliant for another. Further, securities that are Shari'ah-compliant at the time of the offer may not be compliant at a later time after the offer. For example, the issuer may acquire a non-compliant business and thus itself become non-compliant. Standardisation is absent at virtually every level of the compliance process. Special sensitivity will have to be applied to regulatory efforts aimed at clarifying the nature of the compliance determinations and certifications with respect to securities that are averred to be Shari'ah-compliant, which may entail unique disclosure rules at both the inception of an offer and throughout the term of the security.

If regulatory regimes operate so as to preclude the informed use and trading of the Shari'ah-compliant instruments, the result is even more onerous as a market, societal and/or religious matter: a large segment of the global population will be excluded from the markets entirely (with respect to the precluded instrument). Additionally, the benefits of the precluded instruments will go unrealised by the Muslim population, with consequent adverse effects on the conventional markets.

SECURITISATIONS (INCLUDING SUKUK)

In numerous countries, distinct securities laws have been crafted to address securitisations specifically. This is in response to massive growth of securitisations and their unique features.[34] *Sukuk* are the predominant finance-side instrument in the ICM.[35] As discussed in the next section, *sukuk* are securitisations (of an asset, a pool of assets or a whole business). In jurisdictions that have specific securitisation laws, *sukuk* are likely to be governed by those laws. Historically, securitisations have been an effective component of the development and growth of the capital markets, including secondary markets,[36] although the financial crisis of 2007 reveals notable risks inherent in the securitisation process.[37] In the realm of the

---

[34] See, e.g., Jonathan C. Lipson, *Re: Defining Securitization*, 85 CALIFORNIA LAW REVIEW 1229 (2011–2012) ('Lipson, Defining Securitization'), at 1247–56, summarising the state of the markets up to the onset of the 2007 financial crisis, and noting that approximately US$ 2 trillion of securitisations were outstanding in the US at the onset of the crisis. See also the sources cited in note 36, *infra*. For abbreviated histories of securitisation, see, e.g., Steven L. Schwarz, STRUCTURED FINANCE: A GUIDE TO THE PRINCIPLES OF ASSET SECURITIZATION (Adam D. Ford ed., 3d ed. 2010) ('Schwarz Structured Finance'), at § 1.2, Sarah Lehman Quinn, *Government Policy, Housing and the Origins of Securitization, 1780–1968* (2010) ('Quinn'), a Ph.D. dissertation in sociology in the graduate division of the University of California, Berkeley, available at https://escholarship.org/uc/item/7sq3f6xk, and Sarah Quinn, *'Things of Shreds and Patches': Credit Aid, the Budget, and Securitization in America*, Working Paper, University of Michigan.

[35] *Sukuk* are discussed in more detail in '*What are Sukuk?*' below.

[36] There is an extensive literature on asset securitisations. Two practitioner's guides are Patrick D. Dolan and C. VanLeer Davis III, SECURITIZATIONS: LEGAL AND REGULATORY ISSUES (2015) ('Dolan and Davis'), and John Arnholz and Edward E. Gainor, OFFERINGS OF ASSET-BACKED SECURITIES (2007) ('Arnholz and Gainor'). Dolan and Davis addresses the primary substantive bodies of law of relevance to securitisations (e.g. securities, bankruptcy, tax and security interests) and the primary accounting rules. It also discusses various types of securitisation transactions. And it considers legal issues in a range of different countries. Arnholz and Gainor focuses on the legal framework pertaining to public offerings and issuances of ABS, but also includes discussions of tax, legal and accounting issues.

[37] See, e.g., Joshua Coval, Jakub Jurek and Erik Stafford, *The Economics of Structure Finance*, 23 THE JOURNAL OF ECONOMIC PERSPECTIVES 3 (2009) ('Coval, Jurek and Stafford'), Adam B. Ashcraft and Til Schuermann, *Understanding the Securitization of Subprime Mortgage Credit*, FEDERAL RESERVE BANK OF NEW YORK STAFF REPORTS, Number 318 (March 2008), available at http://papers.ssrn.com/sol3/papers.cfm?abstract_id=1071189, Richard Christopher Whalen, *The Subprime Crisis: Cause, Effect and Consequences* (1 March 2008), available at http://papers.ssrn.com/sol3/papers.cfm?abstract_id=1113888, Craig B. Merrill, Taylor Nadauld and Philip E. Strahan, *Final Demand for Structured Finance Securities* (1 August 2014), available at http://papers.ssrn.com/sol3/papers.cfm?abstract_id=2380859, Gary B. Gorton and Andrew Metrick, *Securitized Banking and the Run on the Repo* (9 November 2010), available at http://papers.ssrn.com/sol3/papers.cfm?abstract_id=1440752, Taylor Nadauld and Shane M. Sherlund, *The Role of the Securitization Process in the Expansion of Subprime Credit* (26 May 2009; first draft May 2008), available at http://papers.ssrn.com/sol3/papers.cfm?abstract_id=1410264, Kurt Eggert, *The Great Collapse: How Securitization Caused the Subprime Meltdown*, 41 CONNECTICUT LAW

ICM, *sukuk* function in that same market development capacity. At inception, therefore, it is important to understand the definition, structure, benefits and risks of asset securitisation.[38]

Securitisation is difficult to define, and the definitional proposals are myriad. This chapter considers two definitions as examples. Each touches upon the risk isolation elements of securitisations, emphasising structure and process, and leaving economic and financial consequences to be deduced. The first definition is one that is frequently encountered, in one form or another, in the practice environment:[39]

> *[T]he sale of equity or debt instruments, representing ownership interests in, or secured by, a segregated, income-producing asset or pool of assets, in a transaction structured to reduce or reallocate certain risks inherent in owning or lending against the underlying assets and to ensure that such interests are more readily marketable and, thus, more liquid than ownership interests in and loans against the underlying assets.*

REVIEW 1257 (2008), Stuart M. Turnbull and Michel Crouhy, *The Subprime Credit Crisis of 07* (9 July 2008), available at http://papers.ssrn.com/sol3/papers.cfm?abstract_id=1112467, Benjamin J. Keys, Tanmoy K. Mukherjee, Amit Seru and Vikrant Vig, *Did Securitization Lead to Lax Screening? Evidence from Subprime Loans* (25 December 2008), available at http://papers.ssrn.com/sol3/papers.cfm?abstract_id=1093137, Joseph R. Mason and Josh Rosner, *Where Did the Risk Go? How Misapplied Bond Ratings Cause Mortgage Backed Securities and Collateralized Debt Obligation Market Disruptions* (3 May 2007), available at http://papers.ssrn.com/sol3/papers.cfm?abstract_id=1027475, Yuliya S. Demyanyk and Otto Van Hemert, *Understanding the Subprime Mortgage Crisis* (5 December 2008; first draft 9 October 2007), available at http://papers.ssrn.com/sol3/papers.cfm?abstract_id=1020396, and Atif R. Mian and Amir Sufi, *The Consequences of Mortgage Credit Expansion: Evidence from the U.S. Mortgage Default Crisis* (12 December 2008), available at http://papers.ssrn.com/sol3/papers.cfm?abstract_id=1072304. See also Board of Governors of the Federal Reserve System, REPORT TO THE CONGRESS ON RISK RETENTION (2010). Consider also Shaun Barnes, Kathleen G. Cully and Steven L. Schwarcz, *In-House Counsel's Role in Structuring Mortgage-Backed Securities*, 2012 WISCONSIN LAW REVIEW 521.

[38] The literature analysing the benefits of asset securitisation is voluminous. *See, e.g.*, Joseph C. Shenker and Anthony J. Colletta, *Asset Securitization: Evolution, Current Issues and New Frontiers*, 69 TEXAS LAW REVIEW 1369 (1990–1991) ('Shenker and Colletta'), at 1383–1405, James A. Rosenthal and Juan M. Ocampo, *Analyzing the Economic Benefits of Securitized Credit*, 1 JOURNAL OF APPLIED CORPORATE FINANCE 32 (1992), Steven L. Schwarcz, *The Alchemy of Asset Securitization*, 1 STANFORD JOURNAL OF LAW, BUSINESS & FINANCE 133 (1994–1995) ('Schwarcz Alchemy'), Robert Dean Ellis, *Securitization Vehicles, Fiduciary Duties, and Bondholder's Rights*, 24 JOURNAL OF CORPORATE LAW 295 (1998–1999), and Lipson Defining Securitization, *supra* note 35. Not all observers acclaim the benefits of securitisations. Consider Kurt Eggert, *Held Up in Due Course: Predatory Lending, Securitization, and The Holder in Due Course Doctrine*, 35 CREIGHTON LAW REVIEW 503 (2002), Lois Lupica, *Asset Securitization: The Unsecured Creditor's Perspective*, 76 TEXAS LAW REVIEW 595 (1998), David Gray Carlson, *The Rotten Foundations of Securitizations*, 39 WILLIAM & MARY LAW REVIEW 1055 (1998), and Christopher Frost, *Asset Securitization and Corporate Risk Allocation*, 72 TULANE LAW REVIEW 101 (1997).

[39] Shenker and Colletta, *id.*, at 1374–75.

The second definition focuses on fundamental elements of a securitisation (inputs, a particular intermediate structure, and outputs):[40]

> *A purchase of [1] primary payment rights by [2] a special purpose entity that (i) [3] legally isolates such payment rights from a bankruptcy (or similar insolvency) estate of the originator, and (ii) results, directly or indirectly, in [4] the issuance of securities [5] whose value is determined by the payment rights so purchased.*

The 'segregated, income-producing asset or pools of assets' or 'inputs' are assets, instruments or obligations that involve – are comprised of – some right to payment (such as a lease payment, a residential or commercial real estate loan receivable, a student loan receivable or a royalty) owing to the initial payee that made the loan or generated the receivable or other payment obligation (i.e. the originator). The intermediate structure, for private issuers, typically isolates the payment rights from the credit risks of the originator. This is often accomplished by way of a 'true sale' of those payment rights by the originator to an issuer special purpose vehicle (SPV) (true sales are discussed in the next section). The payment rights are separated from the originator (the seller) and risks associated with the originator-seller, particularly those risks associated with claims of creditors of the originator-seller. The outputs are the securities issued by the SPV (the asset-backed securities (ABS) or *sukuk*). The proceeds from issuance of the ABS are used to pay the purchase price of the inputs, thereby funding the seller of the inputs at a lower cost than if that seller had issued equity or debt, including, especially, at a lower cost than if the seller had obtained financing from a bank or other financial intermediary.[41] Payments on the ABS are derived from cash flow collections on the payment rights that were sold to the issuer SPV.

It is important to note in this context, particularly from the Shari'ah perspective, that payments on the ABS may not constitute payments of principal and interest: that will depend on how the ABS is structured. However, if the underlying payment rights

---

[40] Lipson, Defining Securitization, *supra* note 35, at 1271. Lipson excludes collateralised debt obligations and certain, whole business securitisations and certain other transactions from his definition of 'true' securitisations. *Sukuk* include some transaction types that fall within the concept of whole business securitisations: for example, *mudaraba* and *musharaka* structures. Lipson notes that there are over two dozen regulatory and statutory definitions of securitisations in the US, as well as a raft of non-legal definitions. See the critical discussion of various definitions at 1256–71. In respect of Lipson's definition, see the response in Steven L. Schwarcz, *What is Securitization? And for What Purpose?*, 85 Southern California Law Review 1283 (2011–2012), and Lipson's reply to Schwarcz in Jonathan C. Lipson, *Why (And How To) Define Securitization? A Sur-Reply to Professor Schwarcz*, 85 California Law Review 1301 (2011–2012).

[41] See, e.g., Schwarz Structured Finance, *supra* note 35, at §§ 1.1 and 1.3. Each asset originator, whatever its credit rating or grade, has a definable cost of obtaining funds from direct funding sources (which is often expressed as the interest rate that the originator must pay on those sources). One purpose, and a structuring principle, of an asset securitisation is to isolate certain assets initially owned by that originator in such a manner as will allow an investor in those assets to provide funding at a cost that is lower than that which would be payable on direct funding sources absent such an isolation (taking into account transaction costs). Frequently, this involves accessing the capital markets.

are comprised of assets, instruments or obligations that generate principal and interest, then interest elements will be passed into the ABS payments. Obviously, if the underlying payment rights do not include interest elements, then the ABS payments will not include interest elements.

As a general matter, some or all of the following parties are involved in an ABS transaction:

1. *Originator*: the initial owner of the payment right, being the party that originated or created and was the original payee on the payment right;
2. *Obligor*: the person or entity having the obligation to make payment on the payment right (asset);
3. *Issuer SPV*: the issuer of the security issued in respect of the securitised assets (the ABS, which are equity or debt instruments), usually a special purpose trust,[42] corporation or other entity;
4. *Investment Bankers*: assist in structuring the transaction and underwriting and placing the ABS;
5. *Rating Agency*: assesses the credit quality of the ABS and assigns a credit rating to that security;
6. *Credit Enhancer*: such as a mono-line insurer, surety company, bank or other entity providing credit support through an insurance policy, letter of credit, guarantee or other assurance to ensure that there will be a source of funds available for payments on the ABS as they become due;
7. *Servicer*: for a fee, collects payments due on the underlying payment rights and remits those payments to the security holders or a trustee for the benefit of the security holders;
8. *Trustee*: holds the assets for the benefit of the security holders and deals with the issuer SPV, credit enhancer and servicer; and
9. *Legal Counsel*: assists in structuring the transaction and providing legal opinions to the ratings agencies and the transactional participants.

To understand the regulation of *sukuk*, and thus the regulation of the ICM, it is essential to gain an understanding of the securitisation process.[43] The structures used

---

[42] Anglo-American common law trusts are 'a', if not 'the', primary vehicle for the SPV issuer in asset securitisations. Even where another entity form is used (e.g. a corporation), that entity is structured so as to ensure that it embodies trust elements (e.g. the fiduciary elements). The trust provides greater freedom and flexibility, particularly as regards governance, than the corporation, and (frequently) provides significant tax advantages, and thus is a preferred form. See, e.g., Henry Hansmann and Ugo Mattei, *The Functions of Trust Law: A Comparative Legal and Economic Analysis*, 73 NEW YORK UNIVERSITY LAW REVIEW 434 (1998), at 472–78. Trusts are not existent in civil law systems or those based upon civil law (such as those in the Middle East; although Bahrain has adopted the trust into its secular law, primarily for the purpose of facilitating *sukuk* issuances). The precise type of trust that will constitute the issuer SPV depends upon an array of factors that are not discussed in this chapter.

[43] Schwarcz, Structured Finance, *supra* note 35, Steven L. Schwarcz, Bruce A. Markell and Lissa Lamkin Broome, SECURITIZATION, STRUCTURED FINANCE AND CAPITAL MARKETS (2004) ('Schwarcz, Markell and Broome'), Dolan and Davis, *supra* note 36, Arnholz and Gainor, *supra* note 36, Kenneth C. Kettering, *Securitization and Its Discontents: The Dynamics of Financial Product Development*, 19 CARDOZO LAW REVIEW 1553 (2008) ('Kettering Securitization'), Steven

in securitisation, and the payment rights that have been securitised, are many and varied and beyond the ambit of this chapter.[44]

The payment rights to be securitised (and which serve as the primary source of payment on the ABS) are first identified, evaluated and valued. Evaluation and valuation focus on the credit quality of those rights, particularly the likelihood that payments will be made as and when required pursuant to the terms of the relevant documents. Evaluation and the prediction of default risk are difficult if the focus is any individual right or asset. Assuming that (i) the securitisation is based upon a pool of payment

---

L. Schwarcz, *The Universal Language of International Asset Securitizations*, 12 DUKE JOURNAL OF INTERNATIONAL & COMPARATIVE LAW 285 (2002), and Anna H. Glick, Anna H., *Mechanics of a CMBS Offering*, in CMBS AND THE REAL ESTATE LAWYER 2015: LENDER AND BORROWER ISSUES IN THE CAPITAL MARKETS, PRACTISING LAW INSTITUTE (2015), provide readable introductions to securitisation concepts, structures, and issues regarding commercial mortgage-backed securitisations. U.S. CMBS LEGAL AND STRUCTURED FINANCE CRITERIA OF STANDARD & POOR'S, Standard & Poor's Corporation (2004, with updates), provides a comprehensive and detailed presentation of the many issues that must be considered, and resolved, if asset securitisation *sukuk* are to be posited as a backbone of an Islamic capital market. The various legal criteria are many and are available at http://www.standardandpoors.com/en_US/web/guest/ratings/ratings-criteria/-/articles/criteria/structured-finance/filter/legal. See also *CMBS Rating*, DBRS Ratings Limited (January 2012), available at http://www.dbrs.com/research/244847/cmbs-rating-methodology.pdf, *Standard & Poor's Approach to Rating Sukuk*, RATINGS DIRECT, STANDARD & POOR'S (17 September 2007), *Shari'ah and Sukuk: A Moody's Primer*, INTERNATIONAL STRUCTURED FINANCE: EUROPE, MIDDLE EAST, AFRICA: SPECIAL REPORT, Moody's Investors Service (May 31, 2006), and *A Guide to Rating Islamic Financial Institutions*, Moody's Investors Service (April 2006). COMMERCIAL MORTGAGE-BACKED SECURITISATION: DEVELOPMENTS IN THE EUROPEAN MARKET, Andrew V. Petersen, ed. (2006) ('Petersen') provides an overview of conventional securitisation issues and current European practice in the commercial mortgage-backed securities markets.

[44] For descriptions of the structure of a prototypical securitisation transaction, see Kettering Securitization, *id.*, at 1556–80, and Schwarcz, Markell and Broome, *id.*, at 1–19. Examples of the literature pertaining to specific types of securitisations include Dolan and Davis, *supra* note 36, Patrick D. Dolan, *Lender's Guide to Securitization of Commercial Mortgage Loans*, 115 BANKING LAW JOURNAL 597 (1998), Patrick D. Dolan, *Securitization of Equipment Leases*, NEW YORK LAW JOURNAL, 11 August 1999, at 1, Patrick D. Dolan, *Lender's Guide to the Securitization of State Lottery Winnings and Litigation Settlement Payments*, 115 BANKING LAW JOURNAL 710 (1998), Charles E. Harrell, James L. Rice III and W. Robert Shearer, *Securitization of Oil, Gas, and Other Natural Resource Assets: Emerging Financing Techniques*, 52 BUSINESS LAWYER 885 (1996–1997), Gregory R. Salathé, *Reducing Health Care Costs Through Hospital Accounts Receivable Securitization*, 80 VIRGINIA LAW REVIEW 549 (1994), David J. Kaufmann, David W. Oppenheim and Jordan E. Yarett, *Franchise Securitization Financings*, 27 FRANCHISE LAW JOURNAL 241 (2008) (franchise royalties), Alex Cowley and J. David Cummins, *Securitization of Life Insurance Assets and Liabilities*, 72 THE JOURNAL OF RISK AND INSURANCE 193 (2005), Eli Martin Lazarus, *Viatical and Life Settlement Securitization: Risks and Proposed Regulation*, 29 YALE LAW AND POLICY REVIEW 253 (2010), Robert Plehn, *Securitization of Third World Debt*, 23 THE INTERNATIONAL LAWYER 161 (1989), Claire A. Hill, *Whole Business Securitizations in Emerging Markets*, 12 DUKE JOURNAL OF COMPARATIVE AND INTERNATIONAL LAW 521 (2002) ('Hill'), and *Nursing Homes Securitization Gathers Steam in UK*, INVESTMENT DEALER'S DIGEST, December 8, 1997, at 6.

rights, and (ii) underwriting of those payment rights was appropriately conducted, the focus in a securitisation is predicting the aggregate rate of default for the entirety of the pool. Statistical methods (including those based upon the 'law of large numbers') can be applied to pools of payment rights resulting in a greater degree of confidence as to default predictions.[45] This allows successful securitisation even where there is some risk of uncollectibility on the underlying payment rights. One of the current issues for *sukuk* arises as a result of the fact that they are often based upon a single asset, instrument or obligation, rather than a pool. In such a case, predictions must be made as to the default risk of a single asset: significant predictive uncertainty is the consequence.[46]

After identifying the payment rights to be securitised, the originator of the securitised assets transfers those rights to the issuer SPV, which holds them for the benefit of, and issues the ABS to, the ABS holders. The purpose of this asset transfer is to separate the assets from the risks associated with the originator (including, importantly, the risks associated with the originator's bankruptcy) and place them in a vehicle that has a low likelihood of becoming involved in a bankruptcy proceeding (i.e. is 'bankruptcy remote'). Frequently, the asset transfer transaction will be structured to constitute a 'true sale'; i.e. a sale that is sufficient under the bankruptcy laws to remove the assets from the bankruptcy estate of the originator.

The SPV issues the ABS in the capital markets to raise funds to purchase the transferred payment rights. Because of the transactional structure, the rights and interests of the ABS holders will be limited to the payment rights and collections in respect of those rights (and to and from any credit enhancements). If the transaction is a true sale, there will be relatively little concern about the financial condition or operations of the originator (except to the extent that the originator may have obligations to repurchase assets from the pool or provide other credit enhancement, and except to the extent that the originator's origination practices affect the payment rights comprising the pool at its inception).

The cost of funding through securitisation will be determined by the rate of return (often, in non-Islamic instruments, an interest rate; and, in Islamic instruments, by the profit rate) on the ABS. That cost, in turn, will often be a function of the 'rating' that is assigned to the ABS. Isolation of the underlying assets in the SPV will often allow the financing of those assets at a higher rating, and lower cost, than would be incurred if the assets were not isolated and if the originator sought entity-level funding.

In order to develop strong securitisation capability and related secondary markets, significant market depth and breadth must be obtained. Programme issuers are a critical component, and those issuers must generate considerable volumes on a constant basis. Programme issuers usually include governmental organisations, government-sponsored entities (GSEs)[47] and, of course, primary financial institutions. As an historical matter, the role of GSEs in developing capital markets has been profound. The GSEs

---

[45] Subject to practical constraints, the larger the pool, the better. See, however, Coval, Jurek and Stafford, *supra* note 37.

[46] Contemporary *sukuk* issuances are overwhelmingly sovereign issuances, issuances by entities owned or controlled by sovereigns, or issuances in which the ultimate credit is that of a sovereign or entity owned or controlled by a sovereign. Thus, the default risk is essentially the same as that of the relevant sovereign. Further, financial performance information and basic credit information in many of the jurisdictions of relevance to *sukuk* issuances is weak or lacking altogether, rendering the predictability of default risk significantly more difficult even if pools could be created.

[47] Some of the prominent GSEs in the US include the Federal Home Loan Mortgage Association (Freddie Mac), the Federal National Market Association (FNMA or Fannie Mae), Government National Mortgage Association (GNMA or Ginnie Mae) and the Student Loan Marketing

have played a primary role in the development of the relevant legal and regulatory frameworks, have fostered and overseen the development of standards and standardised documentation, and have helped generate volume and depth of the markets. Governments and GSEs have acted as regulators, enablers, issuers and purchasers of securitised instruments and related securities, with dramatic effects on the capital and secondary markets and the effectuation of monetary policy. In the realm of Islamic finance and ICM, apart from the International Islamic Liquidity Management Corporation (see Chapter 14), there are essentially no programme issuers at the present time.

True Sales

'The concept of "true sale" is profoundly significant in today's commercial world. Defining true sale is the holy grail of the securitisation market. . . .'[48]

The true sale issue relates to the nature of the transfer of the payment rights (assets) from the originator to the issuer SPV. The true sale issue is one of the primary inhibitors to the development of the ICM, particularly as it affects private entity originators that are not owned or controlled by sovereigns. In summary, the inability to determine whether there has been a true sale results in an inability to obtain a true sale legal opinion from legal counsel, which, in turn, may lead to an inability to obtain a rating for the *sukuk* issuance, with consequent adverse pricing effects. In the absence of a true sale, any credit rating would be based on the rating of the originator as obligor. In such a case, the securitised assets would be considered those of the originator, the credit analysis of the originator would take cognisance of all liabilities and competing creditors of the originator, and the issuance would be treated not as 'asset-backed', but as 'asset-based'. Having a clear understanding of the true sale concept is thus imperative.[49]

Association (SLMA or Sallie Mae). See Quinn, *supra* note 35, and Richard D. Jones, *The Emergence of CMBS* in Petersen, *supra* note 43, at 1–17.

[48] Peter V. Pantaleo, Herbert S. Edelman, Frederick L. Feldkamp, Jason Kravitt, Walter McNeill, Thomas E. Plank, Kenneth P. Morrison, Steven L. Schwarcz, Paul Shupack and Barry Zaretsky, *Rethinking the Role of Recourse in the Sale of Financial Assets*, 52 The Business Lawyer 159 (1996–1997) ('Pantaleo et al.'), at 161.

[49] The many articles on true sale characterisation (in different contexts) include the following sampling: Artem Shtatnov, *The Elusive True Sale in Securitization* (2012), available at http://ssrn .com/abstract=2115054; Kettering Securitization, *supra* note 43; Kettering, True Sale, *infra* note 50; Kenneth G. Kettering, *Pride and Prejudice in Securitization: A Reply to Professor Plank*, 30 Cardozo Law Review 1977 (2009): Thomas E. Plank, *The Security of Securitizations and the Future of Security*, 25 Cardozo Law Review 1655 (2004) ('Plank Securitizations'); Thomas E. Plank, *Sense and Sensibility in Securitization: A Prudent Legal Structure and a Fanciful Critique*, 30 Cardozo Law Review 617 (2008); Thomas E. Plank, *The True Sale of Loans and the Role of Recourse*, 14 George Mason Law Review 287 (1981) ('Plank True Sale'); Jonathan C. Lipson, *Secrets and Liens: The End of Notice in Commercial Finance* Law, 21 Emory Bankruptcy Developments Journal 421 (2005); Jonathan C. Lipson, *Enron, Securitization and Bankruptcy Reform: Dead or Dormant?*, 11 West Journal of Bankruptcy Law and Practice 1 (2002); Lois R. Lupica, *Asset Securitization: The Unsecured Creditor's Perspective*, 76 Texas Law Review 595 (1998); Lois R. Lupica, *Revised Article 9, The Proposed Bankruptcy Code Amendments and Securitizing Debtors and Their Creditors*, 7 Fordham Journal of Corporate and Financial Law 3321 (2002); Lois R. Lupica, *Revised Article 9, Securitization*

What is the true sale concept? 'True sale, like true love, is much pursued but sadly elusive.'[50] The answer to the question depends upon the context in which it is posed. The characterisation of a transfer varies depending upon whether the reference to the treatment of the transfer is for accounting, usury, tax, bankruptcy or collateral security purposes, or for yet some other purpose. The criteria vary somewhat in each of these contexts and it is important to consider each of these contexts when analysing any given structure.[51]

Given the previously-cited definitions, a prudent point of beginning is the bankruptcy context. The essence of the concept relates to whether, in a bankruptcy of the originator of the payment rights, a creditor of that originator will have recourse to those securitised payment rights that underlie the ABS issued by the SPV issuer. If the SPV issuer owns the payment rights, its investors will be repaid out of those payment rights in accordance with the terms of the ABS and the bankruptcy of the originator will be of no consequence to the ABS holder. If the SPV issuer does not own those payment rights, the rights of the ABS holders will be suspended and may be subject to impairment or defeat. If the transfer of those payment rights from the originator to the SPV issuer constituted a 'true sale' under bankruptcy law, then the SPV issuer owns the payment rights for bankruptcy law purposes. Alternatively, the transfer may fail to

---

Transactions and the Bankruptcy Dynamic, 9 AMERICAN BANKRUPTCY INSTITUTE LAW REVIEW 287 (2001); Lois R. Lupica, *Circumvention of the Bankruptcy Process: The Statutory Institutionalization of Securitization*, 33 CONNECTICUT LAW REVIEW 199 (2000); Michael Gaddis, *When is a Dog Really a Duck: The True-Sale Problem in Securities Law*, 87 TEXAS LAW REVIEW 487 (2008–2009); Matthew W. Levin and Jennifer M. Meyerowitz, *Buyer Beware: An Analysis of True Sale Issues*, 1 PRATT'S BANKRUPTCY LAW JOURNAL 185 (2005–2006) ('Levin and Meyerowitz'); E. Kristen Moye, *Non-Consolidation and True Sale/Transfer Opinions in Securitized Real Estate Loan Transactions*, 21 PRACTICAL REAL ESTATE LAWYER 7 (2005); Stephen J. Lubben, *Beyond True Sales – Securitization and Chapter 11*, 1 NEW YORK UNIVERSITY JOURNAL OF LAW AND BUSINESS 89 (2004–2005); Steven L. Schwarcz, *The Impact of Bankruptcy Reform on 'True Sale' Determination in Securitization Transactions*, 7 FORDHAM JOURNAL OF CORPORATE AND FINANCIAL LAW 353 (2001); Pantaleo et al., *id.*; Eugene F. Cowell III, *Texas Article 9 Amendments Provide 'True Sale' Safe Harbor*, 115 BANKING LAW JOURNAL 699 (1998); Kenneth Ayotte and Stav Gaon, *Asset-Backed Securities: Costs and Benefits of 'Bankruptcy Remoteness'*, 24 THE REVIEW OF FINANCIAL STUDIES 1299 (2011); Eric J. Higgins, Joseph R. Mason and Adi Mordel, *Asset Sales, Recourse, and Investors Reactions to Initial Securitizations: Evidence why Off-balance Sheet Accounting Treatment does not Remove On-balance Sheet Financial Risk* (2009), available at http://ssrn.com/abstract=1107074 ('Higgins, Mason and Mordel'), Wayne R. Landsman, Kenneth V. Peasnell and Catherine Shakespeare, *Are Asset Securitizations Sales or Loans?*, 83 THE ACCOUNTING REVIEW 1251 (2008) ('Landsman, Peasnell and Shakespeare'); and Soma Bagaria, *Substance v. Form Conflict in True Sale: Hong Kong Court Goes by the Language Used by the Parties* (2012), available at http://ssrn.com/abstract=2042559.

[50] Kenneth C. Kettering, *True Sale of Receivables: A Purposive Analysis*, 16 AMERICAN BANKRUPTCY INSTITUTE LAW REVIEW 511 (2008) ('Kettering True Sale').

[51] A summary of the treatment of the true sale issue in non-bankruptcy contexts (particularly Article 9 of the Uniform Commercial Code which treats sales, including many receivables and rights to payment and broader secured transactions principles) is provided in Kettering True Sale, *id.*, at 526–46. In the bankruptcy context, treated at 555–62, Kettering summarises the importance of avoiding bankruptcy, in the US, as follows (footnotes omitted):

constitute a true sale and be treated as, among other less frequent possibilities, a secured loan by the originator.

In securitisation transactions (and others), the agreement of the parties will state that the originator-seller and the issuer SPV purchaser intend that all rights, title and interest of the seller in the payment rights is conveyed. Despite that expressed intention, courts may recharacterise the transaction as a secured financing: they are 'close cousins'.[52] The intention of the parties is relevant, of course. But so are other factors, including the economic substance, characteristics and the legal structure of the transaction – all determined in the context of the facts and circumstances of the individual transaction.

The critical issue, in most instances, and particularly in the bankruptcy context, is whether the issuer SPV purchaser has assumed enough of the risks relating to the value, and the burdens of ownership, of the subject payment rights, notwithstanding the statements in the relevant agreements. To the extent that the originator-seller continues to participate in the value of the assets (including continuing cash flows and the residual value of the asset), the risks assumed by, and the true sale position of, the issuer SPV transferee are diminished.

Whether viewed from the perspective of the originator-seller or the issuer SPV purchaser the critical question is: how much risk is too much? Among the factors of relevance are the following:[53]

1. whether the originator-transferor continues to exercise control over the transferred property rights and related proceeds of those rights (including pursuant to any 'servicing' arrangements), and, if so, the degree of control;
2. the degree of recourse, if any, that the transferee has against the transferor in respect of deficiencies in the payment rights (recourse is a particularly important factor in the analysis and the term 'recourse' should be read expansively to include

---

[T]he securitization structure frees the financiers from the burdens—usefully denoted by the shorthand "Bankruptcy Tax"—that the Bankruptcy Code would place upon a direct secured lender to the Originator if the Originator later [i.e., after the sale of the transferred assets] goes bankrupt. Those burdens would include (i) the cessation of post-petition payment of the financier's debt, (ii) the stay of any remedies the financiers otherwise would be entitled to exercise against the receivables, and (iii) sufferance of the power of the Originator, as debtor in possession, to use the proceeds of the receivables so long as the financier's interest in the receivables is adequately protected. If the Originator has financed its receivables through securitization, and later goes bankrupt, the securitization financiers [i.e., the issuer SPV purchaser and ABS holders] will be unaffected by the event if the structure of the financing is respected by the bankruptcy court. Relieving the financiers of the Bankruptcy Tax is the purpose of the securitization structure. For the structure to achieve its purpose, the conveyance of the receivables from the Originator to the SPE must remove the receivables from the estate of the Originator in the event of the Originator's subsequent bankruptcy.

Kettering raises the issue, for US law purposes, of whether a true sale of assets (which is a state law matter) might be subject to a separate, and different, true sale test under federal law (specifically federal bankruptcy law). See 557–62.

[52] Kettering Securitization, *supra* note 43, at 1553.

[53] See the sources at note 49, *supra*. Many of the factors listed here are taken from Levin and Meyerowitz, *supra* note 49.

all situations in which the sale and purchase might be undone or unwound to any degree);

3. whether the transferor retains risk related to the value of the transferred payment rights, and, if so, the extent of those retained risks;

4. whether the transferor has some obligation to the transferee to pay principal, interest or other amounts that are in some way related to the value of the transfer price paid for the transferred payment rights;[54]

5. whether the transferee has taken any actions to identify the transferred payment rights as its own, such as obtaining insurance or paying taxes on those payment rights;

6. whether the transferee has performed proper and rigorous due diligence regarding the value of the transferred payment rights;

7. whether the transfer price paid for the transferred payment rights is disproportionate to the value of the transferred payment rights;

8. whether the expected rate of return on the payment rights is more similar to that payable on a loan or a purchase-and-sale transaction;[55]

9. how the transferor and the transferee each account for the transaction;

10. how the transaction was disclosed to stakeholders of the transferor and the transferee;

11. how the transaction was treated for tax purposes by each of the transferor and the transferee;

12. whether there is any indication of an intent to violate public policy or any law or regulatory requirement by virtue of making a sale rather than a loan;

13. whether the transferee took a back-up security interest in the transferred payment rights;

14. whether there are constraints on the ability of the transferee to grant security interests in the transferred assets or the transferee is restricted by the transferor in making any such grants; and

15. whether true sale legal and substantive consolidation legal opinions were provided to the transferor, the transferee and other transaction parties.

It is important to highlight considerations pertaining to interests in the value of the transferred property rights and recourse to the originator-transferor in the *sukuk* context. In this context, it is commonplace practice (at present) (i) for the transferor to agree to repurchase the transferred assets at the end of the term of the *sukuk*, (ii) for the transferor to (often expressly) retain interests in the residual value of the assets, including appreciation (and depreciation) in value,[56] and (ii) for the transferor and related parties to provide various guarantees, make-wholes, supports and/or purchase

---

[54] Landsman, Peasnell and Shakespeare, *supra* note 49, discusses various seller retained interests, and, at 1256, discusses risk retention arrangements that, they posit, would not jeopardise true sale status, such as guarantees in the form of understandings between the originator and the issuer SPV that the originator will not allow the issuer SPV to fail and other 'implicit guarantees' (which would presumably include capital maintenance understandings, for example). The conclusion that such arrangements will not jeopardise true sale characterisation seems a tad optimistic.

[55] Consider Higgins, Mason and Mordel, *supra* note 49.

[56] See Plank True Sale, *supra* note 49, in particular at 288–312.

commitments in respect of either the *sukuk* or the underlying transferred assets in order to provide assurances regarding payment of the *sukuk*.

Admittedly, the existing *sukuk* markets are dominated (overwhelmingly) by sovereign issuances (or issuances in which a sovereign is the ultimate credit) and, for that reason and because of the usufruct-based orientation of the structures, the true sale concept currently is not an imperative consideration. However, in order to open the ICM to private issuers that have no sovereign credit support, the true sale issues (among others discussed in this chapter) will need to be addressed in order to obtain the requisite legal opinions and ratings.

To achieve 'true sale' treatment, 'an originator must limit, if not forgo, its right to the residual value of the receivables [underlying assets or property rights] sold to the SPV,'[57] as well as interests in the cash flows generated by the transferred assets. The amount of this residual value loss may be quite significant due to the necessity of 'overcollateralisation' of the SPV with excess underlying assets in order to assure investors, credit enhancers, liquidity providers and rating agencies that losses will not be suffered as a result of delays or defaults in payments on the underlying assets. The excess assets over those necessary, in the perfect case, to assure payment of the ABS are real costs to the originator.[58] Similarly, retention of interests in the cash flows generated by the transferred assets poses a significant risk, if not an assurance, that true sale treatment will not be forthcoming.

Additionally, many of the assurances provided by originator-transferors and their related parties in the *sukuk* context are likely to jeopardise true sale treatment on both value and recourse grounds.

Substantive Consolidation (Non-Consolidation)

A second set of critical bankruptcy considerations for capital markets transactions—especially securitisations and *sukuk* issuances—is subsumed in the somewhat amorphous and arcane equity concept of 'substantive consolidation'.[59] As a base generality, this is the concept that two or more legally distinct entities might be merged into a single debtor with a common pool of assets and a common pool body of liabilities,[60]

---

[57] See Schwarcz Alchemy, *supra* note 38, at 141.

[58] With respect to structures and techniques for minimising this overcollateralisation cost, see Schwarcz Alchemy, *id.*, at 142–43.

[59] Substantive consolidation is to be distinguished from 'procedural consolidation' (which is also called 'joint administration' or 'administrative consolidation'). In procedural consolidation, two or more related cases involving debtor entities are treated as a single case for procedural purposes only, usually for ease of administration and reduction of expense. Thus, in a procedural consolidation, there may be a single bankruptcy trustee and a single case file. However, the bankruptcy estates of the debtors remain separate and distinct in procedural consolidation. See, e.g., J. Stephen Gilbert, *Substantive Consolidation in Bankruptcy: A Primer*, 43 VANDERBILT LAW REVIEW 207 (1990) ('Gilbert'), at 212–13. Substantive consolidation doctrines do not exist under all bankruptcy regimes.

[60] A 'merger' or other combination of legal entities will not necessarily – or even usually – occur. For example, the court in *In re Owens Corning*, 316 B.R. 168 (Bankr. D. Del.), *rev'd*, 419 F.2d 195 (3d Cir. 2005), *cert. denied*, 126 S. Ct. 1910 (2006) ('Owens Corning'), applied a 'deemed' consolidation in which the various legal entities are not actually combined, but distributions are

and with third-party liabilities[61] of the subject entities being satisfied from the single pool of assets.[62] In the context of securitisations, including *sukuk*, the entities that might be substantively consolidated are the originator and the issuer SPV.[63] Substantive

---

made to creditors as if there had been a business combination. See William H. Widen, *Corporate Form and Substantive Consolidation*, 75 George Washington Law Review 273 (2007) ('Widen'), at 244 and 254–55.

[61] Inter-company liabilities of the substantively consolidated entities are eliminated.

[62] See Mary Elisabeth Kors, *Altered Egos: Deciphering Substantive Consolidation*, 59 University of Pittsburgh Law Review 381 (1997–1998) ('Kors'), Christopher W. Frost, *Organizational Form, Misappropriation Risk, and the Substantive Consolidation of Corporate Groups*, 44 Hastings Law Journal 449 (1992–1993) ('Frost'), Widen, *supra* note 60, J. Maxwell Tucker, *Substantive Consolidation: The Cacophony Continues*, 18 American Bankruptcy Institute Law Review 89 (2010) ('Tucker'), Seth D. Amera and Alan Kolod, *Substantive Consolidation: Getting Back to Basics*, 14 American Bankruptcy Institute Law Review 1 (2006), Gilbert, *supra* note 59, John B. Berringer and Dennis J. Artese, *The ABCs of Substantive Consolidation*, 121 Banking Law Journal 640 (2004), Douglas W. Baird, *Substantive Consolidation Today*, 47 Boston College Law Review 5 (2005–2006), Christopher Ross Steele, *Cross-Border Insolvency: Substantive Consolidation and Non-Main Proceedings*, 7 Pratt's Journal of Bankruptcy Law 307 (2011), Daniel R. Culhane, *Substantive Consolidation and Nondebtor Entities: The Fight Continues*, 7 Pratt's Journal of Bankruptcy Law 514 (2011), Timothy E. Graulich, *Substantive Consolidation—A Post-Modern Trend*, 14 American Bankruptcy Institute Law Review 527 (2006), Jeanne MacKinnon, *Substantive Consolidation: The Back Door to Involuntary Bankruptcy*, 23 San Diego Law Review 203 (1986), Christopher Ross Steele, *Cross-Border Insolvency: Substantive Consolidation and Non-Main Proceedings*, 7 Pratt's Journal of Bankruptcy Law 307 (2011), Patrick C. Sargent, *Bankruptcy Remote Finance Subsidiaries: The Substantive Consolidation Issue*, 44 The Business Lawyer 1223 (1988–1989), William H. Thornton, *The Continuing Presumption Against Substantive Consolidation*, 105 Banking Law Journal 448 (1988), Christopher J. Predko, *Substantive Consolidation Involving Non-Debtors: Conceptual and Jurisdictional Difficulties in Bankruptcy*, 41 Wayne Law Review 1741 (1994–1995), and Baker Ostrin, *A Proposal to Limit the Availability of Substantive Consolidation of Solvent Entities with Bankrupt Affiliates*, 91 Commercial Law Journal 351 (1986).

Substantive consolidation cases in the US (among the legions) setting for various tests and rules and with ramifications for securitisations, *sukuk* and other capital market transactions, include Owens Corning, *supra* note 60, *Union Savings Bank v. Augie/Restivo Banking Company (In re Augie/Restivo Baking Company)*, 860 F.2d 616 (2d. Cir. 1988) ('Augie/Restivo'), *In re Vecco Construction Industries, Inc.*, 4 B.R. 407 (Bankr. E.D. Va. 1980) ('Vecco'), *Nesbit v. Gears Unlimited, Inc.*, 347 F.3d 72 (3d Cir. 2003), *Pension Benefit Guaranty Corporation v. Ouimet Corporation*, 711 F.2d 1085 (1st Cir. 1983) ('Ouimet'), *Drabkin v. Midland-Ross Corporation (In re Auto-Train Corporation)*, 810 F.2d 270 (D.C. Cir. 1987) ('Auto-Train'), and, as the seminal (if tacit) Supreme Court case, *Sampsell v. Imperial Paper & Color Corp.*, 313 U.S. 215 (1941).

[63] Widen, *supra* note 60, at 246, argues that the securitisation industry (which, for present purposes, includes the *sukuk* industry), prefers limits on the use of substantive consolidation primarily because its imposition subjects the assets of the SPV to the automatic stay provisions of the bankruptcy laws, and thus prevents the timely application of the SPV's assets to payments on the security (e.g. *sukuk*) issued by the SPV, which would have an adverse effect on ratings, and thus on pricing. This industry 'hovers between panic and dread' when the substantive consolidation concepts are expanded. Conversely, unsecured creditors 'recoil' at new or tighter limits on substantive consolidation because these restrict their bargaining power to negotiate forms of restructuring that enhance the recoveries of these unsecured creditors.

consolidation is an equitable remedy, and a creature of the courts rather than a statutory construct. It does not require shareholder or creditor votes and avoids many of the administrative procedures of bankruptcy laws.[64]

Substantive consolidation is a doctrine with significant ramifications for creditors and its application has profound effects on creditor recoveries. It effectively denies creditors what they bargained for and their freedom of contract to obtain that bargain: a transaction based upon risk assessments and risk and monetary allocations that are premised upon recourse to the assets of a specific debtor in competition only with other permitted (and limited) creditors of that specific debtor. The pooling concepts, and attendant restructuring of creditor claims, eviscerate that bargain. The substantive consolidation concept abrogates asset partitioning concepts and attendant expectations that are the basis for financier expectations regarding, and transactional definitions of, the assets that are available to repay entity obligations, including indebtedness.[65] It also abrogates the limited liability concept, and the related structural subordination concept,[66]

Many articles (including some in the preceding note) address substantive consolidation as applicable in the securitisation context, especially where the issuer SPV is a subsidiary of the originator. See, e.g., Peter Humphreys and Howard Mulligan, *Substantive Consolidation in the Owens Corning Bankruptcy Case – Impact on Analysis of Structured Finance Transactions*, 122 BANKRUPTCY LAW JOURNAL 54 (2005), and Peter J. Lahny IV, *Asset Securitization: A Discussion of the Traditional Bankruptcy Attacks and an Analysis of the Next Potential Attack, Substantive Consolidation*, 9 AMERICAN BANKRUPTCY INSTITUTE LAW REVIEW 815 (2001). Lahny describes the three traditional bankruptcy attacks as relating to true sales, sales of accounts and chattel paper, and fraudulent transfers, and also notes the pre-bankruptcy attacks on bankruptcy remoteness. With respect to bankruptcy issues pertaining to SPVs, see John A. Pearce II and Ilya A. Lipin, *Special Purpose Vehicles in Bankruptcy Litigation*, 40 HOFSTRA LAW REVIEW 177 (2011–2012), and W. Rodney Clement, Jr. and H. Scott Miller, *Special Purpose Entities (Barely) Survive First Bankruptcy Test*, 25 PROBATE AND PROPERTY 31 (2011). More broadly, and with respect to SPVs after the Enron debacle, see also Steven L. Schwarcz, *Enron and the Use and Abuse of Special Purpose Entities in Corporate Structures*, 70 UNIVERSITY OF CINCINNATI LAW REVIEW 1309 (2001–2002), and Hunter Carpenter, *A Description of the Now Loathed Corporate Financing Tool*, 72 MISSISSIPPI LAW JOURNAL 1065 (2002–2003).

[64] See, e.g., Kors, *supra* note 62, at 383, including footnotes 14 and 15, which include case law citations.

[65] See, e.g., Tucker, *supra* note 62, at 89–90. Tucker, at 91, characterises the application of substantive consolidation concepts in the corporate group context as a 'policy choice between the "entity theory" and the "enterprise theory" of corporate group liability. Under the entity theory of corporate groups, one member of the group is presumed not liable for the debts of the other members. Under the enterprise theory of corporate groups, one member of the group is presumed liable for the debts of the other members.' With respect to the 'asset partitioning' concept, see Henry Hansmann and Reiner Kraakman, *What is Corporate Law?*, in Reinier Kraakman, John Armour, Paul Davies, Luca Enriques, Henry B. Hansmann, Gérard Hertig, Klaus J. Hopt, Hideki Kanda and Edward B. Rock, THE ANATOMY OF CORPORATE LAW: A COMPARATIVE AND FUNCTIONAL APPROACH (2009), at 1 *et seq*. The asset-to-liability ratios of all the individual creditors to the individual pre-consolidation entities (which become joint creditors to a consolidated single entity) are altered in any substantive consolidation.

[66] Structural subordination is a corollary to limited liability. Under the structural subordination concept, creditors of a parent entity may recover from the assets of a subsidiary entity only after the subsidiary entity has paid all of its obligations. See, e.g., Tucker, *id.*, at 90. See Widen, *supra* note 60, at 248–49, noting that guarantees by subsidiaries have the effect of protecting

and attendant expectations.[67] As such, it is a type of corporate disregard doctrine that is similar to, but quite distinct from, 'piercing of the corporate veil'. Further, the substantive consolidation concept, and particularly the unpredictability of its application, have the potential to affect the total costs of aggregating capital and operating businesses by diminishing creditor and shareholder reliance on limited liability principles.[68] That said, commentators take divergent views of the desirability of substantive consolidation.

The judicially-enunciated tests and standards as to whether substantive consolidation is appropriate in a bankruptcy action vary from one jurisdiction to another. One observer has identified four rationales for consolidation: (i) avoiding the costs of disentangling the related entities' financial affairs and similar pragmatic considerations; (ii) protecting the expectations of creditors who relied on the *collective* credit of the entities; (iii) redressing the misappropriation of one entity's assets for the benefit of another entity; and (iv) recognising the control, operational interdependence or lack of corporate formalities that have made the entities 'alter egos' of one another.[69] In summarising the judicial variations, that observer identifies the following four variations:[70]

1. One group of courts has found 'two critical factors: (i) whether creditors dealt with the entities as a single economic unit and "did not rely on their separate identity in extending credit" . . . or (ii) whether the affairs of the debtors are so entangled that consolidation will benefit all creditors.'[71]

2. Another group of courts has applied a detailed balancing test: '. . . the proponent of substantive consolidation must show that (1) there is substantial identity between the entities to be consolidated; and (2) consolidation is necessary to avoid some harm or realise some benefit. . . . Once the proponent has made this prima facie case, the burden shifts to an objecting creditor to show that (1) it has relied on the separate credit of one of the entities to be consolidated; and (2) it will be prejudiced by substantive consolidation.'[72]

3. Still other courts have applied a more generalised balancing test that weighs the benefits of consolidation against the practical harm of consolidation.

---

syndicated lenders to the parent entity against structural subordination, particularly in circumstances such as those of Owens Corning, *supra* note 60.

[67] See, e.g., Frost, *supra* note 62, at 451, and Tucker, *id.*, at 89–91.

[68] The lack of predictability in application of the substantive consolidation concept is noted by most commentators. See, e.g., Frost, *supra* note 62, at 452 ('unprincipled and unpredictable'), Kors, *supra* note 60, at 384 ('impossible to predict . . . decisions espouse numerous standards that are susceptible to broad variations in application'), and Widen, *supra* note 60, at 239 (the substantive consolidation doctrine 'is a mess, leaving courts and parties adrift' and 'in disarray'; it being noted that Widen, at 238, characterises substantive consolidation as 'the most important doctrine in corporate reorganization').

[69] Kors, *supra* note 62, at 385.

[70] Kors, *id.*, at 58–9.

[71] Augie/Restivo, *supra* note 62, at 518.

[72] *Eastgroup Properties v. Southern Motel Association, Ltd.*, 935 F.2d 245 (11th Cir. 1991) ('Eastgroup') (citations omitted). See also Auto-Train, *supra* note 62, at 276, which, in turn, has morphed into a spate of laundry lists: see *Giller*, 962 F.2d at 799 (three-factor test), EastGroup, at 249–50 (two-part test into which a court can incorporate Vecco and Ouimet (each *supra* note 62) factors), and Vecco, *supra* note 62, at 86 footnote 7 (seven factor test).

4. And other courts have compared the facts of a case to a checklist of factors, frequently analysing whether the involved entities are alter egos of one another as a result of control, operational interdependence or lack of corporate formalities.

The Owens Corning case presents a somewhat more restrictive set of standards.[73] It provides that substantive consolidation should be relatively infrequent (the traditional rhetoric), and is permitted in two circumstances: (i) where, prior to bankruptcy, the entities disregard their separateness to such a degree that the creditors of those entities relied upon the breakdown of entity borders and treated them as a single unified entity; and (ii) where the entities' assets and liabilities are so 'scrambled' that separating them during the bankruptcy case is prohibitive and hurts all creditors.

The controversy as to the tests and standards that should guide the imposition of substantive consolidation rages on. The foregoing is intended only to raise the cautions: that the issue is paramount in the sphere of capital markets issuances, including *sukuk* issuances and syndicated financings of other types, and widely used (at least in negotiated restructurings) despite the judicial rhetoric that it should be used rarely;[74] that the tests and standards vary widely from one jurisdiction to another; and that sensitivity to the relevant substantive consolidation concepts is an imperative in every capital markets transaction.

Sukuk

The AAOIFI *sukuk* standard was issued in 2003, and although there had been a few previous *sukuk* issuances,[75] one may consider this standard as being the formal inception of this capital market segment.[76] The standard defines *sukuk* as certificates of

---

[73] *Supra*, note 60. The centralised management of the corporate group that was found to exist in Owens Corning, and which is a factor in inducing the application of substantive consolidation, was dismissed by the appellate court (at 215) as being customary for consolidated corporate groups.

[74] Consider Widen, *supra* note 60, at 251–67.

[75] There had been a small issuance in Malaysia by Shell MDS Malaysia as early as 1990, and a larger issuance also in Malaysia in 2000. The Bahrain Monetary Agency commenced its short-term *salam sukuk* program on June 13, 2001, and the Qatar Global Sukuk was offered on 8 October 2003.

[76] The plural is '*sukuk*'; '*sakk*' is the singular. The '*AAOIFI Sukuk Standard*' is *AAOIFI Shari'a Standard No. (17), Investment Sukuk*, issued 7 Rabi I 1424H corresponding to 8 May 2003, in SHARIA STANDARDS FOR ISLAMIC FINANCIAL INSTITUTIONS, Accounting and Auditing Organisation for Islamic Financial Institutions (2010). With respect to the structure of, and considerations relating to, *sukuk*, including references to a range of *sukuk* issuances over time, see Nathif J. Adam and Abdulkader Thomas, *Islamic Fixed-Income Securities: Sukuk*, in ISLAMIC ASSET MANAGEMENT: FORMING THE FUTURE FOR SHARI'A-COMPLIANT INVESTMENT STRATEGIES, Sohail Jaffer, ed. (2004), at 72–81, ISLAMIC BONDS: YOUR GUIDE TO ISSUING, STRUCTURING AND INVESTING IN SUKUK, Nathif J. Adam and Abdulkader Thomas, eds. (2004), Abdulkader Thomas, *Securitization in Islamic Finance*, in ISLAMIC FINANCE: THE REGULATORY CHALLENGE, Simon Archer and Rifaat Ahmed Abdel Karim, eds. (2007), at 259–70, Mohammed Obaidullah, *Securitization in Islam*, in ISLAMIC CAPITAL MARKETS: PRODUCTS AND STRATEGIES, M. Kabir Hassan and Michael Mahlknecht, eds. (2011) ('Hassan and Mahlknecht'), at 191–99, Michael J. T. McMillen,

equal value put to use as rights in tangible assets, usufructs and services, or as equity in a project or investment activity. It distinguishes *sukuk* from pure equity, notes and bonds. It emphasises that *sukuk* are not debts of the issuer; they are fractional or proportional interests in underlying assets, usufructs, services, projects or investment activities.[77] *Sukuk* may not be issued on a pool of receivables that are not themselves Shari'ah-compliant. Further, the underlying business or activity, and the underlying transactional structures (e.g. the underlying leases), must be Shari'ah-compliant (e.g. no prohibited business activities). As is apparent from the AAOIFI definition, *sukuk* are securitisation structures.

The nature of the securitisation, in terms of the inputs and intermediate structure, depends upon the assets, instruments and/or obligations (payment rights) that are used as inputs and the Shari'ah contract(s) used as the intermediate structure. From a conventional vantage point, *sukuk* may be securitisations of a single asset or a pool of assets or of a whole business.[78] *Ijara*-based *sukuk*, *salam*-based *sukuk*, *istisna'a*-based *sukuk* and some *wakala*-based *sukuk* are securitisations of one or more assets.

Asset Securitization Sukuk and the Islamic Capital Markets: Structural Issues in These Formative Years, 25 Wisconsin International Law Journal 703 (2007) ('McMillen AS Sukuk'), Michael J. T. McMillen, *Contractual Enforceability Issues: Sukuk and Capital Markets Development*, 7 Chicago Journal of International Law 427 (2007) ('McMillen Enforceability'), Michael J. T. McMillen, *Islamic capital markets: developments and issues*, 1 Capital Markets Law Journal 136 (2006) ('McMillen Islamic Capital Markets'), Michael J. T. McMillen, *Islamic Capital Markets: Market Developments and Conceptual Evolution in the First Thirteen Years* (2011) ('McMillen Evolution'), available at http://papers.ssrn.com/sol3/papers.cfm?abstract_id=1781112, Michael J. T. McMillen, *Islamic Capital Markets: Overview and Select Shari'ah Governance Matters* (2013) ('McMillen Capital Markets Governance'), available at http://papers.ssrn.com/sol3/papers.cfm?abstract_id=2293235, Michael J. T. McMillen, *Securities Laws, Enforceability and Sukuk*, in Islamic Finance: Global Legal Issues and Challenges, Rifaat Ahmed Abdel Karim, ed. (2008), Michael J. T. McMillen, *Sukuk in the Sultanate of Oman* (2013), available at http://papers.ssrn.com/sol3/papers.cfm?abstract_id=2276270, Michael J. T. McMillen, *Structuring a Shari'ah-Compliant Real Estate Acquisition Financing: A South Korean Case Study*, in Islamic Finance: Current Regulatory and Legal Issues, S. Nazim Ali, ed. (2005), at 77 ('McMillen Korea'), Michael J. T. McMillen and John A. Crawford, *Sukuk in the First Decade: By the Numbers*, Dow Jones Islamic Market Indexes 3 (December 2008), and Mohamed Ariff, Meysam Safari and Shamsher Mohamad, *Sukuk Securities, Their Definitions, Classification and Pricing Issues* (May 3, 2012) available at http://ssrn.com/abstract=2097847. *See also*, M. Fahim Khan, *Islamic Methods for Government Borrowing and Monetary Management*, in Hassan and Mahlknecht, at 285–301.

[77] From this definitional perspective, they are quite similar to the pass-through certificates that were prevalent in the US in and around 1983. The concepts of 'debt' in the AAOIFI Sukuk Standard, on the one hand, and as contemplated by lawyers, accountants and financiers, on the other hand, are somewhat different. To the latter group, the concept is broader than under the AAOIFI Sukuk Standard and is (generally) a funding arrangement in which the party (the obligor) receiving the funding has an obligation to make certain payments, including, in some instances as a direct obligation of the obligor independent of any assets held by the obligor and/ or, in other instances, as an obligation to pass through or pay through cash flows from assets held by the obligor.

[78] See, e.g., Hill, *supra* note 44, (noting the fixed and floating charges over essentially all of the assets of the business, the secured creditor treatment afforded the issuer SPV, and the probable

Musharaka-based *sukuk*, *mudaraba*-based *sukuk* and (in theory) some *wakala*-based *sukuk* are akin to whole-business securitisations.

The AAOIFI *sukuk* standard provides for 14 eligible asset classes. In summary, they are securitisations: (a) of an existing or to be acquired tangible asset (*ijara*; lease); (b) of an existing or to be acquired leasehold estate (*ijara*); (c) of presales of services (*ijara*); (d) of presales of the production of goods or commodities at a future date (*salam*; forward sale); (e) to fund construction or manufacture (*istisna'a*; construction or manufacture contract); (f) to fund the acquisition of goods for future sale (*murabaha*; sale at a markup); (g) to fund capital participation in a business of investment activity (*mudaraba* or *musharaka*; joint venture and partnership); and (h) to fund various asset acquisition and agency management (*wakala*; agency), agricultural land cultivation, land management and orchard management activities.

Sukuk are often referred to as 'Islamic bonds'. While inaccurate, this characterisation does express the yearnings of many market participants who desire to trade them as bonds in the global markets. Those participants, including some banks and law firms, have structured *sukuk* issuances as tradable fixed income bonds (rather than securitisations that pass-through profits and losses of the underlying asset pool or business). Structuring in this manner makes the *sukuk* much easier to rate and allows law firms to render necessary opinions.[79]

In March of 2008, after a year-long series of meetings, the AAOIFI Shari'ah board issued the AAOIFI Clarification.[80] The AAOIFI Clarification applies to all *sukuk*, although it addresses specific issues pertaining to distinct types of *sukuk* (particularly *musharaka* structures). The AAOIFI Clarification was thought to be necessary because of a series of post-2003 structural developments that rendered many *sukuk* to be, essentially, conventional bonds because: (a) they did not represent ownership in the commercial or industrial enterprises that issued them; (b) they

---

absolute priority treatment afforded the SPV as financier under United Kingdom law), Vinod Kothari, *Whole Business Securitization: Secured Lending Repackaged—A Comment*, 12 DUKE JOURNAL OF COMPARATIVE AND INTERNATIONAL LAW 537 (2002), Matthew Allchurch, *Fosters Closes Australia's First Whole Business Securitization*, 23 INTERNATIONAL FINANCIAL LAW REVIEW 19 (2004), Toshifumi Ueda, *Japan Turns Its Hand to Whole-Business Deals*, 23 INTERNATIONAL FINANCIAL LAW REVIEW 73 (2004), *Malaysian Deals Open the Way to Asian Whole-Business Securitization*, 20 INTERNATIONAL FINANCIAL LAW REVIEW 8 (2001), and Conor Downey, *Whole Business Securitization Comes of Age*, 18 INTERNATIONAL FINANCIAL LAW REVIEW 8 (1999).

[79] Necessary opinions in securitisation *sukuk* are particularly difficult to render, particularly as regards 'true sale' and similar fundamental concepts. See McMillen Enforceability, *supra* note 76, and the discussion under the heading 'Systemic Aspects of Legal Regimes - Legal Opinions in Financing Transactions' in this chapter.

[80] This self-styled 'resolution' or 'advisory' is available at http://www.aaoifi.com (copy on file with the author). See also a previous, insightful paper by Justice Mohammed Taqi Usmani, the chairman of the AAOIFI Shariah board: *Sukuk and Their Contemporary Applications* (undated; prepared in 2007). See Michael J. T. McMillen, *Sukuk in Its Infancy: Misstep and Sequel*, DOW JONES ISLAMIC MARKET NEWSLETTER (2008), at 3, also available at http://papers.ssrn.com/sol3/papers.cfm?abstract_id=2293693.

generated regular payments determined as a percentage of capital, rather than as a percentage of profit; and (c) through various mechanisms, they guaranteed a return of the principal at maturity. These *sukuk* were structured as entitlements to *returns from* entities rather than *ownership of* entities. Others included *murabaha* debt without ownership of tangible assets.[81]

Sukuk have become the defining instrument of the finance side of the ICM, and will remain so for the foreseeable future. It is clear, however, that the *sukuk* markets to date are dominated, overwhelmingly, by sovereign issuances, quasi-sovereign issuances (often with some recourse to the credit of the sovereign), and, to a much lesser extent, private issuances that are often dependent upon sovereign payments and sovereign credits.[82]

It is difficult (often exceedingly difficult) to obtain the necessary legal options, and thus ratings, for private commercial *sukuk* issuances that involve no sovereign or quasi-sovereign credit (direct or indirect) unless the issuances emanate from jurisdictions that apply Anglo-American common law.[83] As a result, and except in the Malaysian markets, there are few *sukuk* issuances from private commercial entities that do not involve direct or indirect resort to sovereign or quasi-sovereign credits. Which is to say that, with some exceptions,[84] the ICM are, at this stage of development, sovereign and quasi-sovereign capital markets.

---

[81] Concerns relating to regularised periodic payment structures focused on (i) payments to the fund manager to the extent that returns exceeded amounts due on the *sukuk* and (ii) loans by fund managers to the *sukuk* holders or their proxies where returns were insufficient to pay fixed amounts on the *sukuk*. The issues pertaining to principal guarantees derived from the use of promises, by the issuer or fund manager, to purchase the subject assets at an amount equal to the original sale price of assets into the *sukuk* structure (i.e. at the principal amount of the *sukuk*).

[82] See, e.g., any of the quarterly or annual reports on *sukuk* issuances, including, Sherine Rafehi, *A Boom Year for Global Sukuk Market*, Thomson Reuters Zawya (January 21, 2015) (summarizing the 2014 markets), available at http://www.zawya.com/story/A_boom_year_for_global_Sukuk_market-ZAWYA20150121105111/, *Sukuk Perceptions and Forecast Study 2014*, Thomson Reuters Zawya (2014), available at http://www.iefpedia.com/english/wp-content/uploads/2014/01/tr-sukuk-perceptions-and-forecast-20143.pdf, *Sukuk Quarterly Bulletin, Issue 20, 4Q 2013*, *Quarterly Sukuk Review, Q4 2014 Edition*, Bloomberg, International Shari'ah Research Academy for Islamic Finance (Q4, 2014), available at http://ifikr.isra.my/documents/10180/16168/Sukuk%20Review%20DEC%20Q4%20v716-02-2015-44.pdf, *Global Sukuk Market: Quarterly Bulletin (July 2014)*, Rasameel Structured Finance (2014), available at http://www.rasameel.com/downloads/RSF_Global_Sukuk_Report_3Q2014 .pdf, and *Global Sukuk Market: Quarterly Bulletin (July 2014)*, Rasameel Structured Finance (2014), available at http://www.rasameel.com/downloads/RSFGlobalSukukReport1H2014-sep11.pdf. With respect to an analysis of virtually all issuances from 2001 to September 2008, see Michael J. T. McMillen and John A. Crawford, *Sukuk in the First Decade: By the Numbers*, Dow Jones Islamic Market Indexes 3 (December 2008).

[83] Some of the reasons are discussed in this chapter under the heading 'Systemic Aspects of Legal Regimes - Legal Infrastructure in Shari'ah-Incorporated Jurisdictions'.

[84] In Malaysia, there have been a number of corporate *sukuk* issuances, Tamweel in Dubai has offered several *sukuk al-ijara*, and in the wake of Basel III several Islamic banks have issued *sukuk* that are intended to qualify as Tier 1 or Tier 2 capital.

Regulatory Regimes for Asset Securitisations

Asset-backed securitisations developed long after the basic legal and regulatory framework for securities and capital markets.[85] Securitisation concepts were 'made up' circa 1977 in the US. This statement is true with respect to the nature of the security as an economic and mathematical matter. It is also true as a legal matter. Securitisation developed and ultimately flourished in the interstices of existing law. Certainly, there have been legislative or regulatory initiatives aimed directly at fostering development of the securitisation markets.[86] But in many ways, most notably the required disclosure in registered offerings and the periodic reporting requirements under the securities laws, securitisation transactions proceeded without the benefit of clear statutory guidance.[87]

Securitisation transactions and concepts present unique and complex issues under many different aspects of the existing legal frameworks. Among others, they present unique tax, collective investment scheme, disclosure and bankruptcy issues. While securitisation concepts could be (and have been) successfully shoe-horned into the interstices of existing laws, there has been a continuing need to modify existing laws to promote effective use of the securitisation device and to realise its benefits. But this pattern of piecemeal adjustment is costly and inefficient. Thus, there has been felt a need for comprehensive treatment of asset-backed securitisations. As stated by the Securities and Exchange Commission of the United States of America (SEC), upon initial proposal of a new set of comprehensive rules for asset-backed securitisations in 2004 (the rules have since been adopted):[88]

> *Asset-backed securities and ABS issuers differ from corporate securities and operating companies. In offering these securities, there is generally no business or management to describe. Instead, information about the transaction structure and the quality of the asset pool and servicing is often what is most important to investors. Many of the [SEC's] existing disclosure and reporting requirements, which [we]re designed primarily for corporate issuers, d[id] not elicit the information that is relevant for most asset-backed securities transactions.*

---

[85] The basic legal framework for regulation of the capital markets in the US was developed in the 1930s and has evolved ever since.

[86] For example, in the US: enactment of the Secondary Mortgage Market Enhancement Act of 1984, Public Law 98–440, October 3, 1984, 98 Statutes 1689, 12 United States Code 1701, available at https://www.law.cornell.edu/topn/secondary_mortgage_market_enhancement_act_of_1984, made mortgage-backed securities ('MBS') easier to sell to a variety of investors; enactment of the real estate mortgage conduit (REMIC) provisions of the tax code in 1986 enabled complex MBS structures; revision of Form S-3 in 1992 permitted shelf registration of many types of ABS; and adoption of Rule 3a-7 under the Investment Company Act, also in 1992, freed many types of non-mortgage ABS from the strictures of the statute.

[87] Arnholz and Gainor, *supra* note 36, at xv-xvi (footnotes omitted).

[88] *Asset-Backed Securities, Securities Act Release No. 33-8518*, 70 FEDERAL REGISTER 1506, 1508 (January 7, 2005), and *Asset-Backed* Securities, *Securities Act Release No. 34-8518*, 17 Code of Federal Regulations Parts 210, 228, 229, 230, 232, 239, 240, 242, 245 and 249, effective date 8 March 2005, located at http://www.sec.gov/rules/final/33-8518.htm (the '*ABS Release*').

The focus in this chapter is the ICM, and *sukuk*, particularly asset-backed securitisation *sukuk*, are and will be an important element of these markets. *Sukuk* will have to comply with the securitisation laws that have been, and increasingly will be, adopted throughout the world. This chapter surveys some of the elements of US law, not because *sukuk* will necessarily be issued from the US, but because laws throughout the world incorporate concepts, to a greater or lesser extent, from the US securitisation legal and regulatory structure.

The changes to the US securities laws in respect of ABS have been implemented in the ABS Rules (including Regulation AB) and in the Offering Reform Rules, as amended and supplemented since the onset of the 2007 financial crisis.[89] These rules apply to public offerings of ABS securities. For purposes of this chapter there are two primary areas of particular interest: the disclosure requirements for ABS and the requirements pertaining to communications to investors in respect of ABS offerings.

The general principle of Section 5 of the Securities Act is that,[90] generally, it is unlawful to sell securities unless a registration statement has been filed and declared effective by the SEC and a prospectus containing certain information about the offering has been delivered (actually or constructively) to the investor in a timely manner. Certain types of securities (such as issuances by government agencies) and certain transactions (such as private placements and secondary market transactions) are exempt from these registration requirements.

Disclosure Matters

Turning to disclosure considerations first, the legal framework moves away from a 'corporate issuer' focus on audited financial statements and disclosure based upon an assumption of an operating company.[91] Regulation AB establishes a disclosure framework that outlines the type of required disclosure, but does not attempt to establish specific rules for each asset class that might be securitised. It is an effort to balance transparency and comparability concerns with rigidity concerns while ensuring that the disclosure requirements would not become out-of-date.[92] Disclosure is thus left in

---

[89]'*Regulation AB*', 17 Code of Federal Regulations, Part 229, Subpart 229.1100, Asset-Backed Securities, is available at https://www.law.cornell.edu/cfr/text/17/part-229/subpart-229.1100. See, e.g., SEC Release Nos. 33-9638; 34-72982; File No. S7-08-10 (4 September 2014) (the '*2014 Release*', which is 683 pages in length), available at http://www.sec.gov/rules/final/2014/33-9638 .pdf (and see Release Nos. 33-9552, 33-9244, 33-9638A; there have been other technical amendments as well). The various amendments, particularly those during 2014, are designed to address some of the weaknesses exposed in the ABS markets during the 2007 financial crisis by (a) providing more information to investors about the assets underlying the ABS in order to allow investors to perform their own due diligence and reduce reliance on credit ratings, (b) ensuring that investors in registered ABS have adequate time to review the collateral characteristics and transaction structure prior to making an investment decision, and (c) ensuring that ABS issued under shelf registration statements (which allow rapid access to the markets) are designed by issuers with greater oversight and care.

[90] Securities Act of 1933, as amended, of the United States of America, available at http://www .sec.gov/about/laws/sa33.pdf.

[91] Prior to Regulation AB, even savvy institutional investors with considerable economic clout found it difficult to obtain the desired disclosure, even when that disclosure was requested. See, e.g., Arnholz and Gainer, *supra* note 36, at § 3.01.

[92] See, ABS Release, *supra* note 88, at 1532.

part to the independent determinations of issuers and their legal counsel as to the materiality of information. There are notes of caution in respect of materiality determinations. For example, the legal framework implies that information provided to rating agencies may well be material.[93] And the liability provisions of the securities laws (Exchange Act – Rule 10b-5, for example),[94] will still be applicable. While material items must be disclosed, disclosure is not limited to material information. There are many items of information that must be disclosed.

Regulation AB requires disclosure regarding third parties that are unaffiliated with the sponsor. These include, as examples, unaffiliated asset originators, servicers, enhancement providers and other obligors. Some of the required disclosure is outside the control of the sponsor, and the sponsors are thus left to perform as much due diligence as possible with respect to the third parties and any information provided by the third parties. Clearly, these requirements increase the liability exposure of sponsors, issuers and underwriters.

Disclosure under Regulation AB is also required with respect to (a) sponsors, (b) depositors, (c) issuers, (d) asset transferors, (e) servicers, (f) trustees, (g) originators, (h) significant obligors, (i) support and enhancement providers, (j) other transaction parties, (k) relationships between and among parties, (l) the asset pool, (m) previous securitisations, (n) the transaction structure and the offered securities, (o) foreign issuers and foreign assets, (p) legal proceedings, and (q) other third parties.

The detailed requirements of Regulation AB are beyond the scope of this chapter. However, it is worthwhile to summarise, in general terms, some of the types of required disclosure.[95] Although not addressed by the ABS Rules themselves, with their promulgation there is an increased emphasis on compliance with the 'plain language' requirements.[96] As a matter of form and presentation, more and longer disclosure is required in the summary section of the prospectus.[97] Regulation AB also emphasises the disclosure of risk factors. Certain risk factors are required to be disclosed. Examples include risks related to the types of assets to be securitised, geographic and other concentrations of assets, legal risks, limitations on liability, risks associated with changes in interest rates and prepayment levels, special risks associated with securities in the asset pool that represent interests in another asset pool (including risks associated with that second pool) and material risks related to security interests (including perfection, priority and enforcement).

Disclosure with respect to a sponsor generally focuses on the character of its business and elements of its securitisation programme, including information with respect to assets, the size, composition and growth of the relevant asset portfolio, and other

---

[93] See, e.g., ABS Release, *supra* note 88, at 1533.

[94] Securities Exchange Act of 1934, as amended, of the United States of America (the '*Exchange Act*'), available at http://www.sec.gov/about/laws/sea34.pdf, and Rule 10b-5 thereunder

[95] In addition to Regulation AB itself (citations follow), see Arnholz and Gainer, *supra* note 36, at § 3.05, which summarises disclosure with respect to each of these categories and discusses some of the practical disclosure issues with respect to each category.

[96] ABS Release, supra note 88, at 1532. And, see Arnholz and Gainer, *id.*, at § 3.09.

[97] See Item 1103 of Regulation AB (with regard to the summary and risk factors) and Item 1102 (with respect to the cover) of Regulation AB, Regulations §§ 229.1103 and 1102, respectively, *supra* note 89.

information that is material to the analysis of the assets in the pool, such as defaults and early amortisations.[98] Thus, the role of programme issuers is acknowledged and addressed.

Overwhelmingly, the issuer entity is a trust.[99] Common law trusts are used where pass-through certificates are issued on the assets, such as in the case of MBS. As contemplated by the AAOIFI *sukuk* standard, most *sukuk* are and will be akin to pass-through certificates. As a result of tax considerations, other asset types are frequently issued pursuant to statutory trusts (or, in some cases, limited liability companies, limited partnerships or corporations), and the securities must be issued as notes pursuant to an indenture. In each case, the form of the entity and its 'governing documents' must be disclosed. If the pooled assets constitute securities, the market price, and the basis for determination of the market price, must be disclosed. Shari'ah principles preclude the securitisation of assets that constitute debt or do not represent an interest in a tangible asset (leaving aside intellectual property for the moment). A pool of assets in which tangible assets constitute the majority is also generally considered acceptable. As Islamic finance and bifurcated structures are developed to securitise other types of assets, the statutory trust concept will be of greater significance than it will be in the early stages of development of ABS *sukuk*.

A major focus of Regulation AB is disclosure with respect to the servicer and every aspect of the servicing function (including sub-servicing).[100] The requirements go not only to transactional participants, but to parties not affiliated with the servicer. There is a significantly enhanced diligence requirement in connection with this category of disclosure. Among the servicer-related disclosure items are (i) the servicing experience, generally and with respect to specific assets types that are the subject of the offering, (ii) material changes in servicing policies during the past three years, (iii) the financial condition of the servicer entities, if material to the servicing function, the asset pool or the offered securities, (iv) material terms of servicing agreements, including in respect of advancing, default and delinquency policies, (v) the ability of the servicer entity to waive or modify terms, (vi) document custody matters, (vii) material terms of custodial arrangements, (viii) limitations on the liability of servicer entities, and (ix) back-up servicing arrangements.

Disclosure regarding asset originators is another area addressed by Regulation AB. As with the servicer, the definitional concept of the SEC is broad.[101] After determining what entities constitute 'originators' for purposes of Regulation AB, the degree of disclosure must be determined. As a basic matter, disclosure will focus on the origination programme, including a general discussion of the assets and a detailed discussion of the securitised assets, a discussion of the size, composition and growth of the relevant asset portfolio, other information material to the asset pool, such as underwriting criteria, and a description of legal proceedings pending in respect of the originator, directly or indirectly.

---

[98] See Regulation AB, *id.*, at § 229.1101.
[99] See Regulation AB, *id.*, at § 229.1107.
[100] See, among other items Item 1108, Item 1101(j), Item 1108(a), 1108(b) and Item 1117 of Regulation AB, *id.*, at §§ 229.1101(j), 1108(a), 1108(b) and 1117.
[101] See Item 1110 of Regulation AB, *id.*, at § 229.1110.

Disclosure regarding credit enhancement providers, other than certain derivative instruments, includes descriptions of both external and internal enhancement and, with respect to external enhancement providers, descriptions of the providers and their business and financial condition (audited and unaudited, depending upon the level of enhancement).[102] Disclosure regarding credit enhancement providers providing certain derivatives instruments will include descriptions of the derivative instruments, the significance percentages of those providers, and descriptions of the providers and their business and financial condition (audited and unaudited, depending upon the level of enhancement).[103]

Regulation AB also requires significant disclosure with respect to the asset pool.[104] It focuses on characteristics of the asset pool. The required disclosure includes tabular disclosure with respect to number, amount and percentages of assets in different asset categories, average balances, average interest rates, average remaining terms, average credit scores, other credit quality criteria, appropriate historical data (including in respect of delinquencies and defaults) and material concentrations of assets. The 2014 Release indicates that standardised asset-level disclosure requirements are being adopted. These requirements include 'data points' pertaining to payment streams on particular assets, collateral related to the assets, performance of the assets over time, loss mitigation efforts by servicers to collect past-due amounts and losses, statistical information on the asset pool, transactional document provisions that allow for modifications of the pool, standardised delinquency presentations, explanations of static pool disclosures and other factors.[105] The 2014 Release also provides for significant asset-specific disclosure regarding specific types of ABS (residential and commercial MBS, automobile loan and lease ABS, debt security ABS and resecuritisations).[106]

Regulation AB mandates significant disclosure regarding the transaction structure and the offered securities, and this disclosure is being enhanced following the 2007 financial crisis.[107] Items of particular concern are fees and expenses, information regarding each security and class of securities that is subject to optional redemption or a termination feature, and descriptions of holders of residual interests and retained interests in the cash flow generated by the asset pool and the nature of those interests.

Disclosure requirements pertaining to foreign ABS issuers, foreign credit enhancers and to ABS sold by US ABS issuers where the issue includes foreign assets or is secured by foreign property include: 'any pertinent governmental, legal or regulatory or administrative matters and any pertinent tax matters, exchange controls, currency restrictions or other economic, fiscal, monetary or potential factors in the applicable home jurisdiction that could materially affect' the ABS or the pool assets,[108] as well as pending legal proceedings. Of particular concern are material effects on the origination of the

---

[102] See Item 1114 and Item 1115 of Regulation AB, *id.*, at §§ 229.1114 and 229.15.

[103] See Item 1115 of Regulation AB, *id.*, at § 229.1115.

[104] See Item 1111 of Regulation AB, *id*, at § 229.1111. There are also extensive and significant disclosure requirements with respect to 'static pools'; see Item 1105 of Regulation AB, at § 229.1105, and see Arnholz and Gainer, *supra* note 36, at § 3.06.

[105] 2014 Release, *supra* note 89, at 17–20 (for summaries of these matters) and subsequent discussions.

[106] See 2014 Release, *id.*, at 49–261, especially at 85–188.

[107] See Item 1113 of Regulation AB, *supra* note 89, at § 229.1113.

[108] See Item 1100(e) of Regulation AB, *id.*, at § 229.1100(e).

asset pool, bankruptcy risks pertaining to the originator or transferor of the assets into the pool, perfection of security interests in pool assets, servicing, trustee duties, pool characteristics and credit enhancements.

Investor Communication Matters

The Offering Reform Rules modified many securities laws provisions pertaining to communications with investors in an effort to acknowledge, and adapt to the realities of, changes in global communications since the Securities Act was initially enacted in 1933. As a correlative, the Offering Reform Rules also buttress the liberalisation in investor communications with stringent liability provisions for misstatements and omissions in marketing materials, whether or not those misstatements or omissions are ultimately corrected in the final prospectus. This sub-section summarises some of the requirements. The Offering Reform Rules take cognisance of the differences between ABS issuers and corporate securities issuers that are noted above.

The historical analytical framework, provided in Section 5 of the Securities Act, with respect to communications with investors in public offerings contemplates three periods. The first is the 'pre-filing' or 'quiet' period before the registration statement is filed.[109] Historically, all communication with the investor was foreclosed and offers of any type were prohibited. The Offering Reform Rules permit certain conditional communications with investors by 'well known seasoned issuers', but not by issuers of ABS. The second period, the 'waiting period', is that between filing of the registration statement and the date it is declared effective and a final prospectus is available. During this period, historically, oral offers are permitted, but written offers generally are not permitted. The Offering Reform Rules provide certain defined exceptions to the historical practice. During the final 'post-effective' period, after the effective date of the registration statement and the delivery of the final prospectus, additional written materials may be delivered without limitation.

Under the Offering Reform Rules, issuers of securities are categorised into one of four categories:

1. 'well known seasoned issuers' are companies eligible to use shelf registrations and that meet specific monetary thresholds pertaining to the minimum public float of common equity held by non-affiliates or registered non-convertible debt securities over a recent period;
2. 'seasoned issuers' are companies eligible to use shelf registrations but not satisfying the public float test applicable for 'well known seasoned issuer' status;
3. 'unseasoned issuers' are companies required to file periodic reports under the Exchange Act or filing such reports voluntarily, but not eligible to use shelf registrations; and
4. 'non-reporting issuers' are companies that are not required to file Exchange Act reports, regardless of whether or not they do so voluntarily.

ABS issuers are categorised as either 'seasoned issuers' (if they offer securities pursuant to a shelf registration statement)[110] or 'non-reporting issuers' (if they offer

---

[109] Most jurisdictions take a somewhat different approach to the concept of relevant time periods and the rules applicable in each period.

[110] The shelf registration requirements are undergoing significant change: see 2014 Release, *supra* note 89, at 300–442.

securities pursuant to a registered offering). However, if the issuer of ABS (or other securities) is an 'ineligible issuer' (primarily because it has not satisfied all required Exchange Act reporting requirements or is the subject of adverse legal, administrative or regulatory determinations or actions), many of the benefits of the Offering Reform Rules are not available to that issuer.

During the pre-filing period, ABS issuers are nearly absolutely prohibited from offering to sell securities. The term 'offer' is broadly construed and includes most types of marketing activities, including those conditioning the public mind or arousing public interest in the issuer or the securities to be offered. There are certain 'safe-harbour' provisions for ABS issuers, largely relating to the dissemination of factual business information in accordance with historical patterns and practices. The Offering Reform Rules establish a bright-line for the commencement of the pre-filing period, assuming that certain conditions are satisfied.

During the waiting period (or the equivalent period in a shelf offering), oral offers (but not written offers) for the sale of the securities may be made. There is an exception for the category of free writing prospectuses (assuming satisfaction of various requirements). There are only limited circumstances when a free writing prospectus is permitted in ABS registered offerings; among them, a copy of the most recent preliminary or final statutory prospectus must be delivered to the investor, not merely filed with the SEC. The 'prospectus' concept is broadly defined to include written and oral materials, including letters, emails, radio and television communications, all forms of electronic media and a wide range of other communications. Any prospectus must satisfy the requirements of Section 10 of the Securities Act (including its technical requirements). If it does not, delivery will constitute a violation of Section 5 of the Securities Act. With respect to ABS issuances, distribution of informational and computational material is prohibited prior to a declaration of the effectiveness of the registration statement. In distillation of the various rules, only preliminary prospectuses (and certain notices) may be delivered during the waiting period. Free writing prospectuses must be filed with the SEC in many cases, and the rules in respect of such filings (and exceptions to those filings) are complex and intricate.

A free writing prospectus is generally any written communication that constitutes an offer to sell or a solicitation of an offer to buy securities relating to a registration, other than certain specified notices and material (the term 'offer' being broadly defined and construed). Free writing prospectuses must satisfy certain specific requirements (Rule 433). The term 'written communication' is a term of art that includes writings, publications (such as radio and television), and graphic materials (including electronic means). A free writing prospectus may include material that is not in the registration statement, but such information may not conflict with the registration statement. Disclaimers of many types may not be included (including those in respect of accuracy or completeness or deference to materials in the registration statement).

As previously noted, the types of requirements discussed in this section are, increasingly, the basis for securitisation law developments around the globe, and will have application to *sukuk* issuances.

SYSTEMIC ASPECTS OF LEGAL REGIMES

Practitioners in the field of Islamic finance are acutely aware that many of the critical inhibiting factors to the development of the ICM (and Islamic finance more generally) relate, directly or indirectly, to the legal and regulatory infrastructure in many of the relevant jurisdictions.[111] Legal and regulatory issues have been a – if not the – major impediment to the issuance of rated *sukuk* by private sector entities and for the overwhelming dominance of sovereign *sukuk* in the ICM. Significant practical issues relate to (a) the ability to enforce the relevant transactional documents (and to obtain the requisite legal opinions in respect of enforcement of those documents), and (b) the consequences of the application of various substantive legal doctrines in securitisation and *sukuk* transactions (and to obtain the requisite legal opinions in respect of the application of those doctrines). Some of the legal and regulatory issues are systemic, such as the weaknesses (in some cases, non-existence – in all cases, the neglect) of bankruptcy regimes,[112] and collateral security regimes,[113] both conventional and Shari'ah-compliant.

---

[111] The matters discussed in this section are discussed in greater detail in Yusuf Talal DeLorenzo and Michael J. T. McMillen, *Law and Islamic Finance: An Interactive Analysis*, in ISLAMIC FINANCE: THE REGULATORY CHALLENGE, Simon Archer and Rifaat Ahmed Abdel Karim, eds. (2007), at 150 *et seq.* ('DeLorenzo and McMillen'), Michael J. T. McMillen, *The UNCITRAL Model Secured Transactions Law: A Shari'ah Perspective*, a chapter in THE DRAFT UNCITRAL MODEL LAW ON SECURED TRANSACTIONS: WHY AND HOW?, edited by Bénédict Foëx, ed. (2016), Michael J. T. McMillen, *Implementing Shari'ah-Compliant Collateral Security Regimes: Select Issues*, a chapter of RESEARCH HANDBOOK ON SECURED FINANCING IN COMMERCIAL TRANSACTIONS, Frederique Dahan, ed. (2015), Michael J. T. McMillen, *Legal Regime for Security Rights in Movable Collateral: An Analysis of the UNCITRAL Model Law from a Shari'ah Perspective*, The World Bank (February 1, 2016), and Michael J. T. McMillen, *The Chapter 11 Bankruptcy Restructuring of Arcapita*, a chapter of GLOBAL TRENDS IN ISLAMIC COMMERCIAL LAW, the International Shariah Research Academy for Islamic Finance and Thomson Reuters Report (2015), McMillen AS Sukuk, *supra* note 76, McMillen Enforceability, *supra* note 76, at 427–58, McMillen Islamic Capital Markets, *supra* note 76, at 1536, McMillen Evolution, *supra* note 76, McMillen Capital Markets Governance, *supra* note 76, Michael J. T. McMillen, *Islamic Capital Markets: A Selective Introduction*, THE INTERNATIONAL WHO'S WHO OF CAPITAL MARKETS LAWYERS (2012), at 2, and Michael J. T. McMillen, *Islamic Capital Markets in the United States and Globally: Overview and Select Shari'ah Governance Elements*, INSIDE THE MINDS: FINANCIAL SERVICES ENFORCEMENT AND COMPLIANCE (2013).

[112] See Abed Awad and Robert E. Michaels, *Iflas and Chapter 11: Classical Islamic Law and Modern Bankruptcy*, 44 THE INTERNATIONAL LAWYER 975 (2010), Jason J. Kilborn, *Foundations of Forgiveness in Islamic Bankruptcy Law: Sources, Methodology, Diversity*, 85 AMERICAN BANKRUPTCY LAW JOURNAL 323 (2011), Michael J. T. McMillen, *The Arcapita Group Bankruptcy: A Restructuring Case Study*, GLOBAL TRENDS IN ISLAMIC COMMERCIAL LAW, International Shari'ah Research Academy and Thomson Reuters (2015), Michael J. T. McMillen, *An Introduction to Shari'ah Considerations in Bankruptcy and Insolvency Contexts and Islamic Finance's First Bankruptcy (East Cameron)* (17 June 2012), available at http://papers.ssrn.com/sol3/papers.cfm?abstract_id=1826246.

[113] See Michael J. T. McMillen, *Implementing Shari'ah-Compliant Collateral Security Regimes: Select Issues*, in RESEARCH HANDBOOK ON SECURED FINANCING IN COMMERCIAL TRANSACTIONS, Frederique Dahan, ed. (2015), at 97 ('McMillen Collateral Security'), and Michael J. T. McMillen, *Rahn Concepts in Saudi Arabia: Formalization and a Registration and Prioritization System*, in Hassan and Mahlknecht, *supra* note 75 ('McMillen Rahn'), at 3, also available in draft (March 9, 2010) at http://papers.ssrn.com/sol3/papers.cfm?abstract_id=1670104.

Others relate to the ability to enforce the Shari'ah in different jurisdictions. And still others relate to the specific legal issues that arise with respect to a transactional type, such as *sukuk*. This section summarises some of the issues of each of these types.

Different Legal and Regulatory Frameworks; Different Modes of Analysis

Many *sukuk* transactions to date have involved small pools of assets as inputs: frequently only a single asset (especially where the issuer or ultimate credit is a sovereign or quasi-sovereign). A small number of other *sukuk* transactions involve larger pools of assets. As the ICM develops, it can be expected that *sukuk* will be comprised of larger asset pools, with assets in different jurisdictions. As the industry globalises, the transactional parties are frequently located in different jurisdictions: the asset originator maybe located in one jurisdiction (say, within the Middle East or Africa), the ABS issuer may be located in another jurisdiction, and the ABS holders will likely (hopefully) be located in multiple and diverse jurisdictions.

Each of the relevant jurisdictions has and will apply a different legal regime with respect to a broad range of legal and regulatory factors. Each of those factors can be considered as a continuum, with the framework and architecture of each jurisdiction falling at a different point on the continuum with respect to the specific factor under consideration. One of those factors, and one of the most important for present purposes, is the degree to which the Shari'ah is incorporated into the secular law of a given nation. '*Purely Secular Jurisdictions*', which take no cognisance of the Shari'ah, are located at one extreme of this continuum. 'Shari'ah-incorporated jurisdictions', which incorporate the Shari'ah into the secular law to some greater or lesser extent, are scattered over a broader portion of this continuum, depending upon the extent, degree and type of incorporation of the Shari'ah into the relevant secular law.[114] Islamic finance

---

[114] For a review of the extent to which, and the manner in which, the laws of various Middle Eastern nations are comprised of, or incorporate, the Shari'ah, see Nayla Comair-Obeid, THE LAW OF BUSINESS CONTRACTS IN THE ARAB MIDDLE EAST (1996), particularly Chapter 3. See also, Noel J. Coulson, COMMERCIAL LAW IN THE GULF STATES: THE ISLAMIC LEGAL TRADITION (1984). The Ottoman Empire adopted many aspects of the French commercial code by 1830, and thereafter adopted many other French codes. Civil law remained largely untouched by this process despite the compilation of the *majelle* (*majalat al-ahkam al-adliyah*). The *majelle* was a codification of civil law following a Western model, but the *majelle* itself was comprised of, and based upon, the Shari'ah as interpreted by the Hanafī school of Islamic jurisprudence. Since 1949, Egypt and Syria have adopted Westernised codifications of certain laws, while retaining the influence of the Shari'ah in many substantive areas. In each of these jurisdictions, the Shari'ah is expressly designated as 'a' source of law. In Egypt, the Shari'ah is to be consulted by a judge after considering the civil code and custom. In Syria, the Shari'ah is to be consulted prior to examination of custom, and is thus a true source of law. Similar concepts are found in the Civil Code of 1976 of Jordan. Kuwait and the United Arab Emirates are examples of nations that have incorporated portions of the Shari'ah into their codes. In certain jurisdictions, such as Saudi Arabia and Oman, there is no civil code and the role of the Shari'ah is predominant, including in respect of contracts. Saudi Arabia recognizes the Shari'ah as the paramount law of the land. However, the various enforcement mechanisms that have been established with respect to the resolution of distinct categories of commercial disputes do influence the application of the Shari'ah to such disputes. One example is the settlement of disputes between a bank and its customers. The 'settlement' of such matters (other than in respect of negotiable instruments) is effected by the Banking Disputes Settlement Committee of the Saudi Arabian Monetary Agency

transactions, such as large *sukuk* issuances, will frequently involve the laws of both purely secular jurisdictions and Shari'ah-incorporated jurisdictions at different points along the aforementioned continuum.[115]

In a purely secular jurisdiction, the legal and regulatory regime is largely based upon a Western interest-based model.[116] So also are the structures, methodologies and documents used in transactions. Institutional parameters, such as those pertaining to risk allocation, risk coverage, underwriting, accounting and collateral security, and the expectations of transactional participants, are all fashioned under and responsive to an interest-based system.

Importantly, in most purely secular jurisdictions, the law will enforce the contractual documentation among the transactional parties as the 'law of the transaction' (assuming that it does not violate laws or public policy). Documentation in many capital markets transactions is highly standardised, reflecting agreed-upon risk allocations and to the end of achieving efficiencies in transactional costs. A prerequisite to standardisation (especially in capital markets transactions, such as securitisations) is

---

(customarily known as the 'SAMA Committee'). The SAMA Committee generally attempts to settle a matter in accordance with the agreement of the parties. Another example in Saudi Arabia is indicated by the jurisdictional authority afforded to the Office of the Settlement of Negotiable Instruments Disputes (NIO), under the aegis of the Ministry of Commerce, which addresses and settles disputes involving negotiable instruments and generally looks only to the 'four corners' of the instrument to which the dispute relates. See McMillen Islamic Project Finance, *supra* note 18, at 1195–203. Consider also the Enforcement of Shari'ah Act 1991, Act X of 1991 of Pakistan, available at http://www.pakistani.org/pakistan/legislation/1991/actXof1991.html.

[115] Consider Michael J. T. McMillen Islamic Project Finance, *id.*, at 1237–63 (discussing transactions in both Purely Secular Jurisdictions (the United States) and Shari'ah-Incorporated Jurisdictions (Saudi Arabia)), McMillen Korea, *supra* note 76 (under the South Korean securitisation laws), Michael J. T. McMillen, *Shari'a-compliant Finance Structures and the Development of an Islamic Economy*, in THE PROCEEDINGS OF THE FIFTH HARVARD UNIVERSITY FORUM ON ISLAMIC FINANCE: ISLAMIC FINANCE: DYNAMICS AND DEVELOPMENT, at 89–102 (2003), Michael J. T. McMillen, *Islamic Finance Review 2005/2006: A Year of Globalization and Integration*, EUROMONEY ISLAMIC FINANCE YEAR IN REVIEW 2005/2006 (2006), and Michael J. T. McMillen, *Raising the Game of Compliance: People and Organizations*, in EUROMONEY ISLAMIC FINANCE YEAR IN REVIEW 2005/2006 (2006).

[116] The Western interest-based transactional paradigm has been dominant for some five centuries, for a number of reasons. Some of those reasons include (a) the dominance of the Western interest-based economic system, (b) the predominance of United States and European financial institutions, lawyers, and accountants in the development and refinement of the most widely used financing techniques, (c) the refinement and exportation of Anglo-American law, (d) the relative infancy of modern Islamic finance, (e) the lack of familiarity with the operation of legal systems in the jurisdictions of the Islamic economic sphere, and (f) the general lack of knowledge of, and familiarity with, the Shari'ah. See, DeLorenzo and McMillen, *supra* note 111, and McMillen Islamic Capital Markets, *supra* note 76, at 144–47. In addition, since the late 1990s many Shari'ah-compliant transactions have been effected in the US and Europe using, exclusively, the secular law of a purely secular jurisdiction as the governing law of the transaction (although the documents themselves have been drafted to be, in and of themselves, compliant with the Shari'ah, as determined by the various Shari'ah supervisory boards that have reviewed those transactions and the related documentation). See, e.g., McMillen Islamic Project Finance, *supra* note 18, at 1237–63. Examples of these early transactions were described in Michael J. T. McMillen, *Special Report U.S. Briefing: Islamic Finance: Breaking the Mould*, 38 MIDDLE EAST ECONOMIC DIGEST (MEED), September 22, 2000 at 28–29.

agreement of all transactional participants and all participants in the broader capital markets on risk allocations for the range of related transactions, from origination through to securitisation, and testing of those allocations by use and, in some cases, litigation. In practice, standardisations reflect risk agreements in and responsiveness to an interest-based environment. In the securitisation field, transactional complexity is highly evolved, and the standardisation reflects agreed-upon risk allocation in transactional models that are markedly more complex than those presently used in Islamic finance.

It is significantly more complicated to summarise the premise of the legal and regulatory system in a Shari'ah-incorporated jurisdiction. There is a broader range of variations.[117] In the Shari'ah-incorporated jurisdictions, provisions of the Shari'ah may be either (a) literally incorporated into the text of the substantive law of the nation; or (b) incorporated as an interpretive matter by the courts or other enforcement bodies, either as 'a' factor or as 'the' paramount factor, with the degree of incorporation varying in accordance with the applicable methodology of incorporation and further influenced by the nature of the judicial and enforcement entity structure of the jurisdiction. In either case, a contract that is governed by the law of the Shari'ah-incorporated jurisdiction will be enforced in accordance with the Shari'ah, to the extent that the Shari'ah is so incorporated and applicable, and whether or not the specific substantive legal provisions are referenced in the contract. In such a jurisdiction the parties cannot by contract alter the applicable Shari'ah provisions, nor will it be necessary for the parties to specifically incorporate applicable Shari'ah provisions.

In order to adequately assess risk (business, financial and legal), both Muslim and Western transactional participants share a desire for transparency, certainty, predictability and stability in the relevant legal frameworks. Their bases of reference and the relevant considerations will vary, however. Muslim transactional participants have greater familiarity with the Western interest-based system than Western transactional participants have with the Shari'ah-based system. A primary focus of Muslim transactional participants will be Shari'ah compliance. Non-Muslim participants may be relatively indifferent to Shari'ah compliance other than to ensure that the transaction works from the vantage point of the Muslim participants. The Western participants will continue to use an analytical framework that proceeds from an interest-based system in analysing rights, obligations, remedies and other risk allocation factors.

One of the challenges in the development of the ICM is how to reconcile these (and other) differences in a manner that assures a perception and realisation of transparency, certainty, predictability and stability for all participants. This must be accomplished in the context of cross-border transactions that must be enforced in a broad range of jurisdictions, even in circumstances such as a *sukuk* offering, where the financing is entirely Shari'ah-compliant.

Further, in order to obtain ratings on ICM instruments, it is necessary to obtain legal opinions as to the enforceability of the transaction documents. These documents must be enforceable under all relevant secular laws, and, from the Shari'ah perspective, must also be compliant with the Shari'ah.

Thus, enforcement is a critical inquiry: will the Shari'ah, as embodied in the transactional documents and the transactional structure, be enforced in different types of jurisdictions and, if so, to what extent?

---

[117] See note 114, *supra*.

Enforceability in Purely Secular Jurisdictions

If ICM are to develop on a globally integrated basis and not remain isolated within relatively limited confines (defined not only by national boundaries, but also by differing interpretations of the Shari'ah), enforceability must be considered (and achieved, concurrently and harmoniously) in both purely secular jurisdictions and in Shari'ah-incorporated jurisdictions. In purely secular jurisdictions, the contracts among the transactional parties will be enforced as governing the relationships among the transactional parties. Enforcement will extend to the agreed risk allocations as evidenced by contractual agreements pertaining to rights, obligations and remedies. Thus, if the parties desire to implement the Shari'ah, they will have to draft the contract in accordance with, and incorporate, the relevant Shari'ah principles (which may be done without explicit reference to the Shari'ah). If New York or English law, or the law of any other purely secular jurisdiction, is chosen as the governing law of a contract, the court will enforce that law, and the contract subject to that law, in accordance with its terms. A Shari'ah-compliant contract will thus be enforced.

If the parties to the contract chose, in the alternative, the Shari'ah itself as the law governing the contract, there is, at present, significantly less transparency, certainty and predictability as to how the contract will be enforced. Two English appellate court cases have addressed the issues of the Shari'ah as governing law for contracts in a purely secular jurisdiction: *Shamil Bank of Bahrain E.C. (Islamic Bankers) v Beximco Pharmaceuticals Ltd. and Others* ('Beximco'),[118] which addressed judicial enforcement of the Shari'ah, and *Musawi v R E International (UK) Ltd & ORS* ('Musawi'),[119] which addressed the issue in the arbitration context.

The determination, in each case, was that the governing law clause did not require consideration of the Shari'ah. That is, the governing secular law will not take cognisance of the Shari'ah, despite the ability of the contractual parties to choose the governing law of the relevant contract.[120]

---

[118] *Shamil Bank of Bahrain E. C. (Islamic Bankers) v Beximco Pharmaceuticals Ltd. and Others*, 1 WLR 1784 (CA 2004) (UK).

[119] *Musawi v R E International (UK) Ltd & ORS*, [2207] EWHC 2981 (Ch) 14 December 2007, 2007 WL 4368227, available at http://www.bailii.org/ew/cases/EWHC/Ch/2007/2981.html.

[120] With respect to the Beximco and Musawi cases and related matters of import for the Islamic capital markets, see, among the many discussions, Nabil Saleh, *A Landmark Judgment of 23 January 2004 by the England and Wales Court of Appeal*, 19 ARAB LAW QUARTERLY 287 (2004), Kilian Bälz, *Shamil Bank of Bahrain v. Beximco Pharmaceuticals and Others*, YEAR BOOK OF ISLAMIC AND MIDDLE EASTERN LAW 509 (2002–2003), Andreas Junius, *Islamic Finance: Issues Surrounding Islamic Law as a Choice of Law under German Conflict of Laws Principles*, 7 CHICAGO JOURNAL OF INTERNATIONAL LAW 537 (2006–2007), Anowar Zahid and Hasani Mohd Ali, *Shariah as a Choice of Law in International Financial Contracts: Shamil Bank of Bahrain Case Revisited*, 10 US–CHINA LAW REVIEW 27 (2013), McMillen Enforceability, *supra* note 76, at 441–50, Geoffrey Fisher, *Sharia Law and Choice of Law Clauses in International Contracts*, 2005 LAWASIA JOURNAL 69, Aisha Nadar, *Islamic Finance and Dispute Resolution: Part 1*, 23 ARAB LAW QUARTERLY 1 (2009), Aisha Nadar, *Islamic Finance and Dispute Resolution: Part 2*, 23 ARAB LAW QUARTERLY 181 (2009), Julio C. Colon, *Choice of Law and Islamic Finance*, 46 TEXAS INTERNATIONAL LAW JOURNAL 411 (2011), Nicholas H. D. Foster, *Islamic Finance Law as an Emergent Legal System*, 21 ARAB LAW QUARTERLY 170 (2007), William Blair, *Global Financial Law*, 1 LAW AND FINANCIAL MARKET REVIEW 395 (2007), Nicholas Poon, *Choice of Law for Enforcement of Arbitral Awards: A Return to the Lex Loci Arbitri?*, SINGAPORE ACADEMY OF LAW JOURNAL 113 (2012), Jason C. T. Chuah, *Islamic Principles Governing International Trade Financing Instruments: A Study of the Morabaha in English Law*, 27 NORTHWESTERN

While affirming the widely-accepted concept that the law of a nation may govern a contract, the court notes that contracts may incorporate provisions of another foreign law or a set of rules as terms of the contract whose enforceability is to be determined by such national law, citing a leading text on conflicts of laws.[121]

Legal Opinions in Financing Transactions

As a condition precedent to closing a financial transaction, including *sukuk* and other capital market transactions, the parties will require that their outside counsel, or opposing outside counsel,[122] provide a series of legal opinions, including third-party opinions.[123] These legal opinions, and others discussed below (such as those pertaining

---

JOURNAL OF INTERNATIONAL LAW AND BUSINESS 137 (2006), Hdeel Abdelhady, *Islamic Law in Secular Courts (Again)*, 27 GPSOLO 36 (2010), Ibrahim Fadlallah, *Is There a Pro-Western Bias in Arbitral Awards*, 9 JOURNAL OF WORLD INVESTMENT AND TRADE 101 (2008), Bruno Zeller, *The UNIDROIT Principles of Contract Law: Is There Room for Their Inclusion into Domestic Contracts*, 26 JOURNAL OF LAW AND COMMERCE 115 (2006–2007), Zheng Tang, *Law Applicable in the Absence of Choice – The New Article 4 of the Rome I Regulation*, 71 MODERN LAW REVIEW 785 (2008), Saad U. Rizwan, *Foreseeable Issues and Hard Questions: The Implications of U.S. Courts Recognizing and Enforcing Foreign Arbitral Awards Applying Islamic Law under the New York Convention*, 98 CORNELL LAW REVIEW 493 (2013), and Russell Sandberg, *Musawi v R E International (UK) Ltd and ORS*, 160 LAW AND JUSTICE – THE CHRISTIAN LAW REVIEW 67 (2008). In simplistic summary, under the applicable legal principles, the Shari'ah is not the law of a nation, but rather a religious and moral code and does not meet the requisite specificity standards.

[121] *Beximco*, *supra* note 118, at paragraphs 48, citing Dicey and Morris, THE CONFLICT OF LAWS (13TH ED.), vol 2, at 32-086 and 32-087 (32-087 addresses the Harter Act and the Hague Rules), which draws the distinction between the law governing the contract and the contractual terms that are to be interpreted.

[122] The use of outside counsel to render these opinions is intended to assure the independence and integrity of the opinions, including through due diligence inquiries by the legal counsel rendering the opinion. See, e.g., Steven L. Schwarcz, *The Limits of Lawyering: Legal Opinions in Structured Finance*, 84 TEXAS LAW REVIEW 1 (2005) ('Schwarcz Legal Opinions'), at 9–10.

[123] The phrase 'third party legal opinions' refers to legal opinions rendered by legal counsel to an entity other than such counsel's client. In financing transactions, third party opinions 'have become far more prevalent than opinions directed to clients.' Schwarcz Legal Opinions, *id.*, at 9, with footnote 46 of that article citing further sources. The practice in financing transactions in the US is to have certain opinions (e.g. the remedies opinion) rendered to the party providing the financing and other transactional parties by counsel to the party obtaining the financing, while the UK practice is to have those opinions rendered to a party by its own counsel. The commonly quoted observation (does it yet approach an aphorism?) is brought to mind: 'When I want your opinion, I'll give it to you.'

Section 7(a) of the Securities Act requires a registration statement to include the information specified in Schedule A of the Securities Act. Paragraph 29 requires the filing of a copy of the legal opinion of counsel regarding the legality of the issue. See Item 601 of Regulation S-K, paragraph (b)(5), of the SEC, 17 Code of Federal Regulations § 229.601 (2003). This legal opinion is included as Exhibit 5 of the registration statement and is thus frequently referred to as an 'Exhibit 5 opinion'. Various legal opinions in the securities law context in SEC filings the United States, including with respect to certain categories of securities and types of offerings, are discussed in Task Force on Securities Law Opinions, American Bar Association Section of Business Law, *Legal Opinions in SEC Filings, Special Report of the Task Force on Securities Law Opinions*, 59 THE BUSINESS LAWYER 1505 (2004).

to true sales and substantive consolidation), are also prerequisites for the rating of capital markets instruments such as securitisations and *sukuk*.[124]

There are four general categories of legal opinions that are required:

1. Opinions addressing the due formation and valid existence of the participating entities under relevant applicable law, generally referred to as the 'entity authority' opinions.
2. Opinions addressing the validity, binding effect and enforceability of the relevant documents, generally referred to as the 'enforceability' or 'remedies' opinions. These are discussed in the succeeding sub-sections of this chapter.
3. Opinions addressing violations of law.
4. Opinions addressing specific matters of substantive law that pertain to the individual transaction (e.g. true sale, substantive consolidation, liens, fraudulent conveyances and a host of other substantive law opinions).[125]

The 'Enforceability' or 'Remedies' Opinion

'A remedies opinion deals with the question of whether the provisions of an agreement will be given effect by the courts.'[126] The essence of the enforceability or remedies opinion is that each of the 'undertakings',[127] in the contracts to which the client is a party, are enforceable under the designated law governing the contracts. The standard wording of

---

[124] See, e.g., Schwarcz Legal Opinions, *id.*, Ronald J. Gilson, *Value Creation by Business Lawyers: Legal Skills and Asset Pricing*, 94 YALE LAW JOURNAL 239, 274-77, Jonathan C. Lipson, *Price, Path & Pride: Third-Party Closing Opinion Practice Among U.S. Lawyers (A Preliminary Investigation)*, 3 BERKLEY BUSINESS LAW JOURNAL 59 (2005), Peter J. Gardner, *A Role for the Business Attorney in the Twenty-First Century: Adding Value to the Client's Enterprise in the Knowledge Economy*, 7 MARQUETTE INTELLECTUAL PROPERTY LAW REVIEW 17 (2003), Seminar, *Business Lawyers and Value Creation for Clients*, 74 OREGON LAW REVIEW 1 *et seq.* (1995), Steven L. Schwarcz, *Explaining the Value of Transactional Lawyering*, 12 STANFORD JOURNAL OF LAW AND BUSINESS 486 (2007), Steven L. Schwarcz, *Lawyers in the Shadows: The Transactional Lawyer in a World of Shadow Banking*, 63 AMERICAN UNIVERSITY LAW REVIEW 157 (2013), Jonathan R. Macey, THIRD PARTY LEGAL OPINIONS: EVALUATION AND ANALYSIS (1995), Scott FitzGibbon and Donald W. Glazer, FITZGIBBON AND GLAZER ON LEGAL OPINIONS (1992), Bryn Vaaler, *Bridging the Gap: Legal Opinions as an Introduction to Business Lawyering*, 61 UNIVERSITY OF MISSOURI KANSAS CITY LAW REVIEW 23 (1992), Kelly A. Love, *A Primer on Opinion Letters: Explanations and Analysis*, 9 TRANSACTIONS: THE TENNESSEE JOURNAL OF BUSINESS LAW 67 (2007–2008) ('Love Opinion Primer'), and Plank Securitizations, *supra* note 49. Lipson challenges the conventional economic analysis as incomplete given the persistence of opinion practice despite inefficiencies. He also notes that non-market factors, such as bar associations, rather than private innovation, appear to be the primary forces for improvement in opinion practice. Schwarcz posits that the value of lawyers in business transactions is primarily the reduction of regulatory costs.

[125] Enforceability opinions are addressed in McMillen Enforceability, *supra* note 76, at 448–58, DeLorenzo and McMillen, *supra* note 111, 168–91, and McMillen Islamic Capital Markets, *supra* note 76, at 153-55. This section draws from those sources. DeLorenzo and McMillen contains a generic example of an enforceability opinion for a Shari'ah-compliant financing transaction in a purely secular jurisdiction.

the opinion is that 'the agreements are valid and binding obligations of the Company, enforceable against the Company in accordance with their terms.'[128] This opinion is

---

[126] The TriBar Opinion Committee, *Third Party 'Closing' Opinions: A Report of the TriBar Opinion Committee*, 53 BUSINESS LAWYER 592 (1998) (the 'TriBar Report'), at 619, which has been supplemented by a range of reports, including The Tri-Bar Opinion Committee, *Special Report of the TriBar Opinion Committee: The Remedies Opinion – Deciding When to Include Exceptions and Assumptions*, 59 THE BUSINESS LAWYER 1483 (2003–2004) ('TriBar Remedies Report'). See also, TriBar Opinion Committee, *Opinions in the Bankruptcy Context: Rating Agency, Structured Financing, and Chapter 11 Transactions*, 46 THE BUSINESS LAWYER 718 (1991) (the 'TriBar Bankruptcy Report'), and Tri Bar Opinion Committee, *Special Report by the TriBar Opinion Committee: Use of the ABA Legal Opinion Accord in Specialized Financing Transactions*, 47 BUSINESS LAWYER 1720 (1992) (the 'TriBar Specialized Financing Report'). And see *Third-Party Legal Opinion Report*, including the *Legal Opinion Accord*, of the Section of Business Law, American Bar Association, 47 BUSINESS LAWYER 167 (1991) at Section 10, 'The Remedies Opinion,' and the definition of 'Remedies Opinion' in the Glossary thereof. See also *First Amended and Restated Report of the State Bar of Arizona Business Law Section Committee on Rendering Legal Opinions in Business Transactions*, October 20, 2004, 38 ARIZONA STATE LAW JOURNAL 47 (2006), and Ad Hoc Committee on Third-Party Legal Opinions, Business Law Section, Washington State Bar Association, *Report on Third-Party Legal Opinion Practice in the State of Washington* (1998), and *Supplemental Report on Third-Party Legal Opinion Practice in the State of Washington Covering Secured Lending Transactions – October 2000*, each available at http://wabuslaw.org/legal-opinion-reports.asp.

Opinions may be unqualified (or clean) or they may be 'qualified'. A qualified opinion is '[a]n opinion that is limited in a way that is not customary for transactions of the type involved'. TriBar Remedies Report, *id.*, at 1486, footnote 18. Opinions may also be 'reasoned' opinions. For example, true sale and non-consolidation opinions are usually reasoned opinions. Reasoned opinions usually state how a judge *should* or *would* rule, if certain assumptions and procedures are valid and the matter is properly presented and argued, on a particular matter and contain discussions of the current status of the law as well as the lack of relevant authority as to particular legal issues or matters. See, e.g., Love Opinion Primer, *supra* note 124, at 68–9.

[127] The TriBar Report, *id.*, at 621, notes that *all* undertakings in the agreements with respect to which the enforceability opinion relates are covered by the opinion. Coverage of all undertakings is based upon New York custom and practice, and the TriBar Report observes that not all jurisdictions interpret opinions in this manner. There are variances in opinion practice from one jurisdiction to another, and the precise formulations in an opinion must be carefully tailored to each jurisdiction. See, e.g., *1989 Report of the Committee on Corporations of the Business Law Section of the State of California Regarding Legal Opinions in Business Transactions*, 45 BUSINESS LAWYER 2169 (1990). The California report endorses a narrower definition of the scope of the enforceability opinion, limiting the coverage of the opinion to only 'material' provisions of the agreements.

[128] There are likely to be exceptions to this general statement of the opinion. Some exceptions, assumptions and limitations are specifically noted in the opinion. See TriBar Report, *id.*, at 620, TriBar Remedies Report, *supra* note 126, and DeLorenzo and McMillen, *supra* note 111, at 168–91. Because the remedies opinion is based upon 'the customary practice of lawyers who regularly give, and lawyers who regularly advise clients regarding, opinions of the kind involved', there are also many unstated exceptions, assumptions and limitations as well as unstated understandings as to matters that are not addressed by the remedies opinion. See TriBar Remedies Report, at 1484 (which includes the quoted language) *et seq*. The remedies opinion focuses, principally, but not exclusively, on the legal effect of the agreement's provisions as a matter of contract law in the specifically identified jurisdiction. TriBar Remedies Report, at 1486, note 22.

customarily delivered at the closing of the transaction as a condition precedent to the closing. Frequently, the opinion is delivered to specific parties to the transaction, often to third parties or parties other than the client of the lawyer that is rendering the opinion (e.g. a rating agency). Those who may rely upon the opinion are the specific addressees of the opinion and others that may be expressly permitted to rely upon the opinion pursuant to a reliance paragraph of the opinion.[129]

As noted in the TriBar Report and TriBar Remedies Report,[130] the remedies opinion covers three distinct, but related, matters: (i) it confirms that an agreement has been formed; (ii) it confirms that the remedies provided in the agreement will be given effect by the courts; and (iii) it describes the extent to which the courts will enforce the provisions of the agreement that are unrelated to the concept of breach.[131]

The remedies opinion addresses 'undertakings'. There are, as a general matter, three types of 'undertakings' in the contracts used in a financial transaction. They are (i) the 'obligations' provisions; (ii) the 'available remedies' provisions; and (iii) the 'ground rules' provisions.

The obligations provisions are those that obligate the company to perform an affirmative act, but say nothing about what will happen if it fails to perform those acts. An example from a lease is the provision requiring the lessee to pay rent. As applied to these provisions, the enforceability opinion 'means that a court will either require the company to fulfill its undertakings as written or grant damages or some other remedy in the event of a breach'.[132]

The 'available remedies' provisions are those specifying a remedy if the company fails to perform particular undertakings. The remedies may be affirmatively stated (e.g. the payment of liquidated damages) or, more frequently, set forth as the right of a party to take a specific action: 'For those provisions, the remedies opinion means that a court will give effect to the specified remedies as written.'[133]

The 'ground rules' provisions establish the basic rules for interpreting or administering an agreement and settling disputes under that agreement. Examples of these provisions include the governing law, choice of courts, notice, and waivers of rights provisions, all of which are actually undertakings of both parties to the agreement: 'Unless excepted from the opinion, these provisions are covered by the remedies opinion, which is

---

[129] See Schwarcz Legal Opinions, *supra* note 122, raising issues pertaining to the duties of a lawyer to the public, and not just to the addressees and those permitted to rely on an opinion. Schwarcz Legal Opinions also notes that others, such as accountants, at times cite legal opinions as their basis for advising on the characterization of certain transactions, such as structured financings being characterized as 'off-balance-sheet financings' based upon the legal opinions rendered as to true sale and non-consolidation.

[130] TriBar Report, *supra* note 126, at 620, and TriBar Remedies Report, *supra* note 126, at 1484.

[131] The remedies opinion (and other closing opinions) state, in the 'coverage limitation', that their coverage is limited to the law (and sometimes specific laws) of specific jurisdictions. See TriBar Report, *id.*, at 631, and TriBar Remedies Report, *id.*, at 1487, note 25.

[132] TriBar Report, *id.*, at 621. Note that a 'representation' in a contract is not an 'undertaking.'

[133] TriBar Report, *id.*, at 621. If the remedy is one that a court in the governing law jurisdiction will not enforce, the opinion will, and must, make an exception for the enforcement of that remedy.

understood to mean that a court will give effect to the provision as written and require the Company to abide by its terms.'[134]

Enforceability opinions in specialised financing transactions are subject to considerations that are not applicable to other enforceability opinions and to requirements for more explicit treatment of different legal topics in the legal opinion.[135] The types of transactions that are 'specialised financing transactions' are not specified in the TriBar Specialized Financing Report. The examples given are leveraged leases, sale–leaseback transactions, and other transactions that are 'reasoned'.[136]

Many Shari'ah-compliant transactions would be considered 'specialised financing transactions' for purposes of the TriBar Specialized Financing Report (and the 'Accord', as defined therein, of the American Bar Association). They involve a significant degree of structuring, the use of multiple agreements to effect the structure, the necessity of considering the entire set of project and financing agreements as a totality to clearly understand the agreement of the parties, the disregard of certain of the entities involved for the purposes of some laws, and multiple characterisations of the transaction.

Specific Substantive Legal Opinions

The issuance of private sector *sukuk*, other securitisations and other capital markets instruments (equity and debt) is critical to the long-term viability of the ICM. A necessary condition to those private sector issuances will be the obtaining of ratings from major international rating agencies. Obtaining those ratings, in turn, is dependent upon obtaining the requisite legal opinions from prominent law firms engaged in these issuance transactions. The major rating agencies have developed ratings criteria that require legal opinions for specific substantive areas of law.[137] Those criteria serve as a paradigm for studying the legal issues that will affect the development and growth of the capital markets, including the secondary markets.[138] The focus of this sub-section, coinciding with the focus of the rating agencies, is on the legal structure of the transaction and the legal opinions with respect to the transaction. Although also of critical import, non-legal matters (such as the credit quality of assets, obligors and enhancers) are ignored.

As previously discussed in connection with securitisations, a *sukuk* transaction involves (a) an asset (payment rights) originator, (b) a *sukuk* issuer SPV, (c) the parent of the issuer, (d) obligors (payors) in respect of the securitised assets, and (e) *sukuk* holders, among others. The asset originator transfers the assets to be securitised to the issuer SPV. The issuer SPV sells *sukuk* to the *sukuk* holders and uses the proceeds of

---

[134] TriBar Report, *id.*, at 621.

[135] See the TriBar Specialized Financing Report, *supra* note 1246.

[136] TriBar Specialized Financing Report, *id.*, at 1726. See also TriBar Bankruptcy Report, *id.*, at 734–36, discussing reasoned and unqualified opinions as to bankruptcy matters in structured financings, including securitisations (and thus *sukuk*).

[137] See the sources at note 41, *supra*.

[138] Other important legal principles are not considered in this chapter, largely because of the tremendous diversity across jurisdictions. These include laws pertaining to tax, real estate, competition, and corporations and other entities, among many others.

that sale to pay the originator for the transferred assets. Over time, the obligors make payments to the issuer SPV who then transfers those payments to the *sukuk* holders.

As a general structural matter, the securitised assets must be isolated for the benefit of the *sukuk* or other holders. In the simplest case, the critical elements are: (i) that all right, title, interest, and estate in and to the securitised assets are transferred in a true sale by the originator to a bankruptcy-remote SPV; and (ii) that SPV grants a first priority perfected (or perfectible) security interest over those assets to secure payments on the *sukuk* or other issued security and other claims of the *sukuk* holders or other holders. Thus, there will be a careful examination of (A) the transfer of the assets from the originator to the SPV, (B) the priority, perfection, and enforceability of the security interests granted in the securitised assets provided as collateral for the benefit of the *sukuk* or other holders, and (C) various bankruptcy-related matters (such as non-consolidation) that may result in modification of the arrangements to which the parties have agreed. This examination focuses on the transactional documentation and the issuance of the legal opinions as to specific matters of relevant substantive law.[139]

In an asset-backed *sukuk* transaction, the following are the primary areas addressed by the legal opinions: (1) true sale of the securitised assets; (2) lien-free transfer of the securitised assets; (3) non-consolidation of the assets in bankruptcy; (4) the collateral security structure; (5) enforceability of the transactional documents; (6) choice of law; and (7) enforcement of judgements and awards. There may be other legal opinions as well, including as to other aspects affecting bankruptcy remoteness.

As a summary statement, in most Shari'ah-incorporated jurisdictions lawyers are not able, at the present time, to render satisfactory legal opinions on many (sometimes any) of the foregoing matters. This inhibits ratings of securities, such as *sukuk*, and thus development of the capital markets. A significant amount of work needs to be undertaken on the legal and regulatory infrastructure, both substantive and procedural, in each of these areas. Some of the more common elements of the items listed in clauses (1) through (4) are reviewed in this section; they are largely matters of local law. In the next section, consideration is given to items (6) and (7); these relate to the broader systemic framework (although they also clearly include local substantive and procedural aspects).

Before considering specific opinion topics, it is important to be mindful that the issuer of the securities in a capital markets transaction is usually an SPV (a wholly-owned subsidiary or other affiliate of the issuer or a trust or unaffiliated corporation) established for the purposes of the financing transaction. The SPV is restricted—usually rigorously restricted—in its activities to participation in the specific financing venture: thus the term 'special purpose vehicle' or 'special purpose entity'. It is usually newly created, and thus has no pre-existing liabilities and only a single creditor—the holders of the *sukuk* or other securities issued by the issuer SPV.[140] The separateness of the SPV

---

[139] This discussion makes no pretence at comprehensiveness. There are numerous other opinion matters that must be addressed in any specific transaction. See, e.g., TriBar Bankruptcy Report, *supra* note 126, which discusses, among other matters, fraudulent conveyances, asset transfers (other than true sale concepts), mandatory stays, advance restrictions on access to bankruptcy, preference matters, court orders approving sales of property during bankruptcy proceedings, and temporary restraints.

[140] In some transactions, there may be a very limited number of other creditors, who are usually specifically identified.

from all other entities and the 'bankruptcy remoteness' of the SPV are critical to the structure, and to the rating, and thus to the pricing.

Bankruptcy remoteness is an amalgamation of concepts (including some that overlap with true sale and substantive consolidation concepts) that focus on minimising the possibility of the initiation of a bankruptcy proceeding against the issuer.[141]

The threshold set of documentary provisions relating to bankruptcy remoteness restrict the business purpose and activities of the issuer SPV exclusively to the specific financing transaction (say, a *sukuk* transaction). These include both affirmative and negative statements of the business purpose of the various entities (particularly the issuer SPV) as well as permissible and prohibited activities of the entities. Rating agencies frequently require that these provisions be included in both the constitutional documents of the issuer SPV and the transactional documents. The required legal opinion will then have to indicate that these provisions will be binding upon the relevant party or parties. The 'separateness covenants' are further provisions of this nature (these also go to the issue of substantive consolidation, and specifically to non-consolidation).[142]

---

[141] In addition to bankruptcy remoteness provisions discussed in the text, there are also requirements for provisions (a) limiting recourse for payments and indemnities to only the securitised assets (and applicable credit enhancements), (b) mandating that the priority of payments set forth in the documents shall govern in all cases, and (c) to the effect that, after full realisation on all securitised assets (and credit enhancements), all payment and indemnity claims are extinguished. These also must be analysed carefully. See also the factors referenced in note 142, *infra*, and the related text.

[142] Separateness covenants frequently require the issuer to: (i) maintain a separate office; (ii) keep separate corporate records; (iii) hold separate board of directors meetings in accordance with specific schedules and legal requirements; (iv) not commingle assets with any other entities; (v) conduct business in its own name; (vi) provide financial statements that are separate from other entities; (vii) pay all liabilities out of its own funds; (viii) maintain strict arm's-length relationships with parent and affiliated entities; (ix) not issue any guarantees; (x) use its own stationery, invoices, checks, and other documents and instruments; (xi) not pledge its assets for the benefit of any other entity; and (xii) hold itself out as separate from its parent and affiliates. This is an area where special care should be exercised. Many of these provisions, in their standard conventional formulations, cannot be implemented in Shari'ah-compliant transactions without modification (and rating agencies resist modifications). This is particularly true where an accommodation title holder is involved (as in an *ijara* transaction). There is, for example, an intermingling of assets as between the lessor (owned by the title holder accommodation party) and the lessee for various tax, regulatory and other purposes, and ownership may be differently characterised for different purposes. Both the lessor and the lessee will grant security interests in the property and their respective interests. The financial statements of the lessee may indicate lessee ownership of the asset despite title being in the lessor. The lessee will frequently have essentially all financial burdens (including those of asset ownership). And the transactions between the lessor and the lessee are not arm's-length. See McMillen, Islamic Finance, *supra* note 20, at 189–227 for a description of a widely-used *ijara* (lease) transaction and various ownership, tax, collateral security and other characterisations and structures.

In both Shari'ah-compliant and conventional transactions, an issue arises as a result of the tension between bankruptcy remoteness on the one hand, and laws pertaining to enterprise liability and corporate governance on the other hand. Consider, for example, corporate governance laws pertaining to *ultra vires* acts of directors of a corporation. Under the laws of some jurisdictions, a director is personally liable for *ultra vires* acts and an indemnification of the director

Whether the foregoing is an appropriate or comprehensive list in any given jurisdiction, or needs to be modified or supplemented in any given jurisdiction, will depend upon a substantive analysis of the specific laws and regulations of each jurisdiction. Those determinations must be made in connection with the structuring of the capital markets (e.g. *sukuk*) transaction and in connection with the rendering of legal opinions.

The analysis of the rating agency requirements in a Shari'ah-compliant transaction is both different from and more complex than the same analysis in a conventional securitisation. The rating agency requirements were developed in the context of a Western interest-based system and its laws and regulations, usually in a purely secular jurisdiction. Most of the early criteria were developed with a focus on, and sensitivity to, the laws of the US and its various states because securitisation was initially developed in the US. Adaptation to the laws of different Shari'ah-incorporated jurisdictions entails a careful analysis of the bases for the existing ratings criteria in light of (a) the differences between the legal regimes, and (b) the fundamental nature of Shari'ah-compliant transactions such as *sukuk* issuances. It is likely that there will be some (negotiated) modifications to the ratings criteria. It is also likely that there will need to be further accommodations to different aspects of the legal regimes, including both substantive and procedural elements, in Shari'ah-incorporated jurisdictions.

Another, more obvious, set of bankruptcy remoteness provisions that are included in most financings relate to non-competition and bankruptcy declarations. The originator, investors, credit enhancers, and others agree in the transaction documents not to initiate involuntary bankruptcy proceedings against the issuer. The issuer also provides, in both its constitutional documents and the transaction documents, not to initiate voluntary bankruptcy proceedings. The substantive and procedural laws of each jurisdiction must be studied to determine whether there are limitations on these types of provisions and how to best implement these concepts in any given jurisdiction.[143]

True Sale

The true sale opinion addresses the issue of whether the issuer SPV purchaser owns the transferred assets or, more specifically, whether the transfer of the income-producing assets from the originator to the issuer SPV will be recognised in a bankruptcy proceeding involving the originator or other transferor of the assets.[144] This is one of two legal concepts that are crucial to isolation of income-producing assets from the risk of the bankruptcy of the originator entity (the other is substantive consolidation, or non-consolidation, in jurisdictions where this concept is present).

---

for violation of those acts, by the corporation or otherwise, is invalid. In the *sukuk* context, if the separateness covenants are included in the constitutional documents, any breach (however immaterial) of the covenants will constitute an *ultra vires* act. In *sukuk* structures, officers of banks, financial institutions (including Islamic financial institutions) and other primary market participants are frequently directors of one or more of the transactional entities. Careful consideration must be given to the legal provisions that relate to corporate governance issues and to how those provisions interact with different Shari'ah-compliant financing structures.

[143] See, e.g., TriBar Bankruptcy Report, *supra* note 126, at 729–30.

[144] See the discussion in the section of this chapter entitled 'Securitisation (Including Sukuk) – True Sales'. For present purposes, it is assumed that the originator is the transferor.

The true sale opinion customarily states that, under the facts and circumstances set forth in the opinion, and in a properly presented and argued proceeding, a bankruptcy court would hold that the transferred payment rights would not be included in the estate of the transferor of those rights or would hold that the transfer of those rights was a sale and not a pledge to secure a debt (or both of the foregoing). As with the substantive consolidation opinion letter, there are various assumptions made in the opinion, and there is a discussion of the relevant case law and statutory law, including a discussion of the application of the relevant law to the relevant facts. These are reasoned opinions.

A related element of the true sale inquiry focuses on the nature of the title to the transferred assets. Many securitisations (including *sukuk*) involve an unperfected transfer of an equitable interest in the assets, rather than a perfected transfer. This is often the case if one of the requirements for perfection of title transfer is that the payor must be notified of the transfer, which is costly, time-consuming and often unpalatable in terms of public relations considerations. In contemporary *sukuk* transactions, sovereign issuers are extremely reluctant, or not permitted by applicable law, to engage in perfected transfers of the assets that underlie the *sukuk* issuance. The transfer must then be perfectible at the election of the issuer SPV.

Two general inquiries must be made in connection with the perfection aspects. First, what are the requirements for a perfected transfer of title under applicable local laws? Second, can a subsequently perfectible title transfer be made under the relevant legal regime and, if so, what are the requirements for subsequent perfection? The answers to these inquiries will then have to be considered in light of the position of the Shari'ah scholars as to whether a separation of legal and equitable title to the securitised assets is permissible. There has been some debate on this issue among prominent Shari'ah scholars, but the weight of opinion seems to acknowledge the permissibility of such a separation of title. Note, in this context, that one of the fundamental premises of the trust is such a separation of legal and equitable title. If separation of legal and equitable title is not permissible, legal title would have to be transferred in a manner that satisfies all of the applicable perfection requirements (including notification of the payor).

Substantive Consolidation (Non-Consolidation)

As previously discussed, substantive consolidation is an equitable doctrine in which the assets and liabilities of one or more entities are combined and treated for bankruptcy purposes as a single entity.[145] In a securitisation or *sukuk*, a substantive consolidation would defeat a major premise of the rating – that the ABS holders or *sukuk* holders can look to the assets segregated in the SPV asset pool without regard to the bankruptcy of the originator of those assets.

Thus, the second crucial aspect of isolation of the income-producing assets is non-consolidation (in jurisdictions that address this concept in one manner or another): the legal separateness of the issuer SPV will be respected in the event of the bankruptcy of the originator, the servicer and/or any other affiliated entity such that the income-producing assets of the issuer SPV will not be drawn back into the bankruptcy proceeding

---

[145] See Gilbert, *supra* note 59. See the section of this chapter entitled 'Securitisations (Including Sukuk) – Substantive Consolidation'.

through the court's power of substantive consolidation. Substantive consolidation opinions (referred to as 'non-consolidation letters' in practice) are often required in connection with securitisation, including *sukuk*, and other structured finance transactions.[146] Customarily, they are rendered to the ratings agencies. An inability to provide the non-consolidation opinion is likely to result in a lower rating (usually below investment grade), with a consequent increase in the pricing of the transaction, possibly to an extent that jeopardises the economic viability of the financing transaction.

The non-consolidation legal opinion states that, in the opinion of the rendering counsel, the SPV will not be substantively consolidated with the originator in the event of the originator's bankruptcy filing, assuming certain steps and procedures are following in the formation and operation of the SPV. These steps and procedures are usually responsive to the tests and standards of the courts in the relevant jurisdiction. For example, they may be structured to avoid an 'identity of interest': between the originator and the issuer SPV.[147] The non-consolidation letter frequently details the factors considered by the relevant courts in determining whether substantive consolidation should be granted. These letters also discuss (a) the equitable remedy nature of substantive consolidation and its discretionary nature, (b) the fact that different courts weight different factual matters differently, (c) the assumptions regarding separateness that must be (and are assumed to have been) drafted into the relevant documents, (d) the assumptions regarding certain objective factual matters of relevance that must be (and are assumed to have been) drafted into the relevant documents,[148] (e) various other subjective or conclusory facts that are assumed in connection with the rendering of the letter, (f) assumptions regarding the absence of factors that are inconsistent with other express assumptions, and (g) qualifications regarding the absence of cases on point with the instant transaction and uncertainties that exist in regard to the rendering of the substantive consolidation letter.[149]

Lien-Free Transfer

Another aspect of the sale analysis relates to whether the transfer of the securitised assets from the originator to the issuer has been made in such a manner that the assets are transferred free and clear of all prior overriding liens. This entails an examination of the nature of liens and the effects of different types of liens under applicable local

---

[146] See Tribar Bankruptcy Report, *supra* note 126, particularly at 725–27, and *Special Report on the Preparation of Substantive Consolidation Opinions, By the Committee on Structured Finance and the Committee on Bankruptcy and Corporate Reorganization of The Association of the Bar of the City of New York*, 53 THE BUSINESS LAWYER 411 (2008–2009) (the 'NYC Bar Bankruptcy Report'). This chapter does not differentiate the many variants of bankruptcy-related actions, such as insolvency, moratorium, receivership, and the like, and, as previously noted, the term 'bankruptcy' is here used to include insolvency. The precise proceedings available or applicable in any given jurisdiction must be carefully considered in structuring any capital markets instrument.

[147] If the identity of interest test is of relevance, as in jurisdictions that apply some variant of the tests set forth in Vecco, *supra* note 62.

[148] See note 146, *supra*, and related text.

[149] See TriBar Bankruptcy Report, *supra* note 126, at 726–27. Frequently, the rating agencies require that assumptions relating to factual matters are supported by factual certificates or documentary covenants.

laws, including the Shari'ah, where appropriate. This jurisdiction-specific examination also will be considered in the relevant legal opinions and is a critical ratings criterion.

Collateral Security Structures

Consideration of the collateral security structure is a critical factor under the ratings criteria, and the subject of legal opinions, in transactions in virtually every jurisdiction. The primary focus is on the type and nature of security interests provided for the benefit of the instrument (e.g. *sukuk*) holders. Those security interests must be first priority (there can be no prior claims) and perfected (or perfectible, if the laws of the relevant jurisdiction so permit). The legal opinions must address the nature of the security interest, its enforceability against third parties, and perfection requirements (such as notices, registration and recordation). The effects of bankruptcy on perfection must also be considered and opined upon. Again, this will entail a careful jurisdiction-specific study of both substantive and procedural laws and regulations, with modifications for each jurisdiction.

This also is a problematic area for Shari'ah-compliant transactions. In many Shari'ah-incorporated jurisdictions the legal regime for collateral security is currently unclear, under-developed (often significantly), or undeveloped.[150] The substantive principles of the law pertaining to security interests are frequently limited. Consider, for example, the possessory nature of security interests (*rahn*: mortgage or pledge) in some of these jurisdictions. A possession-based system, including its prohibitions on grantor use of the encumbered assets, makes it difficult to effect a collateral security structure for *sukuk* transactions. Further, in many jurisdictions of relevance, the perfection and lien priority concepts are undeveloped. Recordation and notice concepts are also frequently absent or of very limited development and application. And, given the state of development of bankruptcy laws (limited), it is difficult to know how security interests will be treated in the bankruptcy context.

Because of these factors, among others, most law firms have found it impossible to render satisfactory opinions on the priority, perfection and other aspects of security interests in most of these jurisdictions.

Legal Infrastructure in Shari'ah-Incorporated Jurisdictions

The general structure of each of the relevant legal systems is of primary relevance to the ability to effect capital markets transactions and thus to the growth and development of the ICM. As a systemic matter, some of the key structural elements that are of relevance are (a) whether the relevant legal regime is based upon a system of *stare decisis* (binding precedents), (b) whether judicial, regulatory and arbitral decisions, and the rationale for those decisions, are published and widely available (in some jurisdictions, whether they are ever available), (c) whether the judicial structure is responsive to continuity and consistency in the application of judicial precedents, (d) the timeframe for enforcement of remedies within the system, and (e) whether *ex post facto* legislation is permissible in a given jurisdiction.

In summary, many of the key structural elements of the legal regime with respect to the foregoing matters are absent or insufficiently developed in jurisdictions of interest for this chapter. The concept of binding precedent is often totally absent. Decisions

---

[150] See McMillen Collateral Security and McMillen Rahn, each *supra* note 113.

are rarely published. In many jurisdictions, each case is considered *de novo* and without regard to other decisions that have been rendered in similar cases. Judges and other adjudicators are afforded wide discretion in determining cases. And the timeframe for enforcement is frequently so long that it precludes effective remedies in fast-moving markets such as the capital markets. *Ex post facto* legislation is often permissible.

Each of these factors is frequently cited by both capital markets lawyers and by international capital markets institutions as a reason for their reluctance to engage in capital markets initiatives in jurisdictions of relevance to the ICM, and particularly so in the case of private sector issuances. These are substantial impediments to growth of the capital markets, including secondary markets, in these jurisdictions, and there should be immediate focus on the removal, or a satisfactory alleviation, of these impediments. Transactional accommodation is not possible in most instances.

If a survey is made of legal opinion practices in Shari'ah-incorporated jurisdictions, it is clear that legal opinions are often deficient because of these systemic factors, as well as the substantive and procedural factors noted in the preceding sub-section. The types of opinion exceptions that are taken in these jurisdictions include the following:

1. the permissibility of *ex post facto* legislation precludes certainty and predictability;
2. the Shari'ah is comprised of general principles, rather than specific legal requirements, and, as such, it is difficult to ascertain how the Shari'ah will be applied in any specific transaction;
3. different *madhahib* interpret relevant Shari'ah principles and precepts differently, and inconsistently, resulting in similar uncertainties as to application in any given transaction;
4. the lack of uniform statements of relevant Shari'ah principles and precepts, even within a given *madhhab*;
5. the lack of binding precedents and published decisions, further exacerbating uncertainties as to application of even agreed-upon Shari'ah principles and precepts;
6. the great degree of discretion in a court in these jurisdictions;
7. the uncertainty of remedies within these jurisdictions;
8. the uncertainty of the application of choice of law principles in these jurisdictions; and
9. the fact that many of these jurisdictions will not enforce foreign judgements and, even where they will enforce foreign arbitral awards, may infuse the Shari'ah into a review of that award pursuant to public policy doctrines.[151]

Some of the foregoing relate to the current degree of elucidation of the Shari'ah itself, at least in a transparent and easily and broadly accessible form. If the Shari'ah principles, and their application, are not transparent, certain, predictable and stable then the secular legal regime (which applies the Shari'ah principles) is not transparent,

---

[151] See the discussion of enforcement of foreign judgements and awards at McMillen Islamic Project Finance, *supra* note 18, at 1199–203, and the sources cited therein. Although this aspect of enforcement is not discussed in any detail in this chapter, it is important to note that considerable uncertainty exists regarding the enforcement of judgements and awards, and the exceptions and exclusions proposed in legal opinions have rendered those opinions insufficient for ratings criteria purposes.

certain, predictable and stable. To date, the rating agencies and the lawyers who have been asked to provide enforceability opinions have been of the opinion that there is insufficient predictability and certainty to permit the rendering of adequate enforceability opinions in these jurisdictions.

The absence of binding precedents and published legal decisions, the degree of judicial discretion, and the permissibility of *ex post facto* legislation are systemic structural matters that are easily addressed if there is the requisite political will and consensus. However, that consensus has been lacking to date. Addressing those fundamental systemic matters would go far towards addressing some of the more substantive legal issues, such as the certainty of available remedies and the matters discussed in this section. Clearly, more needs to be done at the substantive legal and regulatory level.

Consider, as an example, the choice of law opinions that are required in connection with rating of *sukuk* transactions. The opinion must be to the effect that the choice of law will be upheld as valid by enforcing authorities in at least (i) the jurisdiction whose law has been chosen as governing the transactional documentation, (ii) the jurisdiction(s) whose law governs the formation of each of the entities involved in the transaction, and (iii) the jurisdiction in which the assets are located or security interests or security rights in those assets are taken. The analysis of these complex legal opinions is beyond the scope of this chapter, other than to note that this is an area that is deserving of immediate attention in connection with any effort to develop the ICM. As a point of beginning, the choice of law principles in many of the jurisdictions of concern in this report are, at best, unclear and need to be addressed.

Another important factor pertains to whether foreign judgements and arbitral awards will be enforced in any given jurisdiction. Enforcement of foreign judgements and awards often turns on recognition reciprocity as between the two jurisdictions. This also is a legal opinion issue in any capital markets transaction. Some jurisdictions will not enforce foreign judgements and arbitral awards. Some will enforce foreign arbitral awards, but not foreign judgements. In some jurisdictions, the extent and degree of enforcement of foreign judgements and awards is not entirely clear.[152]

Shari'ah-compliant transactions raise these issues in particularly poignant ways. Consider, for example, enforcement of a foreign judgement or award that was rendered or obtained in a purely secular jurisdiction in a Shari'ah-incorporated jurisdiction, and *vice versa*. Will the judgement or award be reviewed *de novo*, in whole or in part, upon attempted enforcement in the Shari'ah-incorporated jurisdiction to determine (x) whether the Shari'ah should have been utilised in reaching the initial decision and/or (y) whether the Shari'ah precludes or limits enforcement in some way? Even in a jurisdiction that is a signatory to the New York Convention on the Enforcement of Arbitral Awards,[153] this issue may arise due to the 'public policy' exception in that Convention.

---

[152] See McMillen Islamic Project Finance, *id.*, at 1195–203, and the sources cited therein, for a discussion of enforcement mechanisms in the Kingdom of Saudi Arabia.

[153] Convention on the Recognition and Enforcement of Foreign Arbitral Awards, United Nations Conference on International Commercial Arbitration, 1958, with the English language version located at http://www.uncitral.org/pdf/english/texts/arbitration/NY-conv/XXII_1_e.pdf.

The question would be whether the Shari'ah is itself a matter of public policy in the enforcing jurisdiction. The answer to this question, and a host of related questions, is unclear. As is the obverse inquiry: will a purely secular jurisdiction decline to enforce a judgement or award rendered in a Shari'ah-incorporated jurisdiction where the basis of the judgement or award is a Shari'ah interpretation of terms not included in the relevant contract?

Clearly, the choice of law and foreign judgement and award enforcement aspects of existing legal and regulatory regimes need to be reconsidered in the context of the expansion and global capital markets integration of Shari'ah-compliant financings.

CONCLUSION

The most rapidly growing area of Islamic finance is ICM activity. This trend is likely to continue unabated for the foreseeable future. The growth is occurring in an environment that has been structured in accordance with interest-based principles, and continues to be dominated by those principles. In particular, interest-based principles underlie and permeate the legal and regulatory regimes to which ICM instruments and activities are subject. This also is likely to be the state of the world for the foreseeable future, whatever growth there might be in ICM activity.

Like the development of securitisation, the development of the ICM (take *sukuk* as a primary example) is occurring in the interstices of existing law and regulatory regimes: regimes to which the ICM will always be subject. This results in distorting stresses and accommodations, given the differently-premised underlying principles. But it also fosters creativity and inventiveness within, and opportunities for, the Islamic finance industry. The ICM industry is adapting, accommodating and growing despite the absence of legal and regulatory regimes that are directly and responsively supportive.

And, like the developmental process that responded (and responds) to securitisations, the legal and regulatory regimes are taking cognisance of, and have initiated sensitive accommodations to, the principles of the Shari'ah that underlie and permeate ICM activity. Awareness seems greatest among central banks and bank and financial regulators. In both purely secular jurisdictions and Shari'ah-incorporated jurisdictions, central banks and bank and financial regulators are initiating, and implementing, legal and regulatory accommodations that are responsive to Islamic finance in a manner that is designed to provide a level playing field for both Shari'ah-compliant and interest-based activities. This has been driven, to a significant degree, by standard setting organisations within the Islamic finance realm (which illustrates the potential for future initiatives).

The response is more muted in the realm of capital markets and securities regulation and capital markets and securities laws. This also presents opportunities for the Islamic finance industry. The ICM industry, in particular, and as a result of its growing financial presence, should take a leading role in spearheading reform in capital markets and securities laws and regulations with the objective of increasing responsiveness to the Shari'ah imperatives that guide a significant portion of the globe's population. Moreover, the ICM industry *must* assume this role if it is to expand beyond its current reliance on sovereign issuances and sovereign credits so as to encompass that significant portion of the globe's population.

The ICM must, for example, address the impediments to private sector involvement in the capital markets. Many of the impediments in the legal and regulatory realms are clear, at least as a matter of identification, if not yet as a matter of precise analysis and implementing formulations. For example, it is clear that bankruptcy (including insolvency) regimes are in a dreadful state in many jurisdictions of immediate and longer-term relevance to the ICM. As are collateral security regimes (which are critical to expanded involvement of small- and medium-sized entities). As are capital markets and securities legal and regulatory regimes. Each at a different level and each at a different stage of development.

Just these examples make clear that the issues faced by the ICM industry (and the broader Islamic finance industry) are the same as those faced by the 'conventional' interest-based (read 'established') capital markets industry. The state of the bankruptcy and collateral security regimes is equally a hindrance to both the established and ICM industries.

This cries out 'opportunity', even 'unparalleled opportunity'. It is an opportunity for participants in the ICM industry to be at the table at inception, to assist in the formation and formulation of these regimes (which affect both established and Islamic industries) from inception. And this, of course, allows for these regimes to be shaped from inception so as to be sensitive and responsive to both the established and the ICM industries from first principles. This opportunity is not always available: witness the third example (capital markets and securities legal and regulatory regimes), where the development of sensitivity and responsiveness to Shari'ah principles will have to proceed as something more akin to an amendatory process.

But what does seem apparent, whether the process is from-inception or amendatory, is that the ICM industry should be at the table. Given the lethargy, inertia and lack of will that has long existed in developing these various regimes (bankruptcy and collateral security being prime examples), the ICM industry *should* take the lead in seeking reform and development, and *must* do so if it is to deliver its potential benefits to the larger population. The ICM industry, having seized the moment to develop, should seize this moment. The undertaking will further global cooperation and mutual benefit. Possibly, there will come a time, even in the near future, when the 'established' capital markets industry will include the ICM industry.

BIBLIOGRAPHY

Abdelhady, Hdeel, *Islamic Law in Secular Courts (Again)*, 27 GPSolo 36 (2010)

Adam, Nathif J., and Abdulkader Thomas, eds., Islamic Bonds: Your Guide to Issuing, Structuring and Investing in *Sukuk* (2004)

_____, *Islamic Fixed-Income Securities: Sukuk*, in Islamic Asset Management: Forming the Future for Shari'a-Compliant Investment Strategies, Sohail Jaffer, ed. (2004)

Aggarwal, Reena, Allen Ferrell and Jonathan Katz, *U.S. Securities Regulation in a World of Global Exchanges*, Discussion Paper No. 569, JOHN M. OLIN CENTER FOR LAW, ECONOMICS AND BUSINESS, HARVARD UNIVERSITY (December 2006)

Aghion, Philippe, and Benjamin Hermalin, *Legal Restrictions on Private Contracts Can Enhance Efficiency*, 6 JOURNAL OF LAW, ECONOMICS AND ORGANIZATION 381 (1990)

Akerlof, George A., *The Market for 'Lemons': Quality Uncertainty and the Market Mechanism*, 84 THE QUARTERLY JOURNAL OF ECONOMICS 488 (1970)

Ali, S. Nazim, ed., ISLAMIC FINANCE: CURRENT REGULATORY AND LEGAL ISSUES (2005)

Allchurch, Matthew, *Fosters Closes Australia's First Whole Business Securitization*, 23 INTERNATIONAL FINANCIAL LAW REVIEW 19 (2004)

Amera, Seth D., and Alan Kolod, *Substantive Consolidation: Getting Back to Basics*, 14 AMERICAN BANKRUPTCY INSTITUTE LAW REVIEW 1 (2006)

American Bar Association, Section of Business Law, *Third-Party Legal Opinion Report, including the Legal Opinion Accord*, 47 BUSINESS LAWYER 167 (1991)

Anabtawi, Iman, and Steven L. Schwarcz, *Regulating Systemic Risk: Towards an Analytical Framework*, 86 NOTRE DAME LAW REVIEW 1349 (2011)

Archer, Simon, and Rifaat Ahmed Abdel Karim, eds., ISLAMIC FINANCE: THE REGULATORY CHALLENGE (2007)

Ariff, Mohamed, Meysam Safari and Shamsher Mohamad, *Sukuk Securities, Their Definitions, Classification and Pricing Issues* (May 3, 2012) available at http://ssrn.com/abstract=2097847

Arnholz, John, and Edward E. Gainor, OFFERINGS OF ASSET-BACKED SECURITIES (2007)

Ashcraft, Adam B., and Til Schuermann, *Understanding the Securitization of Subprime Mortgage Credit*, FEDERAL RESERVE BANK OF NEW YORK STAFF REPORTS, NUMBER 318 (March 2008), available at http://papers.ssrn.com/sol3/papers.cfm?abstract_id=1071189

The Association of the Bar of the City of New York, Committee on Structured Finance and Committee on Bankruptcy and Corporate Reorganization, *Special Report on the Preparation of Substantive Consolidation Opinions*, 64 THE BUSINESS LAWYER 411 (2008–2009)

Awad, Abed, and Robert E. Michaels, *Iflas and Chapter 11: Classical Islamic Law and Modern Bankruptcy*, 44 THE INTERNATIONAL LAWYER 975 (2010)

Ayotte, Kenneth, and Stav Gaon, *Asset-Backed Securities: Costs and Benefits of 'Bankruptcy Remoteness'*, 24 THE REVIEW OF FINANCIAL STUDIES 1299 (2011)

Bagaria, Soma, *Substance v. Form Conflict in True Sale: Hong Kong Court Goes by the Language Used by the Parties* (2012), available at http://ssrn.com/abstract=2042559

Bailey, Warren, Haitao Li, Connie X. Mao and Rui Zhong, *Regulation Fair Disclosure and Earnings Information: Market, Analyst, and Corporate Responses*, 58 THE JOURNAL OF FINANCE 2487 (2003)

_____, G. Andrew Karolyi and Carolina Salva, *The Economic Consequences of Increased Disclosure: Evidence from International Cross-Listings*, 81 JOURNAL OF FINANCIAL ECONOMICS 175 (2006)

Baiman, Stanley, and Robert E. Verrecchia, *The Relation Among Capital Markets, Financial Disclosure, Production Efficiency, and Insider Trading*, 34 JOURNAL OF ACCOUNTING RESEARCH 1 (1996)

Baird, Douglas G., *Substantive Consolidation Today*, 47 BOSTON COLLEGE LAW REVIEW 5 (2005–2006)

Bälz, Kilian, *Shamil Bank of Bahrain v. Beximco Pharmaceuticals and Others*, YEAR BOOK OF ISLAMIC AND MIDDLE EASTERN LAW 509 (2002–2003)

Barnes, Shaun, Kathleen G. Cully and Steven L. Schwarcz, *In-House Counsel's Role in Structuring Mortgage-Backed Securities*, 2012 WISCONSIN LAW REVIEW 521

Berringer, John B., and Dennis J. Artese, *The ABCs of Substantive Consolidation*, 121 BANK-RUPTCY LAW JOURNAL 640 (2004)

Barry, Christopher B., and Stephen J. Brown, *Differential Information and Security Market Equilibrium*, 20 THE JOURNAL OF FINANCIAL AND QUANTITATIVE ANALYSIS 407 (1985)

Beach, Joseph W., *The Saudi Arabian Capital Market Law: A Practical Study of the Creation of Law in Developing Markets*, 41 STANFORD JOURNAL OF INTERNATIONAL LAW 307 (2005)

Becker, Gary, *Crime and Punishment: An Economic Approach*, 76 JOURNAL OF POLITICAL ECONOMY 169 (1968)

Begman, Nittai K., *Investor Protection and the Coasian View*, MIT SLOAN WORKING PAPER 4476-04 (October 2004)

Ben-Shahar, Omri, and Carl E. Schneider, *The Failure of Mandated Disclosure*, 159 UNIVERSITY OF PENNSYLVANIA LAW REVIEW 647 (2010–2011)

Benmelech, Efraim, and Jennifer Dlugosz, *The Alchemy of CDO Ratings*, 56 JOURNAL OF MONETARY ECONOMICS 617 (2009)

Benston, George J., *An Appraisal of the Costs and Benefits of Government-Required Disclosure: SEC and FTC Requirements*, 41 LAW AND CONTEMPORARY PROBLEMS 30 (1977)

_____, *Required Periodic Disclosure Under the Securities Acts and the Proposed Federal Securities Code*, 33 UNIVERSITY OF MIAMI LAW REVIEW 1471 (1978–1979)

_____, *Required Disclosure and the Stock Market: An Evaluation of the Securities Exchange Act of 1934*, 63 THE AMERICAN ECONOMIC REVIEW 132 (March 1973)

_____, *Required Disclosure and the Stock Market: Rejoinder*, 65 THE AMERICAN ECONOMIC REVIEW 473 (1975)

_____, *The Value of the SEC's Accounting Disclosure Requirements*, 44 ACCOUNTING REVIEW 515 (1969)

Beny, Laura, *A Comparative Empirical Investigation of Agency and Market Theories of Insider Trading*, HARVARD LAW SCHOOL JOHN M. OLIN CENTER FOR LAW, ECONOMICS AND BUSINESS DISCUSSION PAPER SERIES, PAPER 264 (1999), available at http://lsr.nellco.org/harvard_olin/264

Bergman, Nittai K., and Daniel Nicolaievsky, *Investor Protection and the Coasian View*, MIT SLOAN MANAGEMENT, MIT SLOAN WORKING PAPER 4476-04 (2004), available at http://papers.ssrn.com/sol3/papers.cfm?abstract_id=517022

Beyer, Anne, Daniel A. Cohen, Thomas Z. Lys and Beverley R. Walther, *The Financial Reporting Environment* (July 2010), available at http://ssrn.com/abstract=1483227

Bhattacharya, Utpal, Hazem Daouk and Michael Welker, *The World Price of Earnings Opacity*, 78 THE ACCOUNTING REVIEW 641 (2003)

Black, Barbara, *Is Stock a Security? A Criticism of the Sale of Business Doctrine in Securities Fraud Litigation*, 16 UNIVERSITY OF CALIFORNIA DAVIS LAW REVIEW 325 (1983)

Black, Bernard, *The Legal and Institutional Preconditions for a Strong Securities Market*, 48 UNIVERSITY OF CALIFORNIA LOS ANGELES LAW REVIEW 781 (2001)

_____, and Reinier Kraakman, *A Self-Enforcing Model of Corporate Law*, 109 HARVARD LAW REVIEW 1911 (1996)

Blair, William, *Global Financial Law*, 1 LAW AND FINANCIAL MARKET REVIEW 395 (2007)

Blomberg, Jeffrey A., and Henry E. Forcier, *But is it a Security? A Look at Offers from Start-Up Companies*, 14 BUSINESS LAW TODAY 48 (2005)

Board of Governors of the Federal Reserve System, REPORT TO THE CONGRESS ON RISK RETENTION (2010)

Botosan, Christine A., *Disclosure Level and the Cost of Equity Capital*, 72 THE ACCOUNTING REVIEW 323 (1997)

Brownlee, E. Richard, III, and S. David Young, *Financial Disclosure Regulation and Its Critics*, 4 JOURNAL OF ACCOUNTING REGULATION 113 (1986)

Brummer, Chris, *How International Law Works (and How It Doesn't)*, 99 GEORGETOWN LAW REVIEW 257 (2011)

_____, *Territoriality as a Regulatory Technique: Notes from the Financial Crisis*, 79 UNIVERSITY OF CINCINNATI LAW REVIEW 499 (2010)

Bushee, Brian J., *Discussion of Disclosure Practices of Foreign Companies Interacting with U.S. Markets*, 42 JOURNAL OF ACCOUNTING RESEARCH 509 (2004)

_____, and Christopher F. Noe, *Corporate Disclosure Practices, Institutional Investors, and Stock Return Volatility*, 38 JOURNAL OF ACCOUNTING RESEARCH 171 (2000)

_____, Dawn A. Matsumoto and Gregory S. Miller, *Managerial and Investor Responses to Disclosure Regulation: The Case of Reg FD and Conference Calls*, 79 THE ACCOUNTING REVIEW 617 (2004)

Carlson, David Gray, *The Rotten Foundations of Securitizations*, 39 WILLIAM & MARY LAW REVIEW 1055 (1998)

Carpenter, Hunter, *Special Purpose Entities: A Description of the Now Loathed Corporate Financing Tool*, 72 MISSISSIPPI LAW JOURNAL 1065 (2002–2003)

Chemmanur, Thomas, and Paolo Fulghierie, *Investment Bank Reputation, Information Production and Financial Intermediation*, 49 THE JOURNAL OF FINANCE 57 (1994)

Chen, Kevin C.W., Zhihong Chen and K.C. John Wei, *Disclosure, Corporate Governance, and the Cost of Equity Capital: Evidence from Asia's Emerging Markets*, HONG KONG UNIVERSITY OF SCIENCE AND TECHNOLOGY WORKING PAPER (June 2003)

Choi, Stephen J., *Law, Finance and Path Dependence: Developing Strong Securities Markets*, 80 TEXAS LAW REVIEW 1657 (2001–2002)

_____, and Andrew T. Guzman, *Portable Reciprocity: Rethinking the International Reach of Securities Regulation*, 71 SOUTHERN CALIFORNIA LAW REVIEW 903 (1998)

Chuah, Jason C. T., *Islamic Principles Governing International Trade Financing Instruments: A Study of the Morabaha in English Law*, 27 NORTHWESTERN JOURNAL OF INTERNATIONAL LAW AND BUSINESS 137 (2006)

Clement, W. Rodney, Jr., and H. Scott Miller, *Special Purpose Entities (Barely) Survive First Bankruptcy Test*, 25 PROBATE AND PROPERTY 31 (2011)

Coase, Ronald, *Economists and Public Policy*, in LARGE CORPORATIONS IN A CHANGING SOCIETY, J. F. Weston, ed. (1975)

_____, *The Problem of Social Cost*, 3 JOURNAL OF LAW AND ECONOMICS 1 (1960)

Coffee, John C., Jr., *Extraterritorial Financial Regulation: Why E.T. Can't Come Home*, 99 CORNELL LAW REVIEW 1259 (2013–2014)

_____, *The Future as History: The Prospects for Global Convergence in Corporate Governance and Its Implications*, 93 NORTHWESTERN UNIVERSITY LAW REVIEW 641 (1998–1999)

_____, *Market Failure and the Economic Case for a Mandatory Disclosure System*, 70 VIRGINIA LAW REVIEW 717 (1984)

_____, *The Mandatory/Enabling Balance in Corporate Law: An Essay on the Judicial Role*, 89 COLUMBIA LAW REVIEW 1618 (1989)

_____, *The Rise of Dispersed Ownership: The Role of Law in the Segregation of Ownership and Control* (January 2001), available at http://papers.ssrn.com/sol3/papers.cfm?abstract_id= 254097

_____, *Understanding Enron: It's About the Gatekeepers, Stupid*, 57 THE BUSINESS LAWYER 1403 (2002)

_____, and Robert E. Verrecchia, *Disclosure, Liquidity, and the Cost of Capital*, 46 THE JOURNAL OF FINANCE 1325 (1991)

Coffey, Ronald J., *The Economic Realities of a 'Security': Is There a More Meaningful Formula?*, 18 CASE WESTERN RESERVE LAW REVIEW 367 (1966–1967)

Colon, Julio C., *Choice of Law and Islamic Finance*, 46 Texas International Law Journal 411 (2011)

Cornelis, Hendrik, and Ton Nederveen, *Civil Liability for Prospectus Misstatements under Dutch Law*, 14 International Financial Law Review 50 (1995)

Cotei, Carmen, Joseph Farhat and Benjamin A. Abugri, *Market Efficiency in Emerging Markets: Does the Legal System Matter?* (May 14, 2009), available at http://papers.ssrn.com/sol3/papers.cfm?abstract_id=1404572

Cowell, Eugene F., III, *Texas Article 9 Amendments Provide 'True Sale' Safe Harbor*, 115 Banking Law Journal 699 (1998)

Cowley, Alex, and J. David Cummins, *Securitization of Life Insurance Assets and Liabilities*, 72 The Journal of Risk and Insurance 193 (2005)

Coval, Joshua, Jakub Jurek and Erik Stafford, *The Economics of Structured Finance*, 23 Journal of Economic Perspectives 3 (2009)

Cox, James D., *Regulatory Duopoly in U.S. Securities Markets*, 99 Columbia Law Review 1200 (1999)

Cross, Frank B., and Robert A. Prentice, *Economics, Capital Markets, and Securities Law*, Law and Economics Research Paper No. 73, The University of Texas School of Law (2006)

Culhane, Daniel R., *Substantive Consolidation and Nondebtor Entities: The Fight Continues*, 7 Pratt's Journal of Bankruptcy Law 514 (2011)

Davidoff, Steven M., *Rhetoric and Reality: A Historical Perspective on the Regulation of Foreign Private Issuers*, 79 University of Cincinnati Law Review 619 (2010)

DBRS Ratings Limited, *CMBS Rating*, DBRS Ratings Limited (January 2012), available at http://www.dbrs.com/research/244847/cmbs-rating-methodology.pdf

DeLong, Bradford, Did J.P. Morgan's Men Add Value? An Economist's Perspective on Financial Capitalism, Inside the Business Enterprise: Historical Perspectives on the Use of Information (1991)

DeLorenzo, Yusuf Talal, and Michael J. T. McMillen, *Law and Islamic Finance: An Interactive Analysis*, in Islamic Finance: The Regulatory Challenge, Simon Archer and Rifaat Ahmed Abdel Karim, eds. (2007), at 150

Demyanyk, Yuliya S., and Otto Van Hemert, *Understanding the Subprime Mortgage Crisis* (December 5, 2008; first draft October 9, 2007), available at http://papers.ssrn.com/sol3/papers.cfm?abstract_id=1020396

Diamond, Douglas W., *Optimal Release of Information by Firms*, 40 The Journal of Finance 1071 (1985)

Dolan, Patrick D., *Lender's Guide to the Securitization of Commercial Mortgage Loans*, 115 Banking Law Journal 597 (1998)

_____, *Lender's Guide to the Securitization of State Lottery Winnings and Litigation Settlement Payments*, 115 Banking Law Journal 710 (1998)

_____, *Securitization of Equipment Leases*, New York Law Journal, August 11, 1999

_____, and VanLeer Davis III, Securitizations: Legal and Regulatory Issues (2015)

Downey, Conor, *Whole Business Securitization Comes of Age*, 18 International Financial Law Review 8 (1999)

Easley, Stephen J., *Recent Developments in the Sale-of-Business Doctrine: Toward a Context-Based Analysis for Federal Securities Jurisdiction*, 39 The Business Lawyer 929 (1984)

Easterbrook, Frank H., and Daniel R. Fischel, *Mandatory Disclosure and the Protection of Investors*, 70 Virginia Law Review 669 (1984)

Edison, Hali J., Ross Levine, Luca Ricci and Torsten Slok, *International Financial Regulation and Economic Growth*, National Bureau of Economic Research Working Paper 9164 (September 2002), available at http://nber.org/papers/w9164

Edwards, Franklin, ed., Financial Regulation (1979)

Eggert, Kurt, *Held Up in Due Course: Predatory Lending, Securitization, and The Holder in Due Course Doctrine*, 35 CREIGHTON LAW REVIEW 503 (2002)

_____, *The Great Collapse: How Securitization Caused the Subprime Meltdown*, 41 CONNECTICUT LAW REVIEW 1257 (2008)

Ellis, Robert Dean, *Securitization Vehicles, Fiduciary Duties, and Bondholder's Rights*, 24 JOURNAL OF Corporate Law 295 (1998–1999)

Enriques, Luca, and Sergio Gilotta, *Disclosure and Financial Market Regulation* (April 2014), available at http://ssrn.com/abstract=24223768

Erel, Isil, Taylor Nadauld and Rene M. Stulz, *Why Did Holdings of Highly Rated Securitization Tranches Differ So Much Across Banks?* (November 2013; first draft December 2012), available at http://papers.ssrn.com/sol3/papers.cfm?abstract_id=1894734

Errico, Luca, and Mitra Farahbaksh, *Islamic Banking: Issues in Prudential Regulations and Supervision*, International Monetary Fund Working Paper WP/98/30 (March 1998)

Fabozzi, Frank J., and Vinod Kothari, INTRODUCTION TO SECURITIZATION (2008)

Fadlallah, Ibrahim, *Is There a Pro-Western Bias in Arbitral Awards*, 9 JOURNAL OF WORLD INVESTMENT AND TRADE 101 (2008)

Fama, Eugene F., *Efficient Capital Markets: A Review of Theory and Empirical Work*, 25 JOURNAL OF FINANCE 383 (1970)

Ferrell, Allen, *The Case for Mandatory Disclosure in Securities Regulation Around the World*, JOHN M. OLIN CENTER FOR LAW, ECONOMICS AND BUSINESS, HARVARD UNIVERSITY (October 2004), available at http://papers.ssrn.com/sol3/papers.cfm?abstract_id=631221

Fischel, Daniel, and Sanford Grossman, *Customer Protection in Futures and Securities Markets*, 4 JOURNAL OF FUTURES MARKETS 273 (1984)

Fisher, Geoffrey, *Sharia Law and Choice of Law Clauses in International Contracts*, 2005 LAWASIA JOURNAL 69

Fisher, Keith R., *The Higher Calling: Regulation of Lawyers Post-Enron*, 37 UNIVERSITY OF MICHIGAN JOURNAL OF LEGAL REFORM 1017 (2004)

FitzGibbon, Scott, *What is a Security? – A Redefinition Based on Eligibility to Participate in the Financial Markets*, 64 MINNESOTA LAW REVIEW 893 (1979–1980)

_____, and Donald W. Glazer, FITZGIBBON AND GLAZER ON LEGAL OPINIONS (1992)

Foëx, Bénédict, ed., THE DRAFT UNCITRAL MODEL LAW ON SECURED TRANSACTIONS: WHY AND HOW?

Forte, Joseph Philip, *From Main Street to Wall Street: Commercial Mortgage-Backed Securities*, 10 PROBATE AND PROPERTY 8 (1996)

Foster, Nicholas H. D., *Islamic Finance Law as an Emergent Legal System*, 21 ARAB LAW QUARTERLY 170 (2007)

Fox, Merritt B., *Civil Liability and Mandatory Disclosure*, 109 COLUMBIA LAW REVIEW 237 (2009)

_____, *Retaining Mandatory Securities Disclosure: Why Issuer Choice is Not Investor Empowerment*, 85 VIRGINIA LAW REVIEW 1335 (1999)

Franco, Joseph A., *Why Antifraud Prohibitions Are Not Enough: The Significance of Opportunism, Candor and Signaling in the Economic Case for Mandatory Securities Disclosure*, 2002 COLUMBIA BUSINESS LAW REVIEW 223

Freeman, John P., *Opinion Letters and Professionalism*, 1973 DUKE LAW JOURNAL 371

Friend, Irwin, and Edward Herman, *The S.E.C. Through a Glass Darkly*, 37 JOURNAL OF BUSINESS 382 (1964)

_____, and Randolph Westerfield, *Required Disclosure and the Stock Market: Comment*, 65 THE AMERICAN ECONOMIC REVIEW 467 (1975)

Frost, Christopher, *Asset Securitization and Corporate Risk Allocation*, 72 TULANE LAW REVIEW 101 (1997)

_____, *Organizational Form, Misappropriation Risk, and Substantive Consolidation of Corporate Groups*, 44 HASTINGS LAW JOURNAL 449 (1992–1993)

Gabaldon, Theresa A., *A Sense of Security: An Empirical Study*, 25 Journal of Corporation Law 307 (1999–2000)

Gaddis, Michael, *When is a Dog Really a Duck?: The True-Sale Problem in Securities Law*, 87 Texas Law Review 487 (2008–2009)

Gambro, Michael S., and Scott Leichtner, *Selected Legal Issues Affecting Securitization*, 1 North Carolina Banking Institute 131 (1997)

Gardner, Peter J., *A Role for the Business Attorney in the Twenty-First Century: Adding Value to the Client's Enterprise in the Knowledge Economy,* 7 Marquette Intellectual Property Law Review 17 (2003)

Gilbert, J. Stephen, *Substantive Consolidation in Bankruptcy: A Primer*, 43 Vanderbilt Law Review 207 (1990)

Gilson, Ronald J., *Value Creation by Business Lawyers: Legal Skills and Asset Pricing*, 94 Yale Law Journal 239

_____, and Reinier R. Kraakman, *The Mechanisms of Market Efficiency*, 70 Virginia Law Review 549 (1984)

Glaeser, Edward, Simon Johnson and Andrei Shleifer, *Coase Versus the Coasians*, 116 Quarterly Journal of Economics 853 (2001)

_____, and Andrei Shleifer, *A Reason for Quantity Regulation*, 91 American Economic Review Papers and Proceedings 431 (2001)

_____, and _____, *Legal Origins*, 117 Quarterly Journal of Economics 1193 (2002)

_____, and _____, *The Rise of the Regulatory State*, 41 Journal of Economic Literature 401 (2003)

Glick, Anna H., *Mechanics of a CMBS Offering*, in CMBS and the Real Estate Lawyer 2015: Lender and Borrower Issues in the Capital Markets, Practising Law Institute (2015), at 91

Gordon, Thomas J., *Securitization of Executory Future Flows as Bankruptcy-Remote True Sales*, 67 University of Chicago Law Review 1317 (2000)

Gorton, Gary B., *The Subprime Panic*, Yale International Center for Finance, Yale ICF Working Paper No. 08-25 (September 30, 2008), available at http://papers.ssrn.com/sol3/papers.cfm?abstract_id=1276047

_____, and Andrew Metrick, *Securitized Banking and the Run on the Repo* (November 9, 2010), available at http://papers.ssrn.com/sol3/papers.cfm?abstract_id=1440752

Goshen, Zohar, and Gideon Parchomovsky, *The Essential Role of Securities Regulation*, 55 Duke Law Journal 711 (2006)

Gouda, Bushra Ali Gouda, *The Saudi Securities Law: Regulation of the Tadawul Stock Market, Issuers, and Securities Professionals under the Saudi Capital Market Law* 2003, 18 Annual Survey of International and Comparative Law 115 (2012)

Gould v. Ruefenacht, 471 U.S. 701 (1985)

Graulich, Timothy E., *Substantive Consolidation – A Post-Modern Trend*, 15 American Bankruptcy Institute Law Review 527 (2006)

Greenberger, Michael, *The Extraterritorial Provisions of the Dodd-Frank Act Protects U.S. Taxpayers from Worldwide Bailouts*, 80 University of Missouri Kansas City Law Review 965 (2012)

Grossman, Sanford, *The Informational Role of Warranties and Private Disclosure About Product Quality*, 24 Journal of Law and Economics 461 (1981)

_____, and Oliver Hart, *Disclosure Laws and Takeover Bids*, 35 Journal of Finance 323 (1980)

Grupo Mexicano de Desarrollo, S.A. v. Alliance Bond Fund, Inc., 527 U.S. 308 (1999)

Hannan, J. Thomas, and William E. Thomas, *The Importance of Economic Reality and Risk in Defining Federal Securities*, 25 Hastings Law Journal 219 (1973–1974)

Hansmann, Henry, and Reiner Kraakman, *The End of History for Corporate Law*, Yale Law School Law and Economics Working Paper No. 235, New York University Law and Economics Working Paper No. 013, Harvard Law School John M. Olin Center for Law,

Economics, and Business Discussion Paper No. 280, and Yale International Center for Finance Working Paper No. 00-09 (January 2000), available at http://papers.ssrn.com/sol3/papers.cfm?abstract_id=204528

_____, and _____, *What is Corporate Law?*, in Reinier Kraakman, John Armour, Paul Davies, Luca Enriques, Henry B. Hansmann, Gérard Hertig, Klaus J. Hopt, Hideki Kanda and Edward B. Rock, THE ANATOMY OF CORPORATE LAW: A COMPARATIVE AND FUNCTIONAL APPROACH (2009), at 1

_____, and Ugo Mattei, *The Functions of Trust Law: A Comparative Legal and Economic Analysis*, 73 NEW YORK UNIVERSITY LAW REVIEW 434 (1998)

Harrell, Charles E., James L. Rice III and W. Robert Shearer, *Securitization of Oil, Gas, and Other Natural Resource Assets: Emerging Financing Techniques*, 52 BUSINESS LAWYER 885 (1996–1997)

Harris, Alton B., *Are 'Synthetic Securities' Securities?*, 2 JOURNAL OF TAXATION OF FINANCIAL PRODUCTS 11 (2001)

Hassan, M. Kabir, and Michael Mahlknecht, eds., ISLAMIC CAPITAL MARKETS: PRODUCTS AND STRATEGIES (2011)

Hay, Jonathan, Andrei Shleifer and Robert Vishny, *Toward a Theory of Legal Reform*, 40 EUROPEAN ECONOMIC REVIEW 559 (1996)

He, Jie, Jun Qian and Philip E. Strahan, *Are All Credit Ratings Created Equal? The Impact of Issuer Size on the Pricing of Mortgage-Backed Securities*, 67 JOURNAL OF FINANCE 2097 (2012)

_____, *Credit Ratings and the Evolution of the Mortgage-Backed Securities Market*, 101 THE AMERICAN ECONOMIC REVIEW 131 (2011)

Higgins, Eric J., Joseph R. Mason and Adi Mordel, *Asset Sales, Recourse, and Investors Reactions to Initial Securitizations: Evidence why Off-balance Sheet Accounting Treatment does not Remove On-balance Sheet Financial Risk* (2009), available at http://ssrn.com/abstract=1107074

Hill, Claire A., *The Future of Synthetic Securitizations—A Comment on Bell and Dawson*, 12 DUKE JOURNAL OF COMPARATIVE AND INTERNATIONAL LAW 563 (2002)

_____, *Latin American Securitization: The Case of the Disappearing Political Risk*, 38 VIRGINIA JOURNAL OF INTERNATIONAL LAW 293 (1998)

_____, *Securitization: A Low-Cost Sweetener for Lemons*, 74 WASHINGTON UNIVERSITY LAW QUARTERLY 101 (1996)

_____, *Whole Business Securitizations in Emerging Markets*, 12 DUKE JOURNAL OF COMPARATIVE AND INTERNATIONAL LAW 521 (2002)

Horton, Joanne, George Serafeim and Ioanna Serafeim, *Does Mandatory IFRS Adoption Improve the Information Environment?*, 30 CONTEMPORARY ACCOUNTING RESEARCH 388 (2013)

Huang, Peter H., *Trust, Guilt, and Securities Regulation*, 151 UNIVERSITY OF PENNSYLVANIA LAW REVIEW 1059 (2003)

Humphreys, Peter, and Howard Mulligan, *Substantive Consolidation in the Owens Corning Bankruptcy Case – Impact on Analysis of Structured Finance Transactions*, 122 BANKRUPTCY LAW JOURNAL 54 (2005)

International Brotherhood of Teamsters v. Daniel, 439 U.S. 551 (1979)

International Organisation of Securities Commissions, *Objectives and Principles of Securities Regulation, International Organization of Securities Commissions* (September 1998), English language version available at http://www.iosco.org/library/pubdocs/pdf/IOSCOPD82.pdf

Investment Dealers Digest, *Nursing Homes Securitization Gathers Steam in UK*, Investment Dealer's Digest, December 8, 1997

J.I. Case v. Borak, 377 U.S. 426 (1964)

Jaffer, Sohail, ed., ISLAMIC ASSET MANAGEMENT: FORMING THE FUTURE FOR SHARI'A-COMPLIANT INVESTMENT STRATEGIES (2004)

Jones, George F., *Footnote 11 of Marine Bank v. Weaver: Will Unconventional Certificates of Deposit Be Held Securities?*, 24 Houston Law Review 491 (1987)

Jones, Richard D., *The Emergence of CMBS* in Commercial Mortgage-Backed Securitisation: Developments in the European Market, Andrew V. Petersen, ed. (2006)

Junius, Andreas, *Islamic Finance: Issues Surrounding Islamic Law as a Choice of Law under German Conflict of Laws Principles*, 7 Chicago Journal of International Law 537 (2006–2007)

Kang, Jane C., *The Regulation of Global Futures Markets: Is Harmonization Possible or Even Desirable?*, 17 Northwestern Journal of International Law and Business 242 (1996)

Kaufmann, David J., David W. Oppenheim and Jordan E. Yarett, *Franchise Securitization Financings*, 27 Franchise Law Journal 241 (2008)

Kettering, Kenneth C., *Pride and Prejudice in Securitization: A Reply to Professor Plank*, 30 Cardozo Law Review 1977 (2009)

_____, *Securitization and Its Discontents: The Dynamics of Financial Product Development*, 19 Cardozo Law Review 1553 (2008)

_____, *True Sale of Receivables: A Purposive Analysis*, 16 American Bankruptcy Institute Law Review 511 (2008)

Keys, Benjamin J., Tanmoy K. Mukherjee, Amit Seru and Vikrant Vig, *Did Securitization Lead to Lax Screening? Evidence from Subprime Loans* (December 25, 2008), available at http://papers.ssrn.com/sol3/papers.cfm?abstract_id=1093137

Khan, M. Fahim, *Islamic Methods for Government Borrowing and Monetary Management*, in Islamic Capital Markets: Products and Strategies, M. Kabir Hassan and Michael Mahlknecht, eds. (2011), at 285

Kilborn, Jason J., *Foundations of Forgiveness in Islamic Bankruptcy Law: Sources, Methodology, Diversity*, 85 American Bankruptcy Law Journal 323 (2011)

King, Mervyn, *International Harmonisation of the Regulation of Capital Markets: An Introduction*, 34 European Economic Review 569 (1990)

Kitch, Edmund W., *The Theory and Practice of Securities Disclosure*, 61 Brooklyn Law Review 763 (1995)

Klee, Kenneth N., and Brendt C. Butler, *Asset-Backed Securitization, Special Purpose Vehicles and Other Securitization Issues*, 35 Uniform Commercial Code Law Journal 23 (2002)

Kors, Mary Elisabeth, *Altered Egos: Deciphering Substantive Consolidation*, 59 University of Pittsburgh Law Review 381 (1997–1998)

Kothari, Vinod, *Whole Business Securitization: Secured Lending Repackaged—A Comment*, 12 Duke Journal of Comparative and International Law 537 (2002)

Kraakman, Reinier, John Armour, Paul Davies, Luca Enriques, Henry B. Hansmann, Gérard Hertig, Klaus J. Hopt, Hideki Kanda and Edward B. Rock, The Anatomy of Corporate Law: A Comparative and Functional Approach (2009)

Kravitt, Jason H.P., Securitization of Financial Assets, 2d ed. (1999, and supplements)

La Porta, Rafael, Florencio Lopez-de-Silanes and Andrei Shleifer, *What Works in Securities Laws?*, 61 The Journal of Finance 1 (2006)

Lahney, Peter J., IV, *Asset Securitization: A Discussion of Traditional Bankruptcy Attacks and an Analysis of the Next Potential Attack, Substantive Consolidation*, 9 American Bankruptcy Institute Law Review 815 (2001)

Landis, James, The Administrative Process (1938)

Landreth Timber Co. v. Landreth, 471 U.S. 681 (1985)

Landsman, Wayne R., Kenneth V. Peasnell and Catherine Shakespeare, *Are Asset Securitizations Sales or Loans?*, 83 The Accounting Review 1251 (2008)

Latimer, Paul, *Securities Regulation Laws: What Are They Trying to Achieve?: A Case Study of the Colombo Stock Exchange*, 2 Asia Pacific Law Review 98 (1993)

Lazarus, Eli Martin, *Viatical and Life Settlement Securitization: Risks and Proposed Regulation*, 29 Yale Law and Policy Review 253 (2010)

Leuz, Christian, and Peter Wysocki, *Economic Consequences of Financial Reporting and Disclosure Regulations: A Review and Suggestions for Future Research* (March 2008; first version May 2006), available at http://ssrn.com/abstract=105398

_____, and Robert E. Verrecchia, *The Economic Consequences of Increased Disclosure*, 38 JOURNAL OF ACCOUNTING RESEARCH 91 (2000)

Levin, Matthew W., and Jennifer M. Meyerowitz, *Buyer Beware: An Analysis of True Sale Issues*, 1 PRATT'S BANKRUPTCY LAW JOURNAL 185 (2005–2006)

Levine, Ross, *International Financial Liberalization and Economic Growth*, 9 REVIEW OF INTERNATIONAL ECONOMICS 688 (2001)

Linsmeier, Thomas J., Daniel B. Thornton, Mohan Venkatachalam and Michael Welker, *The Effect of Mandated Market Risk Disclosures on Trading Volume Sensitivity to Interest Rate, Exchange Rate, and Commodity Price Movements*, 77 THE ACCOUNTING REVIEW 343 (2002)

Lipson, Jonathan C., *Re: Defining Securitization*, 85 SOUTHERN CALIFORNIA LAW REVIEW 1229 (2011–2012)

_____, *Enron, Securitization and Bankruptcy Reform: Dead or Dormant?*, 11 WEST JOURNAL OF BANKRUPTCY LAW AND PRACTICE 1 (2002)

_____, *Price, Path & Pride: Third-Party Closing Opinion Practice Among U.S. Lawyers (A Preliminary Investigation)*, 3 BERKLEY BUSINESS LAW JOURNAL 59 (2005)

_____, *Secrets and Liens: The End of Notice in Commercial Finance Law*, 21 EMORY BANKRUPTCY DEVELOPMENTS JOURNAL 421 (2005)

_____, *Why (And How To) Define Securitization? A Sur-Reply to Professor Schwarcz*, 85 SOUTHERN CALIFORNIA LAW REVIEW 1301 (2011–2012)

Lipton, Martin, and George A. Katz, *'Notes' Are (Are Not?) Always Securities – A Review*, 29 THE BUSINESS LAWYER 861 (1974)

_____, and _____, *'Notes' Are Not Always Securities*, 30 THE BUSINESS LAWYER 763 (1975)

Love, Kelly A., *A Primer on Opinion Letters: Explanations and Analysis*, 9 TRANSACTIONS: THE TENNESSEE JOURNAL OF BUSINESS LAW 67 (2007–2008)

Lowenfels, Lewis D., and Alan R. Bromberg, *What is a Security under the Federal Securities Laws?*, 56 ALBANY LAW REVIEW 473 (1993)

Lubben, Stephen J., *Beyond True Sales – Securitization and Chapter 11* (2004), 1 NEW YORK UNIVERSITY JOURNAL OF LAW AND BUSINESS 89 (2004–2005)

Lupica, Lois R., *Asset Securitization: The Unsecured Creditor's Perspective*, 76 TEXAS LAW REVIEW 595 (1998)

_____, *Circumvention of the Bankruptcy Process: The Statutory Institutionalization of Securitization*, 33 CONNECTICUT LAW REVIEW 199 (2000)

_____, *Revised Article 9, The Proposed Bankruptcy Code Amendments and Securitizing Debtors and Their Creditors*, 7 FORDHAM JOURNAL OF CORPORATE AND FINANCIAL LAW 3321 (2002)

_____, *Revised Article 9, Securitization Transactions and the Bankruptcy Dynamic*, 9 AMERICAN BANKRUPTCY INSTITUTE LAW REVIEW 287 (2001)

Macey, Jonathan, *Administrative Agency Obsolescence and Interest Group Formation: A Case Study of the SEC at Sixty*, 15 CARDOZO LAW REVIEW 909 (1994)

Macey, Jonathan R., THIRD PARTY LEGAL OPINIONS: EVALUATION AND ANALYSIS (1995)

MacKinnon, Jeanne, *Substantive Consolidation: The Back Door to Involuntary Bankruptcy*, 23 SAN DIEGO LAW REVIEW 203 (1986)

Mahoney, Paul G., *Mandatory Disclosure as a Solution to Agency Problems*, 62 UNIVERSITY OF CHICAGO LAW REVIEW 1047 (1995)

_____, *Precaution Costs and the Law of Fraud in Impersonal Markets*, 78 VIRGINIA LAW REVIEW 623 (1992)

_____, *Regulation of International Securities Issues*, 14 REGULATION 62 (1991)

_____, *Securities Regulation by Enforcement*, 7 YALE JOURNAL ON REGULATION 305 (1990)

_____, *The Development of the Securities Law in the United States*, 47 Journal of Accounting Research 325 (2009)

_____, *The Exchange as Regulator*, 83 Virginia Law Review 1453 (1997)

_____, The Political Economy of the Securities Act of 1933 (2001)

_____, Wasting a Crisis: Why Securities Regulation Fails (2015)

Mann, Michael D., Joseph G. Mari and George Lavdas, *Developments in International Securities Law Enforcement and Regulation*, 19 The International Lawyer 729 (1995)

Manne, Henry G., *Economics and Financial Regulation: Will the SEC's New Embrace of Cost-Benefit Analysis be a Watershed Moment?*, 35 Regulation 20 (2012–2013)

_____, *Insider Trading and the Administrative Process*, 35 George Washington Law Review 473 (1966–1967)

Mason, Joseph R., and Josh Rosner, *Where Did the Risk Go? How Misapplied Bond Ratings Cause Mortgage Backed Securities and Collateralized Debt Obligation Market Disruptions* (May 3, 2007), available at http://papers.ssrn.com/sol3/papers.cfm?abstract_id=1027475

Mazando, Frederick H. C., *The Taxonomy of Global Securities: Is the U.S. Definition of a Security too Broad?*, 33 Northwestern Journal of International Law and Business 121 (2012–2013)

Marine Bank v. Weaver, 455 U.S. 551 (1982)

McGinty, Park, *What is a Security?*, 1993 Wisconsin Law Review 1033

McMillen, Michael J. T., *The Arcapita Group Bankruptcy: A Restructuring Case Study*, Global Trends in Islamic Commercial Law, International Shari'ah Research Academy and Thomson Reuters (2015)

_____, *Asset Securitization Sukuk and Islamic Capital Markets: Structural Issues in the Formative Years*, 25 Wisconsin International Law Journal 703 (2007)

_____, *The Chapter 11 Bankruptcy Restructuring of Arcapita*, a chapter of Global Trends in Islamic Commercial Law, the International Shariah Research Academy for Islamic Finance and Thomson Reuters Report 2015

_____, *Contractual Enforceability Issues: Sukuk and Capital Markets Development*, 7 Chicago Journal of International Law 427 (2007)

_____, *An Introduction to Shari'ah Considerations in Bankruptcy and Insolvency Contexts and Islamic Finance's First Bankruptcy (East Cameron)* (June 17, 2012), available at http://papers.ssrn.com/sol3/papers.cfm?abstract_id=1826246

_____, *Islamic Capital Markets in the United States and Globally: Overview and Select Shari'ah Governance Elements*, Inside the Minds: Financial Services Enforcement and Compliance (2013)

_____, *Islamic Capital Markets: Developments and Issues*, 1 Capital Markets Law Journal 136 (2006)

_____, *Islamic Capital Markets: A Selective Introduction*, The International Who's Who of Capital Markets Lawyers (2012), at 2

_____, *Islamic Capital Markets: Market Developments and Conceptual Evolution in the First Thirteen Years* (2011), available at http://ssrn.com/abstract=1781112

_____, *Islamic Capital Markets: Overview and Select Shari'ah Governance Matters* (2013), available at http://papers.ssrn.com/sol3/papers.cfm?abstract_id=2293235

_____, Islamic Finance and the Shari'ah: The Dow Jones Fatwa and Permissible Variance as Studies in Letheanism and Legal Change (2013)

_____, *Islamic Finance Review 2005/2006: A Year of Globalization and Integration*, in Euromoney Islamic Finance Year in Review 2005/2006 (2006)

_____, *Rahn Concepts in Saudi Arabia: Formalization and a Registration and Prioritization System* (March 9, 2010), available at http://papers.ssrn.com/sol3/papers.cfm?abstract_id=1670104

_____, *Rahn Concepts in Saudi Arabia: Formalization and a Registration and Prioritization System*, in ISLAMIC CAPITAL MARKETS: PRODUCTS AND STRATEGIES, M. Kabir Hassan and Michael Mahlknecht, eds. (2011)

_____, *Implementing Shari' ah-Compliant Collateral Security Regimes: Select Issues*, in RESEARCH HANDBOOK ON SECURED FINANCING IN COMMERCIAL TRANSACTIONS, Frederique Dahan, ed. (2015), at 97

_____, *Islamic Shari'ah-compliant Project Finance: Collateral Security and Financing Structure Case Studies*, 24 FORDHAM INTERNATIONAL LAW JOURNAL 1184 (2001)

_____, *Islamic Shari'ah-compliant Project Finance: Collateral Security and Financing Structure Case Studies*, in THE PROCEEDINGS OF THE THIRD HARVARD UNIVERSITY FORUM ON ISLAMIC FINANCE: LOCAL CHALLENGES, GLOBAL OPPORTUNITIES (2000), at 111

_____, *Legal Regime for Security Rights in Movable Collateral: An Analysis of the UNCITRAL Model Law from a Shari'ah Perspective*, The World Bank, February 1, 2016

_____, *A Rahn-ʿAdl Collateral Security Structure for Project and Secured Financings*, in PROCEEDINGS OF THE THIRD HARVARD UNIVERSITY FORUM ON ISLAMIC FINANCE: LOCAL CHALLENGES, GLOBAL OPPORTUNITIES (1999)

_____, *Raising the Game of Compliance: People and Organizations*, EUROMONEY ISLAMIC FINANCE YEAR IN REVIEW 2005/2006 (2006)

_____, *Securities Laws, Enforceability and Sukuk*, in ISLAMIC FINANCE: GLOBAL LEGAL ISSUES AND CHALLENGES, Rifaat Ahmed Abdel Karim, ed. (2008)

_____, *Special Report U.S. Briefing: Islamic Finance: Breaking the Mould*, 38 MIDDLE EAST ECONOMIC DIGEST (MEED), September 22, 2000, at 28

_____, *Shari'a-compliant Finance Structures and the Development of an Islamic Economy*, in THE PROCEEDINGS OF THE FIFTH HARVARD UNIVERSITY FORUM ON ISLAMIC FINANCE: ISLAMIC FINANCE: DYNAMICS AND DEVELOPMENT (2003), at 89

_____, *Structuring a Shari'ah-Compliant Real Estate Acquisition Financing: A South Korean Case Study*, in ISLAMIC FINANCE: CURRENT REGULATORY AND LEGAL ISSUES, S. Nazim Ali, ed. (2005), at 77

_____, *Sukuk in Its Infancy: Misstep and Sequel*, DOW JONES ISLAMIC MARKET NEWSLETTER (2008), at 3, also available at http://papers.ssrn.com/sol3/papers.cfm?abstract_id=2293693

_____, *Sukuk in the Sultanate of Oman* (2013), available at http://papers.ssrn.com/sol3/papers.cfm?abstract_id=2276270

_____, *Trends in Islamic Project and Infrastructure Finance in the Middle East: Re-Emergence of the Murabaha* (February 1, 2011), available at http://papers.ssrn.com/sol3/papers.cfm?-abstract_id=1753252

_____, *The UNCITRAL Model Secured Transactions Law: A Shari'ah Perspective*, a chapter in THE DRAFT UNCITRAL MODEL LAW ON SECURED TRANSACTIONS: WHY AND HOW?, Bénédict Foëx, ed. (2016); draft available at http://papers.ssrn.com/sol3/papers.cfm?ab-stract_id=2526079

_____, and Abradat Kamalpour, *An Innovation in Financing – Islamic CMBS*, in COMMERCIAL MORTGAGE-BACKED SECURITISATION: DEVELOPMENTS IN THE EUROPEAN MARKET, Andrew V. Petersen, ed. (2006)

_____, and John A. Crawford, *Sukuk in the First Decade: By the Numbers*, DOW JONES ISLAMIC MARKET INDEXES 3 (December 2008)

Merrill, Craig B., Taylor Nadauld and Philip E. Strahan, *Final Demand for Structured Finance Securities* (August 1, 2014), available at http://papers.ssrn.com/sol3/papers.cfm?abstract_id=2380859

_____, Taylor Nadauld, René M. Stulz and Shane M. Sherlund, *Why Were There Fire Sales of Mortgage-Backed Securities by Financial Institutions during the Financial Crisis?* (December 1, 2013), available at http://papers.ssrn.com/sol3/papers.cfm?abstract_id=2212684

Mian, Atif R., and Amir Sufi, *The Consequences of Mortgage Credit Expansion: Evidence from the U.S. Mortgage Default Crisis* (December 12, 2008), available at http://papers.ssrn.com/sol3/papers.cfm?abstract_id=1072304

Milgrom, Paul, and John Roberts, *Relying on the Information of Interested Parties*, 17 RAND JOURNAL OF ECONOMICS 18 (1986)

Miller, Merton, FINANCIAL INNOVATIONS AND MARKET VOLATILITY (1991)

Moody's Investors Service, *A Guide to Rating Islamic Financial Institutions*, Moody's Investors Service (April 2006)

_____, *Shari'ah and Sukuk: A Moody's Primer*, International Structured Finance: Europe, Middle East, Africa: Special Report, Moody's Investors Service (May 31, 2006)

Moye, E. Kristen, *Non-Consolidation and True Sale/Transfer Opinions in Securitized Real Estate Loan Transactions*, 21 PRACTICAL REAL ESTATE LAWYER 7 (2005)

Nadar, Aisha, *Islamic Finance and Dispute Resolution: Part 1*, 23 ARAB LAW QUARTERLY 1 (2009)

_____, *Islamic Finance and Dispute Resolution: Part 2*, 23 ARAB LAW QUARTERLY 181 (2009)

Nadauld, Taylor, and Shane M. Sherlund, *The Role of the Securitization Process in the Expansion of Subprime Credit* (May 26, 2009; first draft May 2008), available at http://papers.ssrn.com/sol3/papers.cfm?abstract_id=1410264

_____, and Michael S. Weisbach, *Did Securitization Affect the Cost of Corporate Debt?* (February 4, 2011), available at http://papers.ssrn.com/sol3/papers.cfm?abstract_id=1768862

Newton, William H., III, *What is a Security? A Critical Analysis*, 48 MISSISSIPPI LAW REVIEW 167 (1977)

Obaidullah, Mohammed, *Securitization in Islam*, in ISLAMIC CAPITAL MARKETS: PRODUCTS AND STRATEGIES, M. Kabir Hassan and Michael Mahlknecht, eds. (2011), at 19

Ostrin, Baker, *A Proposal to Limit the Availability of Substantive Consolidation of Solvent Entities with Bankrupt Affiliates*, 19 COMPARATIVE LAW JOURNAL 351 (1986)

Owens, Richard N., *What is a Security?*, 17 THE ACCOUNTING REVIEW 303 (1942)

In re Owens Corning, 316 B.R. 168 (Bankr. D. Del.), *rev'd*, 419 F.2d 195 (3d Cir. 2005), *cert. denied*, 126 S. Ct. 1910 (2006)

Pantaleo, Peter V., Herbert S. Edelman, Frederick L. Feldkamp, Jason Kravitt, Walter McNeill, Thomas E. Plank, Kenneth P. Morrison, Steven L. Schwarcz, Paul Shupack and Barry Zaretsky, *Rethinking the Role of Recourse in the Sale of Financial Assets*, 52 THE BUSINESS LAWYER 159 (1996–1997)

Paredes, Troy A., *Blinded by the Light: Information Overload and its Consequences for Securities Regulation*, 81 WASHINGTON UNIVERSITY LAW QUARTERLY 417 (2003)

Pearce, John A., II, and Ilya A. Lipin, *Special Purpose Vehicles in Bankruptcy Litigation*, 40 HOFSTRA LAW REVIEW 177 (2011–2012)

Petersen, Andrew V., ed., COMMERCIAL MORTGAGE-BACKED SECURITISATION: DEVELOPMENTS IN THE EUROPEAN MARKET (2006)

Petrucci, Angela, *Accounting for Asset Securitization in a Full Disclosure World*, 30 JOURNAL OF LEGISLATION 327 (2003–2004)

Pitt, Harvey L., *Bringing Financial Services Regulation into the Twenty-First Century*, 25 YALE JOURNAL ON REGULATION 315 (2008)

Plank, Thomas E., *The Security of Securitizations and the Future of Security*, 25 CARDOZO LAW REVIEW 1655 (2004)

_____, *Sense and Sensibility in Securitization: A Prudent Legal Structure and a Fanciful Critique*, 30 CARDOZO LAW REVIEW 617 (2008)

_____, *The True Sale of Loans and the Role of Recourse*, 14 GEORGE MASON LAW REVIEW 287 (1981)

Plehn, Robert, *Securitization of Third World Debt*, 23 THE INTERNATIONAL LAWYER 161 (1989)

Polinsky, Mitchell, and Steven Shavell, *The Economic Theory of Public Enforcement of Law*, 38 JOURNAL OF ECONOMIC LITERATURE 45 (2000)

Poon, Nicholas, *Choice of Law for Enforcement of Arbitral Awards: A Return to the Lex Loci Arbitri?*, SINGAPORE ACADEMY OF LAW JOURNAL 113 (2012)

Predko, Christopher J., *Substantive Consolidation Involving Non-Debtors: Conceptual and Jurisdictional Difficulties in Bankruptcy*, 41 WAYNE LAW REVIEW 1741 (1994–1995)

Quinn, Sarah, *Government Policy, Housing and the Origins of Securitization, 1780–1968* (2010), a Ph.D. dissertation in sociology in the graduate division of the University of California, Berkeley, available at https://escholarship.org/uc/item/7sq3f6xk

_____, *Lemon Socialism and Securitization*, 20 Trajectories 3 (2009)

_____, *'Things of Shreds and Patches': Credit Aid, the Budget, and Securitization in America*, Working Paper, University of Michigan

Reese, William, and Michael Weisbach, *Protection of Minority Shareholder Interests, Cross-Listings in the United States, and Subsequent-Equity Offerings*, 66 JOURNAL OF FINANCIAL ECONOMICS 65 (2002)

Reves v. Ernst & Young, 494 U.S. 56, at 61 (1990)

Ringe, Wolf-George, and Alexander Hellgardt, *The International Dimension of Issuer Liability: Liability and Choice of Law from a Transatlantic Perspective*, 31 OXFORD JOURNAL OF LEGAL STUDIES 23 (2011), available at http://papers.ssrn.com/sol3/papers.cfm?abstract_id=1588112

Rizwan, Saad U., *Foreseeable Issues and Hard Questions: The Implications of U.S. Courts Recognizing and Enforcing Foreign Arbitral Awards Applying Islamic Law under the New York Convention*, 98 CORNELL LAW REVIEW 493 (2013)

Rock, Edward, *Securities Regulation as Lobster Trap: A Credible Commitment Theory of Mandatory Disclosure*, 23 CARDOZO LAW REVIEW 675 (2001–2002)

Romano, Roberta, *Empowering Investors: A Market Approach to Securities Regulation*, 107 YALE LAW JOURNAL 2359 (1998)

_____, *The Need for Competition in International Securities Regulations*, 2 THEORETICAL INQUIRIES IN LAW 1 (2001)

Rosenthal, James A., and Juan M. Ocampo, *Analyzing the Economic Benefits of Securitized Credit*, 1 JOURNAL OF APPLIED CORPORATE FINANCE 32 (1992)

Ross, Stephen, *Disclosure Regulation in Financial Markets: Implications of Modern Finance Theory and Signaling Theory*, ISSUES IN FINANCIAL REGULATION, Franklin Edwards, ed. (1979)

Salathé, Gregory R., *Reducing Health Care Costs Through Hospital Accounts Receivable Securitization*, 80 VIRGINIA LAW REVIEW 549 (1994)

Saleh, Nabil, *A Landmark Judgment of 23 January 2004 by the England and Wales Court of Appeal*, 19 ARAB LAW QUARTERLY 287 (2004)

Sandberg, Russell, *Musawi v R E International (UK) Ltd and ORS*, 160 LAW AND JUSTICE – THE CHRISTIAN LAW REVIEW 67 (2008)

Sargent, Patrick C., *Bankruptcy Remote Finance Subsidiaries: The Substantive Consolidation Issue*, 44 THE BUSINESS LAWYER 1223 (1988–1989)

Schwarcz, Steven L., *The Alchemy of Asset Securitization*, 1 STANFORD JOURNAL OF LAW, BUSINESS & FINANCE 133 (1994–1995)

_____, *Diane Sanger Memorial Lecture: Protecting Investors in Securitization Transactions: Does Dodd-Frank Help, or Hurt?* 72 LOUISIANA LAW REVIEW 591 (2013)

_____, *Enron and the Use and Abuse of Special Purpose Entities in Corporate Structures*, 70 UNIVERSITY OF CINCINNATI LAW REVIEW 1309 (2001–2002)

_____, *Explaining the Value of Transactional Lawyering*, 12 STANFORD JOURNAL OF LAW, BUSINESS AND FINANCE 486 (2007)

_____, *The Future of Securitization*, 41 CONNECTICUT LAW REVIEW 1313 (2009)

_____, *The Impact of Bankruptcy Reform on 'True Sale' Determination in Securitization Transactions*, 7 FORDHAM JOURNAL OF CORPORATE AND FINANCIAL LAW 353 (2001)

_____, *Intermediary Risk in a Global Economy*, 50 DUKE LAW JOURNAL 1541 (2000–2001)

_____, *Lawyers in the Shadows: The Transactional Lawyer in a World of Shadow Banking*, 63 AMERICAN UNIVERSITY LAW REVIEW 157 (2013)

_____, *The Limits of Lawyering: Legal Opinions in Structured Finance*, 84 TEXAS LAW REVIEW 1 (2005)

_____, *Marginalizing Risk*, 89 Washington University Law Review 487 (2012)

_____, *The Parts are Greater than the Whole: How Securitization of Divisible Interests Can Revolutionize Structured Finance and Open the Capital Markets to Middle-Market Companies*, 2 Columbia Business Law Review 138 (1993)

_____, *Private Ordering of Public Markets: The Rating Agency Paradox*, 2002 University of Illinois Law Review 1 (2002)

_____, *Protecting Financial Markets: Lessons from the Subprime Mortgage Meltdown*, 83 Minnesota Law Review 373 (2008)

_____, *Regulating Complexity in Financial Markets*, 87 Washington University Law Review 211 (2009)

_____, *Regulating Shadows: Financial Regulation and Responsibility Failure*, 70 Washington and Lee Law Review 1781 (2013)

_____, *Rethinking the Disclosure Paradigm in a World of Complexity*, 2004 University of Illinois Law Review (2004)

_____, *The Roberta Mitchell Lecture: Structuring Responsibility in Securitization Transactions*, 40 Capital University Law Review 803 (2012)

_____, *Securitization Post-Enron*, 25 Cardozo Law Review 1539 (2003–2004)

_____, *Securitization, Structured Finance, and Covered Bonds*, 39 Journal of Corporation Law 129 (2013)

_____, *SMU Dedman School of Law Roy R. Ray Lecture: Markets, Systemic Risk, and the Subprime Mortgage Crisis*, 61 Southern Methodist University Law Review 209 (2008)

_____, Structured Finance: A Guide to the Principles of Asset Securitization (Adam D. Ford ed., 3d ed. 2010)

_____, *Systemic Risk*, 97 Georgetown Law Review 193 (2008)

_____, *Understanding the Subprime Financial Crisis*, 601 South Carolina Law Review 550 (2008–2009)

_____, *What is Securitization? And for What Purpose?*, 85 Southern California Law Review 1283 (2011–2012)

_____, Bruce A. Markell and Lissa Lamkin Broome, Securitization, Structured Finance and Capital Markets (2004)

SEC v. C.M. Joiner Leasing Corp., 320 U.S. 344 (1943)

SEC v. United Benefit Life Insurance Co., 387 U.S. 202 (1967)

SEC v. Variable Annuity Life Insurance Company of America, 359 U.S. 65 (1959)

SEC v. W.J. Howry, Co., 328 U.S. 293, 299 (1946)

Seligman, Joel, *The Historical Need for a Mandatory Corporate Disclosure System*, 9 The Journal of Corporation Law 1 (1983)

_____, *The Mandatory Disclosure System and Foreign Firms*, 4 Pacific Rim Law and Policy Journal 807 (1995)

Seminar, *Business Lawyers and Value Creation for Clients*, 74 Oregon Law Review 1 *et seq.* (1995)

Shenker, Joseph C., and Anthony J. Colletta, *Asset Securitization: Evolution, Current Issues and New Frontiers*, 69 Texas Law Review 1369 (1990–1991)

Shön, Wolfgang, *Corporate Disclosure in a Competitive Environment – The Quest for a European Framework on Mandatory Disclosure*, 6 Journal of Corporate Law Studies 259 (2006)

Shtatnov, Artem, *The Elusive True Sale in Securitization* (2012), available at http://ssrn.com/abstract=2115054

Siems, Mathias M., *The Foundations of Securities Law*, 20 European Business Law Review 141 (2009)

Simon, Carol, *The Effect of the 1933 Securities Act on Investor Information and the Performance of New Issues*, 79 American Economic Review (1989)

Simonds, Richard D., and Stephen S. Kudenholdt, *Fundamentals of Mortgage-Backed Securities and Asset-Backed Securities*, 18 Practical Real Estate Lawyer 39 (2002)

Sitkoff, Robert H., *Trust Law, Corporate Law, and Capital Market Efficiency*, 28 JOURNAL OF CORPORATE LAW 565 (2002–2003)

Sobieski, John, *What is a Security?*, 25 MERCER LAW REVIEW 381 (1974)

Solier, Jean-Luc, and Marcus Best, eds., INTERNATIONAL SECURITIES LAW HANDBOOK, SECOND EDITION (2005)

Standard & Poor's Corporation, U.S. CMBS LEGAL AND STRUCTURED FINANCE CRITERIA OF STANDARD & POOR'S, STANDARD & POOR'S CORPORATION (2003, with updates)

_____, *Standard & Poor's Approach to Rating Sukuk*, Ratings Direct, Standard & Poor's (September 17, 2007)

State Bar of Arizona, Business Law Section Committee on Rendering Legal Opinions in Business Transactions, *First Amended and Restated Report of the State Bar of Arizona Business Law Section Committee on Rendering Legal Opinions in Business Transactions*, October 20, 2004, 38 ARIZONA STATE LAW JOURNAL 47 (2006)

State of California, Business Law Section, *1989 Report of the Committee on Corporations of the Business Law Section of the State of California Regarding Legal Opinions in Business Transactions*, 45 BUSINESS LAWYER 2169 (1990)

Steele, Christopher Ross, *Cross-Border Insolvency: Substantive Consolidation and Non-Main Proceedings*, 7 PRATT'S JOURNAL OF BANKRUPTCY LAW 307 (2011)

Steinberg, Marc I., INTERNATIONAL SECURITIES LAW: A CONTEMPORARY AND COMPARATIVE ANALYSIS (1999)

_____, and William E. Kaulbach, *The Supreme Court and the Definition of 'Security': The 'Context' Clause, 'Investment Contract' Analysis, and Their Ramifications*, 40 VANDERBILT LAW REVIEW 489 (1987)

Stigler, George, *Public Regulation of the Securities Market*, 37 JOURNAL OF BUSINESS 117 (1964)

Stulz, René, *Globalization of Equity Markets and the Cost of Capital*, 12 JOURNAL OF APPLIED CORPORATE FINANCE 8 (1999)

Suchman, Mark C., and Mia L. Cahill, *The Hired Gun as Facilitator: Lawyers and the Suppression of Business Disputes in Silicon Valley*, 21 LAW AND SOCIAL INQUIRY 679 (1996)

Tang, Zheng, *Law Applicable in the Absence of Choice – The New Article 4 of the Rome I Regulation*, 71 MODERN LAW REVIEW 785 (2008)

Taylor, Celia R., *Drowning in Disclosure: The Overburdening of the Securities & Exchange Commission*, 8 VIRGINIA LAW AND BUSINESS REVIEW 86 (2014)

Tcherepnin v. Knight, 389 U.S. 332 (1967)

Thomas, Abdulkader, *Securitization in Islamic Finance*, in ISLAMIC FINANCE: THE REGULATORY CHALLENGE, Simon Archer & Rifaat Ahmed Abdel Karim, eds. (2007), at 259

Thompson, Robert B., *The Shrinking Definition of a Security: Why Purchasing All of a Company's Stock is Not a Federal Security Transaction*, 57 NEW YORK UNIVERSITY LAW REVIEW 225 (1982)

Thornton, William H., *The Continuing Presumption Against Substantive Consolidation*, 105 BANKING LAW JOURNAL 448 (1988)

The TriBar Opinion Committee, *Opinions in the Bankruptcy Context: Rating Agency, Structured Financing, and Chapter 11 Transactions*, 46 THE BUSINESS LAWYER 718 (1991)

_____, *Special Report of the TriBar Opinion Committee: The Remedies Opinion – Deciding When to Include Exceptions and Assumptions*, 59 BUSINESS LAWYER 1483 (2003–2004)

_____, *Special Report by the TriBar Opinion Committee: Use of the ABA Legal Opinion Accord in Specialized Financing Transactions*, 47 BUSINESS LAWYER 1720 (1992)

_____, *Third Party 'Closing' Opinions: A Report of the TriBar Opinion Committee*, 53 BUSINESS LAWYER 592 (1998)

Tucker, J. Maxwell, *Groupo Mexicano and the Death of Substantive Consolidation*, 8 AMERICAN BANKRUPTCY INSTITUTE LAW REVIEW 427 (2000)

_____, *Substantive Consolidation: the Cacophony Continues*, 18 AMERICAN BANKRUPTCY INSTITUTE LAW REVIEW 89 (2010)

Turnbull, Stuart M., and Michel Crouhy, *The Subprime Credit Crisis of 07* (July 9, 2008), available at http://papers.ssrn.com/sol3/papers.cfm?abstract_id=1112467

Ueda, Toshifumi, *Japan Turns Its Hand to Whole-Business Deals*, 23 INTERNATIONAL FINANCIAL LAW REVIEW 73 (2004)

United States of America, The Department of the Treasury, *The Department of the Treasury Blueprint for a Modernized Financial Regulatory Structure*, THE DEPARTMENT OF THE TREASURY, UNITED STATES OF AMERICA (March 2008)

United States Housing Foundation, Inc. v. Forman, 421 U.S. 837, 847–848 (1975)

Vaaler, Bryn, *Bridging the Gap: Legal Opinions as an Introduction to Business Lawyering*, 61 UNIVERSITY OF MISSOURI KANSAS CITY LAW REVIEW 23 (1992)

Verrecchia, Robert E., *Disclosure and the Cost of Capital*, 26 JOURNAL OF ACCOUNTING AND ECONOMICS (1999)

_____, *Discretionary Disclosure*, 5 JOURNAL OF ACCOUNTING AND ECONOMICS 179 (1983)

_____, *Essays on Disclosure*, 32 JOURNAL OF ACCOUNTING AND ECONOMICS 97 (2001)

_____, *Information Quality and Discretionary Disclosure*, 12 JOURNAL OF ACCOUNTING AND ECONOMICS 365 (1990)

_____, *On the Theory of Market Information Efficiency*, 1 JOURNAL OF ACCOUNTING AND ECONOMICS 77 (1979)

Warren, Manning Gilbert, III, EUROPEAN SECURITIES REGULATION (2003)

_____, *Global Harmonization of Securities Laws: The Achievement of the European Communities*, 31 HARVARD INTERNATIONAL LAW JOURNAL 185 (1990)

Welker, Michael, *Disclosure Policy, Information Asymmetry, and Liquidity in Equity Markets*, 11 CONTEMPORARY ACCOUNTING RESEARCH 801 (1995)

Weston, J.F., ed., LARGE CORPORATIONS IN A CHANGING SOCIETY (1975)

Whalen, Richard Christopher, *The Subprime Crisis – Cause, Effect and Consequences*, NETWORKS FINANCIAL INSTITUTE, POLICY BRIEF 2008-PB-04 (March 2008), available at http://papers.ssrn.com/sol3/papers.cfm?abstract_id=1113888

Whitbeck, Jeremy Britton, *The JOBS Act of 2012: The Struggle Between Capital Formation and Investor Protections* (June 15, 2012), available at http://ssrn.com/absract=2149744

Whitehead, Charles K., *Reframing Financial Regulation*, 90 BOSTON UNIVERSITY LAW REVIEW 1 (2010)

Widen, William H., *Corporate Form and Substantive Consolidation*, 75 GEORGE WASHINGTON LAW REVIEW 237 (2006–2007)

Wolfson, Nicholas, *A Critique of the Securities and Exchange Commission*, 30 EMORY LAW JOURNAL 119 (1981)

_____, *Comments on the Proposed Federal Securities Code: Transformation of the Securities Act of 1933*, 33 UNIVERSITY OF MIAMI LAW REVIEW 1495 (1978–1979)

_____, Kenneth I. Rosenblum and Thomas A. Russo, *The Securities Markets: An Overview*, 16 HOWARD LAW JOURNAL 791 (1970–1971)

Wood, Phillip R., ed., INTERNATIONAL LOANS, BONDS, GUARANTEES, LEGAL OPINIONS, 2ND EDITION (2007)

Wysocki, Peter D., *Discussion of Ultimate Ownership, Income Management, and Legal and Extra-Legal Institutions*, 42 JOURNAL OF ACCOUNTING RESEARCH 463 (2004)

Xu, Chenggang, and Katharina Pistor, *Law Enforcement Under Incomplete Law: Theory and Evidence from Financial Market Regulation*, Discussion Paper No TE/02/442 (December 2002), available at http://eprints.lse.ac.uk/3748/1/Law_Enforcement_under_Incomplete_Law_Theory_and_Evidence_from_Financial_Market_Regulation.pdf

Yadav, Yesha, *Beyond Efficiency in Securities Regulation*, Vanderbilt University Law School Law and Economics Working Paper Number 14-8, available at http://ssrn.com/abstract=2400527

Zahid, Anowar, and Hasani Mohd Ali, *Shariah as a Choice of Law in International Financial Contracts: Shamil Bank of Bahrain Case Revisited*, 10 US-China Law Review 27 (2013)

Zarin, David, *Finding Legal Principle in Global Financial Regulation*, 52 Virginia Journal of International Law 683 (2012)

Zeller, Bruno, *The UNIDROIT Principles of Contract Law: Is There Room for Their Inclusion into Domestic Contracts*, 26 Journal of Law and Commerce 115 (2006–2007)

CHAPTER 6

Regulatory Aspects of the Islamic Capital Market and Basel III Requirements

By Musa Abdul-Basser

In the wake of the 2008 global economic and financial crisis, the Basel Committee on Banking Supervision (the Basel Committee) engaged in a massive and concerted effort to strengthen global capital and liquidity rules, with the overall objective of promoting great resilience in the banking sector. Although there would be subsequent revisions and clarifications, in 2010 the Basel Committee released its baseline document, *Basel III: A global regulatory framework for more resilient banks and banking systems* (the Basel III framework). This document, along with the Basel Committee's *Basel III: International framework for liquidity risk measurement, standards and monitoring* (the Basel III liquidity framework), forms the framework guidance for the Basel III regime.[1]

ELIGIBLE CAPITAL AND CAPITAL INSTRUMENTS

In Islamic capital markets, the standards-setting organisation, the Islamic Financial Service Board (IFSB), has also given essential guidance on Basel III, specifically for institutions offering Islamic financial services (IIFS). For its fundamental capital adequacy guidance, the IFSB promulgated IFSB-2 (*Capital Adequacy* Standard) in December and more recently IFSB-15 (Revised Capital Adequacy Standard for Institutions Offering Islamic Financial Services [Excluding Islamic Insurance *(Takāful)* Institutions and Islamic Collective Investment Schemes]) in December 2013, as a contemporaneous

---

[1] 'Basel III: A Global Regulatory Framework for more resilient banks and banking systems', December 2010 (rev. June 2011), Basel Committee on Banking Supervision, Bank for International Settlements.

response to the finalisation of the Basel III framework.[2] In the area of liquidity management, the IFSB has issued its IFSB-12 (Guiding Principles on Liquidity Risk Management for IIFS) in March 2012 and more recently again, more detailed guidance notes, GN-6 (Guidance Note on Quantitative Measures for Liquidity Risk Management in Institutions Offering Islamic Financial Services [Excluding Islamic Insurance (Takāful) Institutions and Islamic Collective Investment Schemes]). In this chapter, we will define the categorical underpinnings of the Basel III capital and liquidity framework documents, as well as discussing the IFSB's analysis of the Basel III categories as they apply to IIFS. Although the Basel III regime focuses on risk-based analysis and the use of ratios, the entire scope of the framework revolves around the classification of different banking assets and liabilities into appropriate categories, as described in the Basel III guidelines. Although both the Basel III regime and the IFSB guidance have complex requirements and exceptions that necessitate detailed analysis, there can be no understanding of either without discussion of the definitional categories that underpin them.

Together with liquidity risk management which was also a major concern, the Basel Committee's primary effort in fortifying the banking sector through the creation of Basel III was to target and strengthen the regulatory capital aspect of the Basel II regime's 'three pillars' framework.[3] Overall, the objective of the Basel III regime's capital adequacy framework is to 'raise both the quality and quantity of the regulatory capital base and enhance the risk coverage of the capital framework', by encouraging banks to keep leveraging low and to contain certain key systemic risks.[4] In focusing on the need to increase both the 'quantity and quality' of regulatory capital, the Basel Committee made some forensic conclusions on some of the drivers of the global financial crises. The Basel

---

[2] The IFSB supplemented IFSB-2 with a number of other publications in subsequent years related to the calculation of capital adequacy requirements in IIFS, in order either to cover additional products and services offered by IIFS or to provide further guidance on the application of various aspects of the current IFSB standards. These publications include:

    a. March 2008: 'GN-1: Guidance Note in Connection with the Capital Adequacy Standard: Recognition of Ratings by External Credit Assessment Institutions (ECAIs) on Shari'ah-Compliant Financial Instruments';

    b. January 2009: 'IFSB-7: Capital Adequacy Requirements for Sukūk, Securitisations and Real Estate Investment';

    c. December 2010: 'GN-2: Guidance Note in Connection with the Risk Management and Capital Adequacy Standards: Commodity Murābahah Transactions';

    d. December 2010: 'GN-3: Guidance Note on the Practice of Smoothing the Profits Payout to Investment Account Holders'; and

    e. March 2011: 'GN-4: Guidance Note in Connection with the IFSB Capital Adequacy Standard: The Determination of Alpha in the Capital Adequacy Ratio for IIFS'.

[3] See, 'Basel III: A Global Regulatory Framework for more resilient banks and banking systems', p. 2. Note, Basel II's framework contained three broad, topical aspects: 'Regulatory Capital' (Pillar 1), 'Supervisory Review' (Pillar 2) and 'Market Disclosure' (Pillar 3).

[4] Ibid. Note, the crux of the capital requirement framework for the capital categories discussed herein is as follows: Banks are required to hold minimum capital of 4.5 percent Common Equity Tier 1, 6.0 percent Tier 1, and total regulatory capital of 8.0 percent. In addition, banks are also required to maintain a 2.5 percent capital 'conservation buffer' (to be held outside of stress periods) as well as an addition 'countercyclical buffer' ranging from 0 to 2.5 percent (to be implemented during a downturn preceded by a period of excess credit growth). These capital requirements all have transitional (phase-in) requirements and other regulatory adjustments that are specified in the Basel III framework document.

Committee found that most banks that had high-risk exposures and suffered losses or write-downs during the crisis took such losses against the bank's retained earnings (a component of common equity), in the absence of adequate loss provisions. In such cases, even banks that appeared to have sufficient capital and assets were actually in poorer financial condition than upon first impression. This obfuscation was exacerbated by inconsistencies in 'the definition of capital across jurisdictions and the lack of disclosure that would have enabled the market to fully assess and compare the quality of capital between institutions'.[5] In light of these conclusions, the Basel Committee transformed the Basel II category of 'Tier 1' capital to 'Common Equity Tier 1' capital, added a new capital category for Basel III called 'Additional Tier 1', refined the 'Tier 2' capital category and eliminated Basel II's 'Tier 3' (short-term subordinated debt) capital category.[6] The three categories or 'components' of capital under the Basel III regime each have 'elements' and 'criteria' that make up the component and are specified below.

Common Equity Tier 1

Common Equity Tier 1 capital consists of the sum of the following elements:

- Common shares issued by the bank that meet the criteria for classification as common shares for regulatory purposes (or the equivalent for non-joint stock companies);
- Stock surplus (share premium) resulting from the issue of instruments included Common Equity Tier 1;
- Retained earnings;
- Accumulated other comprehensive income and other disclosed reserves (unrealised losses here were subject to transitional or phase-in arrangement that are also specified in the Basel III guidelines);
- Common shares issued by consolidated subsidiaries of the bank and held by third parties (i.e. minority interest) that meet the criteria for inclusion in Common Equity Tier 1 capital. See Section 4 for the relevant criteria; and
- Regulatory adjustments applied in the calculation of Common Equity Tier 1.[7]

These broad elements compose the core of the Common Equity Tier 1 capital component and have some regulatory adjustments (related to the phase-in period), caveats and other small exemptions related to non-joint stock banks,[8] but the crux of the definition is that only common equity and retained earning fall into this Common Equity Tier 1 category.

---

[5] Ibid.

[6] For more on Basel II capital adequacy categories, *see* 'Basel II: Revised international capital framework', Basel Committee on Banking Supervision, Bank for International Settlement, 4 June 2006; 'Joint Final Rule: Risk-Based Capital Standards: Advanced Capital Adequacy Framework– Basel II', United States Federal Register, 2 November 2007 – Docket Number R-1261, Board of Governor of the Federal Reserve System; 'Implementation of Basel II: Implications for the World Bank and the IMF', International Monetary Fund, 22 June 2005.

[7] See, 'Basel III: A Global Regulatory Framework for more resilient banks and banking systems', p. 13.

[8] Ibid., p. 14. Note, the criteria also apply to non-joint stock companies such as mutual stock, cooperative or savings institutions. The Basel Committee intended for the criteria here to 'preserve the quality of the instruments by requiring that they are deemed fully equivalent to common shares in terms of their capital quality as regards loss absorption and do not possess features which could cause the condition of the bank to be weakened as a going concern during periods of market stress.'

Criteria

Helpfully, particularly in the case of non-joint stock banks that may have equity instruments other than basic, common shares, the Basel Committee gives further guidance as to just what constitutes Common Equity Tier 1 capital or 'common shares' for the purposes of Basel III. Such equity must:

1. Represent the most subordinated claim in liquidation of the bank.
2. Be entitled to a claim on the residual assets that is proportional with its share of issued capital, after all senior claims have been repaid in liquidation (i.e. claim is not fixed or capped).
3. Have principal that is perpetual and never repaid outside of liquidation (setting aside discretionary repurchases or other means of effectively reducing capital in a discretionary and permissible manner).
4. Be of a bank that does nothing to create an expectation at issuance that the instrument will be bought back, redeemed or cancelled, nor do the statutory or contractual terms provide any feature which might give rise to such an expectation.
5. Have distributions which are paid out of distributable items (retained earnings included). The level of distributions is not in any way tied or linked to the amount paid in at issuance and is not subject to a contractual cap (except to the extent that a bank is unable to pay distributions that exceed the level of distributable items).
6. Contain no circumstances under which the distributions are obligatory. Non-payment is therefore not an event of default.
7. Have distributions which are paid only after all legal and contractual obligations have been met and payments on more senior capital instruments have been made. This means that there are no preferential distributions, including in respect of other elements classified as the highest quality issued capital.
8. Be the issued capital that takes the first and proportionately greatest share of any losses as they occur (including any instrument that has a permanent write-down feature). Within the highest quality capital, each instrument absorbs losses on a going concern basis proportionately and *pari passu* with all the others.
9. Have a paid in amount that is recognised as equity capital (i.e. not recognised as a liability) for determining balance sheet insolvency.
10. Have a paid in amount that is classified as equity under the relevant accounting standards.
11. Be directly issued and paid in and the bank cannot directly or indirectly have funded the purchase of the instrument.

Under the Basel II regime, the Basel Committee had never been as specific or informative in their description of just what constituted basic equity, but with these 11 criteria, Basel III makes it clear that all bank 'equity' is not created the same. By creating such discrete and exacting criteria for this highest category of capital in Basel III, the Basel Committee was able to bifurcate the Basel II 'Tier 1' definition into the Common Equity Tier 1 capital and those forms of basic equity that do not quite meet the Basel Committee definition of 'common shares'. This form of basic equity is categorised as Additional Tier 1 capital.

Additional Tier 1 Capital

As mentioned above, in considering the Basel III regime and the global financial crises, the Basel Committee concluded that one of the primary drivers of bank instability was losses and write-downs taken against retained earnings and common equity. This meant that the bulk of regulatory capital in the new Basel III regime would need to be comprised of the very forms of equity that suffered the most injurious losses during the crisis. However, the Basel Committee also recognised that there is a multiplicity of capital instruments that would be part of the capital structure of modern banks and, yet fall foul of the stringent criteria of Common Equity Tier 1. These forms of bank capital, which fall just short of Common Equity Tier 1, fall into the Additional Tier 1 capital category. The simplest example of this would be a hypothetical bank's preferred stock, where such stock has the right to be paid a dividend (normally a percentage of the nominal value) before the common equity of the bank. Additional Tier 1 capital consists of the sum of the following elements:

- Instruments issued by the bank that meet the criteria for inclusion in Additional Tier 1 capital (and are not included in Common Equity Tier 1);
- Stock surplus (share premium) resulting from the issue of instruments included in Additional Tier 1 capital;
- Instruments issued by consolidated subsidiaries of the bank and held by third parties that meet the criteria for inclusion in Additional Tier 1 capital and are not included in Common Equity Tier 1; and
- Regulatory adjustments applied in the calculation of Additional Tier 1 capital.[9]

Criteria

Notwithstanding certain regulatory adjustments, applicable capital from subsidiaries and the related stock surpluses from Additional Tier 1 capital, we can see above that the definition of Additional Tier 1 capital is completely based upon the related criteria. The following are the so-called 'minimum' set of criteria for an instrument issued by any bank to meet the Additional Tier 1 capital category:

1. Issued and paid in;
2. Subordinated to depositors, general creditors and subordinated debt of the bank;
3. Is neither secured nor covered by a guarantee of the issuer or related entity or other arrangement that legally or economically enhances the seniority of the claim vis-à-vis bank creditors;
4. Is perpetual (there is no maturity date and there are no step-ups or other incentives to redeem);
5. May be callable at the initiative of the issuer only after a minimum of five years:
   a. To exercise a call option a bank must receive prior supervisory approval;
   b. A bank must not do anything which creates an expectation that the call will be exercised; and

---

[9] See, 'Basel III: A Global Regulatory Framework for more resilient banks and banking systems', p. 17.

    c. Banks must not exercise a call unless:
- **i.** They replace the called instrument with capital of the same or better quality and the replacement of this capital is done at conditions which are sustainable for the income capacity of the bank; or
- **ii.** The bank demonstrates that its capital position is well above the minimum capital requirements (by the local regulators) after the call option is exercised;

6. Any repayment of principal (for example, through repurchase or redemption) must be with prior supervisory approval and banks should not assume or create market expectations that supervisory approval will be given

7. Dividend/coupon discretion:
   - **d.** the bank must have full discretion at all times to cancel distributions/payments
   - **e.** cancellation of discretionary payments must not be an event of default
   - **f.** banks must have full access to cancelled payments to meet obligations as they fall due
   - **g.** cancellation of distributions/payments must not impose restrictions on the bank except in relation to distributions to common stockholders

8. Dividends/coupons must be paid out of distributable items;

9. The instrument cannot have a credit-sensitive dividend feature, that is a dividend/coupon that is reset periodically based in whole or in part on the banking organisation's credit standing;

10. The instrument cannot contribute to liabilities exceeding assets if such a balance sheet test forms part of national insolvency law;

11. Instruments classified as liabilities for accounting purposes must have principal loss absorption through either (i) conversion to common shares at an objective pre-specified trigger point or (ii) a write-down mechanism which allocates losses to the instrument at a pre-specified trigger point. The write-down will have the following effects:
    - **h.** Reduce the claim of the instrument in liquidation;
    - **i.** Reduce the amount repaid when a call is exercised; and
    - **j.** Partially or fully reduce coupon/dividend payments on the instrument;

12. Neither the bank nor a related party over which the bank exercises control or significant influence can have purchased the instrument, nor can the bank directly or indirectly have funded the purchase of the instrument;

13. The instrument cannot have any features that hinder recapitalisation, such as provisions that require the issuer to compensate investors if a new instrument is issued at a lower price during a specified time frame; and

14. If the instrument is not issued out of an operating entity or the holding company in the consolidated group (e.g. a special purpose vehicle or 'SPV'), proceeds must be immediately available without limitation to an operating entity or the holding company in the consolidated group in a form which meets or exceeds all of the other criteria for inclusion in Additional Tier 1 Capital.

Although the Additional Tier 1 capital criteria are various, the theme of these criteria is consistent: Additional Tier 1 capital should not be debt, but be generally recognised as being available to absorb unexpected (i.e. unprovisioned) losses while the bank is a going concern without this constituting a default, while possessing payment preference features or other characteristics that make it senior to common stock.

Tier 2 Capital

Under the Basel III framework, Tier 2 capital is now the lowest category of regulatory capital. Unlike the two Tier 1 categories previously mentioned, the purpose of Tier 2 capital is to absorb losses on a 'gone concern' basis, or in other words, losses accrued in insolvency prior to depositors losing any money. Tier 2 capital consists of the sum of the following elements:

- Instruments issued by the bank that meet the criteria for inclusion in Tier 2 capital (and are not included in Tier 1 capital).
- Stock surplus (share premium) resulting from the issue of instruments included in Tier 2 capital.
- Instruments issued by consolidated subsidiaries of the bank and held by third parties that meet the criteria for inclusion in Tier 2 capital and are not included in Tier 1 capital.
- Certain reserves or 'general loan loss provisions' held against future, presently unidentified, losses that are freely available to meet losses which later materialise, as well as the difference between any actual losses that materialise and previously set aside provisions.[10]
- Regulatory adjustments applied in the calculation of Tier 2 capital.

Criteria

Again, as with the Additional Tier 1 capital, the criteria related to the Tier 2 capital definition are crucial and descriptive. The criteria describe a bank instrument that may be equity or debt obligations that have a fixed payment and maturity. The following are a 'minimum' set of criteria for an instrument issued by any bank to meet the Tier 2 capital category:

1. Issued and paid in;
2. Subordinated to depositors and general creditors of the bank;
3. Is neither secured nor covered by a guarantee of the issuer or related entity or other arrangement that legally or economically enhances the seniority of the claim vis-à-vis depositors and general bank creditors;
4. Maturity:
   a. minimum original maturity of at least five years;
   b. recognition in regulatory capital in the remaining five years before maturity will be amortised on a straight line basis; and
   c. there are no step-ups or other incentives to redeem;

---

[10] International Financial Reporting Standards (IFRS) do not consider 'general loan loss provisions' against *unidentified* possible future losses as being either liabilities or contra-assets. However, the new rules in IFRS 9 require impairment provisions (i.e. liabilities or contra-assets) to be made to recognise *lifetime expected credit losses for significant increases in credit risk since initial recognition*, whether on an individual or a collective basis. Expected credit losses are a probability-weighted estimate of credit losses, i.e. *the present value of all cash shortfalls compared to what is contractually due*, over the expected life of the credit instrument (IFRS 9, chapter 5).

5. May be callable at the initiative of the issuer only after a minimum of five years:
   a. To exercise a call option a bank must receive prior supervisory approval;
   b. A bank must not do anything that creates an expectation that the call will be exercised; and
   c. Banks must not exercise a call unless:
      i. They replace the called instrument with capital of the same or better quality and the replacement of this capital is done at conditions which are sustainable for the income capacity of the bank; or
      ii. The bank demonstrates that its capital position is well above the minimum capital requirements in their local jurisdiction after the call option is exercised;
6. The investor must have no rights to accelerate the repayment of future scheduled payments (coupon or principal), except in bankruptcy and liquidation;
7. The instrument cannot have a credit-sensitive dividend feature; that is, a dividend/coupon that is reset periodically based in whole or in part on the banking organisation's credit standing;
8. Neither the bank nor a related party over which the bank exercises control or significant influence can have purchased the instrument, nor can the bank directly or indirectly have funded the purchase of the instrument; and
9. If the instrument is not issued out of an operating entity or the holding company in the consolidated group (e.g. a special purpose vehicle – 'SPV'), proceeds must be immediately available without limitation to an operating entity or the holding company in the consolidated group in a form which meets or exceeds all of the other criteria for inclusion in Tier 2 capital.

SHARI'AH-COMPLIANT INSTRUMENTS AND BASEL III CAPITAL COMPONENTS

The application of Basel III's capital adequacy standards to Islamic banks poses special but seemingly surmountable challenges. At first impression, Islamic banks appear to be already well-capitalised (with high levels of Tier 1 capital that is largely in the form of common equity).[11] Prior to the advent of Basel III, apart from common equity, the treatment of the various components of capital was previously up to the discretion of local supervisory authorities. Still, despite the appearance of healthy capitalisation, Islamic banks undeniably hold unique banking assets that do not fit within the mould of their conventional counterparts. Islamic financial instruments are generally composed of either asset-based contracts (as in the case of *murabaha, salam* and *istisna'a*, which are based on the purchase of an asset, *ijarah*, which is based on selling the usage benefits or usufruct of such an asset), profit sharing (*musharaka* and *mudaraba*), or *sukuk* (securities and investments in structures of the above referenced contractual forms). Such instruments involve exposure to various types of risk, notably market risk as well as credit risk. However, the real differentiation between Shari'ah-compliant

---

[11] Alfred Kammer, Mohamed Norat, Marco Piñón, Ananthakrishnan Prasad, Christopher Towe, Zeine Zeidane (2015) 'Islamic Finance: Opportunities, Challenges, and Policy Options', IMF Staff Discussion Note, April, SDN/15/02, International Monetary Fund, p. 22.

banking assets addressed in IFSB-15 and conventional banking assets arises only in discussion of Basel III's Capital Adequacy Ratio (CAR) requirement and the related 'risk-weighting' of assets connected with the calculation of the CAR.[12] Though discussions of Basel III's CAR and the risk-weighting of bank assets are beyond our more basic topic of the components of capital, a brief word is appropriate on how IFSB-15 approaches this part of Basel III's capital adequacy regime.

IFSB-15 sets the appropriate risk-weighting for assets held in the nine, nominate Shari'ah-compliant transactional forms (*murabaha*, commodity *murabaha*, *salam*, *istis-na'a*, *ijarah*, *musharaka*, *mudaraba*, *qard*, and *wakala*), as well as risk-weighting for *sukuk* related to each of those nominate forms. A complication, however, remains with regard to the calculation of risk-weighted assets given the variation across jurisdictions in the treatment of Profit-Sharing (and loss-bearing) Investment Accounts (PSIA), the assets funded by which are included in the bank's risk-weighted assets according to an alpha factor that varies across jurisdictions.[13] As Islamic banks cannot offer interest-bearing accounts, unrestricted PSIAs have risen as an alternative form of account for depositors who seek a return, but their practical usage has led to complications for IIFS. PSIAs are accounts through which the depositor invests either in a defined and restricted set of investments (restricted PSIA) or in a general pool of any or all of the assets held by the bank (unrestricted PSIA). It is the latter that are used as a substitute for interest-bearing deposit or savings accounts. Generally, these PSIAs can be structured in the

---

[12] 'IFSB-15: Revised Capital Adequacy Standard for Institutions Offering Islamic Financial Services [excluding Islamic Insurance (Takaful) Institutions and Islamic Collective Investment Schemes]', IFSB, December 2013, p. 69.

[13] In principle, under the *mudaraba* contract that typically governs the PSIAs, all losses on investments financed by their funds are to be borne by the Investment Account Holders (IAH) unless there is misconduct, negligence or breach of contract, whereas the profits on such investments are shared between the IAH and the Islamic bank as manager of the investments (*mudarib*) in the proportions specified in the contract. In practice, however, Islamic banks engage in a range of practices that cushion the returns paid to the IAH—thus protecting the cash flows from IAHs funds against variations in the Islamic bank's income from assets financed by those funds—in order to pay market-related compensation to the IAH. These practices expose the bank's share-holders' returns to displaced commercial risk (DCR). IFSB-15 recommends that local regulators should assess the extent of DCR caused by this treatment of PSIAs, based on an IIFS's decision regarding the payout to IAHs, and that banks should reflect these assessments in the computation of their capital adequacy ratio. This is referred to as the 'supervisory discretion formula' for the CAR, which specifies that a fraction 'alpha' of the credit and market risk-weighted assets funded by PSIAs may be included in the denominator of the CAR, where the permissible value for 'alpha' is subject to supervisory discretion. When unrestricted PSIAs fully bear their own risks (credit and market) as specified in their *mudarabah* contract and receive returns equal to the returns on the investments made with their funds, IAHs are treated as investors. In this case, 'alpha' will be zero, and therefore no additional capital requirements are necessary. At the other extreme, when the Islamic bank pays IAHs the market return regardless of the return on assets, and there is no mitigation of DCR by the use of a Profit Equalisation Reserve (PER), then the PSIA cannot be treated as loss-absorbing. In this case, alpha will be set to 1. Therefore, in this case, there will be additional capital requirements to provide the necessary capital buffer. In practice, alpha can be set anywhere between these two extremes, depending on the supervisor's assessment of the magnitude of the displaced commercial risk and the risk mitigating factors in place. See, 'Islamic Finance: Opportunities, Challenges, and Policy Options', p. 21.

form of *wakala*, *musharaka* or, more typically, *mudaraba*. They have become popular but, as we will note below, cannot be considered as part of regulatory capital. Instead, as indicated in footnote 13, ISFB-15 requires their risk-absorbent characteristics to be reflected in the treatment of the assets which they fund in the calculation of the denominator of the CAR.[14] This underscores the importance of efforts to achieve greater consistency of the alpha factor where levels of DCR are similar. It is also important for IIFS to clearly identify their instruments eligible for treatment as Additional Tier 1 and Tier 2 capital and to adhere closely to IFSB-15's guidance on the Basel III framework in this regard.

For our purposes here, IFSB-15's discussion of Basel III's capital component categories does nothing to alter significantly the elements and criteria described in Section A above from the Basel III framework: Generally, common stock for conventional banks is the same for Islamic banks. IFSB reiterates the elements and criteria of Common Equity Tier 1 from the Basel III framework, and generally does the same with the Additional Tier 1 and Tier 2 capital, though there are some interesting points to note for Shari'ah-compliant capital in these last two categories.

Additional Tier 1 Capital and Loss Absorbency for IIFS

As we may recall, and as noted in the Basel III framework, both forms of Tier 1 capital (Common Equity Tier 1 and Additional Tier 1) absorb losses of a bank as a 'going concern'. This means that such forms of capital take losses that the financial institution suffers during the course of its active, solvent business. IFSB-15 notes that IIFS may issue *musharaka sukuk* (with the underlying asset being the entire business of the IIFS). The holders of these *sukuk* are in fact partners with the IIFS common shareholders in the equity capital of the institution and thus fully share the risks of the IIFS' business.[15] Of course, such *musharaka sukuk* would need to comply with the other criteria of the Basel III framework, but most importantly, structure the instrument to abide by the maturity and callability requirements of the framework as well. A problem with such *musharaka sukuk* is that they would rank equally with the bank's common equity of which they would indeed be a non-voting form.

Recently, some Tier 1 *sukuk* issuances have taken the form of *mudaraba sukuk* where the sukuk-holders' rights to the assets financed by their funds are subordinated to the claims of the bank's current account holders and other senior creditors. These structures have received Shari'ah approval.

Tier 2 Capital and Loss Absorption for IIFS

IFSB-15 also asserts that 'it might be possible', subject to Shari'ah compliance concerns, for an IIFS to issue *mudaraba* or *wakala sukuk* as Tier 2 capital, where the underlying assets of such *sukuk* are instruments that are convertible to common stock

---

[14]'IFSB-15: Revised Capital Adequacy Standard for Institutions Offering Islamic Financial Services [excluding Islamic Insurance (Takaful) Institutions and Islamic Collective Investment Schemes]', IFSB, December 2013, p. 10.
[15] Ibid., p. 8.

of the IIFS upon insolvency or cessation of business.[16] Such *sukuk* would adhere to the 'gone concern' criteria under Basel III's framework for Tier 2 capital, insofar as the underlying assets would not be available to meet the claims of the IIFS' creditors or account holders during normal business, but after insolvency and conversion would rank *pari passu* with the common stock of such institutions.[17]

At least one Islamic bank has, however, taken a different approach, similar to that mentioned above, namely a subordinated *mudaraba* structure, but where losses are absorbed only on a 'gone concern' basis, i.e. at the point of the bank's non-viability.

Although there is congruence between the capital components categories set forth in Basel III and the IFSB's Islamic bank-specific guidelines (which are based on Basel III), there are still distinct concerns with interpreting Basel III capital adequacy requirements for Islamic banks, or even applying the IFSB-15 interpretations of such requirements to IIFS in a uniform fashion. Results from a recent survey by the IMF, seem to indicate that the IFSB's well thought out capital adequacy standards are only applied in a limited number of jurisdictions and not uniformly among them.[18] For example, in Ethiopia, Kazakhstan, the UAE and the UK, the chosen Basel capital framework applies to all banks, including Islamic banks. Meanwhile, in Bahrain, Jordan, Malaysia and Sudan the regulatory capital requirements contain prescriptions that are generally based on IFSB standards and principles on needed adjustments to the Basel III framework that cater to IIFS. A specific example of local regulatory discretion previously mentioned is the 'alpha factor'. How different local regulators consider this 'alpha factor' can affect the calculation of the CAR across different countries. Hence, it might be incongruous to compare capital ratios and risk exposures among IIFS in different jurisdictions.[19] As always in the Islamic financial services industry, increased regulatory clarity – set in banking laws and informed by enhanced dialogue among stakeholders – is needed, as is stronger collaboration between Islamic and global standard setters in developing appropriate standards for the industry.

LIQUIDITY RISK MANAGEMENT AND HIGH QUALITY LIQUID ASSETS (HQLA)

The Basel III framework specifically begins its discussion of new liquidity standards by noting that strong capital requirements, though necessary, are insufficient in and of

---

[16] Note, IFSB-15 indicates that the *mudaraba or wakala* contract would need to be particularly careful in defining the trigger point and conversion ratio for such conversion terms in order to avoid *gharrar* in the contract.

[17] IFSB-15, p. 9.

[18] See, 'Islamic Finance: Opportunities, Challenges, and Policy Options', p. 17. Note, of the 29 countries surveyed, IFSB standards regarding risk management and capital adequacy are applied in only six jurisdictions (21 percent of those surveyed).

[19] Ibid., p. 18.

themselves. In more forensic discussion of the global financial crises, the Basel Committee noted that:

> *During the early 'liquidity phase' of the financial crisis, many banks – despite adequate capital levels – still experienced difficulties because they did not manage their liquidity in a prudent manner. The crisis again drove home the importance of liquidity to the proper functioning of financial markets and the banking sector. Prior to the crisis, asset markets were buoyant and funding was readily available at low cost. The rapid reversal in market conditions illustrated how quickly liquidity can evaporate and that illiquidity can last for an extended period of time. The banking system came under severe stress, which necessitated central bank action to support both the functioning of money markets and, in some cases, individual institutions.[20]*

The Basel Committee asserted that it had spoken to the issues of strong liquidity risk management in its 2008 liquidity guidance, *Principles for Sound Liquidity Management and Supervision*, and that the failures of the global financial system occurred in flagrant disregard of these principles (even though the groundwork for the crisis was very much already laid by the time those principles were promulgated).[21] In any case, for the purposes of Basel III, and to complement and strengthen the 2008 liquidity principles, the Basel Committee created two new minimum ratio standards, as well as a group of 'monitoring metrics' to give guidance to local regulators. These two Basel III liquidity management ratios were the Liquidity Coverage Ratio (LCR) and the Net Stable Funding Ratio (NSFR).[22] Basel III developed these two ratios to address two distinct but complementary liquidity management risks. The purpose of the LCR is to increase 'short-term' resilience in a bank's liquidity risk management by ensuring that such an institution has sufficient high quality liquid resources to withstand an acute stress scenario in which there are liquidity shortages lasting for one month. Through the NSFR, the Basel Committee sought to promote such resilience in a bank's liquidity risk profile in the face of such shortage over the course of a one-year time horizon.[23] For the purposes of this section we shall focus on the short-term ratio, LCR, and more specifically what goes into the category of HQLA that makes up its numerator. Indeed, for conventional and Islamic banks alike, the greater concern has seemed to be how to respond to

---

[20] Ibid., p. 8.

[21] Ibid. See also 'Principles for Sound Liquidity Risk Management and Supervision', Bank for International Settlements, 2008.

[22] A bank's LCR = (Stock of HQLA)/(Total net cash outflows over the next 30 calendar days), which must be greater than or equal to 60 percent in times of normal liquidity as of 1 January 2015 (rising 10 percent each year until reaching a cap of 100 percent by 1 January 2019). See, 'Basel III: The Liquidity Coverage Ratio and liquidity risk monitoring tools', Basel Committee on Banking Supervision, Bank for International Settlements, January 2013, for specifics on calculating this ratio. A bank's NSF = (Available amount of stable funding)/(Required amount of stable funding) which must be greater than or equal to 100 percent. See, 'Basel III: the net stable funding ratio', Basel Committee on Banking Supervision, Bank for International Settlements, October 2014, for specifics on the calculation of this ratio.

[23] See, 'Basel III: A Global Regulatory Framework for more resilient banks and banking systems', p. 8.

the Basel III liquidity management requirement surrounding the LCR and its related categorisation of HQLA. In fact, a recent study by the Basel Committee found that had the LCR requirements come into *full* effect in July 2014 (rather than at only 60 percent of the full 100 percent ratio, not required until 2019) a fifth of the 210 monitored banks would have had a shortfall in HQLA, totalling approximately USD341 billion.[24] However, to better understand the specifics of HQLA under Basel III, one needs to consider how the Basel Committee approaches the concept of 'liquidity' in the context of its framework requirements.

Funding Liquidity, Market Liquidity and HQLA

In introducing the LCR and NSFR ratio requirements in the Basel III framework document, the Basel Committee asserts that they were created specifically to address 'funding liquidity'.[25] The Basel Committee also described their 2008 liquidity risk principles document ('Principles for Sound Liquidity Risk Management and Supervision') as an effort to counteract 'funding liquidity risk'. One may wonder what specifically the Basel Committee means when discussing bank 'liquidity' and how, or to what extent, it is reflected in funding liquidity or market liquidity.[26] One need only review the Basel Committee's 2008 liquidity risk principles document for a clear differentiation. In the 2008 liquidity principles document, the Basel Committee defines liquidity as 'the ability of a bank to fund increases in assets and meet obligations as they come due, without incurring unacceptable losses'.[27] In a clarifying footnote in the same document, the Basel Committee not only defines funding liquidity and market liquidity, but also notes that its liquidity risk principles document focuses mainly on 'funding liquidity':

> *This paper [*Principles for Sound Liquidity Risk Management and Supervision*] focuses primarily on funding liquidity risk. Funding liquidity risk is the risk that the firm will not be able to meet efficiently both expected and unexpected current and future cash flow and collateral needs without affecting either daily operations or the financial condition of the firm. Market liquidity risk is the risk that a firm cannot easily offset or eliminate a position at the market price because of inadequate market depth or market disruption.*[28]

In short, funding liquidity and market liquidity, as well as their related risks, are components of overall liquidity. Although the Basel Committee does indeed consider

---

[24] See, Brunsden, Jim (2015) 'Basel Finds Banks $341 Billion Short of Liquidity Rule', Bloomberg Business News, Bloomberg, L. P., 3 March, http://www.bloomberg.com/news/articles/2015-03-03/basel-finds-banks-341-billion-short-of-liquidity-rule

[25] See, 'Basel III: A Global Regulatory Framework for more resilient banks and banking systems', p. 8.

[26] Although in traditional liquidity analysis there are indeed other aspects and sub-sets of liquidity and related risk, including contingent liquidity risk, structural liquidity risk, and term liquidity risk, the focus of this discussion is on the broader categories of funding and market liquidity, as indeed they are the focus of the Basel Committee's liquidity requirement framework.

[27] See, 'Principles for Sound Liquidity Risk Management and Supervision', Bank for International Settlement, 2008, p. 1.

[28] Ibid., at note 2.

market liquidity risk as an aspect of the overall liquidity risk that banks face during liquidity shortages, given that market liquidity is mostly affected by factors exogenous to a bank's management, the bulk the Basel Committee's guidance on liquidity requirements focus on funding risk. This is no different in the current Basel III regime and in the Basel III liquidity framework's discussion of the LCR and NSFR. The Basel Committee does note that banks may affect market liquidity by improperly assessing the value of their own assets and by making large sales of assets on the market (thereby driving down prices).[29] Also, the Basel Committee does recognise that there is an interconnection between funding liquidity and market liquidity, insofar as banks seeking to enhance the former can increase the latter by buying in the secondary markets to build up a stock of liquid assets or selling such assets to obtain cash, and not on-lending in the short-term markets.[30] The potential for banks to contribute to these 'illiquidity spirals' is systemically important to how banks comply with Basel III's liquidity requirements. Still, with the advent of the Basel III global framework, and the Basel III liquidity framework which followed, one will find that when the Basel Committee mentions 'liquidity', they generally mean funding liquidity.

Criteria for HQLA

Systemically, banks' retention and usage of HQLA represent the first line of defence against potential financial crises, as such cyclical events are often preceded and precipitated by liquidity shortages. The Basel III liquidity framework represented the first time that the Basel Committee set specific and detailed criteria for HQLA and set uniform standards as to how they should be defined. This is not to say that the Basel Committee had not made extensive efforts to underline the importance of HQLA or 'liquid assets' (as they were sometimes informally called prior to the advent of Basel III). In fact, the Basel Committee's 2008 liquidity risk principles document emphasises liquid assets in its first of 17 principles, saying in part that '[a] bank should establish a robust liquidity risk management framework that ensures it maintains sufficient liquidity, including a cushion of unencumbered HQLA, to withstand a range of stress events, including those involving the loss or impairment of both unsecured and secured funding sources'.[31] Even in 2011, with the promulgation of its Basel III framework document introducing the LCR requirement, the Basel Committee was light on specifics and descriptions of HQLA. The closest the Basel Committee came to expounding on HQLA in its discussion on LCR in the Basel III framework was the assertion that 'high-quality liquid assets held in the stock should be unencumbered, liquid in markets during a time of stress and, ideally, be central bank eligible'.[32] It was not until January 2013 when the Basel Committee issued its Basel III liquidity framework ('Basel III: The Liquidity Coverage Ratio and Liquidity Risk Monitoring'), as a follow up to the 2011 Basel III framework document, that detailed criteria and categories of HQLA were disseminated. Again, as with Basel III regime's capital adequacy requirements and the CAR, its

---

[29] Ibid., p. 10.
[30] Ibid.
[31] Ibid., at p. 6.
[32] See, 'Basel III: A Global Regulatory Framework for more resilient banks and banking systems', p. 9.

liquidity risk standards and the LCR can be properly implemented only by understanding the categorical underpinnings of the standard. In this case, we must ask, what are HQLA?

HQLA and Credit Quality

HQLA are assets that fit certain 'characteristics' and 'categories' specified in the Basel III liquidity framework. The characteristics are arguably more important than the specific asset categorisations, given that the Basel Committee permits local supervisors significant discretion with respect to discounting assets from HQLA consideration if they do not meet all of the HQLA characteristics, though they might fall into one of the HQLA categories.[33] Two of the characteristics which the Basel Committee lists under its 'fundamental characteristics' relate to an asset's overall credit quality. Specifically, such assets should be characterised by:

1. **Low Risk**: Although Basel III groups a number of risk factors under this characteristic, including low duration risk, low legal risk, low inflation risk and low currency risk, the focus of this 'low-risk' characteristic is the Basel Committee's assertion that 'High credit standing of the issuer and a low degree of subordination increase an asset's liquidity'. The reader will quickly surmise that this form of credit analysis and evaluation of risk is generally conducted by rating agencies or 'recognised external credit assessments institutions' (ECAI) in Basel III terms. If an ECAI determines the credit quality of an asset as low-risk, then it will likely receive a high rating and possess other HQLA characteristics.
2. **Low correlation with risky assets**: Another HQLA characteristic that relates to credit quality and risk is the requirement that an asset have low correlation with risky assets. This means that an asset cannot have any connection to an industry, currency or other characteristic that makes it more illiquid than normal during a period of crisis or illiquidity. The Basel III liquidity framework gives the example of a bank holding an instrument from another financial institution during a period of liquidity shortages for banks.

HQLA and Price Stability

In addition to the fundamental characteristics of HQLA related to credit quality, there are two other 'fundamental characteristics', both related to the valuation dynamics of the HQLA. Both of these price stability characteristics indicate the importance of transparency and availability of market information concerning the asset. Greater information leads to simpler pricing, which in turn creates greater incentive to buy and sell such assets:

1. **Ease and certainty of valuation**: an asset's liquidity increases if market participants are more likely to agree on its valuation. Assets with more standardised, homogenous and simple structures tend to be more fungible, promoting liquidity. The

---

[33] See, 'Basel III: The Liquidity Coverage Ratio and liquidity risk monitoring tool', Basel Committee on Bank Supervision, Bank for International Settlements, January 2013.

pricing formula of an HQLA must be easy to calculate and not depend on strong assumptions. The inputs into the pricing formula must also be publicly available. In practice, this should rule out the inclusion of most structured or exotic products.

2. **Listed on a developed and recognised exchange**: Listed assets have greater 'transparency' and significant amounts of public information on their issuers and associated investment risks. This provides assets that are listed on well-developed exchanges with a more accurate reflection of their actual value in the market and makes them less exposed to price fluctuations that are due to the shallowness of the market. In the absence of such a listing, the asset's issuer may not disclose all significant information to the market, which may give rise to insider trading, price manipulation and other informational asymmetries.

HQLA and Liquidity (Market-Related) Characteristics

In addition to the four fundamental characteristics for HQLA described above, the Basel III liquidity framework also discusses three characteristics of HQLA that relate to whether the asset in question is part of a liquid and resilient marketplace. These 'market-related' characteristics are as follows:

1. **Active and sizeable market:** The purported HQLA must (a) be a part of a deep market that has 'historical' depth and breadth, which may be demonstrated by a combination of anything from high trading volumes to a large diverse group of buyer and sellers and (b) a strong market infrastructure in the asset with multiple market makers making quotes;
2. **Low Volatility:** Again, there should be historical evidence of relative stability of market terms (e.g. prices and haircuts) and volumes during stressed periods. Assets whose prices remain relatively stable and are less prone to sharp price declines have a lower probability of causing institutions to liquidate them at a loss under duress to meet regulatory requirements;
3. **Flight to quality:** Over time, investors and market makers have demonstrated patterns of acquiring the purported HQLA during a systemic crisis.

It seems clear that in setting up these aspects of HQLA characteristics, the Basel Committee was not simply interested in emphasising the importance of market liquidity but, more importantly, the strength of such market liquidity over time. The Basel Committee makes this point, somewhat tautologically, with the assertion that the aforementioned market-related characteristics underscore that 'the test of whether liquid assets are of "high quality" is that, by way of sale or repo, their liquidity-generating capacity is assumed to remain intact even in periods of severe idiosyncratic and market stress'.[34] A relevant concern for this discussion is how much of a 'history' a potential HQLA's market should have before satisfying these market-related characteristics. The Basel III liquidity framework is silent on specifics in this regard, but it seems clear that this means at least one historical occurrence of a systemic event is required before meeting the market-related characteristics.

---

[34] See, ibid., at p. 13.

One HQLA characteristic that neither fits into the 'fundamental', nor 'market-related' groupings is the softer recommendation from the Basel Committee that HQLA, other than the lowest category of HQLA that is defined below, 'should ideally' be eligible at central bank liquidity facilities.[35] Central bank eligibility for an asset not only gives a real liquidity backstop for banks holding such assets, but also provides confidence to the broader market that such assets will remain relatively liquid through a systemic crisis. Another characteristic specified in the Basel III liquidity framework among its operational requirements, is the need for such assets to be unencumbered.[36] As we may recall, the Basel Committee's 2008 liquidity principles (from the period of the Basel II regime) had long recommended 'liquid assets' be free from restraints, pledges or other interests that might prevent them from being liquidated with ease.[37] This 'operational' requirement is universal to all of the categories of HQLA specified below, but should in effect be considered as a required 'characteristic'.

Under the Basel III liquidity framework, HQLA meeting the aforementioned characteristics are divided into two general types, designated as Level 1 assets and Level 2 assets. At a local regulator's discretion, the Level 2 asset category may be further reduced to Level 2A asset and Level 2B assets.[38] Level 2 assets are each assigned a 'haircut' or a percentage discount from their value when calculating a bank's 'total stock of HQLA' and can only represent at most 40 percent of the total HQLA stock of a bank for Basel III purposes. Level 1 assets do not require a 'haircut' and the full value of such HQLA may be attributed to the total stock of a bank for Basel III purposes (though local regulators may assign a haircut to certain Level 1 assets at their discretion) and there is no cap on the percentage of Level 1 assets in the calculation of a bank's total HQLA stock.

Level 1 HQLA

Level 1 assets are the highest category of HQLA under the Basel III framework. They are limited to assets that meet the characteristics discussed above and that are any of the following:

a. coins and banknotes;
b. central bank reserves, to the extent that the central bank policies allow them to be drawn down in times of stress;
c. marketable securities representing claims on or guaranteed by sovereigns, central banks, public sector entities (PSEs), the Bank for International Settlements,

---

[35] Ibid.

[36] See, ibid., at p. 14.

[37] Ibid. Note that assets that have been 'pre-positioned or deposited with or pledged to' a central bank or similar public entity can still be included in a bank's stock of HQLA as long as they have not yet been directly used to generate liquidity for the institution.

[38] See ibid. at p. 17. Note, the Basel Committee has asserted that where regulators allow for Level 2B assets in their jurisdictions there should be a 15 percent cap on the value of such assets on a bank's balance sheet (assessed after applying the required haircuts for the HQLA category and other 30 day repo liquidations that may be unwinding). This 15 percent cap in Level 2B assets is inclusive of the overall 40 percent cap on Level 2 asset that may be held by a financial institution.

the International Monetary Fund, the European Central Bank and European Community, or multilateral development banks, and satisfying all of the following conditions:

  i. assigned a 0 percent risk weight under the 'Basel II Standardised Approach for credit risk' (meaning the security is rated AAA to AA– by an ECAI);
  ii. traded in large, deep and active repo or cash markets characterised by a low level of concentration;
  iii. have a proven record as a reliable source of liquidity in the markets (repo or sale) even during stressed market conditions; and
  iv. not an obligation of a financial institution or any of its affiliated entities.
 d. where the sovereign has a non-0 percent risk weight, sovereign or central bank debt securities issued in domestic currencies by the sovereign or central bank in the country in which the liquidity risk is being taken or in the bank's home country; and
 e. where the sovereign has a non-0 percent risk weight, domestic sovereign or central bank debt securities issued in foreign currencies are eligible up to the amount of the bank's stressed net cash outflows in that specific foreign currency stemming from the bank's operations in the jurisdiction where the bank's liquidity risk is being taken.

Level 2A HQLA

Basel III requires a 15 percent haircut to be applied to the value of each Level 2A asset held in a bank's stock of HQLA. Level 2A assets are limited to assets that meet the HQLA characteristics discussed above and that are any of the following:

 a. Marketable securities representing claims on or guaranteed by sovereigns, central banks, PSEs or multilateral development banks that satisfy all of the following conditions:

  i. assigned a 20 percent risk weight under 'the Basel II Standardised Approach for credit risk' (meaning the security is rated A+ to A– by an ECAI);
  ii. traded in large, deep and active repo or cash markets characterised by a low level of concentration;
  iii. have a proven record as a reliable source of liquidity in the markets (repo or sale) even during stressed market conditions (i.e., maximum decline of price not exceeding 10 percent or increase in haircut not exceeding 10 percentage points over a 30-day period during a relevant period of significant liquidity stress); and
  iv. not an obligation of a financial institution or any of its affiliated entities.
 b. Corporate debt securities (including commercial paper) and 'covered bonds'[39] that satisfy all of the following conditions:

  i. in the case of corporate debt securities: not issued by a financial institution or any of its affiliated entities;
  ii. in the case of covered bonds: not issued by the bank itself or any of its affiliated entities;

---

[39] Note, covered bonds are bonds that are issued or owned by a bank or mortgage company that are subject to specialised law or regulation from a public supervisor to protect the interests of such bond holders.

   iii. either (i) have a long-term credit rating from a recognised ECAI of at least AA–
or in the absence of a long-term rating, a short-term rating equivalent in quality to the long-term rating; or (ii) do not have a credit assessment by a recognised
ECAI but are internally rated as having a probability of default (PD) corresponding to a credit rating of at least AA–;

   iv. traded in large, deep and active repo or cash markets characterised by a low
level of concentration; and

   v. have a proven record as a reliable source of liquidity in the markets (repo or
sale) even during stressed market conditions: i.e., maximum decline of price or
increase in haircut over a 30-day period during a relevant period of significant
liquidity stress not exceeding 10 percent.

Level 2B HQLA

Level 2B assets are the lowest category of HQLA and, as noted above, are only permitted at the discretion of a local regulator or supervisor. The Basel Committee even goes
as far as to strongly caution local supervisors to ensure that purported Level 2B assets
meet the HQLA characteristics discussed above and that local banks have appropriate
internal control and systems in place to monitor the heightened potential risk associated with holding such assets. The three types of Level 2B assets have haircuts ranging
from 25 percent to 50 percent and, of course, are limited to assets that meet the HQLA
characteristics discussed above.

A larger haircut is applied to the current market value of each Level 2B asset held
in the stock of HQLA. Level 2B assets are limited to the following:

  a. Residential mortgage-backed securities that satisfy all of the following conditions
may be included in Level 2B, subject to a 25 percent haircut:

   i. not issued by, and the underlying assets have not been originated by the bank
itself or any of its affiliated entities;

   ii. have a long-term credit rating from a recognised ECAI of AA or higher, or in
the absence of a long-term rating, a short-term rating equivalent in quality to
the long-term rating;

   iii. traded in large, deep and active repo or cash markets characterised by a low
level of concentration;

   iv. have a proven record as a reliable source of liquidity in the markets (repo or
sale) even during stressed market conditions, i.e. a maximum decline of price
not exceeding 20 percent or increase in haircut over a 30-day period not
exceeding 20 percentage points during a relevant period of significant liquidity stress;

   v. the underlying asset pool is restricted to residential mortgages and cannot
contain structured products;

   vi. the underlying mortgages are 'full recourse' loans (i.e. in the case of foreclosure
the mortgagor remains liable for any shortfall in sales proceeds from the property) and have a maximum loan-to-value ratio (LTV) of 80 percent on average
at issuance; and

   vii. the securitisations are subject to 'risk retention' regulations which require issuers to retain an interest in the assets they securitise.

  b. Corporate debt securities (including commercial paper) that satisfy all of the following conditions may be included in Level 2B, subject to a 50 percent haircut:
   - i. not issued by a financial institution or any of its affiliated entities;
   - ii. either (i) have a long-term credit rating from a recognised ECAI between A+ and BBB– or in the absence of a long-term rating, a short-term rating equivalent in quality to the long-term rating; or (ii) do not have a credit assessment by a recognised ECAI and are internally rated as having a PD corresponding to a credit rating of between A+ and BBB–;
   - iii. traded in large, deep and active repo or cash markets characterised by a low level of concentration; and
   - iv. have a proven record as a reliable source of liquidity in the markets (repo or sale) even during stressed market conditions, i.e., a maximum decline of price not exceeding 20 percent or increase in haircut over a 30-day period not exceeding 20 percentage points during a relevant period of significant liquidity stress.

  c. Common equity shares that satisfy all of the following conditions may be included in Level 2B, subject to a 50 percent haircut:
   - i. not issued by a financial institution or any of its affiliated entities;
   - ii. exchange traded and centrally cleared;
   - iii. a constituent of the major stock index in the home jurisdiction or where the liquidity risk is taken, as decided by the supervisor in the jurisdiction where the index is located;
   - iv. denominated in the domestic currency of a bank's home jurisdiction or in the currency of the jurisdiction where a bank's liquidity risk is taken;
   - v. traded in large, deep and active repo or cash markets characterised by a low level of concentration; and
   - vi. have a proven record as a reliable source of liquidity in the markets (repo or sale) even during stressed market conditions, i.e. a maximum decline of share price not exceeding 40 percent or increase in haircut not exceeding 40 percentage points over a 30-day period during a relevant period of significant liquidity.

The categories and characteristics of HQLA detailed in the Basel III framework are specific and set a high standard. Outside of cash, prototypical HQLA is a highly rated, low-risk, fixed income instrument, that is and has a deep and broad market with a historic strength during past crises. However, the question arises, how does the Basel III framework deal with jurisdictions with little to no HQLA or Shari'ah-compliant institutions with limited access to fixed income assets matching the HQLA requirements?

Alternative Liquidity Arrangements and Shari'ah-Compliant HQLA

The Basel Committee recognised that there are some jurisdictions that have insufficient Level 1 assets in their domestic currencies to properly meet the regulatory requirements of the LCR. With this reality in mind, the Basel Committee developed a practical scheme for Alternative Liquidity Arrangements (ALA) for those jurisdictions and currency where HQLA are limited.[40] Although the Basel Committee gives an extensive set of 'qualifying criteria' and subjects potential ALA jurisdictions to a peer review process

---

[40] Note that ALA treatment is not available in the case of insufficient Level 2 assets in a particular jurisdiction, but only in the case of insufficient Level 1 assets.

overseen by the Basel Committee itself before allowing ALA treatment, generally a jurisdiction wishing to use ALA treatment must demonstrate that:

1. There is an insufficient supply of HQLA in its domestic currency;
2. The insufficiency is caused by long-term structural constraints that cannot be resolved within the medium term;
3. It has the capacity, through internal controls, to mitigate the risk that the alternative treatment cannot work as expected in the Basel III framework; and
4. It is committed to observing the obligations relating to supervisory monitoring, disclosure, and periodic self-assessment and independent peer review of its eligibility for alternative treatment.

There has been little anecdotal evidence to date on how the Basel Committee will apply these ALA criteria or which jurisdictions might seek the ALA treatment, but as each year passes and the LCR requirement increases in anticipation of 2019 when the Basel III framework requires a LCR of 100 percent, the Basel Committee's approach to granting ALA will give insight into the overall viability of the LCR framework. As of the Basel Committee's most recent progress report on the adoption of the various Basel regimes in April 2015, none of the 19 member jurisdictions surveyed asserted any need to seek ALA treatment under Basel III.[41] However, this does not rule out any future reliance on ALA treatment, particularly as the liquidity risk management requirements of the LCR strengthen over time. For Shari'ah-compliant instruments and IIFS, the Basel III liquidity framework makes special dispensation in paragraph 68 with respect to the scarcity of technical HQLA. The Basel Committee notes that, 'Shari'ah-compliant banks face a religious prohibition on holding certain types of assets, such as interest-bearing debt securities. Even in jurisdictions that have a sufficient supply of HQLA, an insurmountable impediment to the ability of Shari'ah-compliant banks to meet the LCR requirement may still exist'. The problems of liquidity risk management for Islamic banks are known concerns. Generally, IIFS maintain higher cash liquidity than their conventional counterparts because of the dearth of short-term instruments that offer fixed returns. This reality is exacerbated by a narrow Shari'ah-compliant interbank market and few Shari'ah-compliant lenders-of-last-resort facilities at central banks.[42] Unfortunately, the high HQLA criteria and category requirements of Basel III do not provide any less of an obstacle. In fact, in its liquidity risk guidance document which interprets the Basel III liquidity framework, the IFSB makes the point clearly that most Shari'ah-compliant instruments cannot meet the HQLA criteria because of the market-related characteristics:

> *While some Shari'ah-compliant instruments meet most of the fundamental characteristics of HQLA set out above, they may not fulfil the criteria with regard to market-related characteristics. IIFS tend to hold most of the instruments up to maturity. In addition, few jurisdictions have an active Islamic money market and capital market; thus, Basel III requirements for the instruments to be traded in a large, active and deep repo market are effectively difficult,*

---

[41] See, 'Eighth progress report on adoption of Basel regulatory framework', Basel Committee on Bank Supervision, Bank for International Settlements, April 2015.

[42] See, Song, I., and C. Oosthuizen (2014) 'Islamic Banking Regulation and Supervision: Survey Results and Challenges', IMF Working Paper 14/220, International Monetary Fund, Washington, DC, p. 36; see also, Alfred Kammer et al. (2015) 'Islamic Finance: Opportunities, Challenges, and Policy Options', p. 24.

if not impossible, to meet. Moreover, although some Shari'ah-compliant assets may be less risky than many conventional instruments, such assets are as yet untested during stress conditions as very few jurisdictions in which Islamic finance has been widely developed have experienced a severe financial crisis in the past decade or so.[43]

The inability of Shari'ah-compliant assets to meet the market-related characteristics of the HQLA criteria is largely a function of forces external to the actual quality or risk of the assets, but there is also concern about many Shari'ah-compliant assets meeting even the fundamental characteristics of the HQLA criteria. *Sukuk* tend to not be rated by ECAIs and can often have opaque risk profiles. For example, a recent 2015 survey found that 40 percent of the *sukuk* listed on Dubai's exchanges are not rated (and about 10 percent of those that are rated *sukuk* are below investment-grade).[44] In any case, the cycle of behaviours and conditions (i.e. the prevalence of 'buy and hold' practices) tends to cause low market volumes, which may contribute to the instruments having no central bank eligibility for liquidity facilities, which in turn reduces market liquidity, which leads to the prevalence of unrated *sukuk* that are bought and held, constitutes a chain of cause-and-effect which results in the inability of Shari'ah-compliant instruments to meet the market-related characteristics of the Basel III HQLA criteria. The Basel III liquidity framework allows local regulators and supervisors in jurisdictions where IIFS do business to define which Shari'ah-compliant instruments (such as *sukuk*) can be 'alternative' HQLA for regulatory purposes.[45] These alternative HQLA would be counted towards a bank's computation of its stock of HQLA the same as any conventional asset (if such could be held by the IIFS). The Basel Committee notes that this special dispensation is not intended to allow IIFS to hold less HQLA and IIFS would still need to meet the applicable LCR requirement, inclusive of the 'alternative' HQLA Shari'ah-compliant instruments. The IFSB, in its guidance response to the Basel III liquidity framework, gives more direct advice for local regulators in this regard. The IFSB advises first that such local authorities must develop their own jurisdiction-specific characteristics in lieu of the market-related characteristics that *sukuk* generally fail, and second, suggests that regulators look instead to whether such *sukuk* are eligible for collateral liquidity facilities with the related central bank.[46] It remains to be seen whether IIFS will be able simply to rely on their local regulator's discretion to designate such *sukuk* as HQLA, or whether the local regulator will resort to ALA treatment to meet the Basel III requirements for their IIFS. From the IIFS' point of view, the IFSB's suggestion would be preferable.

---

[43] See, 'GN-6, Guidance Note On Quantitative Measures for Liquidity Risk Management in Institution Offering Islamic Financial Services [Excluding Islamic Insurance (Takāful) Institutions and Islamic Collective Investment Schemes]', Islamic Financial Services Board, April 2015.

[44] 'Dubai must encourage more sukuk rating to encourage Islamic repo development', *Middle East Global Advisor*, 9 July 2015, http://meglobaladvisors.com/dubai-must-encourage-more-sukuk-rating-to-encourage-islamic-repo-development/

[45] See, 'Basel III: The Liquidity Coverage Ratio and liquidity risk monitoring tool', Basel Committee on Bank Supervision, Bank for International Settlements, January 2013, p. 25. Note, the Basel Committee suggests that in such cases the local regulators might also implement haircuts and other requirements for *sukuk* and other Shari'ah-compliant instruments that have been designated as HQLA according to this special dispensation under the Basel III regime.

[46] See, 'GN-6, Guidance Note On Quantitative Measures for Liquidity Risk Management in Institutions Offering Islamic Financial Services [Excluding Islamic Insurance (Takāful) Institutions and Islamic Collective Investment Schemes]', Islamic Financial Services Board, April 2015, p. 13.

In December 2014, on the eve of the advent of the Basel III LCR requirements, International Monetary Fund researchers conducted a survey of IIFS liquidity practices as a part of a working paper on the regulation of Islamic banks. Of the 16 representative IIFS surveyed, 14 respondents disclosed that they rely on interbank *musharaka* transactions and Islamic placement accounts to manage excess liquidity, while 14 respondents use Islamic placement accounts (either *wakala or mudaraba*) and 13 respondents use commodity *murabaha* and interbank *musharaka* to management liquidity shortages.[47] The survey also showed that Islamic banks use a variety of less popular arrangements with conventional banks, such as guarantees, deposits and syndicated loans for liquidity purposes. Although cross-border commodity *murabaha* contracts were considered part of the 'liquid assets' of Islamic banks, (unless jurisdictions are relying on ALA treatment or 'alternative' HQLA discretion) it is unlikely that such Shari'ah-compliant contracts will meet the Basel III HQLA criteria. As IIFS transition from keeping excess liquidity in non-income generating liquid assets (like cash), and as the LCR requirements of Basel III increase, many market analysts expect a greater reliance upon *sukuk* to meet Basel III regulatory demands. The question remains: What types of *sukuk* would meet the HQLA requirements to satisfy the regulatory needs of IIFS in years to come?

Typical corporate *sukuk* are unlikely even to meet the necessary fundamental characteristics for HQLA. Even highly rated sovereign *sukuk* or highly rated *sukuk* sponsored by established multilateral organisations (such as the International Development Bank *sukuk* or International Finance Corporation *sukuk*), which may meet the fundamental characteristics of HQLA on credit quality and price stability, certainly do not pass muster on market-related characteristics, particularly with respect to market depth, history and price volatility. Even uniquely designed highly rated *sukuk* specifically tailored with Basel III in mind, such as the short-term International Islamic Liquidity Management Corporation *sukuk* (the IILM *sukuk*), in spite of the evidence of the volumes of trading in the secondary markets, may not yet have the historical performance necessary to satisfy fully the market-related characteristic test for HQLA. One advantage that the IILM *sukuk* do enjoy, seemingly anticipating the guidance of the IFSB on the designation of such *sukuk* as HQLA for IIFS (by virtue of being accorded the status of eligible collateral by central banks), is that they have already been affirmatively designated as eligible collateral for liquidity facilities at certain of the IILM's member central banks.[48] Although the IILM *sukuk* have also already been deemed as HQLA in some of the same jurisdictions contemporaneously with being deemed 'eligible collateral', this latter categorisation may be thought to anticipate the possession of all the attributes that Shari'ah-compliant instruments will need to hold in order to give local regulators total justification to confer 'alternative' HQLA treatment. Although local regulators will undoubtedly also designate certain Shari'ah-compliant products, such as commodity *murabaha* or *wakala* interbank placements as alternative HQLA, it is likely that markets will see an increase in the number of *sukuk* that actively seek the discretion of their local regulators in qualifying as HQLA.

---

[47] See, Song, I., and C. Oosthuizen (2014) 'Islamic Banking Regulation and Supervision: Survey Results and Challenges', IMF Working Paper 14/220, International Monetary Fund, Washington, DC, p. 36; see also Alfred Kammer et al. (2015) 'Islamic Finance: Opportunities, Challenges, and Policy Options', p. 29.

[48] Note, the IILM *sukuk* has been deemed 'eligible collateral' for central bank facilities by the local supervisors of central banks in Kuwait, Malaysia, Mauritius, Nigeria, Turkey and the UAE.

CHAPTER 7

Shari'ah Foundations of Islamic Equity Investment Criteria and Purification of Investments

By Mohamed A. Elgari

Islam is a religion that governs the life of Muslims in totality. Islamic law which is called Shari'ah in Arabic, governs both one's relationship with God and with one's fellow man. Shari'ah is a very rich and amply detailed legal system. One of the most distinct phenomena in the Muslim world today is that Muslims are keener to adjust all aspects of their life to the commands of Shari'ah. This includes economy and finance. Islamic equity investment criteria came as a response to this trend.

The basic concept of the modern corporation has never been rejected by contemporary Shari'ah scholars since it was introduced in the Muslim world less than 100 years ago. They saw in it a modern form of a well-known Shari'ah acceptable form of partnership called '*Anan* partnership'.[1]

However, the model company upon which all jurisprudent probing was based is one that is free of every prohibited activity, including borrowing on the basis of interest. A company with such purity does not exist today even in Muslim countries. In fact, almost all major business enterprises resort to borrowing if only to manage cash flow. This means that the contemporary form of a company is a far cry from the original model upon which Shari'ah scholars based their judgement.

Only in the wake of colonisation, when Muslim countries witnessed a movement to assert their Islamic identity, did the nature and working of market and business become the subject of Shari'ah scrutiny. In the realm of finance, it was known as the Islamisation of banking. At first appearance, the task was to eliminate interest.

The prohibition of usury in Islam is very firm and uncompromising. In the classification of 'sinful acts' it is at the top of the list. Therefore, the direct effect of realising

---

[1] The problem with such an analogy is that it ignores the most important aspects of modern corporations: legal persons and limited liability.

the fact that interest-based transactions are inescapable by public companies was for Muslims to shun investment in shares, since income from such companies would be tainted with interest. This tendency was even strengthened by the view of contemporary Shari'ah scholars which got firmer and more resolute that interest is usurious at any percentage.

In the early 1990s, the Islamic Jurisprudence Academy of the Organisation of Islamic Cooperation (OIC) could not distance itself from this debate, so at that time the most authoritative jurisprudence body in the Muslim world adopted a decision among several decisions concerning finance and markets, on the definition of 'company share'. It stated that the subject in the sale of shares is an 'undivided portion of company assets'.[2]

This meant that it is possible now to adopt a new approach when looking at companies. This is because the definition made it possible to apply the reasoning of analogy to the case of equity investment. If the problem is the mixture of permissible and non-permissible, then we can rely on the rich heritage of Shari'ah jurisprudence. This is because the case of permissible and prohibited elements getting mixed together is neither new nor novel. It is well covered in the annals of Shari'ah written by classical scholars with well-established rules.

The first attempt to design and set up an Islamic investment programme based on this concept goes back to the same era, i.e. the early 1990s. Unfortunately, the project soon collapsed due to the unfavourable investment environment created by the Gulf war. However, that effort did not go in vain. That attempt clearly paved the way for the revolution that was to take place later in the decade.

Circa 1993, this author and a group of Shari'ah scholars and investment managers were able to design a set of criteria and an investment programme that could be followed by professional fund managers and easily monitored by Shari'ah auditors, based on a new interpretation of the rules of Shari'ah concerning companies and in light of the said declaration of the Fiqh Academy. This set of criteria opened the doors to Muslims to fully engage and participate in the already existing equity markets. The success of these criteria was phenomenal. Not only are billions of dollars now involved in funds that follow the said criteria, but also it became possible to design benchmarks, such as S&P and Dow Jones Islamic Market Indices. Without the aforementioned ruling of the Fiqh Academy such criteria would have not been possible. This chapter tries to illuminate the Shari'ah foundation of the said criteria.

THE ISLAMIC EQUITY INVESTMENT CRITERIA

The Islamic equity investment criteria consist of several screens, each of which satisfies a Shari'ah requirement. If a stock passes all the screens then it is declared part of the Shari'ah-permissible investable universe. Periodically, a process of purification must also be applied. These screens focus on the business of the company and the financial ratios of the same, and are updated every quarter.

---

[2]This is clearly different from the conventional legal definition where a share represents a right to future earning and liquidation proceeds.

The concept of the basic indivision of the company, which was shaped by the Fiqh Academy resolution on the definition of company share, is very simple. A company is seen as a pool of assets which are owned by the shareholders. As a pool, it has inflows which are its sources of funds and outflows which are its investments. The fundamental Shari'ah maxims upon which the Islamic equity investment criteria are based are the following.

Judgement Is Based on the Majority not the Minority

'Judgement is based on the majority not the minority' is a very important maxim in Shari'ah. It dictates that to make a judgement on the permissibility or otherwise of a mixture of things, we should rely on the majority of the content of such mixture, not the minority. The maxim is Shari'ah authentic and was applied by classical *fuqaha* at all times wherever the case involves the mixture of permissible and non-permissible. While this maxim, like most other maxims, is not mentioned in the Quran or Sunnah in so many words, it is derived indirectly from statements in the same and has the unanimous acceptance of scholars since the time of the Prophet (PBUH).

The Rule of One-Third

This is another important Shari'ah maxim. Now if the judgement is based on the majority not the minority, then what is the dividing line between major and minor. The answer is in this maxim. This maxim is also well established in the annals of Shari'ah jurisprudence. It is derived from an authentic narration from the Prophet (PBUH) which declared that the 'third is bordering on the majority'. *Fuqaha* interpret this to mark the dividing line defining what can be considered a majority. Anything less than one-third is considered to be a minority. Although the context of the narration was related to inheritance, *fuqaha* have relied on this rule of one-third in no less than 15 instances in jurisprudence.

The third has no impact on the permissibility or otherwise of a mixture, it is the two-thirds that define the ruling. Anything below the one-third can be just ignored when casting the judgement.[3]

Rule of Dependence

The rule of dependence or subjection is another maxim well established in Shari'ah jurisprudence. This maxim means the Shari'ah injunction will be based on the rule regarding the 'independent' component of the mixture, not the dependent part. What is dependent and what is independent is not based on the size or volume of each part in the mixture but on the intention of the individual Muslim who is susceptible to Shari'ah rules. The interesting thing is that the Fiqh Academy has a ruling which presumably determines what would be the usual intention of the average, non-exceptional individual when investing in equities. It is not trading debt obligations in the books of

---

[3] Refer to: Al-Furuq al-fiqhiyyah Abi al-fadl Muslim ibn Ali al-Dimasqi Tahqiq: Muhammad Abu al Agfan and Hamzah Abu Faris Bayrut: Dar al Garb al Islamic, 1992, Vol (1) p. 83.

the company but receiving a return on their investment from the underlying business in its totality. Hence, in its resolution number 196 (21/2) November 2013 the Fiqh Academy ruled that whenever there is activity and a legal person behind the business in which there is a mix of permissible and non-permissible, we can apply the rule of 'dependence', thus ignoring what is the percentage of debt financing the company assets. This would be true for all forms of companies which are a going concern.

The Maxim of What May Not Be Allowed Initially May Be Tolerated in Continuity

Like all other Shari'ah maxims, this is derived from known Shari'ah rulings, which found their origins in the Quran and Sunnah, albeit not in so many words. The maxim rules that many things may not be acceptable if initiated *de novo*, but may be tolerated if they happened or appear after the transaction was initiated. Hence, while we may not accept initially a company with 40 percent of debt, we may tolerate it if initially it was 33 percent then later the debt increased to 40 percent. Based on this came the part of the programme related to a grace period of 90 days given to fund managers to dispose of the shares that fall out of the criteria. During this period they are assumed to be permissible and any dividend paid will be considered *halal*.

TOTAL ASSETS OR MARKET VALUE

The application of the Islamic equity investment criteria is based on the market value of the company. But there are some applications using total assets of the company as a basis. In fact all the ratios were based, in the early day of the programme, on total assets as expressed in the books of the company and in its financials. This was based on the Fiqh Academy resolution which mentioned 'assets' in the definition of shares. However, later on we moved to market value of the company or capitalisation. The reason for this was that 'assets' and 'total assets' are effectively accounting concepts which are not related to market transactions in the shares of the company, while market value (or enterprise value in the case of non-traded shares) is reality. From a financial point of view, relying on capitalisation widens the selection since this is usually more than the value of the assets.

To this day, some fund managers rely on total assets not market value. This clearly reflects the opinion of their Shari'ah board.

FALLING OUT OF THE CRITERIA

In the reality of markets and companies, things change by the minute. Hence, many companies which passed all the screens may soon fall out of the criteria owing to certain market conditions or corporate actions. The Islamic equity investment programme relies on the Shari'ah maxim of 'what may not be allowed initially can be tolerated in continuity'. Therefore, shares of a company that has fallen out of the criteria can be kept for a short time, usually one quarter, before being disposed of by sale, or kept if they fall back into meeting the criteria. This is what is being applied by most fund managers. In special cases, this period may even be extended to six months. The important point is that they are considered, during this period, as *halal*, though they do not meet the criteria. This is based on the above maxim.

COMPONENTS OF THE PROGRAMME

Now that it becomes possible to reconcile the Shari'ah requirement with the prerequisite of a professionally managed stock portfolio, we need to translate these Shari'ah requirements into an investment programme. This programme requires adopting a filter where only those stocks that meet Shari'ah criteria can be selected for investment. The filter consists of several screens.

The First Screen: Business of the Company

The business of the company must be the production of useful goods and services that are *halal*. Companies such as breweries, casinos or conventional banks are not *halal* and therefore should be screened out. It is to be noted that by 'business of the company' we mean the 'core business'. The modern corporation is rarely limited in its business to one single activity. Therefore, what we need to test is only its core business – 'core' meaning the one from which it draws most of its revenues.

Almost all investment managers, as well as index operators, exclude arms manufacturers of all sorts. This was not in the original design of the criteria as the production of arms is not, *per se*, prohibited from a Shari'ah point of view. However, this is clearly an influence of the ethical investment trend which is now in vogue.

The restrictions on the business of the company are fairly straightforward. Such restrictions are founded on Islamic Shari'ah, the ethical aspects of which are quite apparent, except for the case of gold and silver. Purchase and sale of gold and silver are not impermissible in Shari'ah. Nevertheless, Shari'ah distinguishes between sale of goods and commodities in general and that of money in which gold and silver are included. While goods can be sold spot or on deferred payment basis, money can only be exchanged spot and at nominal value only. Because the whole set of criteria is built on the assumption that a company share is an undivided portion of its assets, sale of a share of a company whose assets are gold effectively means the sale of this undivided portion. While it is possible to make it spot, it is difficult to guarantee that it is exchanged at nominal value. The narration from the Prophet (PBUH) states gold and silver. This is why the majority of scholars adhered to the letter of the narration.

There is some debate on the matter to the effect that gold and silver should be treated as commodities not money, as they no longer are mediums of exchange. It remains, however, that the majority of Shari'ah scholars, even contemporary ones, find it too daring to take a different opinion.

The Second Screen: Financial Ratios

The most innovative part of the Shari'ah equity investment criteria is reaching a solution to the problem of interest. From a Shari'ah point of view, interest paid or received is *riba*, which is staunchly prohibited in Shari'ah. But it is not likely that we could find a company whose shares are traded in organised markets and yet don't deal with other institutions, especially banks as takers or givers of interest. What contemporary scholars were able to do is to rely on certain well-established evidence in Shari'ah, which reasons that what really matters is the 'majority'. The total can be assumed to be represented by the majority. Hence, if the majority of the financing of the company is within Shari'ah permissibility, which is the case for most companies, that small portion must not change the ruling vis a vis permissibility or otherwise. The trick now is to determine what is the dividing line between majority and minority. The rule of 'one-third' as defining minority is well established in Shari'ah literature, albeit in other areas of jurisprudence. It was adopted to define the maximum tolerable non-Shari'ah sources or utilisation of funds.

Borrowing

This is the most important screen in the financial ratios in the Islamic equity investment programme. The Shari'ah is concerned about the sources of funds of the company, which are applied to generate income. If the sources are permissible, then such income should also be permissible (assuming the funds are used for permissible purposes). There are two major sources of such funds for a company: debt and equity. It is rare that a company confines itself to the capital subscribed by its shareholders. In almost all cases, a company is leveraged. Because interest-based transactions are prohibited in Shari'ah, then a portion of the capital structure is not acceptable. But again, if we invoke the concept of a pool, the maxim of majority and minority becomes applicable. If such borrowing is less than a third, then the rule is based on the two-thirds and hence the capital structure is tolerated.

Receivables

Receivables are, in general, funds owed to the company by others. Companies create receivables when they sell on a deferred payment basis. However, we differentiate between receivables created by permissible transactions like deferred payment sale of goods and services and those created by transactions contrary to the requirements of Shari'ah such as (interest-based) lending. Hence, it is assumed that receivables in the companies which are included in Islamic equity funds are all created through sale of goods and services on deferred payment and not lending. The limit would be 33 percent of market value if we apply the rule of majority. This is what has been applied initially. But later, most scholars thought it would be more fitting to apply the rule of dependence. Hence, this limit was increased to 70 percent. But it remains that financial companies whose assets are only receivables are excluded.

Since the Shari'ah position concerning company shares is that a share is an undivided *pro rata* ownership of the assets of the company, then, a sale of a share is effectively a sale of this undivided *pro rata* ownership of these assets.

Shari'ah does not permit the sale of debt except to the debtor and even then only at nominal value. Hence, if the company has only assets in the form of receivables, then sale and purchase of shares of this company would not be permissible as this would amount to a sale of debt to a third party at a price different from the nominal value. This is not permitted. The selection criteria state that receivables in the investee company should be less than 50 percent. The purpose is to make sure that a share represents assets the majority of which is not debt, so as not to boil down to sale of debt.

One may wonder why we adopted a 33 percent limit for debt in the company's capital structure, while the criterion here for receivables is 'less than 50 percent'. The answer is that borrowing on the basis of interest is not permitted. Hence the Shari'ah basis for the rule relates to the mixture of permissible and non-permissible. In the case of receivables, the foundation is different because selling on a deferred price basis (debt) is permitted. But sale of debt is not permissible. This pertains to a different percept.

Lastly, many Shari'ah boards have invoked the rule of dependence. They believe that no investor will buy a share from the debt of the company. They do this to earn income from dividends and capital gain. Hence, receivables are dependent and therefore have no effect on permissibility or otherwise. They went all the way to 70 percent and even more as an acceptable ratio for receivables.

Third Screen: Prohibition of Financial Instruments

It is not permitted for the manager in an Islamic equity fund to use financial instruments that are classified as derivatives. These include the following.

Futures
The Fiqh Academy of the OIC ruled that futures contracts as practised in financial and commodity markets are not permitted in Shari'ah.[4] Futures contracts are standardised forward contracts traded in organised markets. The problem is that offer and acceptance are made today, but the effect happens in the future. In exchange contracts, Shari'ah permits the deferment of either price or delivery of the sold item but not both. In a futures contract, both price and delivery are deferred to a future date. It is not sufficient that a margin is paid. A *salam* contract has some similarity to a futures contract, and indeed is a type of forward contract distinguished by the requirement (which makes it compliant with the Shari'ah) that the total price is paid at the time of contracting.

Options
Not everything can be subject to sale in Shari'ah. Goods, commodities, services and usufructs can all be objects for sale contracts. Certain rights can be subject to exchange contracts but only those which exist and are not artificially created for the purpose of exchange. If we look at the financial options contract, we find that it is a sale contract where one party pays a price to another so that the latter is legally committed to either sell or buy something at a future date for a set price. The subject of the contract is actually this commitment, not the underlying asset, since this will be the subject of another separate contract. Clearly this is a right created for the purpose of speculation (though it may be used for hedging). It is because of this that the Fiqh Academy ruled that financial options are not permitted. Therefore, a fund manager should refrain from investing in options.

Preference Shares
We mentioned earlier that the whole jurisprudence of equity investment is derived from that of the *Anan* company in Shari'ah. The rules governing partnerships in Shari'ah

---

[4] In its session number 6, March 1990.

including *Anan* demand in earnest that fairness and equity is to be maintained by partners. It is apparent that the holder of a preference share is not equal in his rights and obligations to the holder of an ordinary share. It was thought to be because of this that the Fiqh Academy ruled that preference shares were not permitted.

Short Sales

Selling short means that the vendor sells things that they do not own at the time of sale. To be in line with Shari'ah requirements, sold items must be owned by the seller at the time of sale. It is permitted to sell items on a basis of description only, i.e. items not owned by seller the at the time of sale. In this case, however, they have to be 'fungible' in nature and the price must be paid in full at time of sale. Short sales as practised in markets involve the borrowing of papers based on interest and sale of assets that are not owned. They are, therefore, in violation of Shari'ah requirements and must be avoided.

The Five Percent Screen

The original fatwa upon which this investment programme was founded stated that interest earnings, if such exist, should be minimal and insignificant but gave no ratio for that. Fund managers insisted that unless this is quantified, they cannot consider it in the programme. Hence, the figure of 5 percent was adopted by Shari'ah boards. In some cases, 10 percent and 15 percent were also allowed. Neither 5 percent nor 15 percent can be defended from a Shari'ah point of view. Interest is not allowed at any percentage. In fact, such a ratio created a lot of confusion in the minds of investors thinking that only interest above 5 percent is prohibited. It is because of this that several Shari'ah boards, including that of Dow Jones Islamic Market (DJIM) Index, decided to do away with this screen. Since any interest income must be purified, it really does not matter whether it was 5 percent or more or less. On the other hand, there are cases of good companies, which would pass all the screens except this one, because perhaps it is a new venture developing an invention in technology or biological sciences. Because it only has its capital, and has not yet generated any income (except interest earnings), such interest will constitute a higher percentage if related to its assets.

Although such a company is in line with the Shari'ah objectives in investment, it will not pass the screen. In the DJIM Index, another screen was added which states that total cash held by a company combined with interest-bearing securities should not exceed one-third of the market value of the company. This would indirectly screen out interest earnings. If the interest earnings are high, then the cause can only be too much cash and interest-bearing securities on hand. We know that equity investment is a long-term type of investment. Hence, if the company does hold too much cash, but the potential for its growth in the long run (over three years) is high, then we should give the Islamic investor the opportunity to benefit by not excluding such companies just because their interest earnings increased beyond a set percentage. Remember that we will apply the purification formula in any case.

Furthermore, since this 33 percent is related to the market value of the company, those companies which have patents or new formulas that are worth something should not be excluded just because they are in the process of developing their assets.

Moreover, if the rate of interest is very low, interest earnings of the company will be low, despite the fact that the company is holding significant assets in the form of cash.

THE LIMITED APPLICABILITY OF THE SCREENS

While this screen had opened the doors for wider participation of Muslims in stock-markets and guaranteed inclusion of a great number of Muslims into the modern world of investment, this application is limited to already existing companies. The screen must not be used to establish a company on the same basis as envisioned by the criteria. In other words, it would not be permissible to say: 'let us establish a new company and borrow up to 33 percent of our sources of funds from conventional banks'. Such an act has never been allowed by any Shari'ah scholar. Sometimes, this creates confusion in the minds of non-Shari'ah people. But the fact is that the criteria were adopted as a solution, to provide an exit from a situation that is assumed to be very harmful and hence should continue to be so regarded.

PURIFICATION

The financial screens and other filters relating to the business of the company go back only two decades. However, the concept of purification is much older. We can trace the idea of disposing of non-permissible portion, to purify the total income to many centuries ago. In fact, this part of the Islamic equity investment criteria is considered the most solid from a Shari'ah point of view, because of the fact that it has passed the test of time.

The Meaning of Purification

Purification simply means deducting from one's return on investment any income whose source is not compatible with Shari'ah rules and principles. In the case of equity investments, this refers primarily to earned interest and incidental income from other non-permissible sources to the investee company, such as the sale of alcoholic beverages or pork.

However, estimating income from sale of pork and alcoholic beverages is not easy. It is a task that is quite arduous. The basic idea looks simple, but it is not. A company is a going concern. It is a living entity with far-reaching enterprise and widely stretched activities. It is also very complex from an accounting and financial point of view, a far cry from the single partnership of the *Anan* form of company that is described in the Shari'ah texts. Therefore, estimating such income is a formidable task; one that requires excellent knowledge of accounting and corporate finance, as well as an exceptional ability to handle Shari'ah issues – a combination that is rare and not always available.

Shari'ah Basis for Purification

Although the Islamic equity investment programme has now a very wide acceptance from the majority of Shari'ah scholars and the Muslim public at large, some Shari'ah scholars still hold the opinion that the Shari'ah basis for such a programme is not as solid as they would like it to be. However, no part of this programme is on more solid ground from the Shari'ah point of view than the part relating to purification. This is because the issue of purification is not new. Indeed, it has a clear Shari'ah foundation, which is exemplified in the classical annals of *fiqh*, as well as the statements of the majority of the learned scholars of the early centuries based on their understanding of the texts (Quran and Sunnah) from which principles for such procedures were epitomised.

However, articulating these Shari'ah principles into a formal procedure for purification in portfolio investment is quite a heroic task and one with a number of unsettled issues as will be described below.

THE ISSUES

While purification is simple and straightforward as a concept, applying the same to the complex finance of corporations is anything but simple and straightforward. A company is a going concern which has sources of funds and utilisation of funds in a continuous and dynamic manner. Every entry in that company's financials could be tainted by interest or earnings from other Shari'ah non-permissible sources. Hence, the question of what is to be purified needs to be reckoned with.

What is to be purified?

1. Dividend
   There are those who think that non-permissible earnings of a company (such as interest) will transfer into an investor's returns only if the investor collects funds from the company in the form of dividends. Hence what is to be purified is only that part. According to this viewpoint, returns that are derived from capital gains (share price movements), as is typically the case with stock market returns accruing to equity investors, need no purification. According to the argument of those who support this view, such capital gains are a market element. The main implication of this approach is that no cleansing will be needed if dividends are distributed, even if the company does earn interest income.

2. Capital Gains
   Other scholars tend to differentiate between investing in a single company, and being a subscriber in an investment fund. While it makes sense to purify only dividend income in the first case, according to the capital gains approach, the fund itself should be treated as a company, where the investment units are akin to company shares. In this case, the investment returns that one derives from such a fund, which are primarily capital gains, must all be purified as they are not dissimilar to company shares and dividends. This is because no capital gain is realised from the sale of fund units, and hence any income is similar to dividends.

   A third view holds that the increase in share prices in the market (capital gain) is a complex phenomenon. Such an increase can be attributed to a multiplicity of factors, including cash and debt securities (the source of interest income) that can hardly be excluded. This suggests that even capital gains ought to be purified.

3. Assets or Liabilities
   According to the current thinking of some Shari'ah scholars, only company assets need to be purified. This is because the Islamic equity investment programme is based, among other considerations, on the Shari'ah maxim that '*lilkatheer hukm alkull*', the majority has the ruling of all, i.e. the rule is based on the majority, not the minority. Since the bulk of the sources of funds for the company come from permissible sources, i.e. two-thirds, the minority source is then ignored and should not have any consequences on the process of purification.

However, there are those who believe that the above-mentioned maxims only permit investing in companies whose composition of the liability side should be considered for purification. In this case, we need to assign a portion of the income of the company to the debt source of funds and dispose of it.

Profit from Borrowed Funds

Some scholars go further to say that we need to purify income from the profit that is generated from borrowing. So far we have assumed that tainted income emanates from the assets side of the company's balance sheet, and that the liability side is ignored since the Shari'ah criteria that have been applied assume that the judgement is based on two-thirds, not one-third.

According to this view, we further need to treat this debt (or the proportion of the firm's assets that it finances) as if it were a separate venture. These scholars assume that such debt (or debt-financed assets) generated part of the profit that would be equal to its ratio to total liabilities. Since the profit would not have been made without the mixture of capital and labour, then we would assign only half that portion of profit to capital. We then dispose of this half since it is generated through impermissible means. Needless to say, supporters of this view assume that labour is provided by the company and therefore accounts for half of the profit.

Net or Gross

A company deposits some money in a time deposit (or holds government bonds) and earns interest. Such interest will be part of that company's income for the year. But in the case of investment funds should the proportion of such interest income to the whole be considered in relation to total net income or to total revenues? In other words, when we transpose the interest income of a company to the return on investment received by a participant in an equity fund, we need to relate such interest income either to the net income or to the total revenue of the investee company. It appears that income is not a very reliable element, while revenue is less influenced by such factors. By counting interest as part of revenue we indirectly allow charging operational expenses to such a source of income, like any other source. This is not the case when we relate interest to net income.

Purification vs. Screening

It is important to distinguish the method of handling interest as well as all incidental non-permissible earnings in the screening phase of the Islamic investment programme as compared to the method applied in the purification phase. There is no basis in Shari'ah for saying in screening that 5 percent is acceptable while 6 percent is not. In other words, screens that permit investing in a company if its interest earnings are 5 percent or less of its income are clearly founded on expediency, not Shari'ah befittedness. It is because of this that many Shari'ah boards are now moving to more rigorous screening criteria. This is different from the stage of purification where all interest income must be disposed.

Deduct or Inform

Investors in most equity investment funds are advised on a quarterly basis of the percentage of their investment that they need to dispose of to purify their return. It is the duty of every subscriber to purify in person. In other funds, such a burden is entrusted to the fund manager, who is not only required to calculate but also to dispose of the tainted amounts. The first method is clearly more practicable. Because no deduction from the net asset value of the portfolio is made, the fund appears more profitable. Furthermore, this attracts both strict Muslim investors (who would be keen to dispose of this amount every quarter), and the not-so-strict and non-Muslims to invest in the fund.

On the other hand, some Shari'ah scholars think an equity fund will not be truly Islamic unless all returns to investors are 'pure'. Hence the manager must themselves deduct such amounts and dispose of them to charity.

In the writer's view, money itself is neither pure nor tainted. Such things can only take place in the *'dhimma'*.[5] If one earns impermissible income, one will be cleared if one disposes of the same amount from other sources. In the final analysis, those who subscribe to a fund with the intention of earning a pure and clean return will purify.

METHODS OF PURIFICATION

We have deduced from the practices of Islamic equity fund management several methods of purification, which are presented below. Each method is based on assumptions, whose purpose is to embody Shari'ah requirements in a formula that lends itself easily to implementation by fund managers. All the methods presented here are already in practice, and are used by one or more fund managers. However, I am sure that these methods, albeit the most common, are not the only ones in practice.

In each methodology a formula is set up to find factor P, through which interest income can be estimated.

First Method

Let us assume that we have a portfolio of company shares. On 1 January (t_1) we have n investee companies (c) each earning interest equal to i.

Hence, we have interest income i equal to:

$$i_{c1} + \ldots + i_{cn} = a$$

Let us assume that the net operating income for any company in the portfolio is y. Hence the total net operating income for the portfolio is =

$$y_{c1} + \ldots + y_{cn} = b$$

$$\text{Then } H = \frac{a}{b}$$

---

[5] If one becomes obliged from payment of *zakah*, for instance, it suffices if one pays the due amount from funds other than the one on which *zakah* is due. The same thing can be said about any monetary obligation. Fungible obligations are presumed to be kept in a virtual pool and thus can be substituted in place of one another.

Let us assume that the net asset value of the fund on January 1 is equal to NAV_{t1}. Then calculate Z (the increase in NAV for the year) which equals $NAV_{t2} - NAV_{t1}$.

The purification factor P will then equal $ZH = P$.

Hence for every dollar invested, the investor must multiply by P and donate this amount to charity.

If for example, $P = .007$ and the investors $Z = \$ 2,000$ then he must dispose of the amount of $ \$ 14$.

Second Method

Let us assume that we have n companies in the portfolio: $c_1, c_2 \dots c_n$

Then calculate dividend yield (d) where

$$d = \text{Dividend/market value}$$

Therefore, the total annual portfolio dividend yield will be

$$D = d_{c1} + d_{c2} + \dots + d_{cn}$$

Calculate interest income ratio for each company (i)

$$i = \text{interest income/net operating income}$$

For the portfolio the total will be

$$I = i_{c1} + i_{c2} + \dots + i_{cn}$$

Hence, purification factor is $= (D)(I) = P$

This means that for every dollar invested, the amount of $ \$ P$ must be donated annually to charity.

Third Method

Let us assume that reported interest income for each company in the portfolio is X, we will then have X_1 to X_n where $1 \dots n$ denote investee companies.

Let us assume that: T is equal to each company's tax rate and that there is a tax rate for each investee company.

A equals the percentage of the total company shares owned by the fund.

M equals the number of months the share is held in the portfolio. Then we have total after-tax interest income in the portfolio ip equal to:

$$ip = \Sigma_{X(1 \dots n)}(I - T)(X)(A)(M)$$

Our Recommendation

In designing a purification formula we have to take into consideration the following:

1. It needs to be simple and requires data that is standard and available from every company.
2. It satisfies the requirement of 'prudence' from a Shari'ah point of view, which means that if we are to err, we prefer to err on the side of more purification not less.

Hence, the purification suggested by the writer, for purifying in a portfolio of stocks, proceeds as follows:

Step 1: We find the amount of interest and other non-permissible income in each company in the portfolio. Let's say company A earned during the year 2000, $500 from interest and sale of liquor.
If company A paid tax on its income for the year 2000, then interest income should be net of tax. If tax was, say 10 percent then only $450 should considered for purification purposes.

Step 2: We divide this amount by the total number of shares of this company. Let us assume company A has 10,000 shares outstanding in the market. The share price is $.045 per share.

Step 3: We multiply this number by the shares of company A that we hold in the portfolio. For example, if a fund holds 50 shares, then the amount of its investment in this company is $2.25.
If these shares are held in the portfolio for less than one year, then we divide 2.25 by 12 to get a monthly equivalent holding. Let us say we held it for only 9 months. Then only 9/12 of $2.25 = $ 1.69 needs to be disposed of out of the return on investment in this company.

Step 4: We do the same exercise for all the companies in the portfolio. Suppose we ended up with an amount equal to $36.50. This would be the amount we need to dispose of to charity.
We mentioned earlier the view of those who say that only dividends need to be purified. We also mentioned the views of those who believe that even capital gains need to be purified. This formula actually steers away from such a dispute. It aims at purifying the investment itself. The company in which the fund owns a share may have earned impermissible income which needs to be purified even if the company made an overall loss during the year. Accordingly, whether or not the company has paid a dividend, or has made a capital gain or loss, the formula should be applied to the total investment.

CONCLUSION

It is possible to reconcile the economic investment needs of a modern Muslim with the desire to be a devoted Muslim. This can't be done by changing Shari'ah because this is not possible, nor ignoring Shari'ah rules because this is not acceptable to Muslims. The real answer is to believe firmly that Shari'ah is a living order, a body of jurisprudence that is not dead but full of life, if only we can understand it and reinterpret its rules in the light of our contemporary circumstances. The Islamic equity investment criterion is a good example of how the harmonisation can take place. Only those who believe that Shari'ah is empowered with the means to be relevant to humanity at any time and any place can succeed in finding solutions to contrary problems – solutions that are in line with Shari'ah and deliver the legitimate worldly desirable rewards of investors.

In this paper, we tried to shed light on the components of this Islamic equity criteria and their Shari'ah foundation. As a student of Shari'ah, who participated in articulating these concepts two decades ago, I can still think it is work in progress. This paper may provoke some thoughts which will kick-start more development.

CHAPTER 8

Collateralisation in Islamic Capital Markets

By Richard Thomas

In recent years, the development of the breadth and depth of the *sukuk* market in and across borders has demanded consequential development of market infrastructure, and among the most critical areas to be addressed has been the work done on efficient collateralisation in Islamic Capital Markets (ICM).

The demand to regularise the approach to collateralisation is driven by two principal factors: 1) the need for, and current dearth of, High Quality Liquid Assets (HQLA) to meet the changed regulatory environment for Islamic banks; 2) the growth in primary ICM market issuance for structured trade, project and infrastructure purposes, and those which span both issues including growth in issuance of Basel III Tier 1 *sukuk* and covered *sukuk*. Finally, the chapter deals with some specific and unique risks associated with *sukuk*, both idiosyncratic and non-systematic, and some reflections on mitigation.

Looking to the future, and given the continuing challenge of meeting the apparently idiosyncratic requirements of Shari'ah compliance, we might see these factors coming together in a form of clearing for Islamic financial products. Proposals for such a mechanism already have some shape in Malaysia where domestic and foreign investors can buy and sell Islamic debt instruments through exchange and over-the-counter (OTC) markets. Bank Negara's Real Time Electronic Transfer of Funds and Securities (RENTAS) has itself been mooted as a form of Islamic clearing house. I give below an example of the International Islamic Financial Market's (IIFM's) three-party *i'aadat al shari'ah'a* repo alternative, where the introduction of a clearing/custodial institution might assume the role of principal and unlock the potential of this product.

In the meantime, this chapter will address both factors 1 and 2 independently, and from two perspectives, particularly the underlying collateralisation of a Shari'ah-compliant instrument and the use of such an instrument itself as collateral.

THE DEVELOPMENT OF SHARI'AH-COMPLIANT COLLATERALISATION ARRANGEMENTS RELATED TO THE NEED FOR, AND CURRENT DEARTH OF, HQLA TO MEET THE CHANGED REGULATORY ENVIRONMENT FOR ISLAMIC BANKS

Right at the heart of Islamic liquidity risk management and the increased regulatory requirement for HQLA is the consequential requirement for Islamic repos. There are a slew of other closely related issues also dealt with in this chapter, but the Islamic repo itself has until very recently proven too tough a nut to crack in a form that satisfies both Shari'ah scholars and a modern capital market. Some of the most basic aspects of a repo have long been considered fundamentally unacceptable in accordance with Shari'ah. Shari'ah scholars have viewed traditional repos as contravening the ban on borrowing and lending at interest, because traders post securities as collateral for cash and agree to buy them back at a specified date and price, or pay the difference as interest. Recent solutions have been based on collateralised *murabaha*, which is a cost-plus profit arrangement that tries to avoid such issues by having the financier buy the asset at market value and immediately sell the asset to the customer for a mark-up on a deferred payment basis. Because the mark-up price is agreed up front by both parties, this addresses the element of *gharar*, or ambiguity in contracts, that might otherwise exist. The need to avoid *gharar*, described as a 'prohibited risk' by Mohamad Akram Laldin,[1] together with the prohibition of *riba* and *Maisirmaisir* (speculation), is a key principle in Islamic finance: 'It takes place when there is considerable ambiguity related to either the term of the contract, or its object or its counter-value' (Laldin, *loc. cit.*). Transactions can be secured by any Shari'ah-compliant assets, including equities and *sukuk*, but the idiosyncrasy here compared to conventional products is that re-hypothecation (where the financier reuses the collateral pledged as collateral for its own borrowing) is forbidden in Islamic finance.

Despite this restriction, collateralisation remains a valuable tool because although banks cannot use the collateral, it provides comfort from a credit perspective. This is particularly true during the early stages of an Islamic Financial Institution's (IFI's) operations when a preponderance of unrated counterparties results in a need to post collateral.

Aside from repo, perhaps the other thorniest issue for Shari'ah-compliant collateralisation in a market environment has been 'netting', which has historically had similar connotations of basic non-compliance. I will discuss netting more in the next section of this chapter.

Elements of the risks borne in the ICM and by IFIs are now considered 'systemic'. Given the determined geographical spread, growth and sophistication of the Islamic financial market, this development of an efficiently collateralised suite of ICM products has become crucial for practitioners and regulators, and is the subject of

---

[1] Akram Laldin (2012) 'Shari'ah–Non-compliance Risk', in S. Archer and R. A. A. Karim (2012) *Islamic Finance: The New Regulatory Challenge* (Wiley).

considerable constructive energy by key stakeholders. The establishment of the 'Task Force on Islamic Finance and Global Stability' formed in 2009 and chaired by Bank Negara's Governor Zeti of Malaysia has had its own direct impact on the channelling of this constructive energy into workable market practice.

Thus we can see that the matter of collateral in ICM extends both to the basic creation of appropriate instruments, and then to the adoption of those instruments by both regulators and practitioners. The entire 'value chain' of 'collateralisation' in ICM is 'under development', but 2014 has seen a watershed, and developmental theory is now evolving into market product and practice.

THE KEY STAKEHOLDERS IN THE DEVELOPMENT OF THE COLLATERALISATION ELEMENT OF ICM AND THEIR NOTABLE DEVELOPMENTS IN REGULARISING COLLATERALISATION IN ICM ACROSS THE 'VALUE CHAIN'

The institutions that are worthy of mention in this connection are the following:

- The Accounting and Auditing Organisation for Islamic Financial Institutions (AAOIFI) is an Islamic international autonomous not-for-profit corporate body that prepares accounting, auditing, governance, ethics and Shari'ah standards for Islamic financial institutions and is the industry intellectual flagbearer on Shari'ah and financial reporting standards. Until now the relevant reference standards under which guidance on collaterals can be found have been AAOIFI Standards No. 39 – Rahn: Mortgage of financial papers, Sukook 4/1, Shari'ah Standard No. 21 on financial papers, shares and bonds and Shari'ah Standard No. 17 on investment *sukuk*. In November 2014, AAOIFI announced that its *murabaha* standard would be revised to stipulate use of collateral for the recovery of receivables – historically a stumbling block to development of efficiently collateralised instruments. It also announced that it would revise its *sukuk* standard with similar goals in mind, and practitioners anticipate an AAOIFI repo standard to emerge in time. No amendments are expected related to *rahn*, the use of financial paper as collateral/*rahn* or the position on guarantees involving *wakala* contracts. The revisions that emerged during 2015 are likely to have been warmly welcomed.
- The IIFM was established to address the product and documentation standardisation needs of the IFI in the areas of Capital & Money Market, Corporate Finance & Trade Finance, and to provide a universal platform by bringing together regulatory bodies, financial institutions, law firms, stock exchanges, industry associations, infrastructure service providers and other market participants who produce the practical working contracts and market standards. IIFM works closely with AAOIFI, as it also does this with the International Swaps and Derivatives Association (ISDA) from time to time. In fact, the starting point for IIFM standards development is study and inclusion of AAOIFI Shari'ah standards such as the Shari'ah ruling on *rahn*, Shari'ah ruling on unrestricted *wakala* (no guarantee of principal or profit, etc.), then the production of the practical financial contract or product standard which institutions can use in their business activities. As standard-setting organisations, IIFM and AAOIFI complement each other and also avoid duplication. AAOIFI Shari'ah standards do not cover aspects such as market practice,

operational issues, legal etc., which is part of IIFM's work. It is in the areas of practical working contracts that IIFM has had great recent influence, and the nature of those contracts (particularly the IIFM Master Collateralized Murabaha Agreement) and standards are referred to again in more detail later on. I make special note that IIFM has a Credit Support Agreement (CSA) under development. The purpose of this will be to manage the counterparty risk arising from Islamic hedging transactions by providing collateral and margin maintenance requirements. This will also be most valuable and again perhaps a component of an Islamic clearing system. In terms of market standards in use today, we must look at the IIFM standard on Interbank Unrestricted Master Investment Wakalah Agreement, as not only is it used by IFIs but also the Central Bank of Bahrain has introduced an Unrestricted *wakala* facility for retail banks based on IIFM standard.

▪ The Islamic Financial Services Board (IFSB), which issues the global prudential standards and guiding principles for the Islamic Financial Services Industry (IFSI), and acts as an intermediary between the central banks which make up its membership and governing council on the one hand, and the Basel Committee for Banking Supervision on the other hand. Until their issuance of IFSB Guidance Note GN-6 and Standard IFSB-17 *Core Principles for Islamic Finance Regulation: Banking Segment* in April 2015, the most useful guidance on collaterals came in their 2009 Standard IFSB-7 *Capital Adequacy Requirements for Sukuk, Securitisations and Real Estate Investment* (now incorporated into IFSB-15, the revised IFSB standard on capital adequacy). IFSB included in the 2009 standard a section on asset-based *sukuk* structures with a repurchase undertaking (binding promise) by the originator and a so-called pass-through, asset-based *sukuk* structure, where a separate issuing entity (such as CAGAMAS in Malaysia) purchased the underlying assets from the originator, packaged them into a pool and acted as the issuer of the *sukuk*. In section 1.2.1 of the 2009 standard 'Collateral Security Structure', the IFSB identified legal perfection and enforcement of security as areas of critical concern in many jurisdictions. These paragraphs, however, still remain as valuable references and warnings for today's practitioners. Many currently extant *sukuk* issued on a basis of *rahn* (mortgage or other pledge of assets) used this guidance, but IFSB give a stern caveat that there will be obstacles in jurisdictions where *rahn* is possessory in nature and perfection is not certain. It also goes on to highlight that in jurisdictions without *rahn* concepts, the legal regimes for perfection and priority are often not well developed, and in Islamic countries bankruptcy laws too are often poorly developed. (In studying the collateral packages of many primary *sukuk* issuances it will be evident that satisfaction of local law to register or perfect collateral has been more assiduously applied than some aspects of guidance on *rahn*.)

In April 2015, IFSB resolved to adopt the new Guidance Note (GN-6) Quantitative Measures for Liquidity Risk Management in Institutions Offering Islamic Financial Services (Excluding Islamic Insurance (*Takaful*) Institutions and Islamic Collective Investment Schemes). This note seeks to clarify the tools that Islamic banks can use to meet Basel III regulatory liquidity requirements, and defines the types of HQLA that Islamic banks can hold. They describe the three main criteria of HQLA as low correlation with risky assets, an active and sizeable market, and low volatility. At the same time, IFSB also resolved to adopt the standard on Core Principles for Islamic Finance Regulation/CPIFR (IFSB-17) mentioned above. These notes and standards are precursors to new guidance on collateralisation and at the time of their adoption S&P responded by saying 'We expect high credit quality and local currency *sukuk* offerings to increase because these instruments are part of the Level 1 HQLA definition of the IFSB. And we believe sovereigns, central banks, Multilateral Lending Institutions (MLIs) and specialised institutions — such as the International Islamic Liquidity Management Corporation (IILM) — could play a role in further fostering the supply of Islamic liquidity management instruments.'

- The International Islamic Liquidity Management Corporation (IILM) was born out of the 2008 financial crisis as a solution to potential instability in Islamic financial markets, given their previous reliance on conventional organisations. The IILM is a child of the 'Task Force on Islamic Finance and Global Financial Stability' set up under the aegis and chairmanship of Governor Zeti of the Bank Negara. It is an international institution established by central banks, monetary authorities and multilateral organisations to create and regularly issue *sukuk* of short-term Shari'ah-compliant financial instruments to facilitate effective cross-border Islamic liquidity management. The IILM is becoming crucial to the effective operation of more liquid Shari'ah-compliant financial markets for institutions offering Islamic financial services because its *sakk* is deemed by many to be HQLA. The IILM has needed to resolve the critical obstacles to collateralising their own issuances and also to turn their attention to establishing IILM paper itself as eligible collateral for HQLA in both developed and emerging markets. IILM debuted in 2013 with an issue of USD-denominated, highly rated, short-term, tradable, Shari'ah-compliant *sukuk*. The IILM inaugural *sukuk* of USD490 million, rated A-1 by Standard & Poor's rating services, were issued at a tenor of three months and were fully subscribed. As of May 2015, the IILM *sukuk* that had been issued and re-issued amounted to USD9.98 billion, and further sizeable issuances have followed.

There are several important features of the IILM *sukuk* that are intended to assist the establishment of a liquid, cross-border market for IIFS. The IILM *sukuk* are: tradable Shari'ah-compliant USD-denominated short-term financial instruments issued at maturities of up to one year; money-market instruments backed by sovereign assets, distributed and tradable globally via a multi-jurisdictional primary dealer network; they also have strong global support as they represent a unique collaboration between several central banks and a multilateral development organisation with the aim of enhancing the financial stability and the efficient functioning of Islamic financial markets. In looking forward to IILM *sukuk* fulfilling a key role in provision of HQLA as eligible collateral, I would like to see more definition around two promising potential developments:

1. A role in solving the issue of local currency HQLA in most jurisdictions. In 2014, Thomson Reuters opined, 'the need for liquidity management purposes is in the local currency. By allowing the (USD-denominated) IILM Sukuk to be eligible collateral, it provides a way for the central bank to provide fully secured funding via a repo transaction which can be done in local currency where the central bank assumes the currency risk from accepting USD collateral for local currency repo facilities'.

2. Assisting in the reduction of very high haircuts and margins that Islamic banks face when employing current HQLA options that are usually regulatory 'exceptions'.

The IILM is itself proactive in addressing and dealing with the issues on the table. At its third Roundtable on Challenges in Sukuk Issuance, the programme addressed 'Shari'ah aspects of Guarantees and Collaterals on Financial Transactions' and issued a report on the meeting with the pronouncements.

Among central banks most active in creating an appropriate environment are the Central Bank of Bahrain, Bank Negara Malaysia and the UAE Central Bank, with the NASDAQ Dubai also announcing that it is working on introducing Islamic repurchase agreements to boost both the primary and secondary *sukuk* markets. The Bank of England may enter this category as it studies local requirements for a liquidity window for UK Islamic banks. We can say that in 2015 the issue has become critical for Islamic banks because Basel III is in implementation rather than discussion phase, HQLA are in critically short supply and 'exceptions' windows are closing in most jurisdictions.

KEY REGULATORY STAKEHOLDERS IN DEVELOPMENT OF EFFECTIVELY COLLATERALISED ICM PRODUCTS

Bank Negara Malaysia has an enviable track record of well-considered interventions of a constructive nature that have promoted and supported the development of the ICMs in many international jurisdictions. Its influence in the context of collateralisation in ICMs is considerable. One area of note is the work to reduce the influence of *inah*-based contracts on ICM products, which will assist in harmonising standards between GCC, South East Asia and the rest of the world. But we can focus upon the Islamic Financial Services Act 2013 for the purpose of this chapter. In addition to addressing collaterals in more detail, it also begins to address the related issues of restricted and unrestricted (PSIA) investment accounts and fiduciary to the investment account holders.

Central Bank of Bahrain (formerly the Bahrain Monetary Agency), which stands among the foremost in developing a central bank regulatory framework to encourage and develop Islamic financial stability through deep liquid, transparent and regular markets, has recently introduced an unrestricted *wakala* facility for retail banks based on the IIFM standard.

The Securities Commission of Malaysia and Bursa Malaysia. Their contributions to the current state of the market are detailed in this chapter.

The UAE Central Bank, which in April 2015 changed its rules to accept a wide range of *sukuk* as collateral for banks to improve access to its special lending facility.

The Bank of England may enter this category as it studies local requirements for a liquidity window for UK Islamic banks. We can say that in 2015 the issue has become critical for Islamic banks because Basel III is in implementation rather than discussion phase, HQLA are in critically short supply and 'exceptions' windows are closing in most jurisdictions.

THE 'ISLAMIC REPO' AND THE NEED FOR, AND CURRENT DEARTH OF, HQLA TO MEET THE CHANGED REGULATORY ENVIRONMENT FOR ISLAMIC BANKS

Until 2014, the development of an appropriately liquid ICM product for liquidity risk management purposes can be described as slow, because the issue of the Islamic repo could not be effectively resolved. Pre-2014 was a phase of development of theoretical market constructs and regulatory accommodations. Post-2014 is characterised by the emergence of the instruments and standards to transform theory into practice.

Two breakthroughs define 2014 as the pivotal point. Firstly, late in 2014 the IIFM revealed the IIFM Master Collateralized Murabahah Agreement, and this has seen a breakthrough in practical implementation by banks. In this agreement we can also ascertain the seeds of a true Islamic money market. Collateralised *murabaha* is a cost-plus profit arrangement which tries to avoid *riba*, *Maisirmaisir* and *gharar* by removing uncertainty and having the financier buy a Shari'ah-compliant asset such as *sukuk* at market value and immediately selling the asset to the customer for a pre-agreed mark-up on a deferred payment basis. Transactions under this contract can be secured by any Shari'ah-compliant assets, including for example *sukuk* or equities. This agreement 'standard' expressly forbids re-hypothecation, which is the critical factor in the legitimacy of this product from a Shari'ah perspective.

Unlike a straight commodity *murabaha*, the repayment obligation is secured by the Shari'ah-compliant assets held by the customer (and haircuts/overcollateralisation to cover as margin for volatility in mark-to-market value). If the repayment is made on schedule, the *sukuk* are not sold but are returned to the financier. If there is a default, the financier takes possession of the assets.

Secondly, contemporaneously with the realisation of the work done by the IIFM, the IILM has become established as a regular issuer of short-term *sukuk* of such high quality that regulators and market users are calling for their acceptance as the required HQLA collaterals/guarantees.

There are very good examples of appropriately and inappropriately collateralised primary *sukuk* issuance prior to 2014, but these do not fit the subject of HQLA and belong in the second part of this chapter.

Why was progress towards effective collateralisation for liquid products slow prior to 2014? The prominent Shari'ah Scholar Dr Elgari, who sits on over 80 Shari'ah boards around the world, told Reuters in an interview on the subject that, 'Any successful structure has to satisfy the requirements of Shari'ah, and the requirements of regulators, and the requirements of risk managers. To combine all these three factors, it's very difficult.'

The IIFM Master Collateralized Murabaha Agreement is designed to overcome the principal barriers to development of a repo-able product. Prior to 2014, these barriers have been the difficulty in standardising an Islamic repo and harmonising hypothecation, pledge lien or mortgage security structures with Shari'ah in a manner that avoids creating *riba*. The other principal barriers that plagued the repo development included the introduction into transactions, perhaps inadvertently, of *gharar* and *Maisirmaisir* (mentioned above in the context of the IIFM Collateralised Murabaha Agreement). The IIFM has worked with the ISDA to overcome these barriers for many years and it follows their collaboration with the ISDA in drafting a Tahawwut Master Agreement which is widely credited to be the first standardised Shari'ah-compliant OTC derivatives contract.

In addition to IIFM's work, there has been a timely review of *inah* products that have been used in some markets. Malaysia's approach until the Islamic Financial Services Act of 2013 used a sale and buy-back contract identified as *inah*. *Inah* has been widely avoided in the GCC countries, basically because the transfer of ownership of assets is not clearly executed, thus giving rise to uncertainty as regards the transfer. The 2013 Act has regularised this to a great extent, paving the way towards more standardisation in repo, but at the same time reducing the volume of Malaysian government *sukuk* in issue.

The building block for the IIFM Master Collateralized Murabahah Agreement was the 'IIFM Reference Paper on Cost Plus Profit Model I'aadat Al Shira'a (Repo Alternative) and Collateralization' that was released in July 2010. This paper described a bilateral repurchase undertaking, an alternative that replaced the repurchase undertaking with a *wa'ad* and it also contemplated a tri-party structure that was widely held to be the most 'compliant' solution.

The tri-party is still a 'work in progress' because an effective third party is difficult to include in transactional practice. The difference between a conventional tri-party repo and the Shari'ah-compliant version is that in a conventional repo the third party acts as an agent, but in the Shari'ah-compliant version they are obliged to act as a principal and to take risk (another part of the discussion about the need for an Islamic clearing counterparty). Given the issues surrounding tri-party in conventional markets (particularly in the US) since its introduction in the 1970s, and re-exposed in the 2008 crisis at the time of Bear Stearns and Lehman Brothers, it is important that the ICM pays careful attention to resolving collateral allocation and unwind processes. We might suggest that principles of Shari'ah compliance in financial markets might, as they define a compliant dealer/clearer arrangement, offer some guidance to the conventional market in getting its tri-party repo house in order!

After these developments in 2014, the barriers are now more market driven. In the UK, for example, posting collateral means registering a charge at Companies House, which some participants see as potentially damaging from a reputational perspective. Others do not agree and view posting or registering collateral as such a common matter these days. This issue of registration plays out differently in individual markets with ambitions for Islamic ICM participation. In many markets it is simply not legal practice or law. Convergence on these matters will take place among the members of the IFSB and other bodies representing governmental and regulatory interests, at least those with the inclination and authority to seek necessary changes in law to regularise the landscape. The other barriers include those that I have mentioned in the bullet points in the section on the IILM, namely the issue of lack of non-USD or local currency HQLA in most jurisdictions where Islamic finance is prevalent, and the need for a reduction of very high haircuts and margins that Islamic banks face when employing current HQLA options that are often regulatory 'exceptions'.

These post-2014 barriers are heavily influenced by a poor historical track record when it comes to what are ultimately the legal, default, disclosure, resolution and Shari'ah non-compliance risks in collateralised *sukuk*.

DEVELOPING MARKET PRACTICE AND IDENTIFYING AND MITIGATING RISK IN COLLATERALS, GUARANTEES AND COLLATERAL MANAGEMENT

The Bank for International Settlements (BIS) CGFS Paper No 53 of March 2015 tells us that 'it is useful to think about collateral assets as a subset of all financial assets, with their defining feature being market participants' ability to pledge them against borrowed fund' (with the caveat that for 'pledge', a wider range of options may be more appropriately referenced). The paper itself is a report back on a study of whether and how the design of central bank operational frameworks influences private collateral markets, including collateral availability, pricing, market practices and resilience. It is readily accessible online and is very helpful in creating a notional framework through which to analyse the same issues in the specifically Islamic capital market. It provides, for example, some further interesting insights into the development and problems associated with tri-party repo in a conventional sense, which brings some matters to our attention and indicates traps to avoid as the concept of Shari'ah-compliant tri-party repo develops.

Universally there are two common legal methods to set up a collateral arrangement: a) Security or Security Interest, where the assets are appropriated towards payment of a particular debt and available to the secured party upon the occurrence of contractual default; and b) Transfer of Title, where the legal and beneficial interest in the assets is transferred outright to the counterparty as owner, and where arrangements most commonly rely on set-off, or netting. Shari'ah scholars have traditionally specified that actual true ownership of collateral be transferred, and this historical requirement has restricted the credibility of certain products in certain markets. The division between true and beneficial ownership and a combination of both, or simple security over both, is the core aspect of most ICM collateral management packages. Herein lies the basis for the discussion about asset-backed versus asset-based *sukuk*. A failure to document collateral correctly may lead to a court determining that in default, the *sukuk* structure does not transfer the underlying asset to the *sukuk* holders as they might have expected, transfer of ownership is not established and the product is merely an unsecured loan and therefore the *sukuk* holder must join the creditor queue in accordance with whatever resolution regime is in force. Additional differences in treatment of collateral can take place when it is employed in a *musharaka sukuk* or an *ijarah sukuk* structure. In a *musharaka sukuk* structure the assets are jointly owned with the originator, often in an SPV (Trust). In an asset-backed *ijarah sukuk* structure the assets should be owned outright by the *sukuk* holder. This can also lead to greater collateral price risk, which may require further security above the asset itself.

There is a multiplicity of problems, concerns and issues surrounding collateralisation in established conventional finance. Nascent ICMs must thread their way through these issues to reach a consensus Shari'ah-compliant solution. It is clear from the nature of fundamentals of Shari'ah compliance in financial dealings that there will be idiosyncratic matters of import to address and disclose when identifying a permissible asset, establishing any kind of rights over that asset including transfer of ownership, perfection and registration, valuing the asset and permitted action in respect of the asset in an event of default must all be addressed. Some of the case studies referenced in the next section are examples of the consequences of failing to do so.

It is safe to say that the vast majority of structuring tools for establishing the collateral for any legitimate form of financing are essentially non-offensive to Shari'ah in nature. This, we could see, was not true of the mechanisms to make them liquid. It is the specificities of these tools which are important, not their conceptual generalities. For example, a guarantee is a form of collateral and guarantees may be permissible tools in (say) a *sukuk* structure. However there are substantial issues regarding the permissibility of the payment of remuneration (a fee) to a third party for such a guarantee under Shari'ah; in general, it is not permissible to provide an indemnity in return for remuneration, i.e. to sell an indemnity. Also, many of the guarantees issued to collateralise capital markets' instruments are a combination of a pure payment guarantee and a conditional payment guarantee, which may serve to turn the guarantee into an indemnity in some jurisdictions. This is seldom an issue in conventional jurisdictions, but as Dr Elgari notes, 'most of the misconception arises from confusion between indemnities and guarantees; the guarantor provides a guarantee against something, whilst an indemnity makes one party liable for things neither under its influence or control nor related to the transaction itself. Although such conditions clearly violate the Shari'ah, not every indemnity clause is forbidden'.[2] He goes on to recognise that an indemnity is a form of insurance and distinct from a defined obligation. Also, the purpose of merging these forms of guarantee in conventional documentation is usually to make sure that there is both a claim for damages and a debt claim and to cut down on the circumstances that will release a guarantor. Shari'ah treats the issue of damages in very distinct ways, and different jurisdictions apply them in different manners. This focus on guarantees as collateral is not designed to imply that this is the only or principal matter to be dealt with; it is simply to illustrate that when structuring collateral into any form of Shari'ah-compliant contract, attention to the underlying principles of Shari'ah rather than simply matters of local law is important, otherwise unexpected risk of Shari'ah non-compliance may emerge. This maxim is true of every usual aspect, including use of trusts, margining and netting. A full review of each merits a book rather than a chapter, but I think the message is clear that there are specific risks that can be associated with collateralisation distinct from those intended to be Shari'ah-compliant.

RISKS SPECIFICALLY ASSOCIATED WITH ISLAMIC COLLATERALISATION IN ICM

In May 2015, the IMF produced a working paper (WP/15/107) entitled, 'Islamic Finance, Consumer Protection and Financial Stability'. This paper is useful both on its own account but also in cross-referencing a joint publication in 2013 by IFSB, IOSCO (International Organisation of Securities Commissions) and Securities Commission Malaysia of 'Disclosure Requirements for Islamic Capital Market Products', and in drawing our attention to pages 17–18 on Shari'ah Non-Compliance Risk, illustrated in

---

[2]M. A. Elgari (1999) 'Some Recurring Shari'ah Violations in Islamic Investment Agreements Used by International Banking Institutions', Second Harvard University Forum on Islamic Finance Proceedings, pp. 151–154).

defaults by East Cameron Partners Sukuk Al Musharakah, and Investment Dar Company (TID) Sukuk Al Musharakah, Golden Belt 1 (Saad) Ijarah Sukuk and the Nakheel Ijarah Sukuk. References to these four cases are to be found in almost any assessment of default risk in ICM.

The Case of Blom Bank vs. The Investment Dar (TID)

Where there is uncertainty, there is risk. Most of the above chapter deals with uncertainties in Shari'ah rulings governing the treatment of certain aspects of managing collateral. These uncertainties can have unique consequences. In one example, the case of Blom Bank vs. TID, which was heard in the English High Court, was based on a dispute over non-repayment due under a master *wakala* contract. TID argued in front of an appellate court that its constitutional documents prohibited it from entering into Shari'ah non-compliant agreements and that the contract was Shari'ah non-compliant (despite the fact that their own Shari'ah committee had approved it), thus nullifying the contract. The appellate court held that TID raised an arguable case which required consideration at a full trial. The case had many components that are interesting to those looking at taking risk in Islamic financial products. But I wish to highlight the aspect of 'lack of capacity' claimed by TID in this case and the need to understand where, in an ICM structure that likely spans various jurisdictions, the capacity lies to enter into the specific contracts and how Shari'ah non-compliance will be assessed in respect to collaterals in those jurisdictions.

Disclosure Risk, IOSCO Core Principle 16 and International Debt Disclosure Principles

In the 2013 Joint IOSCO, IFSB and Securities Commission Malaysia paper, 'Disclosure Requirements for Islamic Capital Market Products', it was concluded that IOSCO principles, historically assumed to be sufficient for the ICM, were in fact deficient in some key areas. They highlighted the ambiguity that can exist around asset-backed versus asset-based *sukuk*. In proposing a new set of principles for ICM, the paper said that they 'should focus on the ownership of the assets by Sukuk holders and the structure of the particular Sukuk and the material risks involved, Clearly, the key terms of the Sukuk arrangement should be disclosed'. They went on to highlight that particular attention should be paid to the acquisition of the *sukuk* asset from the obligor, the type of transaction conveying the *sukuk* asset to the obligor; and the arrangements for the sale of the *sukuk* asset back to the obligor.

Interestingly, the paper highlighted that IOSCO principles are focused upon the issuer in conventional markets. In the conclusion to this paper, they propose that in new principles for ICM, the focus would be on the obligor. The paper strongly implies that enhanced disclosures will improve the understanding of risks related to the collateralisation of ICM, and the consequences will be a more orderly and efficient market.

Further Aspects of Risks Specifically Associated with Islamic Collateralisation in ICM

From these sections above it can be seen that ICM carries with it some unique risk characteristics that may be described as both idiosyncratic and non-systematic. In addition to those risks identified above, we can also point to other aspects that require special attention when considering (for example) the management of client accounts containing these assets.

Asset Pricing Risk

The risk that collateral will lose value can be considered to be heightened in collateralised ICM products because of risk mitigation problems such as the continuing uncertainty over re-hypothecation, exacerbated by perspectives on put options (which raise issues of Shari'ah compliance). IIFM has done some work on a purchase undertaking to supplement previous work on the subject, but this is currently far from complete. In practical terms, Islamic banks often seek to overcome this problem with a larger initial margin (haircut) to avoid any Shari'ah issue regarding margin variance, with the expectation that the initial margin will be more than enough to cover any underlying move in the collateral. However, this leads to inefficiency in comparison with conventional markets.

Rate of Return Risk (RORR)

Since IFSB published its IFSB-1 'Guiding Principles of Risk Management for Institutions (Other than Insurance Institutions) Offering Only Islamic Financial Services' in 2005, their recognition in Section 6.2, 'Definition and Profiles of Rate of Return Risk', of the unique character of Islamic banks' RORR and their introduction of the concept of 'Displaced Commercial Risk', the market has continued to describe this aspect of risk in Islamic banking as being greater compared to analogous risks in conventional banking (i.e. interest rate risk in the banking book), and this is mirrored in ICMs. A great deal has been written around this subject, and this chapter will focus on addressing only the point that analysts should take this into consideration when considering the risks in collateralised ICM products.

Both of the risks above draw our attention to client account management and in particular the management of assets for holders of PSIAs. Bearing in mind the tools used by Islamic banks to overcome the risks described above in their institutional arrangements, so offering the same solutions for client accounts will be very difficult to achieve when complying with Client Asset Reporting (CASS) to the regulators.

CONCLUSION

The analysis provided in this chapter has highlighted the importance of collateral in ICM transactions, as well as a number of areas in which greater clarity is needed regarding Shari'ah permissibility of certain structures and gaps that need to be filled in the availability of permissible structures. Progress is being made in the development of permissible structures, but as indicated above there are a number of pitfalls to be avoided.

CHAPTER 9

Eligible Capital and Capital Instruments

By Brandon Davies

T his chapter will focus on the structure of capital in banks under the Basel Committee's Basel III regime as amended to date. The implications of Basel III for the capital of Islamic banks will also be considered. Islamic banks may not issue interest-bearing debt instruments, or preferred shares, but there are forms of *sukuk* which may take the place of these. Capital instruments that Islamic banks may issue to meet the Basel III requirements are considered in more detail in Chapter 14.

However, to place into context the new capital regime we have below given an introduction to the reasons behind what amount to very significant changes to the previous regime.

It is important to make the point that the full extent of the changes to the regulatory capital requirements is not yet complete. In particular, this is the case for a new regime for the capital of banks in resolution, the so-called Total Loss Absorbing Capacity (TLAC). Moreover, changes to risk computations and resulting capital requirements for the trading book, known as the Fundamental Review of the Trading Book (FRTB), are not yet finalised.

An additional point made in this introduction is the importance of accounting standards in the computation of capital, as reported under International Financial Reporting Standards (IFRS). Major changes to the computation of banks' published capital and reserves will result from the implementation of the new IFRS9 standard from January 2018.

FLAWS IN THE BASEL II REGIME

Why did the pre-financial crisis capital regime fail to provide the necessary protection to the financial system when the crisis hit?

There were two major flaws with the pre-crisis capital regime:

1. The definition of capital.
2. The capital weights of banking and especially trading book assets.

These two flaws meant that both the numerator and denominator of the capital ratio were wrongly specified and as a result the global banking system was significantly undercapitalised.

THE DEFINITION OF CAPITAL

The flaws of the pre-crisis regime, started with the definition of capital.

Pre-crisis, it was possible to operate with no more than 2 percent of risk-weighted assets in the form of equity.

Quality of Capital Under Basel III

The purpose of holding capital is as a source of funds to absorb losses in excess of those priced into the products provided to customers (known in Basel parlance as unexpected losses).

In general, firms choose to hold a mixture of equity and debt capital that meets the risk and reward preferences of equity shareholders and debt investors. The equity is available to absorb losses while the company remains in business, whereas the debt capital can only absorb losses if the company is put into liquidation.

A firm's capital structure is an important risk indicator for potential investors, as well as for rating agencies and other interested parties. Banks, as regulated institutions, are required by their regulators to hold minimum amounts of capital, and the constituents and structure of capital qualifying for regulatory purposes under the Basel III regulation can be summarised as:

Tier 1 Capital
This consists of:

1. Common Equity Tier 1 capital. The predominant form of Tier 1 capital must be common equity and retained earnings (CET1).
2. Additional Tier 1 capital

The remainder of the Tier 1 capital base must be composed of instruments that are subordinated, have fully discretionary non-cumulative dividends or coupons and have neither a maturity date nor an incentive to redeem.

Basel III does not allow the use in Tier 1 of so-called 'innovative hybrid capital instruments', which under Basel II were limited to 15 percent of the Tier 1 capital base, and consequently this form of capital instrument must be phased out as Basel III regulation is introduced.

Basel III does allow its own version of non-equity capital instruments but these must be able to absorb losses on a going concern basis, either through a write-down or conversion into equity. This has resulted in the issuance of so-called 'contingent capital' instruments, which in general can be summarised as a long-term debt instrument that can be converted into equity should the bank's regulator require it. The conversion effectively allows the regulator to recapitalise a bank with loss-absorbing equity should it suffer losses that threaten its capital adequacy.

In the case of Islamic banks, a form of subordinated *mudaraba sukuk* has been issued by some banks, to take the place of conventional preferred shares, being subordinated to all claims except those of common equity. The Shari'ah does not permit subordinated debt, but *mudaraba* investors are not creditors so Shari'ah scholars have considered such *sukuk* permissible.

The minimum capital adequacy of a bank under Basel III requires:-

- Common equity Tier 1 must be at least 4.5 percent of risk-weighted assets at all times.
- Tier 1 capital must be at least 6.0 percent of risk-weighted assets at all times.
- Total capital (Tier 1 capital plus Tier 2 capital) must be at least 8.0 percent of risk-weighted assets at all times.

Tier 2 Capital

Tier 2 capital continues, as in Basel II, to provide loss absorbency on a 'gone concern' basis. Under Basel II, however, Tier 2 capital was split between Upper Tier 2 which comprised perpetual securities with step-up and call features or other incentives to redeem, and Lower Tier 2 which comprised dated subordinated debt. Given the Basel III focus on the problems of incentives to redeem, only dated subordinated debt remains eligible as Tier 2 capital.

Tier 2 capital must now comprise only debt instruments that have a minimum original maturity of at least five years but, as previously, recognition in regulatory capital in the remaining five years before maturity must be amortised on a straight-line basis. While no step-ups in the interest rate or other incentives to redeem are permitted, and investors must have no rights to accelerate repayment of future scheduled payments except in bankruptcy and liquidation, an option to call the debt after five years but prior to start of the amortisation period is not considered an incentive to redeem. The bank must not, however, do anything to create a prior expectation that redemption will be forthcoming and must ask the regulator's permission to exercise the call, which may result in the regulator imposing conditions on the exercise of the call, such as replacement of the capital with higher quality capital.

Some Islamic banks have issued a type of subordinated *mudaraba sukuk* as Tier 2 capital. Such *sukuk* are subordinated to depositors (including unrestricted investment account holders) and general creditors of the bank, and absorb losses by being written down when the Tier 1 capital ratio falls below a critical level (the 'point of non-viability').

For a Global Systemically Important Financial Institution (G-SIFI) a further layer of gone concern capital known as Total Loss Absorbing Capacity (TLAC) will be required under Basel III (see below).

Hybrid Debt Instruments

The Basel II regime allowed hybrid debt instruments to count as Tier 1 capital, even though they had no principal loss absorbency capacity on a going concern basis.

That is to say that, as a result of the nature of the debt contracts under which these funds were provided, they absorbed losses only after the bank's reserves (equity) were exhausted or the bank was in insolvency, which one would think would be the inevitable result of the bank exhausting its equity capital.

But the insolvency procedure could not in fact be used because the essence of 'too big (or important) to fail' was that large banks could not enter insolvency as the consequences were too damaging for customers, financial systems and economies more broadly.

The big lesson from this history is that going concern capital instruments must be composed mainly of equity, and all other instruments contributing to Tier 1 capital must unambiguously be able to absorb losses when the bank is a going concern.

Deductions from Capital

Moreover, the pre-crisis regime also allowed hybrid debt capital instruments to support the required deductions from the capital calculation, such as:

- goodwill,
- expected losses (introduced later under Basel II with the internal models regime for credit risk) and
- investments in other banks' capital instruments.

However, so far as the balance sheet is concerned, under IFRS any losses arising from these items reduce common equity in the going concern state. Such a discrepancy between numbers produced according to accounting standards and those produced following regulatory requirements was not then, and is not now, unusual, but was in this case a serious failing as it led to overestimating bank equity for regulatory purposes in circumstances where losses through these items were occurring. The result of applying these deductions at the level of total capital had the effect of overstating the core equity capital ratio.

Deferred Tax Assets and Minority Interest Assets

A further flaw was that deferred tax assets were not deducted from capital and minority interest assets were recognised in full. But deferred tax assets depend on future profitability (which is not assured, especially if the firm becomes insolvent) and minority interests are not fully transferable to absorb losses for a group.

Provisions

There were also problems in relation to the treatment of provisions. Under the current international accounting standards, provisions are based on incurred rather than expected losses.

As a consequence, the bank regulatory capital framework *de facto* becomes a partial substitute means of achieving more forward-looking provisioning, through the internal models regime for credit risk, which requires the deduction from capital of expected losses in excess of provisions.

A forward-looking approach to provisioning based on expected losses (now appearing through the adoption from 2018 of IFRS 9) will help move to a more appropriate position where the accounting standard requires a prudent valuation of banking book assets and the capital regime can focus on unexpected loss, thus making the accounting standards closer to the Basel III regulatory regime. However, owing to different definitions, most notably in that of 'expected loss' itself, there will be significant differences between expected loss calculations under Basel III and under IFRS.

QUANTITY OF CAPITAL

The minimum requirement for common equity is raised from the current 2 percent level before the application of regulatory adjustments to 4.5 percent after the application of stricter adjustments for goodwill, deferred tax assets, hedging reserves, provisions shortfalls, gains from the sale of securitisations, changes in own credit, investments in own shares, pension liabilities and shareholdings in financial institutions, as shown in Figure 9.1.

The Tier 1 capital requirement which includes common equity and other qualifying financial instruments will increase from 4 percent to 6 percent.

A 'capital conservation buffer' above the regulatory minimum requirement is to be calibrated at 2.5 percent and to be met with common equity.

A 'countercyclical buffer' with a range of 0 percent to 2.5 percent of common equity or other fully loss-absorbing capital will be implemented according to national circumstances. This buffer will only be in effect when there is excess credit growth that is resulting in a system-wide build-up of risk. The countercyclical buffer when in effect would be introduced as an extension of the conservation buffer range.

'Systemically important' banks should have loss-absorbing capacity beyond the standard announced (see TLAC).

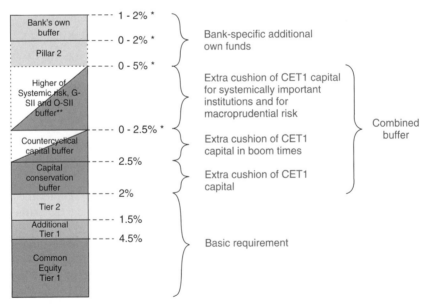

FIGURE 9.1   Basel III – Bank Capital Buffers
Notes:
*Assumed upper bonds (values can be higher)
**In certain cases can be the sum of SII and systemic risk buffer.
Source: European Commission. 'CRD IV/CRR – Frequently Asked Questions' (2013)

The same requirements apply to Islamic banks, as set out in the Islamic Financial Services Board's (IFSB) Standard on Capital Adequacy (IBSB-15, issued in December 2013).

CAPITAL WEIGHTS

Basel I risk weights provided little insight into how firms measured and managed risk and tended to create incentives for banks to increase the average level of riskiness of their assets.

Basel II was not in place properly when the crisis resulting from the insolvency of Lehman Brothers in September 2008 broke, though the Market Risk Amendment to Basel I (incorporated into Basel II) was.

The Market Risk Amendment and Basel II dramatically increased the complexity of the capital framework and while it was intended to increase the scope of risk capture in the regulatory capital measure, it ended up creating new opportunities for 'optimising' (in practice reducing) regulatory capital.

The Basel Committee recognised that across internationally active banks, Basel II would likely lead to an overall reduction in the required capital in respect of credit risk compared with that required under Basel I.

For a set of 17 major international banks (designated as G-SIBs) average risk weights fell almost continuously from 70 percent in 1993 to below 40 percent in 2012.[1] But this fall in average risk weights did not represent a systematic reduction in risk within the banking system; banks were instead able to reduce their capital weights through the implementation of internal models.

The 'gaming' of the regulation through models occurred in a number of ways, some of which (such as the limitation of Value at Risk as a measure of 'tail risk') are only now being addressed through the FRTB.

The level of Pillar 1 risk-weighted capital was therefore wrong – too little capital was required to support the total amount of risk banks were running. So far as market risk was concerned, although this was supposedly corrected by the Market Risk Amendment it is likely that the FRTB will result in significant new additions to the regulatory capital, most especially that required to back the credit risk inherent in trading positions. The so-called Credit Valuation Adjustment (CVA) is to be added to risk capital and represents the difference between the risk-free portfolio value and the true portfolio value that takes into account the possibility of a counterparty's default. The FRTB is also likely to require the capital for trading positions to be calculated using a measure called Expected Shortfall (ES) which for regulatory purposes will replace the widely used Value at Risk (VaR) measure.

---

[1] Data Source: The Banker and Bank of England calculations. Sample comprises: Deutsche Bank, HSBC, BNP Paribas, Barclays, Citigroup, UBS, BAML, BONY, Commerzbank, ING, JPM, LBG, RBS, Santander, State Street, UniCredit, Wells Fargo. The data came from 'The capital adequacy of banks: today's issues and what we have learned from the past', a speech given by Andrew Bailey, Deputy Governor, Prudential Regulation and Chief Executive Officer, Prudential Regulation Authority, at Bloomberg, London, 10 July 2014.

Pillar 2 Capital

Apart from market risk, the lacuna in Basel I was not corrected by the imposition of Pillar 2 capital. In 2008, the major UK banks had a Pillar 2 capital requirement of £22bn which was equivalent to only 10 percent of their then Pillar 1 capital requirement, which as explained above was a significant underestimate in relation to the risk they were running.

In summary, the system was flawed both in terms of the definition of capital, the quality and the quantity of capital that banks were required to hold.

Effect of Basel III on Total Capital

Under the Basel II regime, the Pillar 1 minimum requirement was £38bn of the highest quality capital for the five largest UK banks. Compared to this, taking both capital minima and capital buffers together when Basel III is fully implemented, the equivalent figure as measured in September 2013 (according to the Bank of England) would be £271bn, i.e. seven times the Basel II minimum.

Breaking down this increase of £233bn in Core Tier I capital, £80bn is accounted for by the change in the definition of capital resources, £61bn relates to raising the minimum requirement from 2 percent to 4.5 percent of risk-weighted assets (and changes to the risk weights), £55bn to the Basel III Capital Conservation Buffer, and £37bn to the Basel III Globally Significant Banks Buffer. (Data source: The Banker and Bank of England calculations. Sample comprises: Deutsche Bank, HSBC, BNP Paribas, Barclays, Citigroup, UBS, BAML, BONY, Commerzbank, ING, JPM, LBG, RBS, Santander, State Street, UniCredit, Wells Fargo.)

Stress Testing

A major principle of the new framework is that there is no single 'right' approach to assessing capital adequacy. The very important role that is now given to stress tests illustrates the point. This is a key device to examine and mitigate tail risks, and like all good forecasting exercises, the stress test is designed to probe important issues rather than just to provide a single answer. With regard to Islamic banks, the IFSB issued in March 2012 IFSB-13, *Guiding Principles on Stress Testing for Institutions offering Islamic Financial Services*. A further technical note was issued in December 2016 (TN-2, Technical Note on Stress Testing for Institutions Offering Islamic Financial Services (IIFS)).

Resolution

A second key principle of capital adequacy is that which establishes the boundary between the going and gone concern (or resolution) regimes for loss absorbency. This is one reason why the work on resolution and gone concern loss absorbency (TLAC) is so important, but still outstanding.

In the event that, despite the above reforms, the capital of a big bank – defined as a G-SIFI – proves insufficient to save the bank from liquidation, there is additionally a need to ensure that in liquidation the funds available to the liquidators are sufficient to ensure that depositors are repaid without recourse to the guarantee from the national treasury that typically covers the vast majority of the retail deposits of national banking systems.

The problem that TLAC is designed to eliminate is that in the vast majority of countries (Japan is an exception), depositors' funds are treated in law as having the same rights as other unsecured creditors of the bank, including, of course, the majority of bond holders.

As a result of this, in a bank liquidation, after the claims of preferred creditors such as claims for salary and tax are paid, the remaining funds must be divided between all of the unsecured lenders. If the national treasury is not to stand a significant risk of loss, there is clearly a need for depositor preference in the claims on the available funds.

Rather than a change in the law in respect of preferential claimants on available funds, the Financial Stability Board (FSB) has proposed that GSIFI banks should raise new funding that in large measure would replace existing funding, but with specific provision that repayment of the new funding would, in a liquidation of the bank, be subordinated to the claims of the banks' depositors.

GLOBAL SYSTEMATICALLY IMPORTANT FINANCIAL INSTITUTIONS (G-SIFIS)

The Financial Stability Board (FSB) has published its finalised new rule that will require the world's top 30 banks, known as Global Systemically Important Financial Institutions (G-SIFIs) to issue bonds that can be subordinated to depositors' claims in the event of liquidation of the bank.

The aim is to avoid a failed bank having to rely on taxpayers' funds, as became common after the collapse of Lehman Brothers in 2008. The bonds are in addition to a bank's core capital requirements.

TABLE 9.1   G-SIFI banks

Additional Capital 2.5%	HSBC, JP Morgan Chase
Additional Capital 2.0%	Barclays, BNP Paribas, Citigroup, Deutsche Bank
Additional Capital 1.5%	Bank of America, Credit Suisse, Goldman Sachs, Mitsubishi UFJ FG, Morgan Stanley, Royal Bank of Scotland
Additional Capital 1.0%	Agricultural Bank of China, Bank of China, Bank of New York Mellon, BBVA, Groupe BPCE, Group Crédit Agricole, Industrial and Commercial Bank of China Limited, ING Bank, Mizuho FG, Nordea, Santander, Société Générale, Standard Chartered, State Street, Sumitomo Mitsui FG, UBS, Unicredit Group, Wells Fargo

Value at Risk vs. Expected Shortfall

The Basel Committee is focusing on implementing regulation based on the FRTB which, amongst other changes, will replace VaR-based calculations of market risk with an ES-based calculation.

The difficulties in measuring tail risk are nothing new. When a quarter of a century ago the decision was taken to replace the then jumbled world of customer exposure limits, duration mismatch limits and outright (nominal) position limits, a measure of mean-variance (VaR) and a measure of tail dependency (ES) were both considered (see below). VaR was seen at that time as a usable and reasonably reliable measure of risk in 'normal' circumstances, while ES was seen as very dependent on the choice of the distribution used to project future outcomes.

Figure 9.2 contrasts the VaR at the 95 percent for a normal distribution with the VaR at the 99 percent for both a normal and Generalised Pareto Distribution (GPD) and an ES measure for the GPD. Note the GPD 99 percent is approximately 3x that of the normal distribution and the ES of the GPD is approximately 7x that of the normal 99 percent.

The decision to choose VaR as a measure of risk implied a definition of risk that in many ways was quite unsatisfactory. VaR is a constrained measure and so looks at risk as variance measured at some percentile from the mean (average) outcome. Given this, the constraint on the outcome made for a very much more simple measure of risk than we would need, were we to look for the most extreme outcomes.

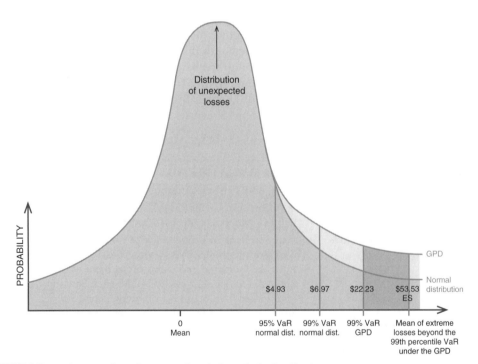

FIGURE 9.2 Value at risk under normal and 'fat tailed' distributions

When anyone thinks of risk, they usually focus on some absolutely bad outcome epitomised, say, by the risk of death, which is a pretty absolute measure of risk! ES is clearly a more appropriate way of measuring extreme outcomes and such outcomes are what most people would think of as risk.

The VaR was chosen because there was no reliable way of predicting the shape of the tail of risk distributions – something that is vital if the computation of ES is to have any practical use. Whether extreme outcomes in financial markets are indeed measurable is very debatable and current research, much of which focuses on so-called 'system dynamics', indicates that the systemic relationships between actors in the financial markets are extremely complex, so that once a crisis moves from being idiosyncratic to being systemic, the tail outcomes change dramatically, and predicting such change is at best work in progress.

LEVERAGE RATIO

US banks have for many years had to conform to a leverage ratio in addition to a relationship between capital and risk-weighted assets. Such a ratio mitigates the inability of a risk-weighted capital adequacy requirement to prevent banks holding assets with zero or very low risk weights from having a very low ratio of equity to assets, i.e. excessive leverage.

The Basel Committee has now proposed the addition of a leverage ratio, to be effective from 2018, to the many other reforms to Basel III. This simple, non-risk-weight based 'backstop' measure is intended to restrict the build-up of excessive leverage in the banking sector, which may in turn create a destabilising deleveraging process that can damage the broader financial system and the economy.

Basel III's leverage ratio is defined as the 'capital measure' (the numerator) divided by the 'exposure measure' (the denominator) and is expressed as a percentage. The capital measure is currently defined as Tier 1 capital and the minimum leverage ratio is 3 percent.

Further to the publication of its initial proposals for the calibration of the ratio, a number of revisions were made by the Basel Committee covering:

- Securities financing transactions (including repo and reverse repo)
- Off-balance sheet items
- Cash variation margin associated with derivative exposures
- Central clearing
- Written credit derivatives

It is possible that in the light of practice further alterations will be made, as one may deduce from the above list of revisions that what may seem a simple idea is in practice not so simple to implement.

There are also a number of areas where the Basel Committee's version of the leverage ratio differs from that used by US regulators – a state of affairs which is unlikely to change owing largely to accounting differences between US GAAP accounting standards and IFRS accounting standards. As a result, no direct comparisons can be made between US banks leverage ratios and those calculated under the Basel III standard.

BASEL III CAPITAL AND ISLAMIC BANKS – FURTHER CONSIDERATIONS

Under Basel II regulations Islamic banks suffered an important handicap as they are not allowed to raise capital through the issue of debt instruments (e.g. bonds). Islamic banks thus typically have much higher equity-to-asset ratios than do conventional banks, which results in their having a lower return on equity than equivalent conventional banks.

Under the Basel III proposals, the results should be less of a problem for Islamic banks, as for them CET1 is typically a much higher percentage of total capital than it is for conventional banks. There is, however, still a role for forms of regulatory capital other than common equity under the going concern capital requirements of Basel III, which would advantage conventional banks if contingent capital were limited to forms of convertible bonds.

Under Basel III, however, it seems possible that contingent capital may also comprise undertakings based on indemnity funds. It is to be hoped that Islamic banks will prove creative enough to develop a contingent capital structure that can be provided on an equivalent basis to both Islamic and conventional banks. In the meantime, as mentioned above, some Islamic banks have issued both Additional Tier 1 and Tier 2 capital instruments using subordinated *mudaraba* structures (see Chapter 14 for further details).

TLAC Capital

Under Basel III the requirement for TLAC is unlikely to apply to any Islamic banks in the near future, as the requirement for TLAC only applies to GSIFI banks. It is, however, something that could possibly apply at some future date, and if it looked remotely likely that an Islamic bank could become a GSIFI, considerable thought would need to be given to the issue as TLAC capital over and above going concern capital is composed solely of bonds. While bailing in unrestricted profit and loss sharing investment (deposit) accounts would be one solution, it would require significant alteration to the contractual obligations between Islamic banks and their unrestricted profit and loss sharing investment account customers, and would make such accounts unattractive. It seems more likely that the type of subordinated Tier 2 *mudaraba sukuk* issued by several Islamic banks will become more common.

While it is unlikely that any Islamic banks will be a GSIFI in the near future, the IFSB considered, in its IFSB-15, the case of a Domestically Significant Islamic Bank (D-SIB), on which the supervisor authority might impose a higher loss absorbency requirement.

Islamic Banks' Competitive Position

The creation of a 'level playing field' between Islamic and conventional banks may be an unintended benefit of Basel III, but it is an important one, as the globalisation of Islamic banking can best be progressed by conforming to an internationally agreed set of regulations that allows and encourages Islamic banks based on different national jurisdictions to compete with one another. Better still, Basel III holds out the prospect of Islamic banks also competing on more equal terms, at least as far as capital is concerned, with conventional banks.

CONCLUSION

Why did the pre-financial crisis capital regime fail to provide the necessary protection to the financial system when the crisis hit? There were two major flaws with the pre-crisis capital regime:

1. The definition of capital.
2. The capital weights of banking and especially trading book assets: i.e. both the numerator and denominator of the capital ratio were wrongly specified!

The Definition of Capital

The flaws of the pre-crisis regime, started with the definition of capital. Pre-crisis, it was possible to operate with no more than 2 percent of risk-weighted assets in the form of equity. This was largely because the then existing regime allowed hybrid debt instruments to count as Tier 1 capital, even though they had no principal loss absorbency capacity on a going concern basis.

But the insolvency procedure could not in fact be used because the essence of 'too big (or important) to fail' was that large banks could not enter insolvency as the consequences were too damaging for customers, financial systems and economies more broadly.

The big lesson from this history is that going concern capital instruments must comprise mainly equity, and all other instruments contributing to Tier 1 capital must unambiguously be able to absorb losses when the bank is a going concern.

Moreover, the pre-crisis regime also allowed hybrid debt capital instruments to support the required deductions from the capital calculation, such as:

- goodwill,
- expected losses (introduced later under Basel II with the internal models regime for credit risk) and
- investments in other banks' capital instruments.

However, as a matter of accounting any losses arising from these items hit common equity in the going concern state. The result of applying these deductions at the level of total capital had the effect of overstating the core equity capital ratio.

A further flaw was that deferred tax assets were not deducted from capital, and minority interest assets were recognised in full and there were also problems in relation to the treatment of provisions.

A forward-looking approach to provisioning based on expected losses (now appearing in the shape of IFRS 9) will help move to a more appropriate position, where the accounting standard requires a prudent valuation of banking book assets and the capital regime can focus on unexpected loss.

The Capital Weights of Banking and Especially Trading Book Assets

Basel I risk weights provided little insight into how firms measured and managed risk and tended to create incentives for banks to increase the average level of riskiness of their assets.

Basel II was not in place properly when the crisis broke, though the Market Risk Amendment was. The Market Risk Amendment and Basel II dramatically increased the complexity of the capital framework, and while it was intended to increase the scope of risk capture in the regulatory capital measure it ended up creating new opportunities for 'optimising' (in practice reducing) regulatory capital.

The level of Pillar 1 risk-weighted capital was therefore wrong – too little capital was required. This was not corrected by the imposition of Pillar 2 capital. In 2008, the major UK banks had a Pillar 2 capital requirement of £22bn (equivalent to 10 percent of then Pillar 1 capital requirement).

In summary, the system was flawed both in terms of the definition of capital, the quality and the quantity of capital banks were required to hold.

Stress Testing

A major principle of the new framework is that there is no single 'right' approach to assessing capital adequacy. The very important role that is now given to stress tests illustrates the point. This is a key device to examine and mitigate tail risks, and like all good forecasting exercises, the stress test is designed to probe important issues rather than just provide a single answer.

Resolution

A second key principle of capital adequacy is that which establishes the boundary between the going and gone concern (or resolution) regimes for total loss absorbency.

Basel III

There can be no doubt that the now much amended Basel III regime addresses many of the problems that the succession of financial crises that have affected the global economy over the last eight years highlighted as failings of Basel II.

It is, however, a very complex regime and it seems likely that it will produce a number of unintended consequences over forthcoming years.

Further amendments are also likely stemming from the better understanding of systemic versus idiosyncratic risk, and it is very important that research in the area of system dynamics is pursued vigorously.

The problem of Basel III being essentially a product of wealthy, slow growth, ageing and risk averse economies will likely magnify and multiply the problems of its implementation in poorer economies with young and rapidly growing populations where economic growth (as against risk avoidance) is more of an issue.

It is also to be hoped it is the last regime to fail to address issues in Islamic bank regulation at source rather than as a series of afterthought amendments as issues arise. In the meantime, the IFSB has issued guidance on capital adequacy and stress testing which adapts the Basel III requirements for application to Islamic banks.

CHAPTER 10

Regulatory Aspects of the Islamic Capital Market and Basel III Requirements – Shari'ah-Compliant Bank Capital Instruments

By Rafe Haneef

The global financial crisis of 2008 resulted in several banks across the globe facing an existential threat. The global panic that ensued dragged the great and the good of the banking fraternity close to the abyss of insolvency, posing a systemic risk to the wider global economic system. Despite massive government bailout programmes, not every bank could be saved from crossing the event horizon, resulting in three of the most venerable names on Wall Street – Bear Stearns, Lehman Brothers and Merrill Lynch – going to the wall, as well as the British bank Northern Rock.

The shock of the global financial crisis prompted regulatory authorities to consider the stability of financial markets and put in place measures that would bolster the shock absorption mechanism of its participants. For banks, the major focus area is on strengthening global capital and liquidity rules.

In December 2010, the Basel Committee on Banking Supervision (BCBS) published the Third Basel Accord (Basel III standards) to replace the Basel II standards, which were considered unsuitable in the post-crisis banking landscape. The Basel III standards aim to improve the quality of bank capital, reduce counterparty risk, constrain over-leverage and improve liquidity risk management.

BANK CAPITAL REQUIREMENTS: BASEL II VS. BASEL III

Basel III refines the definition of bank capital to increase the quality, consistency and transparency of the capital base, as well as imposing higher minimum capital ratios. The main revisions include raising the quality and quantity of Tier 1 capital and simplifying and reducing the proportion of Tier 2 capital. The main differences between the Basel II and Basel III capital requirements are set out in Figure 10.1.

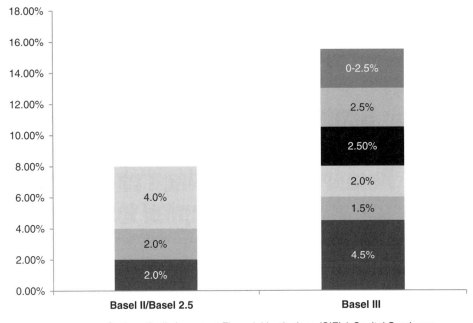

FIGURE 10.1   Basel II/2.5 vs. Basel III capital requirement comparison

As we can see from Figure 10.1, the key differences in capital requirements between Basel II/2.5 and Basel III are as follows:

1. Common Equity Tier 1 capital ratio (CET1) – consisting of common shares and retained earnings – increases from 2 percent to 4.5 percent.
2. Additional Tier 1 (AT1) capital ratio – which may consist of hybrid capital instruments – is reduced from 2.0 percent to 1.5 percent.[1]
3. Tier 2 (T2) capital ratio – which may consist of subordinated debt instruments – is reduced from 4.0 percent to 2 percent.
4. Two additional capital buffers,[2] consisting of CET1 are introduced:
   a. A capital conservation buffer of 2.5 percent (additional buffer intended to ensure that financial institutions are able to absorb losses in stress periods lasting for a number of years).

---

[1] Although Basel III requires financial institutions to maintain a minimum total Tier 1 capital ratio of 6 percent, it allows for AT1 capital of 1.5 percent or more (as long as CET1 meets the minimum 4.5 percent requirement).
[2] This means that banks may be required to have a total CET1 capital ratio of between 7.0 and 9.5 percent.

b. A countercyclical buffer of between 0 and 2.5 percent (intended to protect the banking sector from 'boom and bust' experienced from credit growth – the buffer is required during periods of excessive credit growth and is released during a downturn).

5. Additional capital surcharges between 1 percent and 2.5 percent (extra CET1) for banks that are considered to be systemically important both domestically and globally.[3]

This change in the minimum capital requirements with the emphasis on banks holding a greater amount of CET1 demonstrates that the intention of the Basel III standards is for banks to have greater capacity to absorb losses. This is because losses and write-downs during the financial crisis came from banks' retained earnings, which form a part of CET1.

BASEL III-COMPLIANT COMMON EQUITY TIER 1 (CET1) INSTRUMENTS

CET1 instruments consist of:

1. Qualifying capital instruments (typically common shares or comparable instruments).
2. Share premium accounts.
3. Retained earnings.
4. Accumulated other comprehensive income.
5. Other reserves.
6. Funds for general banking risk.

Qualifying Requirements for Basel III-Compliant CET1 Instruments

A CET1 capital instrument must meet all of the following requirements in order to qualify as Basel III-compliant:[4]

1. It represents the most subordinated claim in liquidation of the bank.
2. It entitles the holder to a claim on the residual assets that is proportional with its share of issued capital, after all senior claims have been repaid in liquidation (i.e. it has an unlimited and variable claim, not a fixed or capped claim).
3. The principal is perpetual and never repaid outside of liquidation (setting aside discretionary repurchases or other means of effectively reducing capital in a discretionary manner that is allowable under relevant law).
4. No expectation is created at issuance that the instrument will be bought back, redeemed or cancelled, nor do the statutory or contractual terms provide any feature which might give rise to such an expectation.
5. Distributions are paid out of distributable items (retained earnings included) and the level of distributions is not in any way tied or linked to the amount paid in at issuance and is not subject to a contractual cap (except to the extent that a bank is unable to pay distributions that exceed the level of distributable items).

---

[3] Still under discussion at time of writing.
[4] 'Basel III: A global regulatory framework for more resilient banks and banking systems' (revised June 2011).

6. There are no circumstances under which the distributions are obligatory – non-payment is therefore not an event of default.
7. Distributions are paid only after all legal and contractual obligations have been met and payments on more senior capital instruments have been made (i.e. there are no preferential distributions, including in respect of other elements classified as the highest quality issued capital).
8. It is the issued capital that takes the first and proportionately greatest share of any losses as they occur (within the highest quality capital, each instrument absorbs losses on a going concern basis proportionately and *pari passu* with all the others).
9. The paid in amount is recognised as equity capital (i.e. not recognised as a liability) for determining balance sheet insolvency.
10. The paid in amount is classified as equity under the relevant accounting standards.[5]
11. It is directly issued and paid in and the bank cannot directly or indirectly have funded the purchase of the instrument.
12. The paid in amount is neither secured nor covered by a guarantee of the issuer or related entity,[6] or subject to any other arrangement that legally or economically enhances the seniority of the claim.
13. It is only issued with the approval of the shareholders of the issuing bank, either given directly by the shareholders or, if permitted by applicable law, given by the board of directors or by other persons duly authorised by the shareholders.
14. It is clearly and separately disclosed on the bank's balance sheet.

Given that CET1 capital instruments consist of common shares or comparable instruments, this paper will instead focus on Basel III-compliant Additional Tier 1 capital and Tier 2 capital instruments which are suitable for structuring as *sukuk* instruments.

BASEL III-COMPLIANT ADDITIONAL TIER 1 CAPITAL (AT1) INSTRUMENTS

AT1 instruments include:

1. Qualifying instruments (considered further below).
2. Share premium accounts related to those qualifying instruments.

---

[5] Under IAS32.16, a financial instrument is an equity instrument only if (a) the instrument includes no contractual obligation to deliver cash or another financial asset to another entity and (b) if the instrument will or may be settled in the issuer's own equity instruments, it is either:

1. a non-derivative that includes no contractual obligation for the issuer to deliver a variable number of its own equity instruments; or
2. a derivative that will be settled only by the issuer exchanging a fixed amount of cash or another financial asset for a fixed number of its own equity instruments.

[6] A related entity can include a parent company, a sister company, a subsidiary or any other affiliate. A holding company is a related entity irrespective of whether it forms part of the consolidated banking group.

Qualifying Requirements for Basel III-Compliant AT1 Instruments

An AT1 capital instrument must meet the following requirements in order to qualify as Basel III-compliant:

1. It is issued and paid in.
2. It is subordinated to depositors, general creditors and subordinated debt of the bank.
3. It is neither secured nor covered by a guarantee of the issuer or related entity or other arrangement that legally or economically enhances the seniority of the claim above other creditors.
4. It is perpetual (i.e. there is no maturity date and there are no step-ups or other incentives to redeem the instrument).
5. It may be callable at the initiative of the issuer only after a minimum of five years.[7]
6. Any payment of principal (e.g. through repurchase or redemption) must be with prior supervisory approval (banks should not assume or create market expectations that supervisory approval will be given).
7. The bank must have dividend/coupon discretion, meaning that it:
   a. may cancel distributions/payments;[8]
   b. such cancellation must not be an event of default;
   c. it must have full access to cancelled payments to meet obligations as they fall due; and
   d. cancellation of distributions/payments must not impose restrictions on the bank except in relation to distributions to common stockholders.
8. Dividends/coupons must be paid out of distributable items.
9. The instrument cannot have a credit-sensitive dividend feature (a dividend/coupon that is reset periodically based in whole or in part on the bank's credit standing).
10. The instrument cannot contribute to liabilities exceeding assets if such a balance sheet test forms part of national insolvency law.
11. If the instrument is classified as a liability for accounting purposes, it must have principal loss absorption through either:
    a. conversion to common shares at an objective pre-specified trigger point, or

---

[7]To exercise a call option a bank must:

1. receive prior supervisory approval;
2. not do anything which creates an expectation that the call will be exercised; and
3. not exercise a call unless:
   1. it replaces the called instrument with capital of the same or better quality and the replacement of this capital is done at conditions which are sustainable for the income capacity of the bank; or
   2. the bank demonstrates that its capital position is well above the minimum capital requirements (as determined by the local regulator) after the call option is exercised.

[8]This means that 'dividend pushers' are prohibited. An instrument with a dividend pusher obliges the issuing bank to make a dividend/coupon payment on the instrument if it has made a payment on another (typically more junior) capital instrument or share. Also, the term 'cancel distributions/payments' means extinguish these payments and therefore does not permit features that require the bank to make distributions/payments in kind.

b. a write-down mechanism which allocates losses to the instrument at a pre-specified trigger point.[9]

12. Neither the bank nor a related party over which the bank exercises control or significant influence can have purchased the instrument, nor can the bank directly or indirectly have funded the purchase of the instrument.

13. The instrument cannot have any features that hinder recapitalisation, such as provisions that require the issuer to compensate investors if a new instrument is issued at a lower price during a specified timeframe.

14. If the instrument is not issued out of an operating entity or the holding company in the consolidated group (e.g. a special purpose vehicle – SPV), proceeds must be immediately available without limitation to an operating entity,[10] or the holding company in the consolidated group in a form which meets or exceeds all of the other criteria for inclusion in Additional Tier 1 capital.

Based on the above requirements, the Islamic finance market has developed Basel III-compliant AT1 *sukuk*, which are considered further in the case studies that follow.

Case Study: Abu Dhabi Islamic Bank (ADIB) USD1 billion, Perpetual Reg S Additional Tier 1 Mudaraba Sukuk

This 2012 Tier 1 offering was the first ever Shari'ah-compliant Tier 1 issue executed in the international markets and the first ever Tier 1 instrument issued by a Middle East bank in the capital markets (Tables 10.1 and 10.2).

Structure overview

1. On the Issue Date, the Issuer (ADIB Capital Invest 1, a Cayman Islands registered SPV[11]) will issue Trust Certificates to Investors in consideration for the proceeds from the issuance (Issuance Proceeds) as shown in Figure 10.2.

2. The Issuer (i.e. the SPV) in its capacity as the Trustee, will declare a trust in favor of the Investors over all rights, title, interest and benefits relating to (i) the assets constituting the Mudaraba & (ii) the Transaction Documents, and monies standing to the credit of the related transaction account.

---

[9] The write-down will have the effect of:

1. reducing the claim of the instrument in liquidation;
2. reducing the amount repaid when a call is exercised; and
3. partially or fully reducing coupon/dividend payments on the instrument.

[10] An entity set up to conduct business with customers with the intention of earning a profit in its own right.

[11] An SPV is required for structural purposes to create an arm's length transaction between ADIB (as *mudarib*) and the Issuer (as *rab-al-maal*) from an Islamic perspective. An offshore SPV formed in a jurisdiction where the concept of a trust is recognised creates an English law trust structure which provides comfort to investors. It is also market practice.

TABLE 10.1   ADIB Tier 1 *mudaraba sukuk* – transaction overview

Issuer	ADIB Capital Invest Ltd.
Obligor	Abu Dhabi Islamic Bank PJSC
Obligor Senior Rating	A2(Moody's)/A+(Fitch) – both stable outlook (the previous 2009 Tier 1 issue is not rated)
Currency/Format	USD/Fixed Rate Regulation S
Structure	*Sukuk mudaraba*
Amount	USD1 billion
Pricing/Settlement Date	8 November 2012/19 November 2012
Optional Call Date	16 October 2018, and on each profit distribution date thereafter
Reset Date	16 October 2018 and every 6 years thereafter to a new fixed rate based on the then prevailing 6yr US mid-swap rate + the initial credit margin
Periodic Distribution	6.375% p.a., semi-annual payments
Issue Price/Re-Offer Spread	100/6 year USD MS+539.3bps
Listing	London Stock Exchange
Governing Law	English law (except *mudaraba* agreement governed under Abu Dhabi and UAE law)

TABLE 10.2   ADIB Tier 1 *mudaraba sukuk* – summary of commercial terms

Maturity	Perpetual
Ranking	Deeply subordinated, senior only to Common Equity Tier 1 (CET1) *Pari passu* with the existing 2009 AED 2bn Tier 1 instrument
Call Date	Callable at year 6 and every 6 years thereafter subject to redemption conditions
Profit Rate	Fully discretionary profit payment cancellation (non-cumulative) Mandatory profit payment cancellation (non-cumulative) if the bank breaches minimum capital ratios or if the bank does not meet solvency conditions Fixed rate 6 year MS + initial margin until first call and reset to a new fixed rate every 6th year thereafter based on then prevailing 6 year USD MS + initial margin
Dividend Stopper	If ADIB chooses not to make a profit payment on the Tier 1 issue, or if there is a mandatory profit payment cancellation, no dividends can be paid on ordinary shares and no profit payments can be made on *pari passu* instruments (2) (ADIB's 2009 Tier 1 issue) Dividends and profit payments on *pari passu* instruments can be resumed when profit payments are made on the Proposed Tier 1 issue, or if one year's worth of payments on the Proposed Tier 1 issue are set aside by ADIB
Optional Early Redemption	Tax event: Imposition of withholding tax – par call capital event: 100% loss of Tier 1 capital treatment

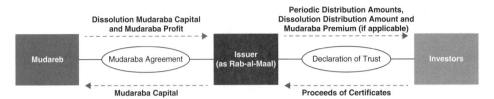

FIGURE 10.2   ADIB Tier 1 *mudaraba sukuk* structure

3. Pursuant to a Mudaraba[12] Agreement between ADIB (as Mudareb) and the Trustee (as Rab-al-Maal), a Mudaraba will be constituted and the Issuance Proceeds will be invested by the Trustee as the Mudaraba Capital.
4. ADIB (as Mudareb) will invest the Mudaraba Capital in the general banking business of ADIB.
5. The objective of the Mudaraba will be to earn profit from the investment of the Mudaraba Capital in the Mudaraba Assets. On each profit payment date, ADIB shall allocate the profit generated by the Mudaraba ("Mudaraba Profit"), after ADIB has deducted any profit earned from its own co-mingled assets, to both the Trustee and the Mudareb. The Trustee shall apply its share of the profit (if any) generated from the Mudaraba to make the profit payment due to the Investors.
6. Payments of the Mudaraba Profit by ADIB (as Mudareb) are at its sole discretion and may only be made in circumstances where ADIB will not be in breach of certain solvency and minimum capital conditions as a result of making such payment.

Transaction highlights

- The transaction was well received by both regional and international investors (see Figure 10.3), culminating in an orderbook in excess of USD15 billion (representing

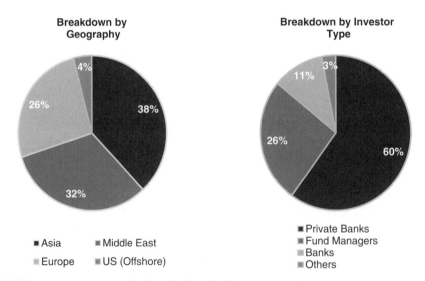

FIGURE 10.3   ADIB Tier 1 *mudaraba sukuk* – distribution statistics

---

[12] *Mudaraba* means a partnership in profit between capital and work in which one partner, the *rab-al-maal* (investor) contributes capital and the other, the *mudarib* (manager), invests time and effort and may contribute its own capital as well.

a 15x oversubscription and the largest oversubscription witnessed in any *sukuk* offering globally).

- The issuance followed a series of investor meetings in Asia, the Middle East and Europe. In light of the unique nature of the transaction, the investor meetings commenced in the UAE with the objective of providing investors with sufficient time to understand the combination of Shari'ah and hybrid capital structuring elements.
- The initial momentum in the orderbook allowed ADIB to release initial price thoughts of a 7 percent area on 7 November 2012, during the Asia morning. The announcement met with an overwhelmingly positive response. As a result, official price guidance was released at 6.50 percent area (+/– 12.5bps), before being tightened again on the back of strong demand. The transaction eventually priced on the afternoon of 8 November 2015 during London hours at the tight end of the guidance at 6.375 percent, representing one of the lowest coupons for USD Tier 1 issuances on the international markets.

Case Study: Dubai Islamic Bank PJSC (DIB) USD1 billion Reg S Perpetual Tier 1 Capital Sukuk

At the time of writing, this USD1 billion *sukuk* offering, the second USD Tier 1 *sukuk* offering by DIB, was the most recent Basel III-compliant Tier 1 *sukuk* issued in the global *sukuk* market (Tables 10.3 and 10.4).

Structure overview

The structure used by DIB was similar to the *mudaraba* structure utilised by ADIB.

Transaction highlights

- DIB opened the 2015 MENA (Middle East and North Africa region) markets and announced the first trade and first perpetual *sukuk* of the year on 6 January. A series of global investor meetings were conducted in Asia, Europe and the Middle East, which were met with strong interest from a diverse range of investors.

TABLE 10.3   DIB Tier 1 *mudaraba sukuk* – transaction overview

Issuer	DIB Tier 1 Sukuk (2) Ltd.
Obligor	Dubai Islamic Bank PJSC
Obligor Senior Rating	Baa1 (Moody's)/A (Fitch) (the Tier 1 issue is not rated)
Currency/Format	USD/Fixed rate Regulation S
Status	Subordinated perpetual non-call 6 Tier 1 capital *sukuk*
Structure	*Sukuk mudaraba*
Amount	USD1 billion
Pricing/Settlement Date	14 January 2015 / 20 January 2015
Issue Price/Re-Offer Spread	100/6 year USD MS+532.5bps
Listing	Irish Stock Exchange and Nasdaq Dubai
Governing Law	English law (except *mudaraba* agreement which is governed by Dubai and UAE law)

TABLE 10.4 DIB Tier 1 *mudaraba sukuk* – summary of commercial terms

Maturity	Perpetual
Ranking	Subordinated, senior only to ordinary shares, payments subject to the solvency conditions
	Pari passu with the existing 2013 6.25% USD1bn Tier 1 instrument
Call Date	20 January 2021 (first call date) and every distribution date thereafter subject to redemption conditions
Distributions	6.75 % fixed p.a. semi-annual until first call date
	Reset to prevailing 6-yr mid-swap rate plus initial margin on first call date and every 6-yr thereafter (each a reset date)
	Non-cumulative cancellation at the issuer's discretion
	Mandatory non-cumulative cancellation if:
	1. distribution exceeds distributable profits;
	2. DIB is in breach of applicable regulatory capital requirements;
	3. regulators requirement; or
	4. insolvency.
Dividend Stopper	Distributions on redemption or purchase of share capital and parity securities, until 1 distribution has been paid in full (or set aside)
Optional Early Redemption	Tax event: Imposition of withholding tax – par call
	Capital event: full or partial loss of Tier 1 capital treatment – 101% call
Variation	Upon capital event or tax event
	Capital securities become or remain Qualifying Tier 1 instruments
Trigger-based Loss Absorption	No (instrument accounted for as equity)
Point of Non-Viability[13] (PONV) and Insolvency-Based Loss Absorption	Full and permanent write-down at the earliest of:
	5. the date the central bank requires contractual non-viability loss absorption, DIB breaching the point of non-viability; or
	6. DIB breaching the solvency conditions; or
	7. a bankruptcy order being issued against DIB.

- Following completion of the roadshow, DIB announced initial price thoughts of a 7 percent area. As soon as the trade was announced, the orderbook grew quickly with strong anchor orders following the roadshow.
- On 14 January, final guidance was released at 6.75 percent. Despite challenging market conditions and the continued oil price volatility, the transaction attracted robust demand which enabled the issuer to price a USD1.0bn transaction.
- With the deal being a *sukuk*, it received overwhelming demand from the MENA investor base and globally there was strong interest from both private banks and high quality institutional accounts.

---

[13] PONV is determined by the relevant financial regulator.

BASEL III-COMPLIANT TIER 2 CAPITAL (T2) INSTRUMENTS

T2 capital ensures loss absorption in case of liquidation and would help ensure that depositors and senior creditors can be paid in such an event. T2 instruments include:

1. Qualifying instruments (considered further below).
2. Share premium accounts related to those qualifying instruments.
3. Certain risk-weighted exposure amounts (using either the Standardised Approach or Internal Ratings Board (IRB) approach under Basel II).

Qualifying Requirements for Basel III-Compliant T2 Instruments

A T2 capital instrument must meet the following requirements in order to qualify as Basel III-compliant:[14]

1. It is issued and paid in.
2. It is subordinated to depositors and general creditors of the bank.
3. It is neither secured nor covered by a guarantee of the issuer or related entity or other arrangement that legally or economically enhances the seniority of the claim above depositors and general creditors.
4. Maturity:
   a. Minimum original maturity of at least five years.
   b. Recognition in regulatory capital in the remaining five years before maturity will be amortised on a straight-line basis.
   c. No step-ups or other incentives to redeem.
5. May be callable at the initiative of the issuer only after a minimum of five years.[15]
6. Investors must have no rights to accelerate the repayment of future scheduled payments (coupon or principal), except in bankruptcy and liquidation.
7. The instrument cannot have a credit-sensitive dividend feature; that is, a dividend/coupon that is reset periodically based in whole or in part on the bank's credit standing.
8. Neither the bank nor a related party over which the bank exercises control or significant influence can have purchased the instrument, nor can the bank directly or indirectly have funded the purchase of the instrument.
9. If the instrument is not issued out of an operating entity or the holding company in the consolidated group (e.g. an SPV), proceeds must be immediately available

---

[14] See note 4 above.

[15] To exercise a call option a bank must:

1. receive prior supervisory approval;
2. not do anything which creates an expectation that the call will be exercised; and
3. not exercise a call unless:
   1. it replaces the called instrument with capital of the same or better quality and the replacement of this capital is done at conditions which are sustainable for the income capacity of the bank; or
   2. the bank demonstrates that its capital position is well above the minimum capital requirements (as determined by the local regulator) after the call option is exercised.

without limitation to an operating entity,[16] or the holding company in the consolidated group in a form which meets or exceeds all of the other criteria for inclusion in Tier 2 capital.

Unlike AT1 capital instruments, T2 capital instruments are more similar in nature to traditional debt instruments which have defined maturities. We have yet to see any Basel III-compliant T2 *sukuk* issuances in the USD *sukuk* market. However, Malaysian Islamic banks have either issued or set up programmes to issue Basel III-compliant T2 MYR *sukuk* which are considered further below.

Case Study: Hong Leong Islamic Bank Berhad (HLISB) MYR400 Million Ten-Year Ijarah Basel III-Compliant Tier 2 Capital Sukuk

On 3 June 2014, HLISB successfully priced the first tranche MYR400 million ten-year *sukuk* out of its MYR1 billion subordinated *sukuk ijarah* programme (see Figure 10.4). The transaction marked the first Basel III-compliant Tier 2 issuance from Hong Leong Group (Table 10.5 and 10.6).

Structure overview

1. On the Issue Date, the Issuer HLISB issues the Subordinated Sukuk certificate (the 'Sukuk') to the investors. Malaysian Trustees Berhad is appointed as Trustee.
2. The Trustee applies the proceeds to purchase the beneficial ownership in certain identified Shariah-compliant leasable assets (the 'Ijarah Assets'). The Ijarah Assets comprise of vehicles owned by HLISB which are currently leased to its customers under hire purchase financing arrangements. There is a short interruption to the hire purchase agreements so that the usufruct of the Ijarah Assets may be leased to HLISB.
3. The Trustee (as Lessor) leases the Ijarah Assets to HLISB (as Lessee).
4. The Lessor will appoint the Lessee as the servicing agent to provide certain services in respect of the Ijarah Assets. Such services include major maintenance and/or

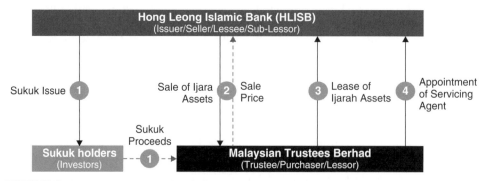

FIGURE 10.4   HLISB Tier 2 capital *sukuk* – inception

---

[16] An entity set up to conduct business with customers with the intention of earning a profit in its own right.

TABLE 10.5 HLISB Tier 2 capital *sukuk* – transaction overview

Issuer	Hong Leong Islamic Bank Berhad (HLISB)
Obligor	HLISB
Rating	AA2 (RAM)
Currency/Format	MYR/Fixed rate *sukuk*
Structure	*Sukuk ijarah*
Amount	MYR200 million
Pricing/Settlement Date	3 June 2014/17 June 2014
Tenor	10 yrs (10 non-callable 5 basis)
Governing Law	Malaysian law

TABLE 10.6 HLISB Tier 2 capital *sukuk* – summary of commercial terms

Non-Viability Event	Following the occurrence of a Non-Viability Event, Bank Negara Malaysia ('BNM') and Malaysia Deposit Insurance Corporation ('PIDM') shall have the option to require the entire principal outstanding or such portion thereof and all other amount owing under the Sukuk be written off, and if BNM and PIDM elects to exercise such option, subject to and as of the date of the occurrence, each of the Sukuk holders hereby: 1. Irrevocably waives its right to receive the principal amount of the Sukuk and to any Ijarah lease payments (including periodic payments accrued and unpaid up to the date of the occurrence of a Non-Viability Event); and 2. Undertakes to transfer his beneficial ownership and interests over the Ijarah Assets to HLISB without consideration, via a Wa'ad. Non-Viability Event means: 1. BNM and PIDM (collectively, the 'Authorities') have notified the Issuer in writing that they are of the opinion that the write off of the Sukuk, together with the conversion or write off of any other Tier 2 Instruments and Tier 1 Instruments which, pursuant to their terms or by operation of law, are capable of being converted into equity or written off at that time, is necessary, without which the Issuer, Hong Leong Bank Berhad or the Hong Leong Financial Group Berhad group would cease to be viable; or 2. The Authorities publicly announce that a decision has been made by BNM, PIDM or any other federal or state government in Malaysia to provide a capital injection or equivalent support to the Issuer, without which the Issuer, Hong Leong Bank Berhad or the Hong Leong Financial Group Berhad group would cease to be viable.

structural repair and the cost associated with procuring sufficient insurance/takaful coverage in respect of the Ijarah Assets.

5. Rental payments from the lease of the Ijarah Assets fund the coupon payments payable throughout the tenor of the Sukuk as shown in Figure 10.5.

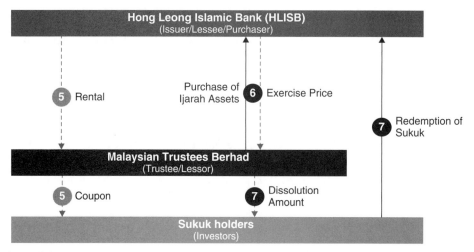

6. Upon dissolution, HLISB purchases the Ijarah Assets for an amount equal to all sums due and payable under the Sukuk. The Exercise Price shall be used to pay the Dissolution Amount that will redeem the Sukuk.
7. HLISB redeems the Certificates by paying the Dissolution Amount to the Investors through the Trustee.

Transaction highlights

- Despite the unfavourable market conditions due to the spike in rates globally and MYR investors being highly selective, the bookbuilding process for HLISB was successfully closed within a day and attracted a strong orderbook of MYR1.2bn to arrive at an oversubscription rate of 2.95x.
- This transaction attracted strong demand high quality accounts and had a strong distribution across a wide investor base among financial institutions (31 percent), asset management companies (10 percent), insurance companies (28 percent), corporates (19 percent) and government agencies (13 percent).

Case Study: Maybank Islamic Berhad (MIB) MYR10 billion, up to 20 years, Basel III-Compliant Tier 2 Murabaha Sukuk Programme

Structure overview

1. Malaysian Trustee Berhad (as Trustee) acting on behalf of the Investors appoints MIB as Purchase Agent to purchase Shari'ah-compliant commodities (the 'Commodities').
2. MIB (as Purchaser) issues a purchase order to MIB (as Purchase Agent) to buy the Commodities from the Trustee, as illustrated in Figure 10.6.
3. MIB issues Sukuk for the proceeds. The proceeds received from the Trustee are used to purchase the Commodities from Commodity Supplier on a spot basis (the 'Commodity Purchase Price').

4. The Trustee sells the Commodities to MIB at a selling price equal to the Commodity Purchase Price plus a margin (the 'Deferred Sale Price') payable on a deferred basis.
5. MIB sells the Commodities to a Commodity Buyer at the Commodity Purchase Price payable on spot basis.
6. MIB makes periodic payments of the Deferred Sale Price over the tenor of the Sukuk on a semi-annual basis.
7. Upon dissolution, MIB makes the final payment of the Deferred Sale Price which is equal to the nominal value of the Sukuk plus accrued but unpaid periodic payments (the 'Redemption Amount') to the Trustee which is applied to redeem the Sukuk, as illustrated in Figure 10.7.

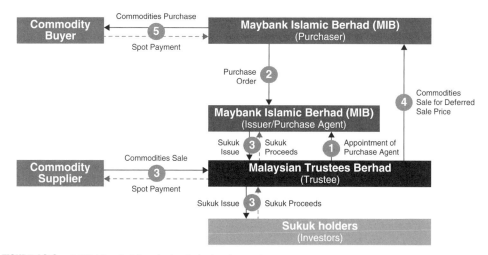

FIGURE 10.6　MIB Tier 2 *Murabaha Sukuk* – inception

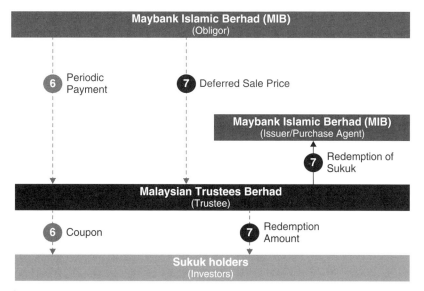

FIGURE 10.7　MIB Tier 2 *Murabaha Sukuk* -- ongoing and maturity

TABLE 10.7   Summary of commercial terms

Non-Viability Event	At the point of a Non-Viability Event, the Issuer shall irrevocably write off the Sukuk in whole or in part, if so required by BNM and/or PIDM at their full discretion. In the event the Sukuk are written off, any written-off amount shall be irrevocably lost and the Sukuk holders will cease to have any claims for any principal, accrued but unpaid periodic profits or any other amount due. The exercise of loss absorption at the point of non-viability shall not constitute an event of default or trigger cross-default clauses.

Note that *murabaha sukuk*, being based on financial assets, would not be considered tradable for Shari'ah reasons in many markets including those in the Gulf Cooperation Council countries.

CONCLUSION

The above transactions highlight the resilience of the Islamic finance industry to quickly adapt to the ever-changing landscape of Basel requirements. The Shari'ah-compliant AT1 capital instruments and T2 capital instruments have been widely accepted and subscribed to by both conventional and Islamic investors. It is hoped that there will be more innovative Basel III-compliant *sukuk* instruments in the future, in particular the issuance of Basel III-compliant T2 *sukuk* issuances in the USD *sukuk*.

CHAPTER 11

Liquidity Risk Management and High Quality Liquid Assets

By Simon Archer and Rifaat Ahmed Abdel Karim

The way in which banks have typically operated as financial intermediaries exposes them to liquidity risk. They seek to earn a 'spread' from an upward sloping yield curve, with the cost of funds increasing as maturities increase, by raising funds through short-term liabilities such as deposits and placing them in longer-term assets such as medium- or long-term loans. This 'maturity transformation' exposes banks to the risk of being caught short of funds to repay short-term liabilities. In such circumstances, a bank may need to realise longer-term assets at distressed prices, and may end up insolvent. To avoid such a fate is the role of liquidity risk management.

While this has long been well known, prudential standards and regulation prior to the Basel Committee for Banking Supervision's (BCBS's) set of Basel III standards largely overlooked liquidity risk, focusing mainly on capital adequacy and related credit and market risks. This was true of the Basel II standards which were introduced in 2004.

The financial and economic crisis of 2007–8 and its grave sequels drew attention to this gap in prudential standards and regulation. The result, in terms of international prudential standards, was Basel III, which placed great emphasis on two major issues: the quantity and quality (loss absorbency) of bank capital, and liquidity risk management.

LIQUIDITY RISK CHALLENGES – FUNDING LIQUIDITY AND MARKET LIQUIDITY

Funding liquidity is provided by access to funds required to meet liquidity needs. Typically, such funds are provided by the interbank market and the money market. In times of liquidity stress, these markets may dry up. In addition, many central banks provide liquidity facilities such as repos and emergency facilities as Lender of Last Resort (LOLR).

Market or asset liquidity is provided by a bank being able to obtain funds by realising substantial amounts of assets quickly and without affecting the price.

Islamic banks face particular challenges for both funding and market liquidity. Operations in the interbank and money markets involve interest-based instruments in which Islamic banks cannot deal. In many jurisdictions, except Malaysia, Islamic banks cannot sell financial assets except at par value.

Market liquidity is provided by a bank holding liquid assets such as high quality short-term papers, for example 90-day treasury bills. In the case of Islamic banks, certain types of *sukuk* may be used. Basel III set a standard for 'high quality liquid assets' (HQLA) which occupy a central position in the new BCBS liquidity risk management framework.

HIGH QUALITY LIQUID ASSETS (HQLA)

HQLA feature prominently in the key BCBS document, *Basel III: The Liquidity Coverage Ratio and liquidity risk monitoring tools* (January 2013). To quote from this document: 'Assets are considered to be HQLA if they can be easily and immediately converted into cash at little or no loss of value' (par. 24). For this purpose, they must be unencumbered, and the following characteristics are 'factors that influence whether or not the market for an asset can be relied upon to raise liquidity when considered in the context of possible stresses' (*ibid.*):

- Low risk, i.e. high credit quality, low market risk, hence low duration, low legal risk, low inflation risk through denomination in a convertible currency with low foreign exchange risk;
- Ease and certainty of valuation;
- Low correlation with risk assets (this excludes instruments issued by financial institutions other than multinational development banks and certain similar institutions);
- Listed on a developed and recognised exchange;
- Active and sizeable market, with active sale or repo markets at all times;
- Low price volatility, which tends to imply low duration;
- Sought after in a context of a 'flight to quality' in a systemic crisis.

Apart from Level 2B HQLA as defined below, HQLA should ideally be eligible at central banks for intraday liquidity needs and overnight liquidity facilities (*op. cit.* par. 26).

Instruments That Qualify As HQLA: A Hierarchy

HQLA are composed of Level 1 and Level 2 assets, with Level 2 assets comprising Level 2A and Level 2B.

The HQLA included in earlier versions of the Liquidity Coverage Ratio (LCR), are:

- Level 1 assets – cash, central bank reserves and high quality marketable securities backed by sovereigns and central banks;
- Level 2 assets (now Level 2A) – lower quality government bonds, covered bonds and at least AA-rated corporate bonds, all subject to a 15 percent haircut and limited to no more than 40 percent of a bank's total HQLA.

The Basel Committee, recognising that in some markets there would be a dearth of HQLA, made a very limited concession in now allowing an additional set of Level 2B assets to be included within their definition of HQLA. These additional assets have to be unencumbered, are subject to a substantial haircut, and can be included only as a limited proportion (15 percent) of a bank's total HQLA, within the 40 percent overall limit on Level 2 assets.

Level 2B assets are the following:

- Corporate debt securities that are rated A+ to BBB–, actively traded and a proven source of liquidity even under stressed market conditions, subject to a 50 percent haircut.
- Unencumbered equities issued by non-financial entities, that are exchange traded, centrally cleared and a constituent of the major stock index where the liquidity risk is taken, denominated in the same currency as the liquidity risk, and a proven source of liquidity under stressed conditions, again subject to a 50 percent haircut.
- High quality residential mortgage-backed securities, rated AA or higher, and with underlying mortgages having a maximum 80 percent Loan-To-Value (LTV) ratio on average at issuance, and liquid (actively traded and a reliable source of liquidity even in stressed conditions), subject to a 25 percent haircut.

Additionally, there were a number of other revisions agreed by the Basel Committee which included special arrangements for Shari'ah-compliant (Islamic) banks, which cannot hold conventional bonds as liquid assets, though to date very little has appeared on this subject and it would appear that central banks with significant Shari'ah-compliant banking systems will need to make the running on this, not least because the practical implementation of the LCR with HQLA is becoming very complex.

In large measure, this is because European regulators in particular are attempting to draft central regulation to address a broad range of different markets with different liquid assets and an equally complex set of allowances and exemptions as to what constitutes cash flows. The practical steer all regulators should take from this is that markets for securities and market practices of banks differ greatly between different countries, and tailoring the Basel III standard to local circumstances is absolutely necessary.

Liquidity Risk Management and HQLA in Islamic Banks

As noted above, Islamic banks face particular challenges with respect to both funding and market liquidity. Because of this, they are obliged to hold cash on hand or at the central bank (without receiving interest) as Shari'ah-compliant HQLA, whereas conventional banks hold interest-bearing instruments. Thus, Islamic banks are at a disadvantage in terms of income.

Basel III offers central banks some discretion in allowing instruments to be accepted as HQLA in jurisdictions where there is an insufficient supply of these assets. In the first place, there are three options under the Alternative Liquidity Approaches (ALA):

- Contractual liquidity facilities for a fee: such facilities could be made available on a Shari'ah-compliant basis;
- Foreign currency HQLA to meet domestic currency liquidity needs;
- Additional Level 2 HQLA with a greater haircut.

The use of the ALA is, however, subject to quite stringent conditions.

In addition, national supervisors in jurisdictions where Islamic banks operate have the option to define Shari'ah-compliant financial products (such as *sukuk*) as alternative HQLA to be used by Islamic banks only, subject to such conditions or haircuts as the supervisors may require. So far, however, there is little evidence of supervisors exercising this option, although some have accepted the medium-term *sukuk* issued by the Islamic Development Bank, in spite of their tenor and lack of secondary market liquidity.

SHARI'AH-COMPLIANT HQLA: THE IILM *SUKUK*

In the context just described, the short-term *sukuk* issued by the International Islamic Liquidity Management Corporation (IILM) are of particular relevance. At the time of writing, there had been 25 issuances of these *sukuk*, for maturities of (predominantly) three and six months, in a programme that started in August 2013. The *sukuk* are rated A-1 by the international rating agency Standard and Poor's (this is a rating of the IILM *sukuk* programme; the issuer itself is not yet rated). The *sukuk* are traded on quite active secondary markets (see Figure 11.1).

The IILM *sukuk* have an asset-backed commercial paper (ABCP) structure based on the *wakalah* contract as shown in Figure 11.2. The underlying assets are at least 51 percent tangible assets and 49 percent receivables. All the IILM assets are sovereign, sovereign linked or supranational assets that are from various countries. The tangible assets are lease-based assets, in *ijarah* leases with different maturities. The beneficial ownership of these assets is transferred from the original owner (asset obligor) in a sale-and-leaseback arrangement to a local Special Purpose Vehicle (SPV) which acts as lessor under the *ijarah* and in turn issues long-term *sukuk* to an IILM Holding SPV in Luxembourg. (The asset obligor thus becomes the *ijarah* lessee under this arrangement and makes rental payments

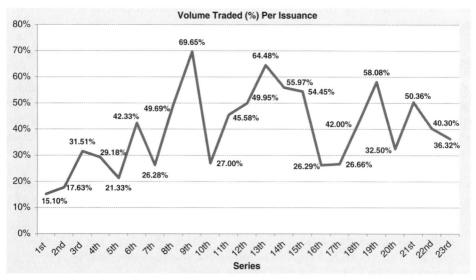

FIGURE 11.1   IILM *sukuk* volume traded (%) per issuance
Data Source: International Islamic Liquidity Management Corporation (IILM)

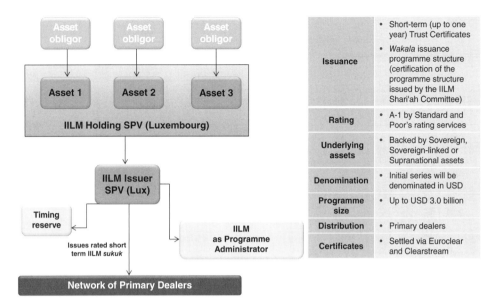

FIGURE 11.2 The IILM programme structure
Data Source: IILM

which provide income to the *sukuk* investors.) The IILM issuer SPV then issues short-term *sukuk* backed by its asset pool, managed by the IILM Corporation as *wakeel* and programme administrator. The short-term *sukuk* are purchased in auctions (in a process similar to that used for short-term government papers) by a network of primary dealers, who act as market makers in an over-the-counter market.

The IILM *sukuk* were designed to meet the Basel III criteria for HQLA, and are generally accepted as meeting the Level 2A criteria, although in some jurisdictions they are accepted as Level 1. Figure 11.3 shows the regulatory treatment for the IILM *sukuk*.

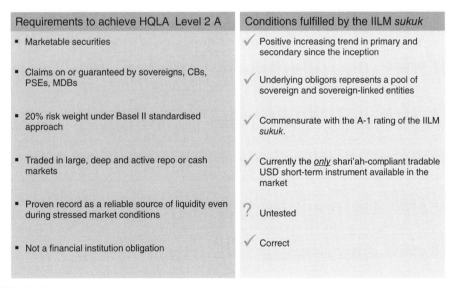

FIGURE 11.3 Regulatory treatment for the IILM *sukuk*
Data Source: IILM

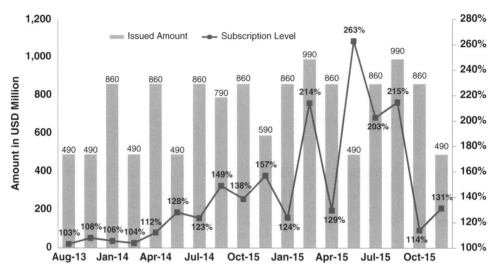

FIGURE 11.4 IILM *sukuk* auction subscription levels
Data Source: IILM

Because the IILM *sukuk* are issued for maturities of less than one year, while the underlying assets have maturities of up to eight years, a major issue in managing the programme is that of liquidity: the proceeds of a new issuance are used to pay the investors in the previous issuance the money due to them on maturity. The IILM has various 'safety devices' to ensure that the necessary funds are available. So far, the issuances of the IILM *sukuk* have always been oversubscribed (see Figure 11.4).

CONCLUSION

The IILM's issuances of up to USD2.2 billion are far from satisfying the needs of Islamic banks for HQLA to manage their liquidity risk, and it is to be hoped for the sake of Islamic banks that other institutions will issue *sukuk* that meet the HQLA criteria.

CHAPTER 12

Malaysia's Islamic Capital Markets – A Case Study

By Obiyathulla Ismath Bacha and Daud Vicary Abdullah

T he capital market plays a very important role in modern economies. Being a part of the financial sector, which it shares with the banking system, capital markets have become the focus of many a government's development plans. Most developing countries' financial sectors tend to be dominated by the banking system. Banks as intermediaries between depositors (surplus units) and borrowers (deficit units) offer indirect financing, in the sense that the depositor has no idea who has borrowed their money, nor the type of project their money has gone into. The bank takes on the intermediation risk in return for the interest spreads. This concentrates risks on a few banks, results in a knife-edge equilibrium and makes the overall economy vulnerable. Governments realising this have started to build capital markets which while also being an intermediary, do it in a way that does not concentrate risk. Capital markets unlike banks require direct financing. That is, the investor, by buying stocks or bonds, has direct exposure to the underlying firm with nothing inbetween. Risks do not get concentrated, but get spread out over a large number of individual/institutional investors. Relative to banks, therefore, the contingent liability to governments from capital markets is much less, in fact almost nothing.

In addition to intermediation, capital markets can be part of the payments system, enable inter-temporal transfers and be a medium for monetary policy transmission. Modern day capital markets also provide the means and avenue for risk management, price discovery and dissemination of market information. The ability to disseminate information in a timely manner and in a cost effective way is a critical value addition of capital markets these days. The efficacy with which a capital market plays these roles ultimately determines the efficient allocation of resources within an economy.

An Islamic Capital Market (ICM) is essentially one that carries out all the above functions but in a Shari'ah-compliant way. The instruments and trading processes/practices are designed to be Shari'ah-compliant. Going by this definition, all components of a conventional capital market – debt, equity, derivative and foreign exchange markets – can be replicated in Shari'ah-compliant ways. While many Islamic countries have replicated parts of the conventional system to do this, Malaysia is the only Muslim country to have developed a fully-fledged ICM. As we will see in this chapter, Malaysia has in place a fully functioning ICM that replicates all the components and functions of a well-developed capital market. In addition to describing the key components and instruments, we evaluate the many initiatives undertaken by the government and identify success factors. This chapter has five sections. Section 2 below provides a brief history of Malaysia's ICM development, including its Shari'ah Governance Framework (SGF). Section 3 describes key components while section 4 examines the market for *sukuk*. Section 5 concludes with a discussion of the challenges in moving forward and whether the Malaysian model can be replicated elsewhere.

THE BEGINNINGS OF AN ISLAMIC CAPITAL MARKET

Researchers of Islamic finance in Malaysia often point to the establishment of the Pilgrims Fund (Lembaga Tabung Haji) in 1963 as the beginning of Islamic finance in Malaysia. While it was an undoubtedly important development, the real impetus came in 1981 with Prime Minister Mahathir's announcement of the 'Inculcation of Islamic values policy'. As a follow-up to this policy, a number of Islamic institutions were established, the most important for the financial sector being the country's first Islamic bank in 1983, Bank Islam Malaysia Berhad (BIMB). This was quickly followed by the first *takaful* operator, Takaful Malaysia Berhad in 1984. Despite the rapid growth of Islamic banking, it was not until the mid-1990s that the Islamisation of capital markets was looked into. The establishment of the Securities Commission (SC) in 1995 to replace and consolidate the work of six different regulators was the turning point. Tasked to initiate a Shari'ah-compliant version of the capital market, the SC established the Shari'ah Advisory Committee (SAC) in 1996, together with an ICM division. This SAC was instrumental in coming up with the world's first Shari'ah stock screening methodology. Around the same time as the SC's establishment, an interesting development was taking place within Islamic banking that was to affect the ICM. Recalling that Islamic banking was established in 1983, given its rapid growth and the obvious latent demand for Shari'ah-compliant financial services, Bank Negara Malaysia came up with the second phase of development. Known as *Skim Perbankan Tanpa Faedah* or interest-free banking scheme, conventional banks were required to offer Islamic banking windows. This, however, presented a new challenge: how would these 'windows' manage their liquidity in a Shari'ah-compliant way? The bilateral arrangement used until then between the sole Islamic bank (BIMB) with Bank Negara Malaysia (BNM) was obviously not workable now that several banks were participating in Islamic finance. In response, and probably in anticipation of this need, Bank Negara established the world's first Islamic interbank money market in January 1994.

Aside from institutions, several regulatory initiatives were undertaken to enable Islamic finance and capital market development. Perhaps the most important of these was the Shari'ah governance framework. Unlike the GCC (Gulf Cooperation Council) countries or other Muslim countries that either have loosely defined, decentralised governance or none at all, Malaysia has a highly centralised Shari'ah governance framework. BNM, the regulator for banks and the SC each have their Shari'ah Advisory

Committees. These national level committees provide the guidance for Shari'ah committees at each reporting institution. The Shari'ah committees at the individual institutions are guided by the rulings of the national SAC and are tasked to ensure Shari'ah compliance within the institution. This Shari'ah compliance is to be executed by both a continuous Shari'ah review and audit process within the institutions. The individual institution is required to provide periodic compliance reporting through its Shari'ah committee to the SAC. Such a structure has not only ensured effective compliance but also standardisation within the country of products and services offered by players.

The above developments of the 1990s laid the foundation for Malaysia to become the Islamic finance hub and world leader in Islamic markets a decade later.

COMPONENTS OF MALAYSIA'S ISLAMIC CAPITAL MARKET

Malaysia's ICM consists of the following.

The Islamic Interbank Money Market (IIMM)

It is obvious that Islamic banks being involved in maturity intermediation would have the same liquidity mismatches that conventional banks have. Thus, the IIMM is designed to play the same role that interbank money markets play, but in a Shari'ah-compliant way. In 'designing' an Islamic interbank money market, Bank Negara Malaysia (BNM) had no existing model, thus the IIMM was created using a conventional money market template. The IIMM like its conventional counterparts has three components: (i) an interbank deposit system, (ii) Shari'ah-compliant money market instruments and (iii) an Islamic cheque clearing system.

Islamic Interbank Deposits

The Islamic interbank deposit facility enables Islamic banks to manage their liquidity position by way of placing or taking deposits among themselves. The underlying Shari'ah contract is *mudaraba*. The interbank deposit works as follows. The bank receiving the deposit will have to repay at maturity, an amount equal to the original deposit plus its declared gross profit before distribution on its one-year investments. This gross profit would be adjusted for the agreed profit-sharing ratio (PSR) and tenor (as percentage by year). What makes this arrangement different from conventional interbank deposits is that the return to the depositor depends on the declared gross profit of the recipient bank. The declared gross profit is being shared according to the agreed PSR – thus the *mudaraba* arrangement. Total interbank volume has over the years shown a steady increase. For 2013, total volume was RM450 billion.

Islamic Money Market Instruments

Several interbank money market instruments are traded in IIMM. As is the case with the conventional money market, institutions in need of short-term funding issue them, while those with surplus funds would buy them. Being an Islamic money market, only Shari'ah-compliant institutions can issue these papers: there is however no such requirement for purchasers. Most of the instruments are a replication of what is available in the conventional money markets. Thus, we have Islamic bankers' acceptances, negotiable Islamic instruments of deposit (NIIDS), Malaysian Islamic treasury bills (MITB), Bank Negara negotiable notes and others. The underlying contract is *bai al inah*. Thus the pricing is very much that of discounting the face values. One key difference, however, is that the discount rate in this case is a market-derived rate. Just as daily, overnight, one-month, three-month and other short tenor rates are determined in conventional money markets through trading and interbank placements, in the IIMM they result in the Islamic interbank rate known as the Kuala Lumpur Islamic Interbank Rate or KLIRR. These rates are reported daily for overnight, one-week, one-month, three-month and six-months. In pricing the traded IIMM instruments, it is the KLIRR rate of appropriate tenor that is used in determining the price. Islamic banks also use these rates in pricing their products.

In addition to the money market instruments above, a number of *sukuk* are also traded. These are usually Malaysian government or quasi-sovereign issues. These *sukuk*, which have maturity of several years, get traded in IIMM in the final year of their maturity, when they are essentially short-term instruments. Figure 12.1 shows volume growth of interbank transactions and the trading performance of Islamic Negotiable Instruments of Deposit (INID), Malaysian Islamic Treasury Bills (MITB) and Bank Negara Negotiable Notes (BNNN).

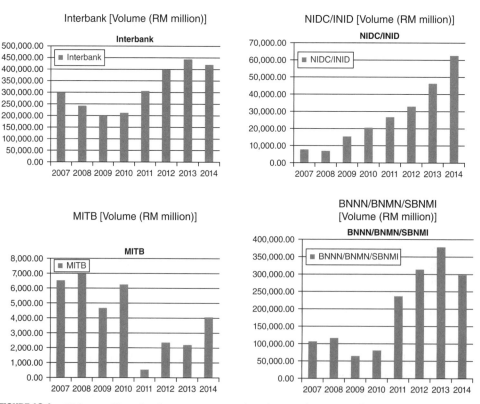

FIGURE 12.1   Volume of Interbank transactions and trading performance of key IIMM instruments
Data Source: Islamic Interbank Money Market, Bank Negara Malaysia

Islamic Cheque Clearing

The Islamic interbank cheque clearing system serves the same purpose as its conventional counterpart but the settlement process is quite different. BNM requires all participating Islamic banks/windows to first establish an *al-wadiah*-based current account with it. All Islamic banks are also required to empower BNM to automatically offset their funding positions when clearing occurs at midnight. On completion of clearing, the deficit bank is deemed to owe the surplus bank an amount of the difference between their offsetting cheques. This amount will have to be settled at opening the next morning with a return due to the surplus bank. The underlying contract is *mudaraba* and settlement is based on a 70:30 PSR. The determination of the amount payable is exactly as in the case of the interbank deposit arrangement described earlier. The most recent one-year gross profit declared by the recipient bank being adjusted for the overnight tenor and the 70:30 PSR.

Bursa Suq Al-Sila

One cannot discuss liquidity management among Islamic financial institutions (IFIs) in Malaysia without discussing *Bursa Suq Al-Sila* (BSAS). Launched in 2009 by Bursa Malaysia, the national stock exchange, BSAS is an electronic trading platform designed to facilitate commodity *murabaha*-based funding. The underlying commodity was crude palm oil (CPO), of which Malaysia is the world's target producer. The fact that palm oil is harvested all year round makes it all the more suitable. *Murabaha*, which is essentially trade financing, is a profit mark-up contract used for working capital and other short-term funding.

An IFI in need of liquidity gets funding through BSAS by buying CPO from another IFI at a price to be paid on deferred terms, as illustrated in Figure 12.2. Once in possession of the commodity, it sells the CPO at spot price through a participating broker of BSAS. Funding gets passed through by way of trade in a commodity. The quick turnaround of buying and selling of CPO is possible given the organised nature of the

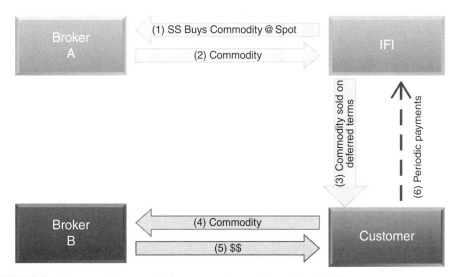

FIGURE 12.2 A commodity *murabaha* transaction on Bursa Suq Al-Sila

trading platform. Execution price risk is eliminated because a single price holds for an entire trading day. The previous day's close price in the spot market is used for an entire day on BSAS. Figure 12.2 shows a typical commodity *murabaha* transaction carried out through the BSAS. Though Malaysian scholars have approved it, some *fiqh* scholars argue that this in essence is organised *tawarruq* and therefore impermissible. Despite the criticism, traded volume on BSAS has increased several folds. Given insufficiency of CPO, BSAS has introduced new commodities on which transactions could be made. These include polyethylene and others. The commodity *murabaha*'s popularity revolves around the ease of trade and the low transaction cost (currently RM15 per million ringgit). The London Metal Exchange (LME) is the only other facility available for commodity *murabaha* trades.

As mentioned earlier, Malaysia's IIMM is the only one of its kind. Other than enabling liquidity management, the IIMM enables price discovery for Malaysian IFIs. Their cost of funds can be determined easily. Elsewhere, in the Middle East – for example, where bilateral arrangements between an IFI and the central bank or its appointed subsidiary are practised – price discovery is not possible. In the absence of such price discovery, the reliance of IFIs on conventional rates cannot be reduced.

Shari'ah-Compliant Equities

Equity financing is philosophically in consonance with the Shari'ah. It is risk sharing, has no fixed returns and one only gets returns if the business makes a profit and declares dividends. Accordingly, there should be no problem with equity financing. However, while equity financing is acceptable, not all stocks listed on an exchange are. There are two potential hurdles. First, the nature of the listed firm's business, and second, the way it has financed itself would be of concern. Given these two concerns, there is a need for a standardised way to evaluate the Shari'ah acceptability of a listed stock.

Malaysia was the first Muslim country to have developed a stock screening methodology. Following this, Dow Jones, the US-based financial information provider, developed its own screening technique. Following this, several others have developed screening methodologies. While these methodologies may differ at the periphery, they all evaluate the underlying business and funding structure. Unlike the Dow Jones, Malaysia's SAC screening allows for mixed businesses. That is, some level of tolerance is allowed for, in the case of listed companies whose main business was *halal* but a portion in a prohibited activity. For example, an airline that serves alcohol or a supermarket chain that may also carry non-*halal* products. In the original 1996 methodology, this tolerance had two levels – 5 percent and 20 percent. That is a 5 percent tolerance level, where the prohibited activity can be measured; for example, sales of alcohol or pork. If these were more than 5 percent, the stock was dropped, otherwise it was considered *halal* for Muslim investors. Where it is not possible to measure the contribution from prohibited products or activity, a 20 percent tolerance level was used. The original Malaysian methodology also did not look at the capital structure but only the interest earned or paid as per the income statement.

The Dow Jones screening did not allow for any mixed business whatsoever. It also evaluated the capital structure, excluding firms with more than 33 percent debt in their capital structure. Thus, it is tighter than the original Malaysian screen. The Malaysian position in allowing for a degree of tolerance is logical, based on two factors. First, the fact that Malaysia has a large non-Muslim minority, whose religious rights are recognised in

Islam. Second, there is the trade-off between purity and strategic need. Using the Dow Jones criteria of zero tolerance for non-*halal* business then, would have meant a very small investible base of acceptable stocks. This would have been too small to support a meaningful asset/portfolio management industry for the Muslim populace.

In November 2013, the SC came out with a revised stock screening methodology. This was much more in line with other internationally used methods. The tolerance for non-*halal* business remained, though it now had four thresholds (5 percent, 10 percent, 20 percent and 25 percent) as opposed to only 5 percent and 20 percent previously. The key change was in financial ratio benchmarks, two new ratios, in line with the Dow Jones, were introduced. These were cash to total assets and debt to total assets. The requirement for both is that they should be below 33 percent. This revision requires the evaluation of the company's balance sheet and leverage, where previously they were not evaluated. As of December 2014, 673 of 906 total listed stocks in Malaysia were deemed Shari'ah-compliant by the new methodology. Thus Shari'ah-compliant stocks were 74.3 percent of total listed stocks but only 61 percent of total market capitalisation.

Aside from Shari'ah-compliant stocks, there are three Shari'ah-compliant stock indices in use. These are (i) FBM EMAS Shariah index, a composite of all listed Shari'ah-compliant stocks, (ii) the FBM Hijrah Shariah index, which is made up of stocks from the EMAS Shariah that meet tighter international screening standards. The third Shari'ah equity index is (iii) the DJIM Malaysia Titans 25. This is an index of 25 highest capitalised Malaysian stocks that pass the Dow Jones filter.[1]

Other Equity Products
Exchange-Traded Funds

Exchange-traded funds (ETFs) are an outgrowth of index funds. Index funds are mutual funds that adopt a passive investment strategy of mimicking the index. Like an index fund, an ETF tracks an underlying stock index or a subgroup within an index. However, unlike an index fund, ETFs are listed on a stock exchange and can be bought and sold like a stock. Given the popularity of ETFs in developed markets, they have been introduced in emerging markets. An Islamic ETF would simply have constituent stocks that have passed a Shari'ah screening filter. Currently, Malaysia has three Shari'ah-compliant ETFs. The oldest and most popular is the MyETFDJIM 25 which has been around since January 2008. It is based on the DJIM's top 25 Shari'ah-compliant stocks of Malaysia. An additional Shari'ah-compliant ETF, the MyETF MSCI Malaysia Islamic Dividend, based on an index of high dividend yielding stocks was launched in May 2014. In May 2015, the My ETF MSCI Malaysia South East Asia Islamic (SEA) Dividend, another index of high yielding South East Asian stocks was introduced. The latter two ETFs, as evident in their name, are based on an index of stocks that have passed the Morgan Stanley (MSCI) Shari'ah screen. As at end of 2014, Islamic ETFs accounted for about 31 percent of total industry by market capitalisation.

Real Estate Investment Trusts (REITs)

Just as ETFs have an underlying basket (index) of stocks, REITs are listed 'stocks' that have as their underlying a group of real estate properties. REITs have been the rage in many Muslim countries, given the popularity of investment in bricks and mortar.

---

[1] The FBM notation stands for FTSE Bursa Malaysia.

Malaysia has a total of 16 listed REITs, three of which are Shari'ah-compliant. All three Shari'ah-compliant REITs are interesting in their diversity. The first, the Al Aqar REIT has a group of private hospitals as its underlying asset. These properties are leased to a health care group. The second is the world's only plantation REIT. The Al Hadharah Boustead REIT has as its underlying plantation land that has been leased to Boustead, a large plantation group. The third REIT is the KLCC REIT, which owns the shopping complex at the Petronas Twin Towers.

Islamic REITs, like their conventional counterparts, depend on rentals for their earnings. However, an Islamic REIT has to endeavour to have zero non-Shari'ah-compliant tenants. A filtering technique is used to determine whether a property is Shari'ah-compliant. Currently, there is a tolerance of 20 percent non-Shari'ah-compliant tenants; that is, a property has to have less than 20 percent of its tenants in non-compliant businesses in order to be deemed eligible for acquisition. However, upon acquisition, the leases of non-compliant tenants are not to be renewed once they have completed their current tenancy; the objective being full compliance at a future date. This zero tolerance has proven to be difficult to achieve. Avoiding pubs or restaurants serving alcohol has not been easy, in particular at destinations where tourists congregate. In view of these externalities, some level of tolerance may have to be accepted. Currently, Islamic REITs account for about 42 percent of total listed REITs by market capitalisation.

Islamic Mutual Funds

Islamic mutual funds, being restricted to investing only in compliant instruments, typically invest in Shari'ah-compliant stocks, *sukuk* and IIMM instruments. This mirrors the asset allocation strategy of conventional mutual funds which is stocks, bonds and cash.

Malaysian Islamic mutual funds have available the full array of instruments, yet they continue to be small. Islamic mutual funds have not seen the type of growth seen in banking or in *sukuk*. This seems ironic, especially as Malaysian Islamic funds have the widest array of investible asset categories. As at end of December 2014, assets under management (AUM) of Islamic funds was only 17.6 percent of total industry. Table 12.1 shows the relative position.

Even though close to a third of all mutual funds in Malaysia are Islamic, they are small relative to the conventional funds. A key reason for this underrepresentation is the presence of a national investment corporation, the Permodalan Nasional Berhad (PNB). PNB was established in the 1980s with the objective of raising *bumiputra* (local Malay) ownership of stocks to targeted 30 percent. This was to be done by pooling the savings of *bumiputras* and channelling them into equities. PNB has proven to be very successful and, given the 'implicit' guarantee of a government-run fund, has attracted most of the savings of Malaysian Muslims.

Shari'ah-Compliant Derivatives

The Malaysian capital market has seen the development of a number of Shari'ah-compliant derivative instruments. As markets develop, risk management needs arise. Innovation had followed demand arising from needs. With the exception of the crude palm oil futures contract, which is the only exchange-traded derivative deemed compliant, the others are Over-The-Counter (OTC) contracts. A number of structured products sold by IFIs within the country, and deemed Shari'ah-compliant, are really derivatives or have embedded options within them. Equity warrants are also deemed compliant if the underlying stocks

TABLE 12.1   Islamic mutual funds

Islamic Assets Under Management – Malaysia 2014

	RM billion – Dec. 2014
Islamic AUM	111.6
Total Fund Management Industry AUM	630
Percent of Islamic AUM	17.6%
Number of Funds	Dec. 2014
Islamic Funds	188 Funds
Total Industry	612 Funds
NAV Islamic Funds	46.7RM bn.
NAV Total Industry	343RM bn.
Percent of Total Industry	13.6%

Data Source: SC website.

are. While there is a range of Shari'ah-compliant derivatives, the most popular are those in the category of foreign exchange and profit rate swaps.

The Islamic Profit Rate Swap (IPRS) is a fairly recent innovation in Malaysia. The IPRS effectively mimics the interest rate swap. A transaction between two IFIs, the institutions exchange cash flows based on a notional principal, a referenced floating rate and a fixed rate over an agreed tenor and time intervals, the objective being to hedge rate exposure. Ironically, Islamic banks in Malaysia have large duration gaps, given their dependence on fixed rate financing. Figure 12.3 shows how an IPRS would enable an IFI to manage the asset liability mismatches on its balance sheet. This Malaysian innovation is now being used in other countries. Variants of the IPRS can have commodity *murabaha* (for the fixed portion) and/or *wa'ad*s. A *wa'ad* is a unilateral promise by one party to the other, in a transaction.

The second category of Shari'ah-compliant derivatives are *wa'ad*-based contracts used in currency risk management. There are two varieties, (i) an Islamic forward and

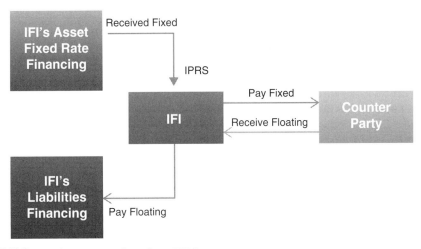

FIGURE 12.3   Hedging rate risk with an IPRS

(ii) an Islamic currency option. In both cases, the customer provides a *wa'ad*, which the IFI accepts. For example, in the case of the forward: a customer wanting to hedge a 100 million yen payable in 90 days would offer a *wa'ad* to purchase (long) 100 million yen on day 90 at the quoted forward rate. A *wa'ad* which is a promise is usually not legally binding. However, the Fiqh Academy in Jeddah has issued a fatwa that a *wa'ad* provided in a commercial transaction is binding if its non-execution could mean monetary losses to the counterparty. As the Shari'ah does not allow bilateral *wa'ad* in a simple transaction, it has become customary for the customer to provide the *wa'ad* to the IFI.

In the case of the *wa'ad*-based currency option, the customer 'buys' a promise from the IFI to either buy or sell a foreign currency at an agreement of rate for an upfront fee. When the customer buys the promise to sell from the bank, he is essentially buying a 'call option' on the underlying foreign currency. The fee he pays is the option premium. A customer buys a 'put option' when he buys a bank's promise to buy an underlying currency at the predetermined exchange rate and maturity date. The advent of these Shari'ah-compliant derivative instruments has gone a long way in providing risk management solutions both to Malaysian IFIs and Shari'ah-compliant businesses.

MALAYSIAN *SUKUK* AND *SUKUK* MARKETS

Sukuk refers to an investment certificate or a trustee certificate. *Sukuk*, which is plural for *sakk*, were used extensively by Muslims in the Middle Ages as papers denoting obligations arising from commercial transactions. A manufacturer may provide a retailer with goods on a *murabaha* basis and receive a *sakk* representing the underlying obligation. In this case the *sakk* is an 'IOU', much like a debt instrument. *Sakk* was also used by governments to pay its soldiers and government servants. These entitled their holders to receive a predetermined amount of commodities from the state treasury on the maturity date. Accordingly, they came to be known as 'grain certificates'. Since the *sakk* represented a state obligation, they were often traded and exchanged among *sukuk* holders. *Sukuk* have therefore been a tradable instrument in Muslim societies in times past. Today, governments and corporates issue *sukuk* to raise external financing. Even so, it would be wrong to compare *sukuk* with bonds. While *sukuk* are intended to raise external financing just like bonds, their operational, legal and regulatory frameworks are vastly different. What makes *sukuk* an asset class by itself is its underlying contract. Depending on what the underlying contract is, a *sukuk* could resemble a conventional bond or an equity instrument. The cash flows, risk profiles and legal obligation could all differ according to the underlying Shari'ah contract.

As was the case with the several Islamic finance products described above, Malaysia had pioneered and issued several *sukuk* domestically before coming up with the *sukuk al ijarah*, when international players woke up to its potential. The *sukuk ijarah* could mimic a fixed rate coupon bond in a Shari'ah-compliant way. Today, *sukuk* are perhaps the most successful and most visible Islamic finance product. Given the range and international diversity of *sukuk* issuers, it is obvious that *sukuk* have become an internationally accepted Islamic financial product. Malaysia, which is currently the world's biggest originator of *sukuk*, has been the product's main supporter and champion. Malaysia's global dominance in *sukuk* is shown in Figures 12.4 and 12.5. Figure 12.4 shows *sukuk* issuance originating from Malaysia and the rest of the world. The percentage of Malaysian issuance relative to global is also shown.

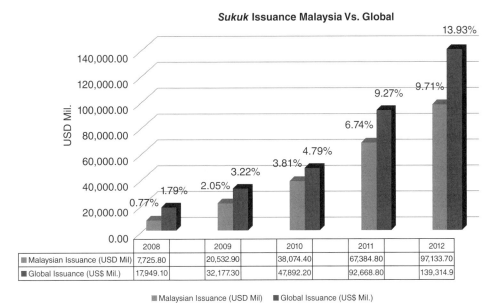

FIGURE 12.4 *Sukuk* issuance, Malaysia vs. Rest of the world
Data Source: Securities Commission Malaysia, RAM (Rating Agency Malaysia)

The chart data table:

	2008	2009	2010	2011	2012
Malaysian Issuance (USD Mil)	7,725.80	20,532.90	38,074.40	67,384.80	97,133.70
Global Issuance (US$ Mil.)	17,949.10	32,177.30	47,892.20	92,668.80	139,314.9

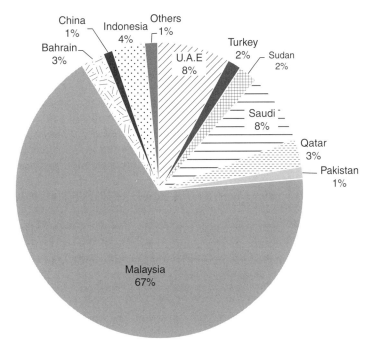

FIGURE 12.5 *Sukuk* issuance by country – 2014
Data Source: IIFM Sukuk Database

Why Malaysia Dominates – Incentives for *Sukuk* Issuance

The obvious dominance of Malaysia in the *sukuk* space, as shown in Figures 12.4 and 12.5, is the result of deliberate government planning and strategy. Aside from the push for Islamisation of the economy from the mid-1980s, the Malaysian government had, as shown above, created a number of supporting institutions. The regulatory framework was refined to make Shari'ah-compliant transactions easy and cost competitive. These initiatives were embedded in two master plans, The Capital Market Master Plans I & II (see box below), which besides building the capital markets had the objective of making the country an Islamic finance hub. A series of special incentives were instituted as part of the programme to make Malaysia attractive for Islamic finance institutions and players. These incentives are summarised in Table 12.2.

MALAYSIA'S CAPITAL MARKET MASTER PLANS

Capital market development in Malaysia owes much to two encompassing plans undertaken by the government. These were the Capital Market Master Plans I & II. Though they came under the ambit of the Ministry of Finance, it was the Securities Commission that steered them and was charged with their execution. These two master plans, each of which was for ten years, were aimed at creating a globally competitive capital market and being an Islamic finance. The first Capital Market Master Plan covered 2001 to 2010, while the second covered 2011 to 2020. These masterplans provided both the synergy and focus needed in building well-functioning markets. While the first plan was focused on deepening and broadening the markets, the second plan aimed at enhancing quality. Its stated objective was growth with governance.

As Table 12.2 shows, Malaysia has been very generous with tax exemptions and deductions for *sukuk* and other Islamic finance activity. *Sukuk* issuers and originators receive a series of tax deductions for cost of issuance, the SPV expenses, cost of establishing SPV and full tax exemption on income accruing to SPV involved in *sukuk* securitisation. Non-resident companies or persons receiving profit paid out on *sukuk* issued in Malaysia receive tax exemption. To ensure tax neutrality with conventional finance, Islamic finance activities that result in multiple sale-purchase activity get tax exemption on subsequent legs of the transaction. Tax incentives are also provided to Islamic stockbroking services and Islamic fund management activity. Interestingly, to attract Islamic finance expertise, non-resident experts of Islamic finance are granted special exemption from income taxes.

In addition to building the infrastructure and providing financial incentives, some amount of flexibility with Shari'ah application has helped. The SAC which sits at the peak of the Shari'ah governance structure has allowed a number of flexibilities with Malaysian issuance of *sukuk*. Some of these are as follows:

i. A buyer/seller to make a prior agreement on sale or purchase. That is, one or more principals of the *sukuk* transaction may make a prior agreement to sell and repurchase or buy back the asset.

ii. Allowing a creditor to forfeit a part of the debt when the debtor pre-pays. That is, an *ibra* (rebate) can be a *syart* (condition) of a *sukuk*. However, the *ibra* must be independent and not be factored into the pricing of the *sukuk*.

TABLE 12.2 Special incentives for the ICM

Capital Market Sectors: Products & Services	Recipient	Incentives	Reference Legislation (if any)
	Issuer	Tax deduction on expenditure incurred for the issuance of *sukuk* pursuant to the principles of *Mudharabah, Musharakah, Ijarah* or *Istisna'a* or any other Shari'ah principles approved by the Minister until the year of assessment 2015.	Income Tax (Deduction for Expenditure on Issuance of Islamic Securities) Rules 2009 – P.U. (A) 420
	Issuer	Tax deduction on expenditure incurred for the issuance of *sukuk* pursuant to the principles of *Murabahah* and *Bai' Bithaman Ajil* based on *tawarruq* until the year of assessment 2015.	Income Tax (Deduction for Expenditure on Issuance of Islamic Securities Pursuant to Principles of Murabahah and Bai' Bitahaman Ajil) Rules 2011 – P.U. (A) 355
Sukuk	Issuer	Tax deduction on expenditure incurred for the issuance of *sukuk* pursuant to the principle of *Wakalah* (comprising a mixed component of debt and assets) until the year of assessment 2015.	Income Tax (Deduction for Expenditure on Issuance of Islamic Securities) Rules 2011– P.U. (A) 443
	Issuer	Tax deduction on expenditure incurred for the issuance of AgroSukuk pursuant to the principles of *Musharakah, Mudharabah, Wakalah bi al-Istithmar* (comprising a mixed component of debt and assets) and *Ijarah* until the year of assessment 2015.	Income Tax (Deduction for Expenditure on Issuance of Agro Sukuk) Rules 2013 – P.U. (A) 305
	Issuer/Special Purpose Vehicle (SPV)	The SPV issuing the *sukuk* (excluding asset-backed securities in a securitisation transaction) is exempted from income tax given that the SPV is established solely to channel funds.	i. Income Tax (Exemption) (No. 14) Order 2007 – P.U. (A) 180 ii. Income Tax Act 1967 (Revised 1971) – Section 60I

(Continued)

TABLE 12.2 (*Continued*)

Capital Market Sectors: Products & Services	Recipient	Incentives	Reference Legislation (if any)
	Originator	The company that established the SPV is also given a deduction on the cost of issuance of the *sukuk* incurred by the SPV;	i. Income Tax (Deduction on the Cost of Issuance of The Islamic Securities) Rules 2007 – P.U. (A) 176 ii. Income Tax Act 1967 (Revised 1971) – Section 60I
	Investor	Profit paid or credited to non-resident companies in respect of RM denominated *sukuk* (other than convertible loan stock) approved by the SC is exempted from income tax.	Income Tax Act 1967 (Revised 1971)– Schedule 6 – Exemption from Tax: Section 33A
	Investor	Profit paid or credited to any person in respect of non-Ringgit *sukuk* originating from Malaysia (other than convertible loan stock) and approved by the SC is exempted from income tax.	Income Tax Act 1967 (Revised 1971)– Schedule 6 – Exemption from Tax: Section 33B
	Investor	Profit paid or credited to any individual, unit trust and listed closed-end fund in respect of *sukuk* (other than convertible loan stock) approved by the SC is exempted from income tax.	Income Tax Act 1967 (Revised 1971) – Schedule 6 – Exemption from Tax: Section 35
	Issuer	To ensure neutrality with conventional schemes of financing, any tax on profits received or incurred on transactions or duty chargeable on additional instrument pursuant to a scheme of financing approved by the SC is exempted provided that the scheme is in accordance with the principles of Syariah and such instrument is required for the purpose of complying with those principles.	i. Income Tax Act 1967(Revised 1971) – Section 2(8) ii. Stamp Act – Schedule 1 "General Exemptions"

Islamic Stockbroking Services	Stockbroking company	Establishment expenditure incurred for the commencement of an Islamic stock broking business are allowed to be tax deductible, subject to the company commencing its business within a period of 2 years from the date of approval from the Bursa Malaysia. (effective for applications received by the Bursa Malaysia until 31 December 2015).	Income Tax (Deduction on Expenditure for Establishment of an Islamic Stock Broking Business) (Amendment) Rules 2009 – P.U. (A) 401
Islamic Fund Management		Fund management companies managing Islamic funds of local investors to be given income tax exemption on income received from fund management services. To be effective from the year of assessment 2008 until the year of assessment 2016. The funds must be managed in accordance with Shari'ah principles and certified by the SC.	Income Tax (Exemption) (No.6) Order 2008 – P.U. (A) 255
	Islamic fund management company	Islamic fund management companies are allowed to have 100% foreign ownership.	–
	Islamic fund management company	Islamic fund management companies are permitted to invest 100% of assets abroad.	–
	Islamic fund management company	A sum of RM7 billion fund will be channeled by EPF to be managed by Islamic fund management companies.	–
Non Resident Experts in Islamic finance	Non Resident Experts in Islamic finance	Income tax exemption to be given to income received by non-resident experts in Islamic finance until 31 December 2016. The experts have to be verified by the MIFC Secretariat.	Income Tax (Exemption) (No.3) Order 2008 – P.U. (A) 114

Source: Securities Commission Malaysia

iii. *Sukuk* originators can arrange for third-party guarantee on the capital. For example, an originator can get a bank to provide a guarantee of the face value of the *sukuk* amount. This would be particularly relevant to *musharaka/mudaraba sukuk*.

iv. Contracts awarded by the government or its agencies can be the underlying asset for a *sukuk*. Here, the underlying asset is obviously not a physical or tangible asset but a contractual undertaking awarded by the government to the entity originating the *sukuk*.

v. *Sukuk* can be on a 'when-issued' basis, i.e. some form of shelf-registration is possible.

vi. A floating rate mechanism can be used when determining profit rates for *sukuk* based on *bay bithaman ajil* (BBA), *murabaha* and *istisna'a* contracts. The *ibra* (rebate) to be used in determining profit rate.

vii. For *sukuk* involving the sale/purchase of assets as in *ijarah*, BBA, *murabaha* and the like, the SAC has determined that if the sale price involves a premium over market price/value, the price must not exceed 1.33 times the market price. An asset sold at a discount should not be at a price lower than 67 percent (0.67) of the market price. Where the market price is indeterminate, pricing can be on a 'willing buyer–willing seller' basis.

The above resolutions from the SAC have gone a long way in enabling the growth and development of *sukuk* in Malaysia. For example, enabling an issuer to make a prior agreement on sale or purchase of the underlying asset at maturity would substantially reduce the risk associated with a *sukuk*. The repurchase agreement ensures a known cash flow at maturity. The reduced risk would mean reduced required return. To an issuer this translates into lower cost of capital, a huge advantage in relative terms. When contracts awarded by the government or its agencies can be the underlying asset for a *sukuk*, it makes the use of *sukuk* possible for infrastructure financing. The ability to shelf register makes it possible to stagger the issuance over a period of time to fund projects as and when needed. For long-dated *sukuk*, the ability to use a floating rate mechanism reduces duration and the attendant rate risk. In addition to giving Malaysian *sukuk* a leg up against foreign originators, these resolutions also levelled the playing field for *sukuk* vis-à-vis conventional bonds.

Malaysian Sukuk Issuance – Innovation, A Key Driver

Interestingly, Malaysia's first *sukuk* issuers were private entities, and at that foreign ones. Shell MDS Sdn. Berhad, the Malaysian subsidiary of the Anglo-Dutch oil giant, was the first Malaysian *sukuk* issuer. The issue was in 1990. Based on the BBA contract, it consisted of two tranches: a five-year maturity for RM75 million and a RM50 million tranche with an eight-year maturity. This first issuance was followed in 1991 with a *musharaka*-based *sukuk* by Sarawak Shell Berhad, yet another subsidiary of the Dutch firm. This was a RM600 million, 'guaranteed' *musharaka* with participating certificates. The third ringgit-denominated *sukuk* was issued in 1993 by Petronas Dagangan. This consisted of RM300 million of unsecured redeemable papers with RM120 million of detachable warrants. In a sense, this *sukuk* was a variant of the convertible bond in that the warrants could be converted into shares of the listed Petronas Dagangan.

Following these three issues, the market gained traction. A number of highly innovative *sukuk* structures were unveiled. Among these were a 'redeemable' *sukuk* by KFC

(Kentucky Fried Chicken) in 1997. These redeemable *sukuk* came with warrants that enabled the holder to purchase KFC Holdings stock at predetermined prices. This was followed in 2001 with the first global *sukuk*. Issued by Guthrie, a plantation firm, the USD-denominated *ijarah sukuk* had semiannual payments referenced on LIBOR. The year 2001 also saw the first sovereign *sukuk* issued by the Malaysian government. Again, this *sukuk* was USD-denominated and referenced on LIBOR. A number of Malaysian institutions have pushed the frontier of innovation with *sukuk*, two of them being Khazanah, the sovereign wealth fund and Cagamas, the national home mortgage corporation. Khazanah has issued a series of 'exchangeable *sukuk*' that are convertible at maturity to different stocks of Malaysian public listed firms held within its portfolio. The most recent innovative *sukuk* by Khazanah is an SRI (Sustainable and Responsible Investment) *sukuk*. Another notable innovation was one of the world's first perpetual *sukuk* issued by MAS (Malaysia Airlines) in 2013. Regulators, particularly the Securities Commission, have been accommodative of these innovations. In 2014, it approved the potential use of intellectual property as an underlying asset for *sukuk* issuance.

Sukuk Issuance – The Evolution

There has been a fundamental change taking place within the Malaysian *sukuk* space. This has to do with the type of *sukuk* issued or underlying contract used. In the early years, most Malaysian *sukuk* issues were based on debt-like contracts like *bay al bithaman ajil* (BBA) and *murabaha*. Given the unease with such fixed rate instruments in the Middle East, and thereby their acceptability, there was a clear attempt by Malaysian issuers to move away from the heavy reliance on BBA-type *sukuk*. Figure 12.6 shows this evolution. In 2004, BBA and *murabaha*-based issues accounted for 95 percent of total *sukuk* issued. By 2008, BBA-based issues had shrunk to a mere 3 percent while *murabaha*-based *sukuk* to a miniscule 1 percent. The big growth had been in *ijarah* and *musharaka*-based issues. By 2010, *mudaraba* and *sukuk* based on combined contracts had increased. It is clear that a major evolution had taken place in the Malaysian market for *sukuk* issuance. Where previously Malaysian issuers had targeted domestic investors, today it is clearly the global marketplace.

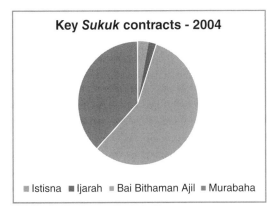

FIGURE 12.6 The evolution in *sukuk* issuance
Data Source: Securities Commission Malaysia

CONCLUSION

Despite the huge strides and the obvious successes that Malaysia has had in building its ICM, there remain several challenges in moving on from here. First and foremost is the continued heavy reliance on debt-like contracts, *murabaha*, *ijarah* and the like. In fact, the reliance on commodity *murabaha* appears to have increased. Risk-sharing contracts like *mudarabah* and *musharaka* remain small. Ironically, even where the label *mudaraba* or *musharaka* is used, clauses are introduced to render the contract less of a risk-sharing one; this being done in the name of reducing 'uncertainties' and marketability. The preponderance of debt-like instruments reduces the value proposition of Islamic finance, which is based on risk sharing. A second challenge is that despite three decades of growth and recreation of all the different components of a well-developed capital market, Islamic finance has not been able to shake off its reliance on interest rates in pricing instruments, while Malaysia's IIMM is unique in enabling the trading of short-term instruments, opening the way for price discovery. This, however, is yet to happen, largely due to the free flow of funds between the Islamic and conventional sectors. While non-Shari'ah-compliant institutions are not allowed to issue instruments in the IIMM, there is nothing to stop them investing in them. The arbitrage potential that this gives rise to ensures that the two markets, the IIMM and the conventional money market, have the same prevailing rates. The conventional money market being several times larger dictates the direction and the IIMM being smaller, follows.

A third problem is liquidity or the lack of it. Illiquidity in the Islamic markets is not just a Malaysian phenomenon, but a global one. Secondary market trading of *sukuk* is plagued with illiquidity. The imbalance between demand and supply and the large-sized denominations are often blamed. However, the retail *sukuk*, which have much smaller denomination and are listed on the stock exchange, do not seem to fare any better. The clustering of instruments, particularly *sukuk* at the short and medium tenors, is another challenge. While there have been a few 'perpetual' *sukuk*, there is a dearth of instruments in the 10–30 year range. A final challenge is one that is unlikely to be solved any time soon: the need for harmonisation in Shari'ah interpretation. Malaysia has come thus far by being progressive in its interpretation and willingness to push the frontier in many pioneering ways. However, it has had its criticism. With the passage of time, many Islamic nations now see the benefit of Malaysia's experimentation and willingness to move forward. But, orthodoxy will continue to challenge development.

As we end, it would be worth asking if the Malaysian model can be replicated elsewhere. The ability to implement or construct an Islamic finance framework depends very much on the 'state of play' within a jurisdiction of the current STARS:

S   Shari'ah and legal framework
T   Tax environment
A   Accounting framework
R   Regulatory framework
S   Standards framework (documentation, professional education etc.)

Malaysia had a unique state of play, with regard to all of the above, when it commenced its journey in Islamic finance, and it is extremely unlikely that any other country would be in exactly the same position. For example, Malaysia has a legal framework based on

English common law, whereas a country such as Indonesia has a framework based on the Dutch civil code. These two, very different starting points would have a very significant impact on the implementation of an IF environment.

While good lessons can be learned from the Malaysian model, it would be incorrect to assume that it could be implemented in totality in any other environment. An analysis of the 'as is' in relation to the STARS would need to be done, as would a design for the future 'to be' environment. This would then give a reasonable framework to assess the degree of fit and relevance of the Malaysian model.

BIBLIOGRAPHY

Aidid, S. I. (2008) *Malaysia at 50, achievements and aspirations* (IIUM and Thomcon Learning, Singapore).

Bank Negara Malaysia. http://www.bnm.gov.my/

ISRA and Securities Commission, Malaysia (2015) *Islamic Capital Markets. Principles and Practices* (Pearson Publishing, Malaysia).

Obiyathulla, I. B and Abbas, M. (2013) *Islamic Capital Markets – A Comparative Approach* (Wiley, Singapore).

Securities Commission, Malaysia. http://www.sc.com.my/

CHAPTER 13

Bahrain's Islamic Capital Markets – A Case Study

By Dr Hatim El-Tahir

Increased insights and development of Islamic capital markets (ICMs) and their asset classes are tremendously important for both government and private sectors. In relation to the development of instruments and the regulations in capital markets, the discussion about the changing landscape of the global financial market in recent years is crucial. The fundamental changes have been introduced in governance, risk and capital management. These changes increased the idea of investing in real sectors of economies to stimulate growth. They also encouraged academicians, practitioners and policy-makers to consider alternative business models to address the capital and risk regulatory requirements, such as the 'equity-based' and risk-participatory financing models offered by Islamic finance.

The Kingdom of Bahrain (Bahrain) leverages its position as a leading regional financial hub. In this new landscape, mentioned above, Bahrain responds proactively to address the new economic and financial orders. The Central Bank of Bahrain (CBB) leads a set of regulatory and government support initiatives, all of which aim at enhancing financial stability strategies and introducing ways to stimulate sustainable economic growth.

This chapter addresses the rationale for developing an ICM in Bahrain. It begins with identifying the achievements made in building its architectural framework. Next, it analyses the factors that provide the stimulus for the development and the expansion of the Bahraini ICM. This leads to the discussion of the leading products, markets and industries that shaped the country's ICM. Then it presents case studies from a leading innovative corporate *sukuk* issuances industry. The chapter concludes by stating the gaps that could impact Bahrain's competitiveness and cites feasible strategies that could support the development of the ICM.

THE RATIONALE FOR CAPITAL MARKET DEVELOPMENT

A vast body of economic literature supports the view that financial development is a prerequisite for economic development. For nations to sustain long-term economic growth, it is imperative to have a sound and well-functioning financial system. Such a system can yield several benefits to the economy as it helps mobilise savings to more productive sectors, improves resource allocation, facilitates diversification and promotes better mechanisms of risk sharing. It can also promote financial stability as deep and liquid financial systems with diverse instruments. With the presence of a strong regulatory framework, it can provide buffers against shocks emanating from volatile markets.[1]

Growing awareness of and demand for investing in accordance with Shari'ah principles on a global scale have been the catalyst for making the Islamic financial services industry a flourishing industry. It also is a reflection of the increasing wealth and capacity of investors, both Muslim and non-Muslim, to seek and invest in new investment products that serve their needs.[2]

The government stays in pace with these developments through its regulatory agency, the CBB. The CBB has continuously revised its regulatory infrastructure and introduced guidelines that promote international best practices. Important directional strategies have been introduced over recent decades to build a sound and efficient regulatory framework in the country.

More recently, and in a bid to enhance Bahrain's competitiveness, the CBB led a consolidation strategy in the Islamic banking sector which aimed at restructuring the sector's resources, capabilities and capital. Over ten successful transactions took place and produced healthier, management-sound, capitalised and resource-efficient institutions. The success of this strategy is set to be replicated in the *takaful* industry. However, more generally now, institutions offering Islamic financial services (IIFS) cover almost every aspect of Islamic finance, including asset management, mutual funds, *sukuk* issuance and insurance. With the CBB taking a leading role, IIFS have been at the forefront of developing Islamic financial products.[3]

THE PATH TO A SOUND MARKET

A high level overview of the Financial Development (FD) index published by the International Monetary Fund (IMF), as shown in Figure 13.1, reveals an interesting growth pattern in Bahrain's financial system position compared with other GCC countries and leading developed economies. The ranking in the index is largely derived from two sub-indices: the Financial Institutions (FI) index and the Financial Market (FM) index.

Figure 13.2 shows the ICD-Thomson Reuters Islamic finance development indicator for the top 15 countries.

---

[1]Deloitte Research and Analysis.
[2]The OICU-IOSCO, Report of the Islamic Capital Market Task Force of the International Organization of Securities Commissions, July 2004, p. 3.
[3]Economic Development Board (EDB), Financial Services Report, 2015, p. 4.

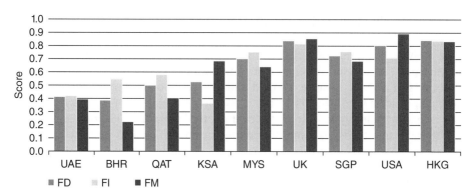

FIGURE 13.1 IMF financial development index 2015
Sources: Deloitte (2015), IMF

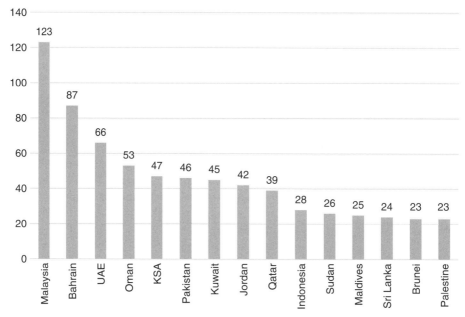

FIGURE 13.2 Islamic finance development indicator for the top 15 countries in the world
Source: ICD-Thomson Reuters (2016)

Table 13.1 shows a selection of financial development indicators in Bahrain and other economies in 2012. While Bahrain's stock market is the largest market in the GCC by capitalisation in absolute terms, it is average relative to the country's GDP (i.e. 54.4 percent of GDP in 2012) when compared to other GCC economies, or low when compared other major international centres such as Hong Kong, Singapore, the US or the UK. In terms of debt security issuances, Bahrain comes first within the GCC in the value of its international debt issuances relative to its GDP (33 percent). It also outperforms advanced economies, such as Singapore (25 percent) and the US (19 percent)

TABLE 13.1 Financial development indicators in Bahrain and other economies (2012)

Country	Corporate bond issuance to GDP (%)	Credit to government and state enterprises to GDP (%)	International debt issues (1) to GDP (%)	Private credit by FIs to GDP (%)	Stockmarket capitalisation to GDP (%)
UAE	1.6	20.2	28.1	60.3	18.4
Bahrain		**20.7**	**32.7**	**97.6**	**54.4**
Qatar	1.1	23.7	22.8	35.7	66.2
Saudi Arabia	0.3	7.9		46.5	48.4
Malaysia	5.8	11.9	15	111.3	142.1
Hong Kong	7.6	38.1	37.6	194.4	378.4
Singapore	5.3	27.4	24.7	112.5	126.3
USA	4.8	5.1	18.6	176.6	107
UK	4.9	5.3	107	168.2	112.1
World	2.4	6.8	12.9	38.8	30.8

Data Source: The Global Financial Development Database, World Bank
Note 1: International debt issues cover long-term bonds and notes and money market instruments placed on international markets.
Note 2: Private credit to FIs includes private credit to banks.

in its international debt issuances. In fact, the latter economies have a well-developed domestic debt securities markets where they issue most of their debt instruments and attract external issuers to issue securities in their markets.[4]

THE ECONOMIC OUTLOOK

The Bahrain Economic Development Board (EDB) forecasts that Bahrain will record average annual real GDP growth of 3.3 percent in 2015–2017, as shown in Table 13.2. However, lower oil prices will undoubtedly impact on the drive for investment projects across the region, reducing demand for Bahrain's services-oriented economy. Shari'ah-compliant assets in the country have risen from USD1.9 billion in 2000 to USD25.1 billion in June 2015 and now account for around 13 percent of the Kingdom's total banking assets. It is also worth noting that financial services account for around 17 percent of the country's GDP (the second-largest contributor after oil).

Clearly Bahrain, with its historic growth in GDP, and the depth and scale of its financial services and human capital, stands a good chance of becoming a regional global centre of excellence in ICMs. To attain this, the CBB and other government agencies have designed a series of policy initiatives and regulatory changes and upgrades, aligning the industry regulatory framework to best international practices and standards.

---

[4]Based on the Deloitte Report, 'Developing Dubai's debt market to promote investment and growth', 2015.

TABLE 13.2   Bahrain economic outlook

	2013	2014f	2015f	2016f	2017f
Real GDP growth, %	5.3%	4.2%	3.6%	3.3%	3%
Non-hydrocarbons sector	3.0%	4.6%	4.5%	3.9%	3.6%
Hydrocarbons sector	15.3%	2.9%	0.0%	0.5%	0.5%
Nominal GDP growth, %	8.3%	3.1%	2.1%	5.8%	5.3%
Inflation (CPI %)	3.3%	3.0%	3.0%	3.0%	2.6%
Current account (% of GDP)	7.8%	5.7%	2.9%	2.0%	–2.5%
Fiscal balance (% of GDP)	–3.3%	–3.9%	–4.0%	–1.5%	–6.1%
Crude Oil Arabian Medium (USD)	106.4	96.0	80.0	80.0	60.0

Data Source: Bahrain Economic Development Board (2015)

THE EMERGENCE OF THE MODERN FINANCIAL MARKET

In the last three decades, Bahrain's focus was largely driven by growth in size and importance of the financial services sector. This was attributed largely to the pressing need for a diversification policy of the country's economy to reduce dependence on the depleting oil resources. A number of institutions, regulation and financial products have evolved in this era.

Bahrain Bourse

June 2014 marked the twenty-fifth anniversary of trading on the exchange, which began operating as the Bahrain Stock Exchange in 1989. Bahrain Bourse (Bourse) was established as a shareholding company in 2010. The official exchange was created after the collapse of an unofficial trading centre called the Al Jowhara Market and its equivalent in Kuwait, the Souk Al Manakh, in the 1980s.[5]

With an 18.9 percent year-on-year increase in market capitalisation and a 17.2 percent hike in the Bahrain All-Share Index, 2013 was a positive year for the Bourse. This positive trend continued into 2014, with a 21.7 percent rise in market capitalisation to BD8.47 billion (USD22.45 billion) at the end of September 2014 and a 23.63 percent increase year to date in the Bahrain All-Share Index, which ended the third quarter at 1,476.02, exceeding highs last seen in early 2011.[6]

A landmark regulatory change in 2002 took place when the legislative and regulatory authority and supervision of the Bourse were transferred from the Ministry of Commerce to the CBB, so that the CBB regulates and supervises all the Bourse's activities. This change sparked development of the Bourse, in which the latter witnessed a catalogue of product and service offerings. Government institutions and companies started issuing several investment instruments, taking advantage of the legislative and technical infrastructure established by the Bourse. Some of these included the listing

---

[5]Oxford Business Group Report.
[6]Ibid.

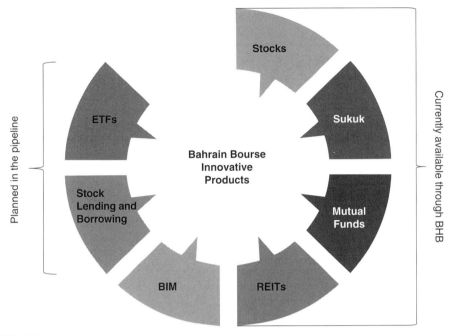

FIGURE 13.3 Bahrain Bourse innovative products
Source: Bahrain Bourse

and registration of preferred shares, bonds, *sukuk* and mutual funds, making it the first bourse to list such instruments in the region.[7] Figure 13.3 provides a portrait of the Bourse's innovative product suite. The list includes all aspects of investment and financing instruments.

In July 2014, there were 50 firms listed on the Bourse, two mutual funds and nine bonds or *sukuk*. Initial public offering (IPO) activity had slowed since the early 2000s. This is attributed to the slowdown of the government's privatisation programme. As elsewhere in the Gulf, the local corporate debt market remained insignificant and underdeveloped, largely because medium-sized and large firms were largely dependent on classic bank lending.

Market Capitalisation

As at end of June 2015, market capitalisation of the Bourse stood at BD8.0 billion, as shown in Table 13.3 and Figure 13.4. This level of market capitalisation is 3.2 percent lower than the level as at end of December 2014 and 0.7 percent lower year-on-year.[8] A breakdown of market capitalisation by sector indicates that 'Industrial' recorded the highest year-on-year increase in market capitalisation (12.9 percent) followed by 'Hotel and Tourism' (7.7 percent) and 'Services' (5.2 percent). The rest of the sectors witnessed a year-on-year decrease in market capitalisation.

---

[7]Bahrain Bourse Publications.
[8]Central Bank of Bahrain, Financial Stability Report, August 2015.

TABLE 13.3 Bahrain All-Share Index (Feb 2011 – June 2015)

(BD)

Sector	June 2014	Dec. 2014	June 2015	Dec 2014–June 2015 (% Change)	June 2014–June 2015 (% Change)
Commercial banks	3,825,790,134	3,793,805,442	3,664,820,365	-3.4%	-4.2%
Investment	2,159,672,680	2,295,082,815	2,121,193,355	-7.6%	-1.8%
Insurance	174,549,943	163,878,591	161,883,489	-1.2%	-7.3%
Services	1,099,045,952	1,125,569,854	1,156,482,718	2.7%	5.2%
Industrial	647,368,316	751,120,639	730,756,917	-2.7%	12.9%
Hotel and Tourism	207,494,503	197,610,963	223,467,892	13.1%	7.7%
Total	8,113,921,529	8,327,068,303	8,058,604,736	-3.2%	-0.7%

Source: Central Bank of Bahrain

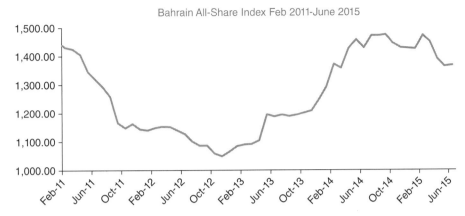

FIGURE 13.4 Market capitalisation on the Bahrain Bourse
Source: Bahrain Bourse

INTRODUCTION OF AN ISLAMIC FINANCE INDEX

In 2015, the Bourse introduced a trading index of Shari'ah-compliant companies. The Islamic finance index in the region should enable investors, brokers and advisors to take better-informed investment decisions and helps investors track the performance of companies' stocks listed on the index.

Initially the index included the shares of 17 companies, all of which comply with the technical and financial standards set by the Bourse's Shari'ah committee. According to Khalid Hamad, Executive Director of Banking Supervision at CBB, the new venture will encourage Islamic banks and other companies 'to take new initiatives in the capital market, through mutual funds and securities that comply with the Islamic Sharia'.[9]

Bahrain Financial Exchange (BFX)

The Bahrain Financial Exchange (BFX) – an international derivatives, structured products, Shari'ah-compliant and cash instrument exchange – began trading in October 2010. Foreign exchange, gold and natural gas futures were traded. The BFX, which is regulated by the CBB, has developed an Islamic finance trading platform named 'Bait Al Bursa' which offers electronic exchange traded Islamic financial instruments and aspires to introduce innovative solutions that meet the demand of today's Islamic finance market.

Some of its main products include the following:

- *e-tayseer*, the first of Bait Al Bursa's products, is a fully automated platform for transactions in the supply, purchase and sale of assets for facilitating *murabaha* transactions. *e-tayseer* allows suppliers to place their assets onto the platform ready to be purchased by financial institutions. Financial institutions can then purchase

[9]http://www.bahrain.com/en/media-centre/Pages/Bahrain-Bourse-launches-regions-first-Islamic-Finance-Index.aspx#.Vm7GsUp97IU

TABLE 13.4   The BFX product portfolio

Cash Instruments	Equities, bonds, notes, certificates of deposit, depository receipts, Exchange Traded Funds (ETFs), Exchange Traded Commodities (ETCs), Real Estate Investment Trusts (REITs)
Derivatives Instruments	Swaps, futures and options. Underlying can be commodities, currencies, equities, financial instruments or indices
Shari'ah-Compliant Financial Instruments	Equities, *sukuk*, *murabaha*, *wakala*, Islamic options, Islamic repo, Islamic ETFs, Islamic REITs

Data Source: Bahrain Financial Exchange

these assets and conduct *murabaha* transactions with counterparties to fulfil their liquidity management requirements in a secure online environment.

- **The BFX platform** for multi-asset class trading offers market participants the ability to trade multiple asset classes on one market. The BFX product portfolio is split into three main categories, as shown in Table 13.4 and explained in Table 13.5.

TABLE 13.5   The BFX conventional market products

Commodities	**Gold: BFX provides products booklet and contract specifications** ■ The BFX Gold Futures facilitates market participants to mitigate risk against volatile Gold prices. The BFX Gold Futures (Symbol: BFXGOLD) are available for trading in the contract size of 32 troy ounces. ■ The BFX MCX $ Gold Futures facilitates hedgers, arbitrageurs and investors to directly obtain exposure to Gold prices benchmarked to the Indian bullion markets. **Silver: BFX provides products booklet and contract specifications** ■ The BFX Silver Futures (Symbol: BFXSLVR) enables market participants to hedge against price volatility. ■ The launch of the BFX MCX $ Silver Futures shall benefit global market participants to trade on Silver priced on the Indian markets. This is also expected to bridge the price differential across global markets, thereby, providing uniformity in the global price discovery mechanism.
Currencies	■ Increasing volatility in the EURUSD exchange rate has necessitated exporters, importers, corporates, financial institutions and investors to hedge against currency price risk using futures contracts. ■ The BFX Euro versus the US dollar (EUR-USD) currency futures (Symbol: BFXEUUS) has a lot size of EUR 25,000 and is quoted in US dollars and cents per one Euro.
Energy	■ The BFX Natural Gas Futures (Symbol: BFXNG) futures contract enables market participants to mitigate risk against volatile Natural Gas prices. ■ The contract size is 2,500 mm Btu and is quoted in US dollars and cents per one million Btu.

Data Source: Bahrain Financial Exchange

Access to Government Debt

In January 2015, the CBB launched a new product aimed at increasing access to government debt by allowing both institutions and individual investors to directly purchase government bonds and *sukuk* from the primary market via licensed brokers.

Islamic Money Market Instruments

In June 2001, the CBB offered, for the first time in the Gulf, government bills that were structured to comply with Shari'ah Islamic law. The bills were worth USD25 million, and were designed in the form of three-month papers, referred to as *sukuk salam* securities.

Islamic Asset Management

The wave of regulatory reform in investment heralded a new dawn when the CBB announced changes and regulatory updates in its collective investment schemes. In particular, in August 2006, the Financial Trust Law was issued to govern the establishment of financial trusts, and set a precedent in the region. One year later, in June 2007, the Collective Investment Undertakings (CIUs) Law was passed – an investment law that forms part of volume six of the CBB Rulebook, which regulates capital markets in Bahrain. The investment module widened the range of services and products available for investment to include hedge funds and derivatives. In addition, the CBB also introduced rules to govern Real Estate Investment Trusts (REITs) and Private Investment Undertakings (PIUs), which would hopefully help boost flexibility of structuring of Shari'ah-compliant investment instruments and attract wider portfolios of investors and requirements.

The investment rules also catered for overseas domiciled CIUs, which are required to register with the CBB before they can be marketed in Bahrain. In this respect, the country is challenged by pressures to invest more in its infrastructure and to provide more economic incentives to attract European and other Western investment funds.

Growth of Mutual Funds

Despite the global financial downturn, Bahrain continued to see growth in funds domiciliation averaging about 15 percent in recent years. The number of authorised funds in Bahrain reached 2,743 with a Net Asset Value (NAV) totalling USD9.74 billion, as shown in Figure 13.5. It is also reported that there are 88 Islamic funds incorporated and registered in Bahrain with total assets of USD1.4 billion as of March 2015.[10]

Islamic Real Estate Investment Trusts (REITs)

The year 2015 saw a new development in capital market instruments when new listing rules for REITs were introduced by the Bourse. This new development is set to revitalise the troubled real estate industry in the country and help restore confidence

---

[10]http://www.cbb.gov.bh/page-p-11th_annual_world_islamic_funds_and_financial_markets_conferences_2015.htm

FIGURE 13.5 Mutual fund providers, (USD '000)
Source: Central Bank of Bahrain, 2015

in real estate investment. Some of the key features of this development include the following:

- New listing rules for REITs issued by the Bourse came into effect on 17 May 2015, with requirements including a minimum of two properties with a combined asset value of no less than USD20 million.
- REITs are regulated and authorised by the CBB before they can be listed. According to CBB regulations, the dividend pay-out ratio of a REIT has to be at least 90 percent of its net realised income.

The Listing Requirements

REITs licensed by the CBB are mandated by law to list on the stock exchange within a period of six months after obtaining approval from CBB.

The Case of the First REIT

Eskan Bank appointed SICO as lead arranger for the first REIT to be listed on the Bourse by an IPO, and only the second Shari'ah-compliant listed REIT in the Gulf region. As arranger, SICO is responsible for managing the entire process, which includes internal property valuations along with independent real estate values, legal structure, regulatory submissions and the IPO.

The Shari'ah-compliant REIT is expected to have a total value of BD20 million, with a tranche that will be offered to the public through the IPO:

- Eskan Bank's REIT will consist of two income-generating and unleveraged properties – Segaya Plaza in Segaya and Danaat Al Madina in Isa Town.
- A listed REIT is a regulated investment vehicle that invests directly in real estate with its units traded like a stock on exchanges. REITs generally provide investors with access to real estate, a regular and stable income stream and diversification, and enhance the liquidity of their portfolios.[11]

The *Sukuk* Market

The CBB pioneered the development of the local *sukuk* market by undertaking a regular programme of sovereign issues. It has released one *ijarah* and one *salam sukuk* each month, in addition to long-term Islamic leasing securities every now and then.

However, the CBB took many steps on the supply side in 2001 by providing short-term as well as long-term, tradable, asset-backed *sukuk*. On the demand side, the Liquidity Management Centre was established to facilitate the creation of an interbank money market.

The CBB, and to a greater extent Bank Negara Malaysia (BNM), are also perceived to have been proactive in issuing short-term *sukuk* that could be used to meet the recent Basel III requirements such as the Liquidity Coverage Ratio (LCR) and the creation of level 1 High Quality Liquid Assets (HQLA). Most of the government's *sukuk* are either not listed on developed markets or listed but not actively traded.[12]

---

[11]Bahrain Bourse Publications.
[12]Standard and Poor's 'Islamic Finance Outlook 2015'.

However, it is envisaged that the creation of the International Islamic Liquidity Management Corporation (IILM) will address this industry regulatory requirement and develop a programme of HQLA issuances.

On the corporate *sukuk* side, there have been only nine issues since 2004. The latest was Gulf International Bank's USD300 million *sukuk al-murabaha* in 2011, which was issued through a special purpose vehicle incorporated in the Cayman Islands, Horizon Sukuk.

An Anchor *Sukuk*: Mumtalakat

Bahrain's Sovereign Wealth Fund (SWF), Mumtalakat Holding Company, set a new sign of development in corporate *sukuk* history when it tapped the *sukuk* market in Malaysia. This move is considered to be the first of its kind in the oil-rich Gulf countries, and was welcomed by many business and capital market analysts. The transaction was well received by market participants. The dual-listing of Mumtalakat *sukuk*, a ringgit denominated security, amounted to a market value just less than the equivalent of USD1 billion. The main objective of this capital raising is to manage the holding firm's long-term finances and partly pay off some of its maturing corporate debts. The 20-year Medium-Term Notes (MTNs) *sukuk* have secured an AA2 rating from RAM Ratings.

Table 13.6 shows some of the main corporate *sukuk* issues in the Kingdom. The CBB also remains active in the sovereign *sukuk* market through the issuance of medium- to long-term *sukuk*, complemented by a regular programme of short-term issuance. A landmark development in this respect was the recent and unprecedented 30-year bond. The issuance raised USD1.25 billion and met with strong investor demand, with orders reportedly reaching USD5.75 billion. The bond was priced to yield 6 percent.

Key Transactional Process

Some of the recently developed investment instruments by the Bourse include fixed income investment instruments (*sukuk al ijaraha*) which are offered to both retail and corporate investors (see Figure 13.6). The trust certificates are issued in multiples of BD500 (USD1,325). The underlying assets used for this type of investment products are generally government *sukuk*, and hence the product is widely known in the market as *sukuk al ijaraha*.

Figure 13.6 illustrates the structure of the *sukuk al ijaraha* where the government of Bahrain (the obligor) sells its assets and leases them back to fund a particular project. The government of Bahrain also acts as issuer and trustee (the SPV) and issues the trust certificates to investors or *sukuk* holders (1) and receives proceeds (2). The government of Bahrain being the obligor sells its assets (3) at the agreed price (4). The trustee leases back the assets (5) to the government – the originator and pays rentals (6). Periodic distributors, mostly half-yearly, are paid to investors as in (7). At maturity the SPV, being the trustee, sells back the assets in question to the government (8) at the exercise price (9) and the investment process ends with paying back investors their principal (10).

However, it is worth noting that the role of the Bourse in this investment platform is limited to the role of a broker to promote the government *sukuk* as retail and corporate investment instruments.

TABLE 13.6 List of corporate *sukuk* issued, 2005–2012

Status	Issuer	Sukuk Name	Sukuk	Country	Currency	Subscription	Issue	Tenor	Arranger
Matured	Gulf International Bank	GIB/Horizon Sukuk limited	Murabaha	Bahrain	USD	3-Jul-05	300 M	3 years	JP Morgan Chase Bank
Matured	Al Marfa'a Al Mali Sukuk Company	Bahrain Financial Harbour Sukuk	Ijarah	Bahrain	USD	30-Jun-05	134.0M	5 Years	Dubai Islamic Bank P.J.S.C.
Matured	Durrat Sukuk Company	Durrat Al Bahrain Sukuk	Ijarah-Istisnaa	Bahrain	USD	25-Jan-05	152.5M	5 Years	Kuwait Finance House Liquidity Management Centre
Closed	Bahrain Mumtalakat Holding Company	Bahrain Mumtalakat Sukuk (2017) (IMTN 1)	Murabaha	Bahrain	MYR	4-Oct-12	91.1M	5 Years	CIMB Investment Bank Berhad
Closed	Horizon Sukuk Limited	Gulf International Bank Sukuk	Murabaha	Bahrain	USD	7-Dec-11	300.0M	3 Years	JPMorgan Chase Bank
Matured	Arcapita Bank	Arcapita MultiCurrency Sukuk	Murabaha	Bahrain	USD	19-Oct-05	210.0M	5 Years	Bayerische Hypo-und Vereinsbank Bahrain
Matured	Diyaar Sukuk Company	Diyaar Sukuk	Musharaka	Bahrain	USD	17-May-07	200.0M	4 Years	Kuwait Finance House

Source: Deloitte Research and Analysis

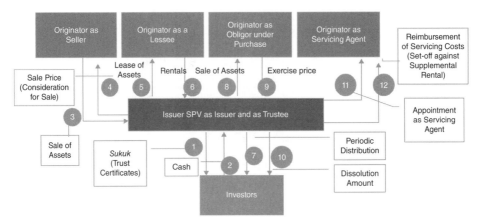

FIGURE 13.6 *Sukuk al ijarah* – New product for an existing market
Source: Bahrain Bourse

CONCLUSION

In this chapter, we looked at the different aspects that have influenced the growth of the financial service sector and ICM. The analysis reveals that while the market size is limited in dollar figures, there were significant regulatory and product development initiatives, all of which are aimed at keeping the country's position – as industry hub – at the forefront globally.

It is evident that there are some gaps that require more efforts to address and resolve. At the start, the country is constrained by capacity with a small market and limited growth prospects, given its small population and current regional economic and geopolitical risks. However, for the country to remain competitive as a regional ICM, there are a number of strategy and policy considerations that regulators need to consider in developing an ICM strategy.

In this context, there are four key inter-related elements of building a sound and efficient ICM in the country, as illustrated in Figure 13.7:

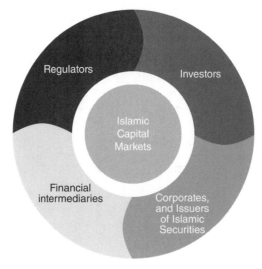

FIGURE 13.7 Four key elements for building a sound and efficient Islamic capital market

- Regulators: National regulators need to engage market participants and other stakeholders to address issues of governance, risk and corporates' debt and equity requirements.
- Investors: To promote public understanding of the Shari'ah principles and business models, best practices and limitation of excessive and speculative investments (derivatives).
- Issuers' integrity: To instil a culture of good practice in transparency and disclosure among corporates and issuers of Islamic securities.
- Financial intermediaries: To provide sound investment advice and maintain a high code of business conduct practices.

For this strategy to work efficiently, industry stakeholders need to work more closely and initiate industry dialogue platforms to ensure constant updates and knowledge and skill sharing. Government support is key to this, to ensure better alignment of business and objectives and to create an enabling regulatory and investment environment.

CASE STUDY: MUMTALAKAT USD600 MILLION *SUKUK*

Mumtalakat was established in June 2006 as an independent holding company for the government of Bahrain's stakes in non-oil and gas-related assets. The perceived SWF company owns stakes in strategic non-oil and gas assets of the Kingdom of Bahrain, and significantly contributes to the Kingdom's national economy.

The SWF company's portfolio of firms spans a variety of sectors, including aluminum production, financial services, telecommunications, real estate, aviation, tourism and food production. The firm is strategically created to align and implement the execution of the government's initiatives to improve governance and transparency, pursue value-enhancing opportunities and help achieve operational excellence for its state-owned non-oil and gas-related assets.

In November 2014, Bahrain Mumtalakat Holding raised USD600 million from the sale of *sukuk* in an attempt to refinance its debt. Table 13.7 outlines the transaction summary and terms of the sale. The innovative *sukuk* structure (a hybrid structure comprised of a Commodity *murabaha* and a *wakala* based on Mumtalakat's holding in its portfolio companies) allowed the SWF company to capitalise on the strong Islamic pool of liquidity.

Rating Considerations

Bahrain Mumtalakat Holding has been rated BBB (stable) by both Fitch and Standard & Poor's. The transaction represents Mumtalakat's first USD *sukuk* issuance, which was executed as a drawdown under its recently established USD1,000 million Regulation Multicurrency Trust Certificate Issuance Programme, which is listed on the Irish Stock Exchange. It also marks the company's return to the USD debt capital markets following its inaugural bond issuance in 2010.

TABLE 13.7   Transaction Summary – Terms and Lead Managers

Transactional Features

Issuance	Issuer/Trustee	Mumtalakat Holding Sukuk 2021
	Issuance Price	USD 600 million
Transaction Terms	Tenure	7 years
	Coupon Rate	4% profit rate, Coupon frequency twice per year
	Payments	Nominal, minimum settlement amount USD200,000
	Currency	USD
	Use of proceeds	To refinance their debt
Regulatory and Legal	Legal Advisor/ Counsel	Legal Advisor (Domestic law): Hassan Radhi & Associates Attorneys & Legal Consultants. Issuer Legal Advisor (Domestic law): Zu'bi & Partners
	Listing	Irish Stock Exchange
	Joint Lead Managers	BNP Paribas, Deutsche Bank, MUFJG and Standard Chartered Bank acted as Joint Lead Managers on the issuance, while Arab Banking Corporation and National Bank of Bahrain acted as Co-Lead Managers

Data Source: Mumtalakat Holding Company

MUMTALAKAT *SUKUK*: THE MURABAHA PROGRAMME

Table 13.8 and Figure 13.8 outline the details of the Mumtalakat *sukuk*.

TABLE 13.8   Transaction Summary of Bahrain Mumtalakat – Terms and Lead Managers

Transactional Features

Issuance	Issuer/ Trustee	Trustee Deutsche Trustees Malaysia Berhad
	Program size	RM3.0 billion
Transaction Terms	Tenure	The tenure of the *sukuk murabaha* programme is 20 years from the date of issue of the first series of *sukuk murabaha*.
	Coupon Rate	The profit rate is determined and agreed prior to the issuance of *sukuk murabaha* of each such series. Each series shall be on a semi-annual or quarterly basis
	Currency	Malaysian ringgit, RM
	Use of Proceeds	Used for Mumtalakat's general corporate purposes
Regulatory and Legal	Legal Advisor/ Counsel	Lead Arranger and Principal Advisor: Chartered Saadiq Berhad Sharia' Committee
	Listing	Bursa Malaysia Securities Berhad
	Joint Lead Managers	Lead Arranger: Chartered Saadiq Berhad Sharia' Committee, SCSB. Lead Managers: CIMB Investment Bank Berhad

Data Source: Deloitte Research and Analysis

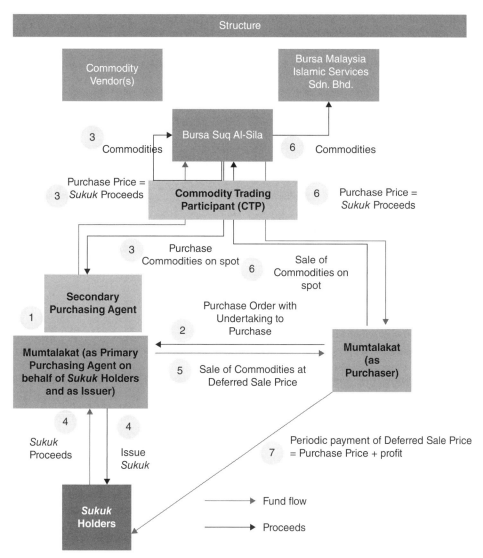

FIGURE 13.8   The structure type – *sukuk al-murabaha*
Source: The Mumtalakat Sukuk Prospectus

Rating Considerations

Fitch Ratings (Fitch) has assigned an expected rating of BBB to the *sukuk murabaha* programme and RAM Rating Services Berhad (RAM Ratings) has assigned an indicative rating of AA2.

CHAPTER 14

Sukuk Issued as Regulatory Capital Instruments for Basel III Compliance – A Case Study

By Abdullah Haron

Basel III is a set of international banking regulations developed by the Bank for International Settlements in order to promote stability in the international financial system. Basel III builds on the Basel I and Basel II documents, and seeks to improve the banking sector's ability to deal with financial and economic stress, improve risk management and strengthen the banks' transparency and disclosures. In combination with other regulations, Basel III is expected to reduce the ability of banks, including Islamic banks, to damage the economy by taking on excess risk.

One of the reforms initiated by the Basel Committee on Banking Supervision (BCBS) is intended to strengthen the regulatory capital framework. Banks must hold more or higher quality capital than before in order to absorb losses on a going concern basis. This ensures the continuing ability of the banks to meet their obligations as they fall due, while also maintaining the confidence of customers, depositors, creditors and other stakeholders in their dealings with the banks. Capital requirements also seek to give further protection to depositors and other senior creditors in a 'gone concern' situation (i.e. at the point of non-viability) by providing an additional cushion of loss absorbency that can allow senior claims to be met in liquidation.

REGULATORY CAPITAL IN BASEL III AND IFSB-15

Basel III's total regulatory capital consists of the sum of the following elements:

1. Tier 1 capital (going concern capital)
   a. Common Equity Tier 1 (CET1)
   b. Additional Tier 1 (AT1)
2. Tier 2 capital (gone concern capital)

Basel III requires banks to maintain a minimum ratio of 4.5 percent for CET1 capital. Basel III also set the minimum requirement for the non-common equity AT1 capital and Tier 2 capital at 1.5 percent and 2 percent, respectively. AT1 capital is a layer of additional going concern capital which is perpetual in nature.

Together, the CET1 and the AT1 constitute subordinated paid-in capital capable of absorbing losses while the bank is still solvent. As for the Tier 2 capital, it is considered as gone concern capital, which absorbs losses when the bank is 'at the point of non-viability', i.e. a 'bail in' to avoid or limit a 'bail out'.

Basel III also requires banks to maintain a 2.5 percent capital preservation buffer and 0–2.5 percent countercyclical capital buffer. Banks will have until 2019 to implement these changes, giving them plenty of time to do so.

In order for an instrument to be included in these components of capital, Basel III provides a set of relevant criteria. The eligibility of various types of instruments for inclusion in Tier 1 or Tier 2 is a matter for consideration by the supervisory authority in the light of the relevant criteria.

In line with the revised BCBS' capital adequacy requirement, the Islamic Financial Services Board (IFSB) released IFSB-15 in December 2013, with the purpose of enhancing its framework for capital adequacy and liquidity requirements to suit the specificities of Islamic banks. *Sukuk* currently play an instrumental role in addressing the capital adequacy and liquidity needs of Islamic banks as stipulated by the Basel III. Briefly, for both Basel III and IFSB-15, CET1 will comprise ordinary share capital, retained profits and some other reserves.

For the AT1 and Tier 2, *sukuk* issued against assets owned by an Islamic bank may be used by that bank as additional capital to meet the regulatory minimum requirements. Owing to Shari'ah requirements, there are similarities and differences between Basel III and IFSB-15.

The focus of this case study is on AT1 and Tier 2.

Key Criteria for Basel III

According to Basel III, the key criteria of AT1 and Tier 2 instruments issued by banks, among others, are outlined in Table 14.1.

Challenges for *Sukuk* Issuance in the Context of Basel III's Key Criteria

Sukuk represent the holder's proportionate ownership in an undivided part of an underlying asset, where the holder assumes all rights and obligations to such an asset. The features of asset-backed *sukuk* are similar to conventional asset-backed securities (ABS) in many aspects. First of all, the return on both types of securities is based on a pool of assets; both involve the transfer of beneficial/legal ownership of the assets from the issuer to the buyer of the securities. Secondly, the holders of both types of securities derive the risk and return from the cash flows of the underlying asset, as well as having recourse to the asset, not the issuer, in case of default. Finally, both types of securities are intended to generate a stable and predictable return for investors from the cash flows generated by the assets.

TABLE 14.1   Key Criteria of AT1 and Tier 2 instruments

Additional Tier 1	Tier 2
1 Issued and paid-in.	Issued and paid-in.
2 Subordinated to depositors, general creditors and subordinated debt of the bank.	Subordinated to depositors and general creditors of the bank.
3 Is neither secured nor covered by a guarantee of the issuer or related entity or other arrangement that legally or economically enhances the seniority of the claim vis-à-vis bank creditors.	Is neither secured nor covered by a guarantee of the issuer or related entity or other arrangement that legally or economically enhances the seniority of the claim vis-à-vis depositors and general bank creditors.
4 Is perpetual, i.e. there is no maturity date and there are no step-ups or other incentives to redeem.	Maturity: a minimum original maturity of at least five years. b recognition in regulatory capital in the remaining five years before maturity will be amortised on a straight-line basis. c there are no step-ups or other incentives to redeem.
5 May be callable at the initiative of the issuer only after a minimum of five years.	May be callable at the initiative of the issuer only after a minimum of five years.
6 Any repayment of principal (e.g. through repurchase or redemption) must be with prior supervisory approval and banks should not assume or create market expectations that supervisory approval will be given.	The investor must have no rights to accelerate the repayment of future scheduled payments (coupon or principal), except in bankruptcy and liquidation.
7 Dividend/coupon discretion: 1. The bank must have full discretion at all times to cancel distributions/payments. 2. Cancellation of discretionary payments must not be an event of default. 3. Banks must have full access to cancelled payments to meet obligations as they fall due. 4. Cancellation of distributions/payments must not impose restrictions on the bank except in relation to distributions to common stockholders.	
8 Dividends/coupons must be paid out of distributable items.	
9 The instrument cannot have a credit-sensitive dividend feature; that is, a dividend/coupon that is reset periodically based in whole or in part on the banking organisation's credit standing.	The instrument cannot have a credit-sensitive dividend feature; that is, a dividend/coupon that is reset periodically based in whole or in part on the banking organisation's credit standing.

TABLE 14.1   (*Continued*)

Additional Tier 1	Tier 2
10 The instrument cannot contribute to liabilities exceeding assets if such a balance sheet test forms part of national insolvency law.	
11 Instruments classified as liabilities for accounting purposes must have principal loss absorption through either (i) conversion to common shares at an objective pre-specified trigger point or (ii) a write-down mechanism which allocates losses to the instrument at a pre-specified trigger point.	
13 Neither the bank nor a related party over which the bank exercises control or significant influence can have purchased the instrument, nor can the bank directly or indirectly have funded the purchase of the instrument.	Neither the bank nor a related party over which the bank exercises control or significant influence can have purchased the instrument, nor can the bank directly or indirectly have funded the purchase of the instrument.
14 The instrument cannot have any features that hinder recapitalisation, such as provisions that require the issuer to compensate investors if a new instrument is issued at a lower price during a specified timeframe.	
15 If the instrument is not issued out of an operating entity or the holding company in the consolidated group (e.g. a special-purpose vehicle – SPV), proceeds must be immediately available without limitation to an operating entity or the holding company in the consolidated group in a form which meets or exceeds all of the other criteria for inclusion in AT1 capital.	If the instrument is not issued out of an operating entity or the holding company in the consolidated group (e.g. an SPV), proceeds must be immediately available without limitation to an operating entity or the holding company in the consolidated group in a form which meets or exceeds all of the other criteria for inclusion in Tier 2 capital.
	a Provisions or loan-loss reserves held against future, presently unidentified losses are freely available to meet losses which subsequently materialise and therefore qualify for inclusion within Tier 2.
	b Provisions ascribed to identified deterioration of particular assets or known liabilities, whether individual or grouped, should be excluded.
	c Furthermore, general provisions/general loan-loss reserves eligible for inclusion in Tier 2 will be limited to a maximum of 1.25 percentage points of credit risk-weighted risk assets calculated under the standardised approach.

However for ABS to be Shari'ah-compliant, there must be two-level screening: asset-level and contract-level. On the asset level – such as real estate, infrastructure, car fleets or aircraft – the underlying asset must be Shari'ah-compliant, while on the contract level, the contract governing the ownership and use of the assets must comply with Shari'ah rules and principles, for example *ijarah*, *murabaha* or *mudaraba*. Furthermore, in order for the *sukuk* to be tradable, the majority of the underlying assets must be non-financial assets (i.e. not *murabaha*, *salam* or *istisna'a* receivables).

Due to these specific natures in structuring *sukuk* and in compliance with international standard setting, Islamic banks may face certain challenges to meet some of the Basel III AT1 and Tier 2 criteria. Key challenges facing Islamic banks, among others, are the following:

Loss Absorbency Through Subordination

In complying with the Basel III key criteria where loss absorbency is concerned, there seems to be a limit to the type of Shari'ah-compliant structures that can be utilised. Basel III requires that instruments would have to be ranked senior or junior to others to enable them to bear losses under either going concern or gone concern scenarios.

From the Shari'ah perspective on some of the structures, it is not possible to maintain Basel III's ranking order of CET1 (ordinary shares) representing the most subordinated claim in the event of liquidation, to be followed by AT1 and then Tier 2 capital, if both AT1 and Tier 2 are structured using *musharaka* contracts. It is therefore not possible for one partner to be subordinated vis-à-vis another partner, whereby one partner has a priority in receiving payments. *Musharaka sukuk* are thus similar to non-voting ordinary shares and should be ranked *pari passu* with common equity.

So far, most Islamic banks have raised regulatory capital via equity-based *sukuk* such as *musharaka* and *mudaraba* structures in order to meet both Basel III requirements. Although some of the equity-based *sukuk* are structured using *mudaraba*, the structure is essentially a *musharaka* whereby a partnership is formed between the *sukuk* holders and the bank, as the capital raised from the *sukuk* holders (investors as *rab-al-maal*) is commingled with that of the issuer (Islamic bank as *mudarib*, who manages the *musharaka* venture) and used to meet the general obligations of the Islamic bank.

Convertibility at the Point of Non-Viability

Basel III stipulates that an instrument must have a term to allow conversion or write off at the point of non-viability (PONV), i.e. AT1 converts to ordinary shares while Tier 2 is either written off or convertible to ordinary shares.

The assets underlying the *sukuk* would be converted into ordinary shares at a pre-agreed exchange ratio on the occurrence of the trigger event. An issue may arise when the ordinary shares provided in exchange for the underlying assets would almost certainly have a lower value. This raises a potential Shari'ah issue of *ibra* with respect to such a shortfall in counter value being a condition of the issuance of the *sukuk*.

For this reason, in respect of instruments issued by an Islamic bank, only conversion into ordinary shares is possible for capital instruments structured using unrestricted non exchange-based contracts (e.g. *musharaka*, *mudaraba* or capital *wakala*) while instruments structured using exchange-based contracts (e.g. *murabaha*, *tawarruq* or *ijarah*) can either be written off or converted into ordinary shares.

IFSB-15's Key Criteria for AT1 and Tier 2

In order to address these challenges, the IFSB has adapted certain Basel III requirements in order to ensure a certain level of consistency in the Islamic financial services industry.

It should be noted that the intention of the introduction of IFSB requirements is to reaffirm Basel III's primary goal to increase the level, quality and global consistency of regulatory capital and, at the same time, to address the specific features of the contracts and operation for adherence to Shari'ah rules and principles in the *sukuk* issuance. Table 14.2 outlines the key specific requirements set out by the IFSB in connection with the Basel III requirement.

TABLE 14.2 Key requirements set by IFSB

	Additional Tier 1	Tier 2
Loss Absorbency	Subject to Shari'ah approval, an IIFS may issue *musharaka sukuk* (with the underlying assets as the whole business of the bank) that are able to absorb losses so as to qualify for inclusion in AT1 capital. In these *musharaka sukuk*, the *sukuk* holders are partners with the common shareholders in the equity capital of the IIFS, as per the terms of the *musharaka* agreement, and thus fully share the risks and rewards of the IIFS's operations.	It might be possible, subject to Shari'ah compliance, for an IIFS to issue T2 capital instruments in the form of *mudaraba* or *wakala sukuk*, the underlying assets of which would be convertible (as specified in the contract) into shares of common equity at the PONV or insolvency. It is essential that the terms of conversion, notably the trigger point and the conversion ratio, are clearly specified in the *sukuk* contract so as to avoid *gharar*. Prior to conversion, the underlying assets of such *sukuk* would not be available to meet the claims of the IIFS's current account holders or other creditors. After conversion of the *sukuk* in case of the IIFS's non-viability or insolvency, T2 capital would rank *pari passu* with CET1, along with AT1 capital.

(Continued)

TABLE 14.2   (*Continued*)

	Additional Tier 1	Tier 2
Issuance Process and Procedure	The instrument is issued and paid-up, and neither the IIFS nor a related party over which the IIFS exercises control or significant influence can purchase the instrument, or fund its purchase, either directly or indirectly. Repayment of principal through repurchase or buy-back is allowed subject to supervisory approval without any expectation of repayment being created by the IIFS.	The instrument is issued and paid-up, and neither the IIFS nor a related party over which the IIFS exercises control or significant influence can purchase the instrument or fund the purchase of the instrument, either directly or indirectly. Issuance that takes place outside an operating entity of the IIFS or the holding company in the consolidated group, such as through a Special-Purpose Entity (SPE), must follow specific requirements. For instance, the proceeds of issuance must be made immediately available to an operating entity or holding company in the consolidated group, in a form that meets or exceeds all the other criteria of Tier 2.
Maturity and Callability	The *musharaka sukuk* are perpetual in nature and have no maturity date. They must not have step-up features (i.e. periodic increases in the rate of return) and are without any other incentive to the issuer to redeem them. If the instrument is callable, the issuer is permitted to exercise a call option only after five years and subject to certain requirements, such as: (i) prior supervisory approval; (ii) no call expectation is created by the IIFS; and (iii) ability to replace the called instruments with the same or better quality of capital, either before or concurrently with the call. The IIFS shall not exercise a call unless it successfully exhibits that its capital position is above the regulatory capital requirement after the call option is exercised. Instruments which qualify for AT1 capital cannot have any features that hinder recapitalisation (provisions that require the IIFS to compensate	The original minimum maturity shall be at least five years. The instrument shall not have step-up facilities and be without any incentive to redeem by the issuer. For recognition in regulatory capital, any amortisation of the principal will be on a straight-line basis in the remaining five years before maturity. If the instrument is callable, the issuer is permitted to exercise a call option only after five years and subject to certain requirements, such as: (i) prior supervisory approval; (ii) there is no call expectation created by the IIFS; and (iii) ability to replace the called instruments with the same or better quality of capital, either before or concurrently with the call. The IIFS shall not exercise a call unless it successfully exhibits that its capital position is above the regulatory capital requirement.

TABLE 14.2   (*Continued*)

	Additional Tier 1	Tier 2
	investors if a new instrument is issued at a lower price during a specified timeframe). If an instrument is issued out of an SPE, proceeds must be immediately available without limitation to the IIFS in a form which meets or exceeds all of the other criteria for inclusion in AT1 capital.	
Distribution of Profits	The contract should provide that non-distribution of profits would not constitute a default event. Distributions should not be linked to the credit rating of the IIFS, either wholly or in part.	The distribution of profits to the holders of the instruments should not be linked to the credit rating of the IIFS, either wholly or in part. Future scheduled payments should not be accelerated at the option of investors, except in the case of liquidation or bankruptcy.
Unsecured in Nature	The amount paid at issuance is neither secured nor guaranteed by the IIFS or any related entity. In addition, there should not be any arrangement that legally or economically increases the seniority of the instrument's claim.	The amount paid during issuance is neither secured nor guaranteed by the IIFS or any of its related entities. Besides, there should not be any arrangement that legally or economically increases the seniority of claim in case of liquidation.

SUKUK AS CAPITAL INSTRUMENTS IN BASEL III

Since the implementation of Basel III in January 2013, a number of Basel III-compliant *sukuk* issuances have been made. Auctioned by a few different issuing banks across Malaysia, Saudi Arabia and the United Arab Emirates (UAE), the deals raised approximately USD4.93 billion. Over the past two years, there was Tier 1 *sukuk* issuance from three UAE Islamic banks totalling USD2.5 billion. Issuers of these *sukuk* claim that they qualify as AT1 capital under Basel III. However, at this juncture, the Central Bank of the UAE has yet issued any specific guidance on Basel III for banks operating in the UAE.

According to MIFC (2013), the gradual implementation of Basel III accords has led Islamic banks to turn towards Basel III-compliant *sukuk* instruments to satisfy the revised capital standards. More issuances are expected to come to the market with Basel III-compliant features. Out of the USD4.93 billion outstanding Basel III *sukuk*, 59 percent was issued in accordance with Basel III's Tier 2 capital requirements, while the other 41 percent was raised complying with the Additional Tier 1 capital requirements.

Various structures were utilised by issuers, the most preferred being the *mudaraba* structure (67 percent), followed by hybrid structures (22 percent) and the *murabaha* structure (11 percent). A *mudaraba sukuk* provides an ideal Shari'ah-compliant structure to accommodate the features of AT1 capital, such as the discretionary profit payments. In the case of the Abu Dhabi Islamic Bank (ADIB), the *sukuk*, which were based on the contract of *mudaraba*, are classified as equity. Therefore, they do not include principal loss absorption or equity conversion features. Periodic distributions are fully discretionary and non-cumulative.

It should be noted that the IFSB only mentioned *musharaka sukuk* to be eligible for AT1 inclusion, where the underlying asset is the whole business of the issuing bank. Moreover, the IFSB specifies that these *sukuk* should be able to absorb losses. Further reading indicated that even when the *sukuk* is called a *mudaraba*, essentially the *sukuk* represented a *musharaka* structure, with the partnership formed between the *sukuk* holders and the Islamic banks.

The first issuance of Basel III-compliant *sukuk* came from ADIB on 19 November 2012. The USD1 billion *sukuk* complied with AT1 capital requirements and generated an overwhelming response from the investors. The deal was more than three times oversubscribed on the initial benchmark size at an order book of USD15.5 billion, with an expected profit rate of 6.37 percent – the lowest ever coupon for an instrument of this type.

Following ADIB's successful issuance, Dubai Islamic Bank (DIB) issued the second Basel III-compliant *sukuk* in March 2013. Towards the beginning of 2014, there were three more issuances in Saudi Arabia, namely, Saudi Hollandi Bank, Saudi British Bank and National Commercial Bank. Unlike the UAE banks, the Saudi banks issued *sukuk* in order to increase their Tier 2 capitals. Al Hilal Bank (AHB) then issued Tier 1 *sukuk* in June 2014. AHB is the first bank from the MENA region to issue an AT1 offering which includes a contingent PONV clause.

Key features of the UAE *sukuk* issuance are illustrated in Table 14.3.

TABLE 14.3 Key features of the UAE *sukuk* issuance

	Al Hilal	Dubai Islamic	Abu Dhabi Islamic
Issuer Size	USD500 million	USD1 billion	USD1 billion
Issue Date	24 June 2014	13 March 2013	8 November 2012
Benchmark Rate	5Yr MS – 1.77%	6Yr MS – 1.29%	6Yr MS – 0.96%
Profit Rate	5.50%	6.25%	6.375%
Status	Subordinated	Subordinated	Subordinated
Type of Structure	*Mudaraba*	*Mudaraba*	*Mudaraba*
Embedded Option	Callable after 5 years	Callable after 6 years	Callable after 6 years
Coupon Discretion	Non-cumulative discretionary distributions Non-payment upon: i. AHB having insufficient distributable profits, ii. breach by AHB of applicable regulatory capital requirements, iii. the request of the regulator, iv. solvency condition not being met, or v. AHB electing not to pay.	Non-cumulative discretionary distributions Non-payment upon: i. DIB having insufficient distributable profits, ii. breach by DIB of applicable regulatory capital requirements, iii. the request of the regulator, iv. solvency condition not being met, or v. DIB electing not to pay.	Non-cumulative discretionary distributions Non-payment upon: i. ADIB having insufficient distributable profits, ii. breach by ADIB of applicable regulatory capital requirements, iii. the request of the regulator, iv. solvency condition not being met, or v. ADIB electing not to pay.

TABLE 14.3   *(Continued)*

	Al Hilal	Dubai Islamic	Abu Dhabi Islamic
Dividend Stopper/ Pusher	Stopper/ No pusher	Stopper/ No pusher	Stopper/ No pusher
Going Concern Loss – Absorption Trigger	No principal loss absorption	No principal loss absorption	No principal loss absorption
Non-viability Loss Covered through permitted Risk factor on potential Risk factor on potential Absorption (PONV)	Covered through permitted amendment via full and permanent write-down	Risk factor on potential statutory regime, but no contractual PONV clause	Risk factor on potential statutory regime, but no contractual PONV clause

The successful experience in the Gulf Cooperation Council countries was emulated by Islamic banks in Southeast Asia, especially Malaysia with the issuance of *sukuk* by AmIslamic Bank, Maybank Islamic, RHB Islamic and Public Islamic Bank with the purpose of boosting their Tier 2 capital.

Figure 14.1 illustrates an example of a Basel III-compliant *sukuk mudaraba* structure. The notable difference is that unlike some of the previous *sukuk* issuances, payments

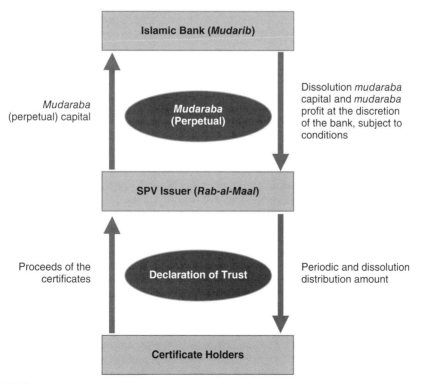

FIGURE 14.1   An example of a Basel III-compliant *sukuk mudaraba* structure

of *mudaraba* profit by Islamic banks (as *mulamic*) are at the sole discretion of the bank and may only be made if it meets certain conditions. The certificates are perpetual securities in respect of which there is no fixed redemption date and accordingly, the *mudaraba* is a perpetual arrangement with no fixed end date. Subject to certain conditions set out in the *mudaraba* agreement, the Islamic bank may at its option liquidate the *mudaraba* in whole, but not in part, on the basis of an actual liquidation of the *mudaraba*.

AL HILAL BANK TIER 1 SUKUK LIMITED

Al Hilal Bank (AHB) was founded by the Abu Dhabi Investment Council, an investment arm of the Abu Dhabi government, with an authorised capital of AED4 billion. The first four branches of the bank in UAE were opened on 19 June 2008 in Abu Dhabi. Since then, the bank has taken off in achieving remarkable successes in various areas of banking to the present day.

The AHB successfully issued Perpetual Tier 1 USD500 million *sukuk* on 24 June 2014. The bank also successfully priced its USD500 million perpetual (non-call 5) AT1 *sukuk* at the lowest coupon ever achieved by any bank for a USD Tier 1 issuance outside of the United States since 2008. The success of the transaction was further reflected in the strong and healthy order book, which closed at over USD4.5bn, representing 9.0x oversubscription, from over 200 accounts. Joint bookrunners/joint lead managers for the issue included AHB, Citigroup, Emirates NBD Capital, HSBC, National Bank of Abu Dhabi (NBAD) and Standard Chartered Bank.

Description

The Issuer will issue Certificates (which shall be perpetual and accordingly shall not have a fixed redemption) to the Certificate holders and collect the trust certificate proceeds therefrom. [As shown in Figure 14.2.]

Pursuant to a Mudaraba Agreement between AHB (as Mudarib) and the Issuer (as Rab-al-Maal), a Mudaraba will be constituted whereunder the Trust Certificate Proceeds will be contributed by the Issuer as the initial Mudaraba Capital. The Mudaraba shall commence on the date of the payment of the Mudaraba Capital to AHB by the Issuer and shall terminate on the date that the Trust Certificates are redeemed in full, following the liquidation of the Mudaraba in accordance with the terms of the Mudaraba Agreement.

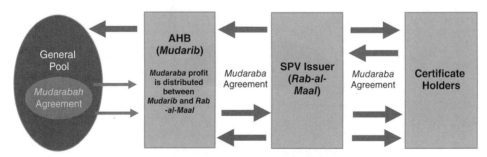

FIGURE 14.2　The Al Hilal Bank's *sukuk* structure and cash flows

AHB (as Mudarib) will invest the Mudaraba Capital in the general business of AHB in accordance with an agreed Investment Plan. The Mudaraba Capital as so invested will be converted into undivided assets in the General Pool as the Mudaraba Assets. AHB shall be entitled to commingle its own assets with the Mudaraba Assets.

Pursuant to the terms of the Mudaraba Agreement, AHB will pay (after deducting its share of the profit in respect of its commingled assets and in accordance with an agreed profit sharing ratio – 99 percent to the Rab-al-Maal and 1% to the Mudarib) the Rab-al-Maal Mudaraba Profit to the Issuer and the Issuer will utilize the Rab-al-Maal Mudaraba Profit to pay the Periodic Distribution Amounts to the Certificate holders pursuant to the terms of the Certificates.

Payments of the Rab-al-Maal Mudaraba Profit by AHB (as Mudarib) are at the sole discretion of AHB (as Mudarib) and may only be made in circumstances where AHB will not be in breach of certain solvency and minimum capital conditions, before or as a result of making such payment.

If the Certificates are not redeemed or purchased and cancelled on or prior to the date falling on the 5th anniversary of the date of the Mudaraba Agreement (the 'First Call Date'), Periodic Distribution Amounts shall be payable at a fixed rate to be reset on the First Call Date and every five years thereafter, equal to the Relevant Five Year Reset Rate plus a margin.

Subject to certain conditions, at the discretion of AHB (as Mudarib), AHB (as Mudarib) may liquidate (on the basis of a constructive liquidation) the Mudaraba in whole, either:

i. on the First Call Date or any Mudaraba Profit Distribution Date after the First Call Date; or

ii. on any date on or after the date of the Mudaraba Agreement upon the occurrence of (i) a Tax Event or (ii) Capital Event.

The Mudaraba shall be automatically liquidated upon a winding-up, bankruptcy, dissolution or liquidation (or other analogous event) of the Mudarib and/or if a Dissolution Event occurs.

Subordination

From a Shari'ah perspective, subordination is permitted whereby the *mudaraba* is authorised by certificate holders to use the amount due to the certificate holders to pay depositors and senior creditors for their due right before making payment to certificate holders. Strictly speaking, the certificate holders are not creditors.

Sukuk proceeds were totally or partially commingled in the general Shari'ah-compliant financial services business of the AHB, such that the AHB would have a general obligation to pay the *sukuk* holders. The principle of subordination was also applied to these equity-based *sukuk* issued, whereby in the event of losses there would be an obligation to pay deposit liabilities and other senior creditors first, and the equity-based *sukuk* would be paid thereafter. Moreover, the *sukuk* represented unsecured obligations of the issuer, and no collateral was given to back their repayment. It should be noted, however, that in the absence of the subordination clause, the *sukuk* holders (or the issuer SPV on their behalf) would have had an ownership claim as *rab-al-maal* to the *mudaraba* assets so that the *sukuk* would not have been 'unsecured obligations'.

Payment of *Mudaraba* Profit

Payment of *mudaraba* profit by the Islamic bank (as *mudarib*) is at the sole discretion of the bank and may only be made if certain conditions are met. The certificates are perpetual securities in respect of which there is no fixed redemption date and accordingly, the *mudaraba* is a perpetual arrangement with no fixed end date. Subject to certain conditions set out in the *mudaraba* agreement, the Islamic bank may at its option liquidate the *mudaraba* in whole, but not in part, on the basis of an actual liquidation of the *mudaraba*. In all instances, the bank will only liquidate the *mudaraba* to the extent that, on a dissolution, the *mudaraba* capital would be equal to the nominal amount of the *sukuk* to be repaid. To the extent that the bank (as *mudarib*) breaches this obligation, it is required to indemnify the issuer (SPV) in respect of this shortfall.

MAYBANK ISLAMIC'S RM1.5 BILLION SUBORDINATED *SUKUK MURABAHA* ISSUANCE

Maybank Islamic Berhad (Maybank Islamic) is the largest Islamic banking group in Malaysia and Asia Pacific and third largest in the world by asset size, with 29 percent market share in Malaysia and Shari'ah-compliant assets of RM125.1 billion (USD38.1 billion) as at December 2013.

In April 2014, Maybank Islamic successfully established a Basel III-compliant Tier 2 Subordinated *sukuk* programme of up to RM10.0 billion in nominal value. This programme provides flexibility to Maybank Islamic to issue subordinated *sukuk murabaha* (subordinated *sukuk murabaha*) within the tenure of the *sukuk* programme of up to 20 years from the first issue date of the subordinated *sukuk murabaha*. During this tenure, Maybank Islamic has the option to issue subordinated *sukuk murabaha* with maturity of at least five years and up to 20 years from the issue date with a call option, if applicable. The maiden RM1.5 billion (USD0.5billion) subordinated *sukuk murabaha* issuance was issued on 7 April 2014. To date, Maybank Islamic's subordinated *sukuk murabaha* issuance is the largest single issuance of a Basel III-compliant Tier 2 capital *sukuk* denominated in ringgit Malaysia by an Islamic banking institution in Malaysia.

Maybank Islamic's first subordinated *sukuk murabaha* carry a maturity period of 10 years on a 10 non-callable 5 basis. The *murabaha* (via *tawarruq* arrangement) structure was chosen, taking into consideration the currency of issuance and target investors who were predominantly Malaysian-based, wherein such structure is widely accepted. (*Sukuk murabaha* would not be accepted as tradable in other countries.) It was lead arranged and lead managed by Maybank Investment Bank Berhad.

Description

Pursuant to a service agency agreement, Maybank Islamic will be appointed by the Sukūk Trustee (acting on behalf of the Sukūk holders) as the purchase agent ('Purchase Agent') to purchase the Commodities. [As illustrated in Figure 14.3.]

Maybank Islamic (as the 'Purchaser') will issue a purchase order to Maybank Islamic (as the Purchase Agent) to buy the Commodities from the Sukūk Trustee (acting on behalf of the Sukūk holders) at the Deferred Sale Price.

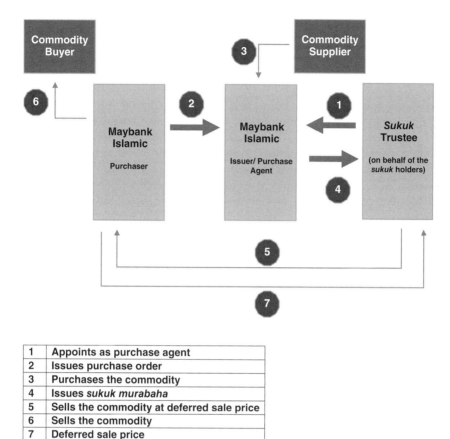

1	Appoints as purchase agent
2	Issues purchase order
3	Purchases the commodity
4	Issues *sukuk murabaha*
5	Sells the commodity at deferred sale price
6	Sells the commodity
7	Deferred sale price

FIGURE 14.3   Maybank Islamic's subordinated *sukuk murabaha* structure

The Purchase Agent will purchase the Commodities from a commodity supplier ('Commodity Supplier') in the Bursa Suq Al-Sila' commodity market on a spot basis at a purchase price equivalent to the proceeds of the Subordinated Sukūk Murābahah ('Commodity Purchase Price').

Maybank Islamic as the Issuer will, from time to time, issue Subordinated Sukūk Murābahah which evidences the Sukūk holders' ownership in the Commodities and Purchaser's obligation to pay the Deferred Sale Price to the Sukūk holders upon sale of the Commodities to the Purchaser. The proceeds received from the Sukūk holders shall be used by the Purchase Agent to pay the Commodity Purchase Price.

Subsequently, the Sukūk Trustee (on behalf of the Sukūk holders) will sell the Commodities to the Purchaser at a selling price equivalent to 100% of the nominal value of the relevant tranche of the Subordinated Sukūk Murābahah plus the aggregate periodic profits ('Periodic Profits') on deferred payment terms ('Deferred Sale Price').

The Purchaser shall sell, on a spot basis, the Commodities to a commodity buyer ('Commodity Buyer') for a cash consideration equal to the Commodity Purchase Price.

The Purchaser shall make periodic payments on each Periodic Payment Date and final payment of the Deferred Sale Price at the maturity date of the Subordinated Sukūk Murābahah to the Sukūk holders. Upon declaration of an Event of Default or early settlement pursuant to the Call Option, the Tax Redemption or the Regulatory

Redemption, the Purchaser shall pay the outstanding Deferred Sale Price (subject to ibra') as final settlement of the same to the Sukūk holders.

Provision for Non-Viability Loss Absorption

As part of the Basel III requirement pursuant to the Capital Adequacy Framework for Islamic Banks (Capital Components) issued by the Central Bank of Malaysia, Bank Negara Malaysia (BNM), the subordinated *sukuk murabaha* includes a provision for non-viability loss absorption. At the point of a non-viability event, Maybank Islamic shall irrevocably write off the subordinated *sukuk murabaha* in whole or in part thereof. Any written-off amount of the subordinated *sukuk murabaha* shall be irrevocably lost and the *sukuk* holders of such subordinated *sukuk murabaha* will cease to have any claims on the amount due in respect of such subordinated *sukuk murabaha* which have been written off. Notwithstanding this, the exercise of the loss absorption at the PONV does not constitute an event of default or trigger any cross-default clauses.

From a Shari'ah perspective, the write-off mechanism applies the concept of *ibra*, which refers to an act by a person relinquishing his claims or rights to collect payment due from another person whether partially or in whole. The *sukuk* holders agree to relinquish their rights to receive payment on the amount due under the subordinated *sukuk murabaha* which have been written off. According to the majority of jurists, *ibra* is defined as an absolute relinquishment of a debt and the scholars do not place restrictions as to whether the relinquishment shall only be applicable to the profit portion of the outstanding sale price. This satisfies the above scenario where the *sukuk* holders shall relinquish the outstanding sale price payable by Maybank Islamic pursuant to such write-off.

Occurrence of non-viability events, principally determined by BNM and Malaysia Deposit Insurance Corporation or Perbadanan Insurans Deposit Malaysia (PIDM) at their full discretion, can be defined to include among others:

1. failure by an Islamic banking institution to maintain its capital at an adequate level, hence detrimentally affecting its depositors especially when the Islamic banking institution is unable to recapitalise on its own;
2. failure by an Islamic banking institution to follow any directive of compliance issued by BNM necessary to preserve or restore its financial soundness; or
3. the Islamic banking institution's assets are insufficient to provide protection to its depositors and creditors.

The subordinated *sukuk murabaha* may also, at the option of BNM and PIDM, be written off upon the occurrence of a trigger event in relation to Malayan Banking Berhad (Maybank), a parent company of Maybank Islamic, since the subordinated *sukuk murabaha* are included as capital at the consolidated level of Maybank.

Other features of the subordinated *sukuk murabaha* which are structured to comply with Basel III requirements are that the instrument has an original maturity of at least five years, and there can be no step-up features or other incentives for the Islamic banking institution to redeem the instrument.

Lastly, as with other Tier 2 capital instruments, the subordinated *sukuk murabaha* will, in the event of a winding-up or liquidation of Maybank Islamic, be subordinated in right of payments to the claims of all depositors and senior creditors.

The subordinated *sukuk murabaha* has only two events of default prescribed in its terms: if Maybank Islamic defaults in payment of principal or profits or any amount under the *sukuk* programme and such default continues for seven business days; or if a court or an agency or regulatory authority in Malaysia with such jurisdiction shall have instituted proceeding for liquidation of Maybank Islamic and such decree or order remains in force for 60 days.

In general, the proceeds raised from the maiden issue of Maybank Islamic's subordinated *sukuk murabaha* are utilised to strengthen its capital position, as well as for its business expansion programme, general banking and working capital purposes.

CONCLUSION

The above cases highlight the regulatory capital requirements under Basel III and the IFSB-15 and deliberate on the qualifying AT1 and Tier 2 capital instruments that can be issued by Islamic banks to meet Shari'ah requirements, and Basel III criteria and objectives.

Shari'ah issues in the subordinated *sukuk*, in both equity-based and exchange-based contracts, were examined for the purpose of structuring AT1 and Tier 2 capital instruments. It may be concluded that there are two possible approaches to complying with Basel III and Shari'ah requirements (as highlighted by some researchers).

First, is to avoid the Shari'ah issues related to the issue of subordination altogether and instead recommend *musharaka* instruments for both AT1 and Tier 2 capital whereby CET1, AT1 and Tier 2 will all be ranked *pari passu* with one another. This approach will still be compliant with the philosophy of Basel III which in substance aims to strengthen the resilience of the banking sector via increasing the total equity of the Risk-Weighted Assets (RWA), thus enabling Islamic banks to absorb losses in the case of financial stress. However, the Tier 1 *sukuk* would rank *pari passu* with the ordinary shares, and there would in effect be no Tier 2 *sukuk* if all were ranked *pari passu*.

The second approach is to comply fully with the ranking order as required by Basel III by using subordinated *mudaraba sukuk* for AT1, and exchange-based contracts in the form of *murabaha* and *ijarah sukuk* for structuring T2 capital instruments along with the use of a conversion mechanism to achieve the effect of subordinating Tier 2 capital instruments to current and saving accounts and general creditors. However, certain Shari'ah issues surrounding the current structures of exchange-based contracts (namely *murabaha* and *ijarah sukuk*) need to be resolved first before this approach can become a reality.

BIBLIOGRAPHY

Archer, Simon (2013) *Regulatory Treatment of Sukuk in the Light of Basel III and Sharī'ah Compliance Issues.* INCEIFC.

Beebee Salma, S., M. Marjan, and M. Madaa Munjid (2013) 'Instruments for Meeting Capital Adequacy Requirements of Additional Tier 1 and Tier 2 under Basel III: A Sharī'ah Perspective', Proceeding of the 5th Islamic Economics System Conference (iECONS 2013), 'Sustainable Development through the Islamic Economics System', Organised by Faculty Economics and Muamalat, Universiti Sains Islam Malaysia, Berjaya Times Square Hotel, Kuala Lumpur, 4–5 September.

Cheong, L. S. (2014) 'Al Hilal Bank Perpetual Tier 1 Sukuk Al – Muārabah Based Structure', IIFM Sukuk Report, November.

Collins, Nick (2013) 'Abu Dhabi Islamic Bank leads the way with the world's first Basel III Compliant Tier 1 Sukuk issuance', *Islamic Finance News*, March.

Kanan, O. (2015) 'Regulatory and Supervisory Challenges of Islamic Banking after Basel-III', COMCEC Financial Cooperation Working Group Meeting Ankara, March.

MIFC (2013) 'Innovation for Growth Basel III Creates a Golden Opportunity', www.mifc.com.

Mohamed, D. (2014) 'BASEL III Offers an Opportunity for Islamic Banks to Strengthen Their Capitalization and Liquidity Management', in Standard & Poor's Islamic Finance Outlook 2015, September.

Muzzafar, H. (2014) 'Basel II & III Sukuk by Islamic Institutions', presentation at the IIFM Industry Seminar on Islamic Capital and Money Market, May.

Promod, D. (2014) 'A Credit Rating Agency's Perspective on Basel III Sukuk', presentation at the IIFM Industry Seminar on Islamic Financial Market at the 21st Annual World Islamic Banking Conference, December.

Rahail, A. (2011) Sukuk *and Islamic Capital Markets* (Globe Law and Business).

Shearman & Sterling LLP (2011) 'The New Basel III Framework: Implications for Banking Organizations', client publication, March.

Siew, S. M. (2014) 'Basel III Sukuk as Bank Capital. How Do We See It?', IIFM Industry Seminar on Islamic Capital and Money Market Singapore, June.

Sutan Amir, H. (2014) 'The Important Role of Sukuk in the Basel III Era', Thomson Reuters, 15 Dec.

Wilson, Rodney (2013) 'Challenges for Islamic Banks in Complying with Basel III', The First Annual Conference of Islamic Economics & Islamic Finance at ECO-ENA, Inc., Canada, August.

CHAPTER 15

Concluding Remarks

By Simon Archer and Rifaat Ahmed Abdel Karim

The development of the ICM internationally provides a good illustration of the institutional interdependence between the market and the state. The country in which the ICM is the most developed is Malaysia, where the public authorities have made a point of facilitating the development of the various branches of Islamic finance, including banking and the capital market. The Bank Negara (central bank) and the Bursa Malaysia (stock exchange) each has a Shari'ah Committee to provide overall guidance on Shari'ah compliance. The Islamic Financial Services Board and the International Islamic Liquidity Management Corporation have also been made welcome in the country. The legal and institutional infrastructure has been conducive to the development of Islamic finance, including the ICM. Malaysia benefits from being a sizeable country with an economy and a conventional capital market that are relatively well-developed, and its legal system based on common law has been able to accommodate Islamic finance without too much difficulty.

Hardly any other Muslim majority country is able to offer such support to Islamic finance. One that must be mentioned is Sudan, where the economy is operated on a Shari'ah-compliant basis. The Khartoum Stock Exchange inaugurated its electronic trading system in March 2016. Another country in which Islamic finance is well-established is Bahrain, where the central bank provides regulation, supervision and guidance to Islamic banks and *takaful* (insurance) undertakings, and where a number of institutions concerned with Islamic finance are established. In the UAE, the Dubai Financial Services Authority has been set up to regulate the Dubai International Financial Centre, which is host to various ICM activities.

Various other Muslim majority countries are developing their financial sector and, in the process, an infrastructure that helps to support the ICM. However, this is a challenging and time-consuming task. Some idea of this can be gained from Chapters 5, 6 and 8 above. Given the benefits which Islamic finance generally, including ICMs, is able to offer in terms of financial inclusion and the mobilisation of funds for economic development, it is to be hoped that the public authorities in such countries will continue to take up this challenge.

Nominate Contracts Employed as a Basis for Shari'ah-Compliant Financial Transactions

WAKALA

Wakala is an agency relationship between the *wakeel* (agent) and *muwakil* (principal) whereby the *wakeel* will invest the *muwakil*'s funds in certain Shari'ah-compliant assets. The *wakeel* is entitled to a fee for their services and, in addition, any profit made above an agreed profit rate to be paid to the *muwakil* may also be paid to the *wakeel* as an incentive fee pursuant to the term of a *wakala* agreement.

MUDARABA

Mudaraba is a partnership between two or more parties where one party (the *mudarib*) is the active partner who contributes their effort and management skills but no capital, while the other party or parties – the sleeping partner(s) – contribute(s) capital. The parties may share profits, but losses can only be borne by the capital provider. A *mudaraba* contract can be for any period of time, at the end of which the contract is liquidated. The capital provider is not entitled to claim a fixed amount as profit, although the percentage of the profit payable to the capital provider is stipulated in the financing agreement. Accordingly, there should be no guaranteed return for the investors with this type of financing.

MUSHARAKA

Musharaka is a partnership between two or more parties with each partner contributing to the capital of the joint venture (in cash or in kind). The capital is invested in a Shari'ah-compliant manner with profits resulting from the venture being shared between the partners according to contractually agreed proportions, while losses are shared according to the ratios of capital provided. One partner may be designated as the manager of the partnership and others as sleeping partners. A *mudaraba* can thus be seen as a limiting case of a partnership where the managing partner contributes no capital and therefore bears no losses. A *mudaraba* may be nested within a *musharaka*, wherein the *mudarib* contributes capital on which they receive a share of profit in addition to their share of the *mudaraba* profit. This structure is typically used by Islamic banks when they accept unrestricted profit-sharing investment accounts in place of conventional interest-bearing deposits.

There is also a form of *musharaka* (diminishing *musharaka*) which is used for financing and especially for home purchase plans. The party wishing to acquire an asset enters into a *musharaka* with the party providing the finance and contributes a small part (say 20 percent) of the purchase price while the other party (typically an Islamic bank) provides the balance. The contract provides that the purchaser will progressively buy out the bank's share of the asset by instalments. This arrangement is typically accompanied by an *ijarah* contract (see below) whereby the purchasing partner leases the asset and pays rent on the proportion of the price which has not yet been bought out.

MURABAHA

Murabaha is defined as the sale of goods at cost plus an agreed mark-up, normally for deferred payment either by instalments or at maturity. This contract is frequently used in business for working capital finance, and for retail credit including home purchase plans. In this type of transaction, an asset is purchased by the purchaser (typically a bank) at the request of another party (the borrower) from a third party (a supplier) and then resold to the borrower at an agreed mark-up for immediate or deferred payment. The mark-up includes any expenses incurred by the purchaser. For the contract to be valid, it must specify the quantity, full description and the terms of delivery of the asset, as well as the cost of the asset, the profit payable to the bank and the payment terms (see *Gharar*).

SALAM

Salam is a form of working capital financing which takes the form of a sale agreement whereby the seller agrees to deliver goods at a future date in exchange for advance payment of the price in full. Although the goods typically do not exist at the time of the contract, a full description or specification of the goods is required at the outset as well as the date and terms of delivery. Further, the goods must also be of a type that is generally available in the market, i.e. commodities that are fungible goods. *Salam* may be used in conjunction with a parallel *Salam* contract whereby the buyer agrees to deliver a part or all of the goods at an agreed price to another party when they have been received.

IJARAH

Ijarah is a leasing contract whereby the owner of an asset (bearing all risks associated with the ownership of the asset) leases it to the lessee for a rent which is either agreed in advance or adjusted regularly throughout the lease period, either by consent, by reference to an 'expert' or in some cases by reference to an external benchmark (e.g. LIBOR). An *ijarah* can be structured so that the lessor retains ownership of the asset after the termination of the lease period or can include an option for the lessee to purchase the asset on a specified date. A common version of the latter type of *ijarah* (lease-to-buy) is known as *ijarah muntahia bittamlik* (IMB), where the lessee's payments include a capital element and the final purchase is for a token amount. This is an alternative to the combined diminishing *musharaka* plus *ijarah* arrangement described above, the difference being that with IMB the ownership of the asset does not pass until the final payment is made.

ISTISNA'A

Istisna'a is a form of working capital or project finance which takes the form of a sale contract whereby a party (a construction company) undertakes to manufacture or construct a specified asset according to agreed specifications and price in exchange for a series of progress or stage payments to be made as the construction work reaches certified stages of completion. In order for the contract to be Shari'ah-compliant, the price of the asset must be fixed at the time the contract is entered into along with the specifications of the asset. The terms of delivery must be clearly stated. An *istisna'a* contract is typically used in conjunction with a parallel *istisna'a* contract, whereby an Islamic banks acts as a financial intermediary between the construction company and a final purchaser, and the latter makes payment of an agreed price to the bank either as stage payments as the work progresses or on completion.

MUSATAHA

Musataha is a right to use, develop and benefit from land for a specified period, regardless of who the owner is or who else might have an interest in it. This right may be used as the asset underpinning an *ijarah*-based *sukuk*.

USUFRUCT

Usufruct is not a contract, but a right to use and derive profit or benefit from property belonging to another, regardless of who the owner is or who else might have an interest in it. This right may be used as the asset underpinning an *ijarah*-based *sukuk*.

WA'AD

Wa'ad means an undertaking or promise by one party in favour of another to do a Shari'ah-compliant act such as selling or buying an asset on a future date or on the occurrence of a certain event. In *Fiqh al Muamalat*, Wa'ad is considered to be a unilateral contract. There are different opinions regarding the promisee's rights as against the promiser in case of non-fulfilment; for example, according to one opinion the promisee is entitled to be indemnified against any loss suffered as a result of relying on the promise, but not all scholars agree with this.

ARBOUN

Arboun means 'advance payment', but is usually taken to refer to a specific sale contract whereby the purchaser pays a deposit forming part of the purchase price for the purchase of a particular asset. The purchaser is granted a period of time to determine whether to proceed with the sale. If the purchaser chooses not to proceed with the sale the deposit is forfeited to the seller. This is similar to an option to buy, but this type of agreement is controversial as some scholars do not accept as fair the forfeiting of the deposit without any consideration or loss to the seller other than either time or loss of opportunity, both of which cannot be compensated for under Shari'ah.

A Note on Market Index Providers

Concentration in the number of index providers is quite dramatic, the market being dominated by only four providers, S&P provides indices for around USD4.3 trillion of US fund assets, Barclays, which dominates bond indices provides them for USD3.0 trillion, Russell for USD2.3 trillion and MSCI for USD2.2 trillion.

Given the size of the assets under management of these tracker funds and ETFs, any change in an index is likely to have significant effects on asset markets. Changes are nevertheless frequent and final decisions on re-weighting of assets in an index are controlled by the index provider.

For equity indices such as the S&P 500 index, the changes in the index over time are very substantial; only 36 percent of the companies covered by it today were in the index in 1994 and the composition by industry has also changed with technology companies rising over that period from 8 percent to 13 percent. Moreover, the different index providers have very different indexation processes; while S&P update their S&P 500 index 20 times a year, Russell indices are updated only once annually.

Bond indices are one particular issue, weighted as they are by the amount of tradable debt a country or company has issued, which means that the more heavily indebted a bond issuer becomes the bigger the share it takes in the index. Funds that passively track indices are therefore effectively forced to become exposed to these highly indebted issuers. For bond investors this feature has significant consequences. The Barclays Global Aggregate, the dominant index of sovereign bonds, has over 50 percent of its USD42.5 trillion covered by the US, Italy and Japan, while Brazil, Russia, India and China account for only 1 percent.

This contrasts with equity indices, which are usually weighted by company size, e.g. the S&P 500 composite, though it can be argued that active investors more usually buy equal amounts of their target stocks. S&P do publish an index on this basis, the S&P 500 equal weight index (each stock = 0.2 percent of the index), which since the year 2000 has regularly outperformed the more widely used composite index. Significantly, the equal weight index requires frequent rebalancing through the taking of profits from stocks rising in value and buying those that have recently fallen, and over-weights smaller and cheaper stocks which in general outperform larger companies in the long term.

The obvious answer to the issues indices have for investors is for them to allocate more of their funds to fund managers who operate on a different basis such as absolute return funds or funds using so called 'smart' indices; with sovereign weighting according to an economy's absolute size, based on (say) absolute gross domestic product (GDP), or for companies equal weighted indices or indices based on companies' financial health.

Index

Note: Page references followed by 'f' refer to Figures; those followed by 't' refer to Tables